GOSPEL STUDIES SERIES

Your Study of
The Book of Mormon
Made Easier

Part 1
1 Nephi through Words of Mormon

Books
by David J. Ridges

The Gospel Studies Series

- *Isaiah Made Easier, Second Edition*
- *The New Testament Made Easier, Part 1 (Second Edition)*
- *The New Testament Made Easier, Part 2 (Second Edition)*
- *Your Study of The Book of Mormon Made Easier, Part 1*
- *Your Study of The Book of Mormon Made Easier, Part 2*
- *Your Study of The Book of Mormon Made Easier, Part 3*
- *Your Study of The Doctrine and Covenants Made Easier, Part 1*
- *Your Study of The Doctrine and Covenants Made Easier, Part 2*
- *Your Study of The Doctrine and Covenants Made Easier, Part 3*
- *The Old Testament Made Easier, Part 1*
- *The Old Testament Made Easier—Selections from the Old Testament, Part 2*
- *The Old Testament Made Easier—Selections from the Old Testament, Part 3*
- *Your Study of the Pearl of Great Price Made Easier*
- *Your Study of Jeremiah Made Easier*
- *Your Study of The Book of Revelation Made Easier, Second Edition*

Additional titles by David J. Ridges

- *Our Savior, Jesus Christ: His Life and Mission to Cleanse and Heal*
- *Mormon Beliefs and Doctrines Made Easier*
- *The Proclamation on the Family: The Word of the Lord on More Than 30 Current Issues*
- *65 Signs of the Times and the Second Coming*
- *Doctrinal Details of the Plan of Salvation: From Premortality to Exaltation*

GOSPEL STUDIES SERIES

Your Study of
The Book of Mormon
Made Easier

Part 1

1 Nephi through Words of Mormon

David J. Ridges

Springville, Utah

Copyright © 2004, 2012 David J. Ridges

All Rights Reserved.

No part of this book may be reproduced in any form whatsoever, whether by graphic, visual, electronic, film, microfilm, tape recording, or any other means, without prior written permission of the author, except in the case of brief passages embodied in critical reviews and articles.

This book is not an official publication of The Church of Jesus Christ of Latter-day Saints. The opinions and views expressed herein belong solely to the author and do not necessarily represent the opinions or views of Cedar Fort, Inc. Permission for the use of sources, graphics, and photos is also solely the responsibility of the author.

ISBN 13: 978-1-55517-725-6

Published by CFI, an imprint of Cedar Fort, Inc., 2373 W. 700 S., Springville, UT 84663
Distributed by Cedar Fort, Inc., www.cedarfort.com

Library of Congress Control Number: 2003114914

Cover design by Nicole Williams
Cover design © 2010 by Lyle Mortimer

Printed in the United States of America

10 9 8 7 6 5 4 3 2 1

Printed on acid-free paper

The Gospel Studies Series

Welcome to Volume 4 in the Gospel Studies Series, which covers the first portion of the Book of Mormon. In this volume, we will study First Nephi through The Words of Mormon. As with other books in this series of study guides, we will use the Book of Mormon as published by The Church of Jesus Christ of Latter-day Saints as our basic text. Any references to the Bible come from the King James Version of the Bible as published by The Church of Jesus Christ of Latter-day Saints. The entire text from First Nephi through The Words of Mormon is included, with brief notes of explanation between and within the verses to clarify and help with understanding.

This work is intended to be a user-friendly, introductory study to this portion of the Book of Mormon as well as a refresher course for more advanced students of the scriptures. It is also designed to be a quick-reference resource which will enable readers to look up a particular passage of scripture for use in lessons, talks, or personal study as desired. The author hopes that readers will write in their own scriptures some of the notes given in this book in order to assist them as they read and study the Book of Mormon in the future.

David J. Ridges

The JST References in Study Guides by David J. Ridges

Note that some of the JST (The Joseph Smith Translation of the Bible) references I use in my study guides are not found in our LDS Bible in the footnotes or in the Joseph Smith Translation section in the reference section in the back. The reason for this, as explained to me while writing curriculum materials for the Church, is simply that there is not enough room to include all of the JST additions and changes to the King James Version of the Bible (the one we use in the English speaking part of the Church). As you can imagine, as was likewise explained to me, there were difficult decisions that had to be made by the Scriptures Committee of the Church as to which JST contributions were included and which were not.

The Joseph Smith Translation of the Bible in its entirety can generally be found in or ordered through LDS bookstores. It was originally published under the auspices of the Reorganized Church of Jesus Christ of Latter Day Saints in Independence, Missouri. The version of the JST I prefer to use is a parallel column version, *Joseph Smith's "New Translation" of the Bible*, published by Herald Publishing House, Independence, Missouri, in 1970. This parallel column version compares the King James Bible with the JST side by side and includes only the verses that have changes, additions, or deletions made by the Prophet Joseph Smith.

By the way, some members of the Church have wondered if we can trust the JST since it was published by a breakaway faction from our Church. They worry that some changes from Joseph Smith's original manuscript might have been made to support doctrinal differences between us and the RLDS Church. This is not the case. Many years ago, Robert J. Matthews of the Brigham Young University Religion Department was given permission by leaders of the RLDS Church to come to their Independence, Missouri, headquarters and personally compare the original JST document word for word with their publication of the JST. Brother Matthews was thus able to verify that they had been meticulously true to the Prophet's original work.

Contents

Foreword	ix
Introduction	xi
First Nephi	1
Second Nephi	157
Jacob	330
Enos	380
Jarom	385
Omni	388
The Words of Mormon	393
Sources	396
About the Author	415

Foreword

In over thirty-five years of teaching in the Church and for the Church Educational System, I have found that members of the Church encounter some common problems when it comes to understanding the scriptures. One problem is understanding symbolism. Another common concern is how best to mark their own scriptures and perhaps make brief notes in them. Yet another concern is how to understand what the scriptures are actually teaching. In other words, what are the major messages being taught by the Lord through His prophets?

This book is designed to address each of the concerns mentioned above for First Nephi through The Words of Mormon in the Book of Mormon. The format is intentionally simple, with some license taken with respect to capitalization and punctuation in order to minimize interruption of the flow. It is intended to help readers:

- Quickly gain a basic understanding of these scriptures through the use of brief, italicized explanatory notes in brackets within the verses, as well as occasional notes between verses. This paves the way for even deeper testimony and understanding later.

- Better understand the beautiful language of the Book of Mormon. This is accomplished in this book with in-the-verse notes which define difficult terms.

- Mark their scriptures and put brief notes in the margins which will help them understand now and remember later what particular passages of scripture teach.

- Better understand symbolism, especially in the writings of Isaiah that Nephi included in the Book of Mormon.

Over the years, one of the most common expressions of gratitude from my students has been, "Thanks for the notes you had us put in our scriptures." This book is dedicated to that purpose.

Complete sources for the notes given in this work are found in the back of this book and also include the standard works of The Church of Jesus Christ of Latter-day Saints and the Joseph Smith Translation of the Bible.

The author hopes that this book will serve effectively as a "teacher in your hand" for members of the Church as they seek to increase their understanding of the writings and teachings found in the Book of Mormon. Above all, if this work serves to bring increased understanding and testimony of the Atonement of Christ, all the efforts to put it together will have been far more than worth it. A special thanks goes to my wife, Janette, and to my sons and daughters who have encouraged me every step of the way.

David J. Ridges

Introduction

The Book of Mormon—Another Testament of Jesus Christ is indeed a witness for Christ. On average, Christ is mentioned every 1.7 verses in the Book of Mormon. No wonder it is "the keystone of our religion, and a man would get nearer to God by abiding by its precepts, than by any other book." (See "Introduction" at the beginning of the Book of Mormon. Joseph Smith made this statement to the Twelve Apostles in Brigham Young's home in Nauvoo on November 28, 1841.)

About the Title Page

The title page, found at the beginning of the Book of Mormon, is a literal translation of Moroni's last statement, last page, left-hand side of the plates. (See *History of the Church*, Volume 1, p. 71.) The title page is a fascinating example of non-punctuated near eastern languages. In and of itself, it is a strong witness that the Book of Mormon is a translation of an ancient record.

If you will take a look at the title page of your Book of Mormon (which begins with the words, "The Book of Mormon, an account written by the hand of Mormon upon plates taken from the plates of Nephi"), you will note that there are only two periods in the whole text, one at the end of each paragraph. In near eastern languages, the words are all "run on," that is to say, there aren't any spaces between them and it is up to the reader to separate them. An example, in English, might be as follows:

THISISANEXAMPLEOFASENTENCEINWHICHALLOFTHEWORDSRUNTOGETHERANDTHEREADERHASTOSEPARATETHEMINORDERTOMAKESENSEOUTOFTHEM.

Properly punctuated, with individual words separated by spaces, in English the above would read, "This is an example of a sentence in which all of the words run together, and the reader has to separate them in order to make sense out of them."

It is interesting to note as you read the title page that Joseph Smith dictated the translation to his scribe, who then wrote it down. When it was taken to the printer, it was left up to the printer to punctuate it. In this case, the printer chose to use dashes to separate the various phrases, along with a few commas and an occasional semicolon.

For instance, if you read the last phrase of the first paragraph where it says, "The interpretation thereof by the gift of God," you will sense the problem the printer faced in punctuating a translation from an ancient language. If it were normal English, it would need some additional words to make a proper English sentence out of it. As it is, it is just there, as is the case with such ancient languages, one thought coming after the previous thought, in a manner typical of near eastern languages. This is what is known as an "internal witness." It is a witness that the Book of Mormon was translated from an ancient language, whose origins were in the area of the Holy Land.

In fact, Nephi tells us that the language he used to write the record on his plates consisted of "the learning of the Jews and the language of the Egyptians" (see 1 Nephi 1:2.). In other words, the origins of the language he used are found in the Near East.

The title page is Moroni's last statement to us. In the first paragraph, he tells us to whom the Book of Mormon is addressed, namely, the Lamanites, the Jews and the Gentiles, in other words, to all people. It is not just another book; rather, it is "written by way of commandment." Thus, it is the revealed word of God to be brought forth to the world in the last days, translated by the gift of God.

Moroni instructs us that it is an abridgment (a shortened or condensed version) of the record of the Nephites as well as an abridgment of the record of the Jaredites (the book of Ether). In the second paragraph of the title page, he tells us that he had three major purposes in mind for us as he prepared the gold plates for Joseph Smith to translate, namely:

1. To show us, who are a remnant of Israel (who are descendants of Abraham) what great things the Lord did for our ancestors. Among other things, this reminds us who we are and what our potential really is when we follow Christ faithfully.

2. To testify to us of the vital role which covenants play in bringing us back to God. Nephi reminds us that covenants were taken away as

"plain and precious things" (1 Nephi 13:26–29). They were removed from the gospel because of apostasy. You may recall also that covenants are only required for entrance into celestial glory and exaltation. No covenants are required for entrance into terrestrial or telestial glory. Thus, when we make and keep covenants, we are qualifying to return to God and to live in His presence forever.

3. To convince all of us "that JESUS is the CHRIST, the ETERNAL GOD, manifesting himself unto all nations." As stated above, the Book of Mormon mentions the Savior, one way or another, on average, every 1.7 verses. Every time we read from its sacred pages, we are giving the Holy Ghost many specific opportunities to bear direct witness to us that Jesus is the Christ and that His Atonement can be completely effective in our personal lives.

One could perhaps summarize the above-mentioned three major purposes of the Book of Mormon as follows: the Book of Mormon is a sacred, inspired volume of scripture in which the Savior teaches us about the history of His dealings with people in the past, about His desire to make covenants with us for our safety and well-being, and about the role of His Atonement in bringing peace and optimism into our lives.

This peace and optimism is emphasized in the last phrase of the title page wherein Moroni assures us that through the Atonement of Christ we "may be found spotless at the judgment-seat of Christ."

THE TESTIMONY OF THE THREE WITNESSES AND THE EIGHT WITNESSES

It is of great worth to take a careful look at the testimony of the Three Witnesses and the Eight Witnesses. These testimonies stand as powerful witnesses of the Book of Mormon as well as of the Prophet Joseph Smith. The fact that six of these eleven men left the Church but never denied that they had seen the plates gives strong validity to their testimonies. A list of each of these men, accompanied by a note as to whether or not they remained faithful, follows:

THE THREE WITNESSES

Oliver Cowdery: Left the Church, came back later.

David Whitmer: Left the Church, never came back.

Martin Harris: Left the Church, came back later.

THE EIGHT WITNESSES

Christian Whitmer: Remained faithful.

Jacob Whitmer: Left the Church, never came back.

Peter Whitmer, Junior: Remained faithful.

John Whitmer: Left the Church, never came back.

Hiram Page: Left the Church, never came back.

Joseph Smith, Senior: Remained faithful.

Hyrum Smith: Remained faithful.

Samuel Smith: Remained faithful.

As you study the testimony of the Three Witnesses, located near the beginning of your Book of Mormon, you will note that theirs is a spiritual witness. They keep it very simple and straightforward, certifying that:

1. They have seen the plates.
2. They know that the plates were translated by the gift and power of God.
3. They heard the voice of God so testifying.
4. They know the work is true.
5. They have personally seen the engravings upon the plates, and they were shown them by the power of God.
6. An angel brought the plates and showed them to the three men.

It is interesting to note that both Oliver Cowdery and Martin Harris personally handled the plates as the angel showed them to them, whereas David Whitmer chose not to handle them (see *Investigating the Book of Mormon Witnesses*, by Richard Lloyd Anderson, p. 81).

As you read the testimony of the Eight Witnesses, you will note that it is primarily a physical witness. In other words, they did not see an angel nor hear the voice of God. Rather, they bear sober witness that Joseph Smith showed them the plates, that they had "the appearance of gold" (these were honest, careful men), that they handled the leaves which had been translated, that the engravings had "the appearance of ancient work" (again, very honest and careful wording), that they had seen and lifted the plates and knew for certain that Joseph Smith had them in his possession.

These two testimonies, one of the Three and one of the Eight, have gone forth and continue to go forth to all the world bearing witness of the Book of Mormon and of the Prophet Joseph Smith. Each of us who prayerfully studies this sacred record can add our testimony to theirs.

THE FIRST BOOK OF NEPHI

Four different sets of metal plates or engraved records are spoken of in the Book of Mormon itself. For more information about these sets of plates, see "A Brief Explanation About the Book of Mormon" in the introductory pages to your Book of Mormon.

The first six books of the Book of Mormon (1 Nephi, 2 Nephi, Jacob, Enos, Jarom, and Omni) are taken from the small plates of Nephi. According to 2 Nephi 5:28–33, Nephi began the small plates thirty years after Lehi's family had left Jerusalem. It was to be a special record emphasizing spiritual things and teachings. Another set of plates, known as the large plates of Nephi, had been kept since they left Jerusalem. This set contained more of the history and secular records of the people.

As we begin our study of First Nephi, we see the importance of the small plates of Nephi. For one thing, after Joseph Smith had translated 116 handwritten pages of the large plates of Nephi, Martin Harris, who was serving as his scribe, begged him to let him take the precious manuscript pages home to Palmyra, New York, to stop the wagging tongues and gossip which was being spread about Martin. It was said that he had been fooled and taken in by Joseph Smith. After repeated requests by Martin, Joseph allowed him to take the 116 pages. They were lost and never recovered.

After a difficult period of waiting, Joseph was allowed to take up the work of translating the plates again. We learn from D&C 10:30, 38–41 that Joseph was instructed by the Lord not to retranslate the plates from which the lost 116 manuscript pages had been taken. Rather, he was to translate from the small plates of Nephi (which were contained in the gold plates he had taken from Hill Cumorah) to make up for what had been lost. Joseph obeyed, and we have 1 Nephi, 2 Nephi, Jacob, Enos, Jarom, and Omni in place of the material which had been translated from the large plates. In fact, we came out ahead because we are now privileged to read and study the more spiritual matters contained in the small plates as opposed to the things contained in the large plates which covered the same period of time and whose translation was lost with the 116 pages. As usual, the Lord triumphs over Satan's efforts to halt the work.

By the way, the main heading to First Nephi, given in italics at the very beginning of the book starting with *"An account of Lehi . . .,"* is a direct translation from the plates. However, the headings at the beginning of each chapter, such as *"Nephi begins the record of his people—Lehi sees . . ."* at the beginning of the first chapter, were written by Elder Bruce R. McConkie of the Quorum of the Twelve Apostles by assignment from the First Presidency, to help us have an overview of each chapter's contents.

FIRST NEPHI 1

It is interesting to consider how old Nephi might be as he writes this. As mentioned above, we know from 2 Nephi 5:28–33 that he started engraving his small plates thirty years after they left Jerusalem. If we assume that Nephi was somewhere between fifteen and twenty years old when Lehi and his family left Jerusalem, it would make Nephi perhaps forty-five to fifty years old as he begins engraving the first verse of our Book of Mormon.

Thus, it would be reasonable to think that he is looking back with tender memories and is somewhat nostalgic as he thinks about his parents and the events which have taken place over the last thirty years.

1 I, NEPHI, having been born of goodly [*an Old Testament word which means "praiseworthy, morally good, noble," according to* Strong's Exhaustive Concordance of the Bible, *word #2570*] parents, therefore I was taught somewhat in all the learning of my father; and having seen many afflictions in the course of my days, nevertheless, having been highly favored of the Lord in all my days; yea, having had a great knowledge of the goodness and the mysteries of God, therefore I make a record of my proceedings in my days.

We learn many things about Nephi from verse 1, above. First, he is appreciative of righteous parents. Second, he emphasizes the positives in his life. After mentioning that he has "seen many afflictions" in his days, which is an understatement, he immediately tells us that he has been "highly favored of the Lord" in **all** his days, thus underscoring the kind of lives positive personalities enjoy.

For perspective, we might just take a quick look at a few of the "many afflictions" in Nephi's life up to this point. He was nearly murdered four times by his own brothers (1 Nephi 7:16, 1 Nephi 16:37, 1 Nephi 17:45, 2 Nephi 5:4). Laban tried to kill him and his brothers (1 Nephi 3:25). They spent eight difficult years in the wilderness. He had much opposition in building the ship (1 Nephi 17), plus he was tied up on the ship (1 Nephi 18).

In spite of such afflictions, Nephi focused on the great blessings he had received from the Lord, which included "a great knowledge of the goodness and the mysteries of God" (verse 1, above). We might note that the word "mysteries" as used here means basic doctrines such as correct knowledge of the Godhead, the plan of salvation, priesthood authority, resurrection, and so forth, rather than strange, mysterious trivia or secret teachings (see Bible Dictionary, p. 736, under "Mystery" in your Bible).

2 Yea, I make a record in the language of my father, which consists of the learning of the Jews and the language of the Egyptians.

3 And I know that the record which I make is true; and I make it with mine own hand; and I make it according to my knowledge.

Next, Nephi will mention Zedekiah, king of Judah. This is about 600 B.C.; Zedekiah is a wicked, twenty-one-year-old king (see 2 Kings 24:18–19). He will reign for eleven years, during which time, among other evil deeds, he will imprison the Prophet Jeremiah in a miserable dungeon with deep mire (see Jeremiah, chapters 38–39). Finally, after Lehi and his family have fled Jerusalem, King Zedekiah will be captured by King Nebuchadnezzar's forces of Babylon about 587 B.C. Zedekiah's sons (except for Mulek) will be killed before his eyes, and he will be blinded and carried as a prisoner to Babylon (see 2 Kings 25).

4 For it came to pass in the commencement of the first year of the reign of Zedekiah, king of Judah, (my father, Lehi, having dwelt at Jerusalem in all his days); and in that same year there came many prophets [*including Jeremiah, Nahum, Habakkuk, and Zephaniah*], prophesying unto the people that they must repent, or the great city Jerusalem must be destroyed.

5 Wherefore it came to pass that my father, Lehi, as he went forth prayed unto the Lord, yea, even with all his heart, in behalf of his people.

You may wish to underline in your own Book of Mormon several words and phrases from verses 6 through 16, which point out to us that Lehi, himself, was indeed a great prophet. We will underline and **bold** some of them now, and then return to these verses for some additional teaching.

6 And it came to pass as he prayed unto the Lord, **there came a pillar of fire and dwelt upon a rock before him**; and **he saw and heard much**; and because of the things which he saw and heard he did quake and tremble exceedingly.

7 And it came to pass that he returned to his own house at Jerusalem; and he cast himself upon his bed, being **overcome with the Spirit** and the things which he had seen.

8 And being thus overcome with the Spirit, he was **carried away in a vision**, even that he **saw the heavens open**, and he thought he **saw God sitting upon his throne, surrounded with numberless concourses of angels in the attitude of singing and praising their God**.

9 And it came to pass that **he saw One descending out of the midst of heaven, and he beheld that his luster was above that of the sun at noon-day**.

10 And he also **saw twelve others following him**, and their brightness did exceed that of the stars in the firmament.

11 And they came down and went forth upon the face of the earth; and **the first came and stood before my father, and gave unto him a book, and bade him that he should read**.

12 And it came to pass that as he read, he was filled with the Spirit of the Lord.

13 And he read, saying: Wo, wo, unto Jerusalem, for I have seen thine abominations! Yea, and **many things did my father read concerning Jerusalem—that it should be destroyed**, and the inhabitants thereof; many should perish by the sword, and **many should be carried away captive into Babylon**.

14 And it came to pass that when **my father had read and seen many great and marvelous things**, he did exclaim many things unto the Lord; such as: Great and marvelous are thy works, O Lord God Almighty! Thy throne is high in the heavens, and thy power, and goodness, and mercy are over all the inhabitants of the earth; and, because thou art merciful, thou wilt not suffer those who come

First Nephi 1

unto thee that they shall perish!

15 And after this manner was the language of my father in the praising of his God; for his soul did rejoice, and his whole heart was filled, because of the things which he had seen, yea, which the Lord had shown unto him.

16 And now I, Nephi, do not make a full account of the things which my father hath written, for he hath written many things which **he saw in visions** and in **dreams**; and he also hath written many things which he **prophesied** and spake unto his children, of which I shall not make a full account.

> Now that we have paid attention to certain words of Nephi which point out what a great prophet his father, Lehi, was, we will repeat verses 6 through 16 and add a few notes for teaching purposes.

6 And it came to pass as he prayed unto the Lord, there came a pillar of fire and dwelt upon a rock before him; and he saw and heard much; and because of the things which he saw and heard he did quake and tremble exceedingly.

7 And it came to pass that he returned to his own house at Jerusalem; and he cast himself upon his bed, being overcome with the Spirit and the things which he had seen.

> Next, in verse 8, we run into an interesting phrase which causes some readers to ask, "Why doesn't it come right out and say that Lehi saw God, rather than saying that he thought he saw God?"
>
> The answer is simple. In order to avoid even the slightest chance of using the name of God inappropriately, ancient prophets sometimes used the "polite" indirect reference rather than using "God" outright. Lehi did see God the Father, but in writing about it, Nephi uses the indirect "thought he saw God." We see other examples of this indirect mode in the scriptures. For instance, in Abraham 3:24, Abraham refers to the premortal Christ as one "that was like unto God." In Daniel 3:25, Christ is referred to as "like the Son of God." In Revelation 1:13, Jesus is referred to as "one like unto the Son of man."

8 And being thus overcome with the Spirit, he was carried away in a vision, even that he saw the heavens open, and he thought he saw God [*the Father; compare with Revelation 4:2, 5:7*] sitting upon his throne, surrounded with numberless concourses of angels in the attitude of singing and praising their God.

9 And it came to pass that he

[*Lehi*] saw One [*Christ*] descending out of the midst of heaven, and he beheld that his luster [*brightness*] was above that of the sun at noon-day.

10 And he also saw twelve others [*the Twelve Apostles*] following him [*the Savior*], and their brightness did exceed that of the stars in the firmament [*the heavens*].

11 And they came down and went forth upon the face of the earth; and the first [*Christ*] came and stood before my father, and gave unto him a book [*symbolic of a mission to perform—compare with D&C 77:14 and Revelation 10:2 and 9*], and bade him that he should read [*asked him to read the book*].

12 And it came to pass that as he read, he was filled with the Spirit of the Lord.

13 And he read, saying: Wo, wo, unto Jerusalem, for I have seen thine abominations [*terrible wickedness*]! Yea, and many things did my father read concerning Jerusalem—that it should be destroyed, and the inhabitants thereof; many should perish by the sword, and many should be carried away captive into Babylon [*a powerful enemy nation headquartered about five hundred miles east of Jerusalem*].

14 And it came to pass that when my father had read and seen many great and marvelous things, he did exclaim many things unto the Lord; such as: Great and marvelous are thy works, O Lord God Almighty! Thy throne is high in the heavens, and thy power, and goodness, and mercy are over all the inhabitants of the earth; and, because thou art merciful, thou wilt not suffer those who come unto thee that they shall perish!

15 And after this manner was the language of my father in the praising of his God; for his soul did rejoice, and his whole heart was filled, because of the things which he had seen, yea, which the Lord had shown unto him.

16 And now I, Nephi, do not make a full account of the things which my father hath written, for he hath written many things which he saw in visions and in dreams; and he also hath written many things which he prophesied and spake unto his children, of which I shall not make a full account.

17 But I shall make an account of my proceedings in my days. Behold, I make an abridgment

[*a shortened version or summary*] of the record of my father, upon plates which I have made with mine own hands [*this brief summary of his father's writings goes through 1 Nephi, chapter 8*]; wherefore, after I have abridged the record of my father then will I make an account of mine own life.

18 Therefore, I would that ye should know, that after the Lord had shown so many marvelous things unto my father, Lehi, yea, concerning the destruction of Jerusalem, behold he went forth among the people, and began to prophesy and to declare unto them concerning the things which he had both seen and heard.

19 And it came to pass that the Jews did mock him because of the things which he testified of them; for he truly testified of their wickedness and their abominations; and he testified that the things which he saw and heard, and also the things which he read in the book [*referred to in verse 11*], manifested plainly of the coming of a Messiah, and also the redemption of the world.

20 And when the Jews heard these things they were angry with him; yea, even as with the prophets of old, whom they had cast out, and stoned, and slain; and they also sought his life, that they might take it away. But behold, I, Nephi, will show unto you that the tender mercies of the Lord are over all those whom he hath chosen, because of their faith, to make them mighty even unto the power of deliverance.

Nephi tells us in verse 20, above, that one of his major goals in his writing is to show us the "tender mercies" of the Lord. Verse 20 of course is in the first chapter of the Book of Mormon. In the last chapter of the Book of Mormon (Moroni 10:3), Moroni expresses a hope that we will have noticed "how merciful the Lord hath been unto the children of men" as we studied this precious volume of scripture.

To me, these two verses, one at the beginning and one at the end, form "bookends" for the content of the Book of Mormon. They serve as a reminder that the Lord loves to extend kindness and mercy to each of us. The whole book is a reminder of this. One of my friends once found more than four hundred "tender mercy" statements or experiences, in one form or another, within the Book of Mormon.

FIRST NEPHI 2

In this chapter, Lehi is warned by the Lord to take his family and flee into the wilderness. He, of course, obeys, leaving his wealth and worldly possessions behind. Some readers are inclined to ask why he didn't just leave Laman and Lemuel home also, rather than being subjected to the problems they continued to cause. While Lehi and Sariah are best qualified to respond to this question, perhaps we may venture a few responses. First of all, faithful parents continue to hope that wayward children will repent and they often do. Another facet of the answer may be that in each family, it is not just the wayward or rebellious members who need to learn lessons, but the faithful members also have the need to grow in patience, wisdom, forgiving, striving to bring them back, etc., and to learn almost countless other attributes of exalted beings.

1 FOR behold, it came to pass that the Lord spake unto my father, yea, even in a dream, and said unto him: Blessed art thou Lehi, because of the things which thou hast done; and because thou hast been faithful and declared unto this people the things which I commanded thee, behold, they seek to take away thy life.

2 And it came to pass that the Lord commanded my father, even in a dream, that he should take his family and depart into the wilderness.

3 And it came to pass that he was obedient unto the word of the Lord, wherefore he did as the Lord commanded him.

4 And it came to pass that he departed into the wilderness. And he left his house, and the land of his inheritance, and his gold, and his silver, and his precious things, and took nothing with him, save it were his family, and provisions, and tents, and departed into the wilderness.

> Just an interesting "internal evidence" that the Book of Mormon is a translation from an ancient Near-Eastern (Semitic) language. Count the number of times "and" is used in verse 4, above. This usage is very typical of such languages.

5 And he came down by the borders near the shore of the Red Sea [*about 180–200 miles from Jerusalem*]; and he traveled in the wilderness in the borders which are nearer the Red Sea; and he did travel in the wilderness with his family, which consisted of my mother, Sariah, and my elder brothers, who were Laman, Lemuel, and Sam.

> According to 2 Nephi 5:6, Lehi's family increased in the

wilderness to include two more sons (Jacob and Joseph, plus daughters).

6 And it came to pass that when he had traveled three days in the wilderness, he pitched his tent in a valley by the side of a river of water.

> The phrase "a river of water" in verse 6, above, is another internal evidence that the Book of Mormon account is a translation of an ancient record which originates in the area of the Holy Land. In that arid country, there are many "rivers" which are usually dry river beds and are commonly called "wadis." Here, Nephi indicates that the "river" actually has water flowing in it at the time they camp by it.

7 And it came to pass that he built an altar of stones, and made an offering unto the Lord, and gave thanks unto the Lord our God.

> Building an altar and giving an offering to the Lord, in verse 7, above, is a reminder that Lehi and his family worship God according to Old Testament laws and ceremonies (compare with Exodus 20:24–26). The Book of Mormon people will continue to keep the law of Moses until the Savior appears (3 Nephi) and gives them the higher laws of the New Testament.

8 And it came to pass that he called the name of the river, Laman [*this was quite an honor given to Laman*], and it emptied into the Red Sea; and the valley was in the borders near the mouth thereof.

9 And when my father saw that the waters of the river emptied into the fountain of the Red Sea, he spake unto Laman, saying: O that thou mightest be like unto this river, continually running into the fountain of all righteousness! [*Perhaps meaning that he wishes that Laman's deeds and desires would always merge with the Lord's will and the course of righteousness.*]

10 And he also spake unto Lemuel: O that thou mightest be like unto this valley, firm and steadfast, and immovable in keeping the commandments of the Lord!

> We will take a moment here to look at some possible reasons for recording Laman and Lemuel's murmuring and rebellious behavior. One reason for so doing is to avoid such behaviors ourselves. Another reason is so that we can perhaps better understand why they continue to cause trouble as Nephi's record continues. Yet another reason might be so that we gain better insight into how patient the Lord is with all of us as He gives us opportunity after opportunity to repent and change our ways.

Neither Laman nor Lemuel appear to honor their father, which is one of the Ten Commandments that they were no doubt taught. Both seem to be materialistic, according to Nephi (verse 11, next). They do not seem spiritual or sensitive to the things of God (verse 12). They obviously don't believe the words of other prophets about the fate of Jerusalem, according to verse 13. Yet another reason for such rebellion and spiritual insensitivity may be revealed by Nephi in the last half of verse 13. This is a rather startling and serious insight. Nephi says that "they were like unto the Jews who were at Jerusalem."

With this in mind, let's see what the Prophet Jeremiah said about the evils indulged in by the Jews at Jerusalem during this period in history. Jeremiah 9:2–3 says (**bold** added for emphasis):

2 Oh that I had in the wilderness a lodging place of wayfaring men; that I might leave my people, and go from them! for **they** *be* **all adulterers**, an assembly of treacherous men.

3 And **they bend their tongues** *like* **their bow** *for* **lies**: but they are not valiant for the truth upon the earth; for **they proceed from evil to evil**, and they know not me, saith the LORD.

Jeremiah 6:15 tells us that the Jews had gotten to the point of such spiritual insensitivity that they were no longer embarrassed by wickedness. We read (**bold** added for emphasis):

15 Were they ashamed when they had committed abomination? nay, **they were not at all ashamed, neither could they blush**: therefore they shall fall among them that fall: at the time *that* I visit them they shall be cast down, saith the LORD.

Sexual immorality seems to have run wild among the Jews at this time as stated in Jeremiah 5:7–8 (**bold** added for emphasis):

7 How shall I pardon thee for this? thy children have forsaken me, and sworn by *them that are* no gods: when I had fed them to the full, **they** then **committed adultery**, **and assembled themselves by troops in the harlots' houses.**

8 They were *as* fed horses in the morning: **every one neighed after his neighbour's wife.**

D&C 42:23, which follows next, tells us one of the awful consequences of continued sexual immorality. It is the loss of the Spirit. When people lose the Spirit, they no longer see evil as being wrong or even dangerous. And they see righteous people and principles as foolish.

FIRST NEPHI 2

D&C 42:23

23 And he that looketh upon a woman to lust after her shall deny the faith, and shall not have the Spirit; and if he repents not he shall be cast out.

While we cannot know for sure that Laman and Lemuel were involved in such evil, Nephi's statement that they "were like unto the Jews" gives us strong reason to wonder, and is powerful counsel to avoid such evils in our own lives. Whatever the case, Laman and Lemuel had become very selfish and insensitive to spiritual things. It became a downward spiral in their lives and even led to murderous desires in their hearts.

11 Now this he [*Lehi*] spake because of the stiffneckedness of Laman and Lemuel; for behold they did murmur in many things against their father, because he was a visionary man, and had led them out of the land of Jerusalem, to leave the land of their inheritance, and their gold, and their silver, and their precious things, to perish in the wilderness. And this they said he had done because of the foolish imaginations of his heart.

12 And thus Laman and Lemuel, being the eldest, did murmur against their father. And they did murmur because they knew not the dealings of that God who had created them.

13 Neither did they believe that Jerusalem, that great city, could be destroyed according to the words of the prophets. And they were like unto the Jews who were at Jerusalem, who sought to take away the life of my father.

14 And it came to pass that my father did speak unto them in the valley of Lemuel, with power, being filled with the Spirit, until their frames did shake before him. And he did confound them, that they durst not utter against him; wherefore, they did as he commanded them.

We might learn at least two lessons from verse 14, above. One would be that even though Laman and Lemuel were so rebellious, the Lord still gave them a miraculous experience to help them repent and become righteous, if they so chose. Another lesson is that when people ignore the gentle whisperings of the Spirit and continue in wickedness, the Lord "turns up the volume" to try to get them to listen and repent. It is so in our day, with the forces of nature in an uproar—storms, earthquakes, pestilence, natural disasters—because so many of the inhabitants of the earth have ignored the gentler invitations to come unto Christ (see D&C 88:88–90).

15 And my father dwelt in a tent.

16 And it came to pass that I, Nephi, being exceedingly young, nevertheless being large in stature, and also having great desires to know of the mysteries [*the basic truths and doctrines, see Bible Dictionary, p. 736, under "Mysteries"*] of God, wherefore, I did cry [*pray mightily*] unto the Lord; and behold he did visit me, and did soften my heart that I did believe all the words which had been spoken by my father; wherefore, I did not rebel against him like unto my brothers.

There is an important lesson to learn from Nephi in verse 16, above. Some people ask whether or not it is wrong to doubt or wonder about matters related to the gospel. Given the fact that individual agency is a gift from God, the answer has to be "No." But it is wrong and foolish to rebel. It is what we do about doubts when they arise in our hearts that makes or breaks us. When doubts about their father and his visions arose in Laman and Lemuel's minds, they chose to murmur and rebel. A careful reading of verse 16 may indicate that Nephi also had doubts in his heart, because he tells us that the Lord "did soften my heart that I did believe all the words which had been spoken by my father; wherefore, I did not rebel." Nephi's approach was different from that of his two older brothers. He had an honest heart, a great desire to know the basic truths and doctrines of the gospel, and a desire to know the truthfulness of what his father taught. He humbly prayed to the Lord until he received the sweet, reassuring answer about the truthfulness of his father's revelations. Thus, he had full ownership of faithfully following his prophet father.

17 And I spake unto Sam, making known unto him the things which the Lord had manifested unto me by his Holy Spirit. And it came to pass that he believed in my words.

Sam is one of my favorite people in the Book of Mormon. I have tender feelings for him and hope to meet him someday. Though older than Nephi, he faithfully follows him and assists him. He reminds me of Hyrum Smith, Joseph Smith's older brother. Though they were older brothers, both Sam and Hyrum seemed to have the gift of believing the words of others, a gift of the Spirit spoken of in D&C 46:14. They both followed and faithfully supported their younger prophet brothers throughout the rest of their lives.

18 But, behold, Laman and Lemuel would not hearken unto

my words; and being grieved because of the hardness of their hearts I cried unto the Lord for them [*Nephi really cares about his rebellious older brothers*].

19 And it came to pass that the Lord spake unto me, saying: Blessed art thou, Nephi, because of thy faith, for thou hast sought me diligently, with lowliness of heart [*humility*].

20 And inasmuch as ye shall keep my commandments, ye shall prosper, and shall be led to a land of promise; yea, even a land which I have prepared for you; yea, a land which is choice above all other lands [*symbolic of heaven, celestial glory, exaltation*].

21 And inasmuch as [*if*] thy brethren shall rebel against thee, they shall be cut off from the presence of the Lord.

There is probably quite an important lesson here for us. It may be that Nephi did not get the answer he wanted. He had obviously been praying for the souls and salvation of Laman and Lemuel. Instead of being reassured that they would be saved, he is reminded that they have agency, and their judgment will depend on how they use it. However, in the next verse, he is reassured that if he continues to keep the commandments, he will be saved. Thus, we are reminded that we need to do all we can to save others, including praying continually for them. But we cannot force anyone to salvation against his or her agency.

22 And inasmuch as thou shalt keep my commandments, thou shalt be made a ruler and a teacher over thy brethren [*this prophecy is fulfilled as the Book of Mormon continues*].

23 For behold, in that day that they shall rebel against me, I will curse them even with a sore curse, and they shall have no power over thy seed [*Nephi's posterity*] except they shall rebel against me also.

24 And if it so be that they [*Nephi's posterity*] rebel against me, they [*Laman and Lemuel's posterity*] shall be a scourge [*trouble*] unto thy seed, to stir them up in the ways of remembrance. [*In other words, if necessary, the Lamanites will cause the Nephites trouble in order to try to get them to repent.*]

FIRST NEPHI 3

In this chapter, Lehi's sons will be asked to go back to Jerusalem to get the brass plates of Laban. There are many major messages and lessons for us here. For one thing, this is certainly a mission to which the brothers are called by the Lord. Sometimes we find ourselves thinking that since the call comes from the Lord, everything ought to work out smoothly, with every potential obstacle removed. We forget sometimes that life is a "schooling" provided for our growth and development, and that if every time we went on the Lord's errand, things were to go perfectly well because of the Lord's blessings, we would be deprived of much of our education.

Another issue which students sometimes bring up as they study this chapter is the question, "Since the Lord knew that they would need the brass plates, why didn't He tell Lehi before they left the Jerusalem area, instead of having the boys go back 180–200 miles, one way, through a very dangerous wilderness filled with robbers, murderers, and wild beasts?"

Again, the answer lies in the fact that mortal life is for our learning and development. Nephi and his brothers each had many opportunities for increased faith and testimony during the hardships they encountered. Some of them grew spiritually, and some did not.

There is one major blessing which came as a result of this commandment of the Lord to go back and get the brass plates, which we may sometimes overlook. It has to do with strengthening Sariah's testimony. In order to see this, we will skip ahead to 1 Nephi, chapter five, for a moment. As we do so, we will focus on the difficult unknowns Sariah faced as a mother and wife as her boys were gone on such a dangerous undertaking. At best, her sons would have been gone for at least a month, perhaps closer to two months. It was a long and treacherous journey to Jerusalem and back, and there were dangers that could befall Nephi and his brothers while in the Jerusalem area. Remember, the Jews had tried to kill Lehi, and perhaps felt animosity for his family members too.

We are told by Nephi, in 1 Nephi 5:1, that his mother "truly had mourned" for her sons while they were gone. Verse 2 tells us that she had eventually assumed that they had died in the wilderness, and that she had complained rather bitterly against her husband, Lehi, accusing him of leading them away from the comforts of home, getting their sons killed in the wilderness, and that they, too, would die.

According to 1 Nephi 5:4–6, Lehi was able to "comfort" Sariah somewhat, but when their sons actually returned safely to camp (verse 7), she indeed *was* comforted! In fact, her testimony that they were working under the direction of the Lord thus became "a surety" (verse 8), and we never hear another complaint nor lack of support from her again. Such a firm testimony is priceless, and the whole journey back to Jerusalem would have been well worth it if only to provide noble Sariah with such strength and sure knowledge that they were on the Lord's errand.

Regardless of the reasons the Lord had for commanding Lehi's sons to return for the brass plates, we know that it was worthwhile because the Lord commanded it. Now, let's return to Nephi's account.

1 AND it came to pass that I, Nephi, returned from speaking with the Lord, to the tent of my father.

2 And it came to pass that he spake unto me, saying: Behold I have dreamed a dream, in the which the Lord hath commanded me that thou and thy brethren shall return to Jerusalem.

3 For behold, Laban hath the record of the Jews and also a genealogy of my forefathers, and they are engraven upon plates of brass.

> It would appear that Laban was probably Lehi's relative and that he was the one in the family who possessed the family genealogy and records. Among other things, the brass plates contained what we know as the Old Testament, from Genesis up to and including some of the writings of Jeremiah (see 1 Nephi 5:11–13).

4 Wherefore, the Lord hath commanded me that thou and thy brothers should go unto the house of Laban, and seek the records, and bring them down hither [*here*] into the wilderness.

5 And now, behold thy brothers murmur [*complain*], saying it is a hard thing which I have required of them; but behold I have not required it of them, but it is a commandment of the Lord.

> Verse 5 is a valuable reminder to us all that when our prophet speaks to us, it is not his instructions we are hearing; rather, it is the word of the Lord.

6 Therefore go, my son, and thou shalt be favored of the Lord,

because thou hast not murmured.

> Verse 7, next, is one of the most famous verses in the Book of Mormon, with a very valuable message.

7 And it came to pass that I, Nephi, said unto my father: I will go and do the things which the Lord hath commanded, for I know that the Lord giveth no commandments unto the children of men, save he shall prepare a way for them that they may accomplish the thing which he commandeth them.

8 And it came to pass that when my father had heard these words he was exceedingly glad [*very, very glad*], for he knew that I had been blessed of the Lord.

9 And I, Nephi, and my brethren took our journey in the wilderness, with our tents, to go up to the land of Jerusalem.

> Even the phrase "up to the land of Jerusalem" is a bit of internal testimony of the truth of the Book of Mormon. Those of you who are familiar with the geography of the Holy Land realize that Jerusalem is up high in the mountains, and most other sites are "down" from Jerusalem. Therefore, most people in that area, as they travel to Jerusalem, are indeed traveling "up."

10 And it came to pass that when we had gone up to the land of Jerusalem, I and my brethren did consult one with another.

11 And we cast lots—who of us should go in unto the house of Laban. And it came to pass that the lot [*the short straw, the short stick, or whatever they used*] fell upon Laman; and Laman went in unto the house of Laban, and he talked with him as he sat in his house.

12 And he desired of Laban the records which were engraven upon the plates of brass, which contained the genealogy of my father.

13 And behold, it came to pass that Laban was angry, and thrust him out from his presence; and he would not that he should have the records. Wherefore, he said unto him: Behold thou art a robber, and I will slay thee. [*This false accusation would be a shock and a major disappointment, especially since Laman had been assured by Nephi and Lehi that the Lord had sent them to get the brass plates.*]

14 But Laman fled out of his presence, and told the things which Laban had done, unto us. And we began to be exceedingly sorrowful, and my brethren were

about to return unto my father in the wilderness.

> As mentioned earlier, this was the work of the Lord, and the Lord could have caused things to go well on this first attempt to get the brass plates from Laban. However, as you know, sturdy and lasting growth does not come from constant ease. By the way, it appears from verse 14, above, that this setback was hard on all four sons, including Nephi, because he says, "**We** began to be exceedingly sorrowful." However, Nephi was completely determined to keep the commandment of the Lord to get the plates and did not join with his brethren in their desire to go back to their father in the wilderness. Therefore, Nephi grew from this experience, and Laman and Lemuel weakened. We don't know about Sam but suspect that he also grew.

> In verse 15, next, Nephi uses the strongest possible oath in his Semitic culture to express his commitment to fulfill the commandment of the Lord. In his culture, to promise or swear by any living thing was a very strong oath. But to swear by one's own life was stronger still, and to promise by the living God was the strongest of all promises or oaths.

15 But behold I said unto them that: As the Lord liveth, and as we live, we will not go down unto our father in the wilderness until we have accomplished the thing which the Lord hath commanded us.

16 Wherefore, let us be faithful in keeping the commandments of the Lord; therefore let us go down to the land of our father's inheritance [*indicating probably that Lehi and his family lived somewhere near Jerusalem but outside of the actual city limits*], for behold he left gold and silver, and all manner of riches. And all this he hath done because of the commandments of the Lord.

> True Saints, past and present, are like Lehi in that they willingly give up whatever it takes in order to do the work of the Lord. This certainly includes missionaries, both young elders and sisters as well as senior couples and sisters.

17 For he knew that Jerusalem must be destroyed, because of the wickedness of the people.

> Verse 18, next, is highly symbolic and significant. The destruction of Jerusalem will of course be literal, as history shows. However, when we see such verses in scripture, we would do well to shift our mind into "symbolism mode" and note the many possible messages provided in symbolism. Symbolism is almost infinitely deep and thus allows the Holy Ghost to point out different messages

to our minds each time we encounter the same passages of scripture.

For instance, the phrase "if my father should dwell in the land after he hath been commanded to flee out of the land, behold, he would also perish" in verse 18 could have many different applications. It could apply literally to a family camping in a steep-walled canyon who are prompted by the Spirit to flee because a flash flood is coming. It could likewise apply to a member who is in a relationship which threatens to compromise the moral standards of the gospel. If he or she does not flee the circumstance, danger of great spiritual damage or even perishing spiritually could follow.

Yet another example of the symbolic lesson in verse 18 might be that of a younger or older member of the Church who has fallen in with the wrong crowd. If he or she does not heed the warnings of the Spirit to flee and get away from the temptations, dire consequences may follow. Such warnings of the Holy Ghost could be with respect to reading material, financial dealings, physical danger, military dangers, political trends and philosophies, social philosophies, and disobeying the wisdom and counsel of parents, bishops, grandparents, or whomever. The list goes on and on, as do the symbolic applications of verse 18.

18 For behold, they have rejected the words of the prophets. Wherefore, if my father should dwell in the land after he hath been commanded to flee out of the land, behold, he would also perish. Wherefore, it must needs be that he flee out of the land.

> Nephi next reminds his brothers why it is so important for them to follow through and get the brass plates. As mentioned in the previous note, there is much symbolism in scripture, and you will readily see how the next verses symbolically apply to the importance of scriptures and family history in your own life.

19 And behold, it is wisdom in God that we should obtain these records, that we may preserve unto our children the language of our fathers;

20 And also that we may preserve unto them the words which have been spoken by the mouth of all the holy prophets, which have been delivered unto them by the Spirit and power of God, since the world began, even down unto this present time. [*All this was contained on the brass plates.*]

21 And it came to pass that after this manner of language did I persuade my brethren, that they might be faithful in keeping the commandments of God. [*The prophecy, given in 1 Nephi 2:22, that Nephi would*

become "a ruler and a teacher" over his brothers is already coming to pass.]

22 And it came to pass that we went down to the land of our inheritance, and we did gather together our gold, and our silver, and our precious things.

23 And after we had gathered these things together, we went up again unto the house of Laban.

24 And it came to pass that we went in unto Laban, and desired him that he would give unto us the records which were engraven upon the plates of brass, for which we would give unto him our gold, and our silver, and all our precious things.

25 And it came to pass that when Laban saw our property, and that it was exceedingly great, he did lust after it [*Laban was a greedy man*], insomuch that he thrust us out, and sent his servants to slay us, that he might obtain our property. [*Laban was willing to murder for selfish gain.*]

26 And it came to pass that we did flee before the servants of Laban, and we were obliged to leave behind our property, and it fell into the hands of Laban.

27 And it came to pass that we fled into the wilderness, and the servants of Laban did not overtake us, and we hid ourselves in the cavity of a rock [*probably meaning a cave*].

> Next, we are reminded again that when circumstances become difficult, some people weaken while some grow stronger as a result. Usually, those who weaken try to find someone other than themselves to blame. Common companions to blame are anger and violence.

28 And it came to pass that Laman was angry with me, and also with my father; and also was Lemuel, for he hearkened unto the words of Laman. [*Lemuel seems to be a follower but is unwise in his choice of whom to follow.*] Wherefore Laman and Lemuel did speak many hard words unto us, their younger brothers, and they did smite [*hit*] us even with a rod.

29 And it came to pass as they smote us with a rod, behold, an angel of the Lord came and stood before them, and he spake unto them, saying: Why do ye smite your younger brother with a rod? Know ye not that the Lord hath chosen him [*Nephi; see 1 Nephi 2:22*] to be a ruler over you, and this because of your iniquities [*evil doings*]? Behold ye shall go up to Jerusalem again,

and the Lord will deliver Laban into your hands.

> This is a promise. Therefore, they know that they will succeed in obtaining the brass plates if they go back for them again. What it takes for Nephi to actually take possession of them, though, will become one of the most difficult trials of his young life so far. Yet, after the severe trial of his faith, he will succeed, and he will have grown tremendously in his ability to follow the commandments of God. Likewise, he will have obtained great blessings.

30 And after the angel had spoken unto us, he departed.

31 And after the angel had departed, Laman and Lemuel again began to murmur, saying: How is it possible that the Lord will deliver Laban into our hands? Behold, he is a mighty man, and he can command fifty, yea, even he can slay fifty; then why not us?

> We are left almost stunned by Laman and Lemuel's response to the appearance of the angel. How could they possibly be so boldly foolish and rejecting of his message? How could they immediately turn such a wonderful thing as the appearance of an angel into a strong negative? We are left to conclude that wickedness does not promote rational thought. This is, in fact, a major message of the scriptures.

FIRST NEPHI 4

So far, the four sons of Lehi have done everything in their power to accomplish their mission and still have failed. There seems to be a lesson here for all of us. In many things and responsibilities, we succeed on the first try. The Lord encourages us to use our mind to solve problems and tells us that it is not necessary for Him to "command" us "in all things" and that "the power is in us" to solve many situations (see D&C 58:26–28). However, it seems that we need to be reminded of our complete dependence upon the Lord from time to time. For instance, this is absolutely the case with respect to our dependence on the Atonement. When we need to revisit this lesson, it seems that nothing we try succeeds. Then the Lord steps in and shows forth His power, and we succeed in His way.

1 AND it came to pass that I spake unto my brethren, saying: Let us go up again unto Jerusalem, and let us be faithful in keeping the commandments of the Lord; for behold he is mightier than all the earth, then why not mightier than Laban and his fifty, yea, or even than his tens of thousands? [*In other words, even if Laban had tens of*

thousands of soldiers, the Lord could still overcome them and bless us with success in obtaining the plates.]

2 Therefore let us go up; let us be strong like unto Moses; for he truly spake unto the waters of the Red Sea and they divided hither and thither, and our fathers came through, out of captivity, on dry ground, and the armies of Pharaoh did follow and were drowned in the waters of the Red Sea.

It seems that many people who read the Bible, along with most Bible scholars today, do not believe that Moses and the children of Israel literally had the Red Sea part for them and that they went through on dry ground with the armies of Pharaoh drowning as they pursued them. In fact, some scholars say that it was the "Reed" Sea, not the Red Sea, which Moses and his people crossed, that the water was very shallow, and that the hot desert wind just happened to push it back for the Israelites.

In verse 2, above, we see the Book of Mormon supporting and verifying the Bible. The Israelites did experience the miracle of the parting of the Red Sea and they did go through on dry ground, a major miracle in and of itself. The prophecy of Ezekiel in Ezekiel 37:15–17 is being fulfilled before our eyes. The Bible and the Book of Mormon, the stick of Judah and the stick of Ephraim, have "become one in thine hand."

3 Now behold ye know that this is true; and ye also know that an angel hath spoken unto you; wherefore [*how*] can ye doubt? Let us go up; the Lord is able to deliver us, even as our fathers, and to destroy Laban, even as the Egyptians.

4 Now when I had spoken these words, they were yet wroth [*angry*], and did still continue to murmur; nevertheless they did follow me up until we came without [*outside of*] the walls of Jerusalem.

5 And it was by night; and I caused that they should hide themselves without [*outside of*] the walls. And after they had hid themselves, I, Nephi, crept into the city and went forth towards the house of Laban.

As mentioned in a previous note, Nephi is about to encounter a very severe test of faith. He will pass the test, but not before he has been through an internal struggle of deepest proportions. There is a lesson in this for each of us. Sometimes, as we strive to faithfully live the gospel, and to carry out our callings and responsibilities at home and in the Church organization, we encounter obstacles which we most certainly did not expect, especially in the light of the Lord's promises to the faithful. At such times, Nephi's experience in the next verses can be most helpful and reassuring.

6 And I was led by the Spirit, not knowing beforehand the things which I should do.

7 Nevertheless I went forth, and as I came near unto the house of Laban I beheld a man, and he had fallen to the earth before me, for he was drunken with wine.

8 And when I came to him I found that it was Laban.

9 And I beheld his sword, and I drew it forth from the sheath thereof; and the hilt thereof was of pure gold, and the workmanship thereof was exceedingly fine, and I saw that the blade thereof was of the most precious steel.

> Just a thought. We know that Nephi was still a young man when he encountered Laban. We can't help but note his admiring, detailed description of Laban's fine sword in verse 9, above. It is what we would expect from a typical young man.
>
> Next, we see and feel the struggle in Nephi's mind and heart as he seeks to sort out the teachings of his youth about not killing people, his commitment to follow God, and the commandment to kill Laban. It is a profoundly deep struggle, and we can learn much from it.

10 And it came to pass that I was constrained [*compelled, obligated*] by the Spirit that I should kill Laban; but I said in my heart: Never at any time have I shed the blood of man. And I shrunk [*held back*] and would [*wished*] that I might not slay him.

11 And the Spirit said unto me again: Behold the Lord hath delivered him into thy hands. Yea, and I also knew that he had sought to take away mine own life; yea, and he would not hearken unto [*listen to; obey*] the commandments of the Lord; and he also had taken away our property [*Laban was a robber*].

12 And it came to pass that the Spirit said unto me again: Slay him, for the Lord hath delivered him into thy hands;

13 Behold the Lord slayeth the wicked to bring forth his righteous purposes. It is better that one man should perish than that a nation should dwindle and perish in unbelief [*a very famous quote from the Book of Mormon*].

14 [*Nephi's intense internal struggle continues.*] And now, when I, Nephi, had heard these

words, I remembered the words of the Lord which he spake unto me in the wilderness, saying that: Inasmuch as thy seed [*posterity*] shall keep my commandments, they shall prosper in the land of promise [*literally, the Americas; symbolically, heaven*].

15 Yea, and I also thought that they could not keep the commandments of the Lord according to the law of Moses, save [*unless*] they should have the law [*the scriptures*].

16 And I also knew that the law was engraven upon the plates of brass.

17 And again, I knew that the Lord had delivered Laban into my hands for this cause—that I might obtain the records according to his commandments.

18 Therefore I did obey the voice of the Spirit, and took Laban by the hair of the head, and I smote off his head with his own sword.

> As mentioned previously, this was a most difficult choice for Nephi. It seems that Nephi has always been quick to obey, yet, in this instance, it takes 9 verses for him to obey, signifying the struggle within his soul. However, having passed this extreme test, he will now be able to quickly obey the Lord when it comes to future difficult assignments. For instance, when asked to build a ship, a rather startling assignment for one without any shipbuilding experience, he simply asks, "Whither shall I go that I may find ore to molten, that I may make tools to construct the ship?" (1 Nephi 17:9)

19 And after I had smitten off his head with his own sword, I took the garments of Laban [*Laban's clothes*] and put them upon mine own body; yea, even every whit [*every bit*]; and I did gird on his armor about my loins [*I put his armor on*].

20 And after I had done this, I went forth unto the treasury of Laban. And as I went forth towards the treasury of Laban, behold, I saw the servant of Laban [*Zoram, see verse 35*] who had the keys of the treasury. And I commanded him in the voice of Laban, that he should go with me into the treasury.

21 And he supposed me to be his master, Laban, for he beheld [*saw*] the garments [*Laban's clothes*] and also the sword girded about my loins.

22 And he spake unto me concerning the elders [*religious leaders, see verse 26*] of the Jews, he knowing that his

master, Laban, had been out by night among them.

23 And I spake unto him as if it had been Laban.

24 And I also spake unto him that I should carry the engravings, which were upon the plates of brass, to my elder brethren, who were without the walls [*outside the city walls*].

25 And I also bade [*requested*] him that he should follow me.

26 And he, supposing that I spake of the brethren of the church, and that I was truly that Laban whom I had slain, wherefore [*therefore*] he did follow me.

27 And he spake unto me many times concerning the elders of the Jews, as I went forth unto my brethren, who were without [*outside of*] the walls.

28 And it came to pass that when Laman saw me he was exceedingly frightened, and also Lemuel and Sam. And they fled from before my presence; for they supposed it was Laban, and that he had slain me and had sought to take away their lives also.

29 And it came to pass that I called after them, and they did hear me; wherefore they did cease to flee from my presence.

Imagine how surprised and startled Zoram must have been when Nephi spoke in his own voice, and his brothers actually stopped!

30 And it came to pass that when the servant of Laban beheld [*saw*] my brethren he began to tremble, and was about to flee from before me and return to the city of Jerusalem.

31 And now I, Nephi, being a man large in stature, and also having received much strength of the Lord, therefore I did seize upon the servant of Laban, and held him, that he should not flee.

Nephi is certainly humble about his size and strength, and sets a good example by giving the Lord credit for his ability to restrain Zoram. Next, we see again the use of the strongest possible oath in Jewish culture (see note prior to 1 Nephi 3:15 in this book) as Nephi talks to Zoram and Zoram responds.

32 And it came to pass that I spake with him, that if he would hearken unto my words, as the Lord liveth, and as I live, even so that if he would hearken unto our words, we would spare his life.

33 And I spake unto him, even with an oath, that he need not fear; that he should be a free man

like unto us if he would go down in the wilderness with us.

34 And I also spake unto him, saying: Surely the Lord hath commanded us to do this thing; and shall we not be diligent in keeping the commandments of the Lord? Therefore, if thou wilt go down into the wilderness to my father thou shalt have place with us.

> Next, we see the confidence which Nephi's oath gives Zoram. Zoram's oath in return frees Nephi of any concerns about him.

35 And it came to pass that Zoram did take courage at the words which I spake. Now Zoram was the name of the servant; and he promised that he would go down into the wilderness unto our father. Yea, and he also made an oath unto us that he would tarry [remain] with us from that time forth.

36 Now we were desirous that he should tarry with us for this cause, that the Jews might not know concerning our flight into the wilderness, lest they should pursue us and destroy us.

37 And it came to pass that when Zoram had made an oath unto us, our fears did cease concerning him.

38 And it came to pass that we took the plates of brass and the servant of Laban [Zoram], and departed into the wilderness, and journeyed unto the tent of our father.

FIRST NEPHI 5

Imagine the joy and relief for all concerned as the sons returned safely to camp, along with Zoram! As mentioned in the note at the beginning of 1 Nephi, chapter three, in this book, many things had been accomplished by fulfilling the commandment of the Lord to return and get the brass plates of Laban, not the least of which was the strengthening of Sariah's testimony of her husband's prophetic calling.

1 AND it came to pass that after we had come down into the wilderness unto our father, behold, he was filled with joy, and also my mother, Sariah, was exceedingly glad, for she truly had mourned because of us.

2 For she had supposed that we had perished in the wilderness; and she also had complained against my father, telling him that he was a visionary man; saying: Behold thou hast led us forth from the land of our inheritance,

and my sons are no more, and we perish in the wilderness.

3 And after this manner of language had my mother complained against my father.

4 And it had come to pass that my father spake unto her, saying: I know that I am a visionary man; for if I had not seen the things of God in a vision I should not have known the goodness of God, but had tarried at Jerusalem, and had perished with my brethren.

5 But behold, I have obtained a land of promise [*literally, the Americas; symbolically, heaven*], in the which things I do rejoice; yea, and I know that the Lord will deliver my sons out of the hands of Laban, and bring them down again unto us in the wilderness.

6 And after this manner of language did my father, Lehi, comfort my mother, Sariah, concerning us, while we journeyed in the wilderness up to the land of Jerusalem, to obtain the record of the Jews [*the brass plates*].

7 And when we had returned to the tent of my father, behold their joy was full, and my mother was comforted.

> Listen now to Sariah's testimony and imagine Lehi and Nephi's joy and comfort as they and the others listened to it.

8 And she spake, saying: Now I know of a surety [*for sure*] that the Lord hath commanded my husband to flee into the wilderness; yea, and I also know of a surety that the Lord hath protected my sons, and delivered them out of the hands of Laban, and given them power whereby they could accomplish the thing which the Lord hath commanded them. And after this manner of language did she speak.

9 And it came to pass that they did rejoice exceedingly, and did offer sacrifice and burnt offerings unto the Lord; and they gave thanks unto the God of Israel.

> Verse 9, above, reminds us that they were still living the law of Moses, including animal sacrifices, symbolic of the coming Atonement of Christ. In this sense, we are still in Old Testament times at this point in the Book of Mormon and will be until the visit of the resurrected Savior in Third Nephi.
>
> And, speaking of this part of the Book of Mormon as being Old Testament, it is very significant to note that the Book of Mormon gives us a more accurate understanding of Old Testament teachings about Christ than our current version of the Old Testament does.

10 And after they had given thanks unto the God of Israel,

my father, Lehi, took the records which were engraven upon the plates of brass, and he did search them from the beginning.

> Apostle Bruce R. McConkie said the following about the brass plates: "The brass plates . . . contain more of the word of the Lord for the comparable period than does our present Old Testament. They will also come forth in due time as part of the restoration of all things" (McConkie, *Millennial Messiah*, p. 113).
>
> Now Nephi gives us a detailed description of the contents of the brass plates of Laban.

11 And he beheld that they did contain the five books of Moses [*Genesis, Exodus, Leviticus, Numbers, and Deuteronomy*], which gave an account of the creation of the world, and also of Adam and Eve, who were our first parents [*our first ancestors; in other words, this is as far back as our mortal genealogy goes*];

> Perhaps one quote from the First Presidency would be helpful here, in conjunction with verse 11, above. The question as to whether or not organic evolution was the means by which our ancestors eventually came on the scene seems to be answered in the last phrase of verse 11.
>
> Concerning the origins of mankind, the First Presidency said:
>
> "It is held by some that Adam was not the first man upon this earth, and that the original human being was a development from lower orders of the animal creation. These, however, are the theories of men. The word of the Lord declares that Adam was 'the first man of all men' (Moses 1:34), and we are therefore in duty bound to regard him as the primal parent of our race . . . Man began life as a human being, in the likeness of our heavenly Father." (Smith, Winder, and Lund, *Messages of the First Presidency of The Church of Jesus Christ of Latter-day Saints*, p. 4:205–6)

12 And also a record of the Jews from the beginning, even down to the commencement of the reign of Zedekiah, king of Judah; [*In other words, down to about 600 B.C.*]

13 And also the prophecies of the holy prophets, from the beginning, even down to the commencement of the reign of Zedekiah; and also many prophecies which have been spoken by the mouth of Jeremiah. [*This would be basically the words of the prophets, including those contained in our Old Testament, up to and including much of Jeremiah.*]

14 And it came to pass that my father, Lehi, also found upon the plates of brass a genealogy of his fathers; wherefore he knew that he was a descendant of Joseph [*through Manasseh, see Alma 10:3*]; yea, even that Joseph who was the son of Jacob, who was sold into Egypt, and who was preserved by the hand of the Lord, that he might preserve his father, Jacob, and all his household from perishing with famine.

15 And they were also led out of captivity and out of the land of Egypt, by that same God who had preserved them.

> There is symbolism in verse 15, above. The Lord literally led the children of Israel out of Egyptian bondage, but the symbolism, as is the case for so many literal events in scripture, is that if we faithfully follow the Lord, we will be led out of the "captivity" of sin, and out of the world (Egypt) into the "promised land" (heaven).

16 And thus my father, Lehi, did discover the genealogy of his fathers. And Laban also was a descendant of Joseph, wherefore he and his fathers had kept the records.

> Verse 16, above, is where we learn that Laban was a relative, near or distant, of Lehi.

17 And now when my father saw all these things, he was filled with the Spirit, and began to prophesy concerning his seed [*posterity*]—

18 That these plates of brass should go forth unto all nations, kindreds, tongues, and people who were of his seed.

19 Wherefore, he said that these plates of brass should never perish; neither should they be dimmed any more by time. And he prophesied many things concerning his seed.

> We learn from verse 19, above, that the brass plates of Laban still exist. They have been preserved by the Lord and, no doubt, someday the faithful will be able to see them.

20 And it came to pass that thus far I and my father had kept the commandments wherewith the Lord had commanded us.

21 And we had obtained the records which the Lord had commanded us, and searched them and found that they were desirable; yea, even of great worth unto us, insomuch that we could preserve the commandments of the Lord unto our children. [*A major reason for having the scriptures and studying and teaching them.*]

22 Wherefore, it was wisdom in the Lord that we should carry them with us, as we journeyed in the wilderness towards the land of promise. [*Again, the "land of promise" also symbolizes celestial glory and living in the presence of God forever.*]

FIRST NEPHI 6

Next, Nephi refers to the special record which the Lord commanded him to write thirty years after they left Jerusalem (see 2 Nephi 5:28–33). We usually refer to this record as the small plates of Nephi. He carefully limits what things he engraves on these small plates to more spiritual matters, lessons and messages, with just enough history to provide background and setting for what he wants to teach us, as well as his own people, as we read and study his writings. Another set of plates had been kept over the years and are commonly referred to as the large plates of Nephi (see "A Brief Explanation About the Book of Mormon" at the beginning of your Book of Mormon for more about the various sets of plates referred to in it; see also the note at the beginning of First Nephi in this book).

1 AND now I, Nephi, do not give the genealogy of my fathers in this part of my record; neither at any time shall I give it after upon these plates [*the small plates*] which I am writing; for it is given in the record which has been kept by my father [*the large plates*]; wherefore, I do not write it in this work [*the small plates*].

2 For it sufficeth me to say that we are descendants of Joseph.

3 And it mattereth not to me that I am particular to give a full account of all the things of my father, for they cannot be written upon these plates [*the small plates*], for I desire the room that I may write of the things of God.

4 For the fulness of mine intent [*in engraving these small plates as well as everything else I do*] is that I may persuade men to come unto the God of Abraham, and the God of Isaac, and the God of Jacob [*in other words, the only true God*], and be saved.

5 Wherefore, the things which are pleasing unto the world I do not write, but the things which are pleasing unto God and unto those who are not of the world [*the righteous*].

6 Wherefore, I shall give commandment unto my seed [*my posterity*], that they shall not

occupy these plates [*the small plates*] with things which are not of worth unto the children of men.

FIRST NEPHI 7

It is interesting to observe that this time when the sons of Lehi and Sariah are asked to go back to Jerusalem, Laman and Lemuel do not murmur, probably because there is something in it for them, namely, wives. This may be another clue to their personalities.

There is another point we will mention before we start this next chapter. We see the hand of the Lord in providing a family, in advance, with just the right number of unmarried daughters. We note that there are five who need wives, namely, Laman, Lemuel, Sam, Nephi, and Zoram. Ishmael's family has five unmarried daughters plus two married sons and their families. Also, we are given to understand that Ishmael's two sons had married into Lehi's family. Apostle Erastus Snow said that Joseph Smith said that this was the case. From this we would gather that Lehi and Sariah had two older daughters, and that they had married Ishmael's sons

and already had families of their own. Here is the quote from Elder Erastus Snow (**bold** added for emphasis):

"The Prophet Joseph informed us that the record of Lehi, was contained on the 116 pages that were first translated and subsequently stolen, and of which an abridgement is given us in the first book of Nephi, which is the record of Nephi individually, he himself being of the lineage of Manasseh; but that Ishmael was of the lineage of Ephraim, and that **his sons married into Lehi's family, and Lehi's sons married Ishmael's daughters.**" (Snow, *Journal of Discourses,* 23:184.)

1 AND now I would that ye might know, that after my father, Lehi, had made an end of prophesying concerning his seed [*posterity, descendants*], it came to pass that the Lord spake unto him again, saying that it was not meet for him [*not good for him*], Lehi, that he should take his family into the wilderness alone; but that his sons should take daughters to wife, that they might raise up seed [*children*] unto the Lord in the land of promise.

2 And it came to pass that the Lord commanded him that I, Nephi, and my brethren, should

again return unto the land of Jerusalem, and bring down Ishmael and his family into the wilderness.

3 And it came to pass that I, Nephi, did again, with my brethren, go forth into the wilderness to go up to Jerusalem.

> There may be some rather significant symbolism containing a very important lesson for us in the fact that the four brothers are asked to return to Jerusalem again. We noted in their previous return to Jerusalem that difficulties while on the Lord's errand tend to provide growth or emphasize weaknesses, depending on how we choose to use our agency. Laman and Lemuel weakened. Nephi and Sam strengthened.
>
> Now, they are given another opportunity to make the journey. This can be symbolic of the fact that we are given many, many chances during our mortal lives, to take the same tests over and over. For instance, if we "fail" the Word of Wisdom "test" we get to "retake" it, via the principle of repentance. If we fail the "be kind to others" test, we get plenty of additional opportunities to take it again. If we fail the "keep the Sabbath Day holy" test, we get plenty of additional Sabbaths in which we can do better.
>
> At this point in the Book of Mormon, the Lord is kind enough to give Laman and Lemuel a chance to "retake" the "return to Jerusalem" test, along with Nephi and Sam, who passed the test last time. In fact, it seems that whenever we fail one of the Lord's tests, we get to retake it with faithful Saints who have already passed it. They are good examples for us.

4 And it came to pass that we went up unto the house of Ishmael, and we did gain favor in the sight of Ishmael, insomuch that we did speak unto him the words of the Lord.

5 And it came to pass that the Lord did soften the heart of Ishmael, and also his household, insomuch that they took their journey with us down into the wilderness to the tent of our father.

> It will be interesting when we get the rest of the details of this meeting of Nephi and his brothers with Ishmael and his family. We note that, whereas Nephi took the brunt of the responsibility for getting the brass plates on their last journey to Jerusalem, this time it seems that they all participated in the responsibility. At least, the use of the word "we" in verse 4, above, leads us to that conclusion. The Lord was involved this time also, and softened the hearts of Ishmael and his family (verse 5, above) so they came. No doubt they

had all felt the Spirit of the Lord and thus had at least the beginnings of testimonies. If so, their level of accountability for obeying the Lord's commandments would have increased, at least a bit.

We also understand, from the quote from Erastus Snow in the note at the beginning of this chapter, that Ishmael was from the tribe of Ephraim. We will repeat a part of the quote here and add **bold** for emphasis:

"The Prophet Joseph informed us that **Ishmael was of the lineage of Ephraim**, and that his sons married into Lehi's family, and Lehi's sons married Ishmael's daughters, thus fulfilling the words of Jacob upon Ephraim and Manasseh in the 48th chapter of Genesis, which says: 'And let my name be named on them, and the name of my fathers Abraham and Isaac; and let them grow into a multitude in the midst of the land.' Thus these descendants of Manasseh and Ephraim grew together upon this American continent." (Snow, *Journal of Discourses,* 23:184)

6 And it came to pass that as we journeyed in the wilderness, behold Laman and Lemuel, and two of the daughters of Ishmael, and the two sons of Ishmael and their families, did rebel against us; yea, against me, Nephi, and Sam, and their father, Ishmael, and his wife, and his three other daughters.

7 And it came to pass in the which rebellion, they were desirous to return unto the land of Jerusalem. [*They obviously did not believe that Jerusalem would be destroyed, even though many prophets had said so.*]

8 And now I, Nephi, being grieved for the hardness of their hearts, therefore I spake unto them, saying, yea, even unto Laman and unto Lemuel: Behold ye are mine elder brethren, and how is it that ye are so hard in your hearts, and so blind in your minds, that ye have need that I, your younger brother, should speak unto you, yea, and set an example for you?

9 How is it that ye have not hearkened unto the word of the Lord?

One way we keep our testimonies strong is by remembering past blessings from the Lord to us. This is emphasized in Alma 5:6, among other places. Nephi will use the term "forgotten" three times in the next three verses. "Forgetting" past blessings from the Lord is one way to lose or ignore one's testimony.

10 How is it that ye have forgotten that ye have seen an angel of the Lord?

First Nephi 7

11 Yea, and how is it that ye have forgotten what great things the Lord hath done for us, in delivering us out of the hands of Laban, and also that we should obtain the record [*the brass plates*]?

12 Yea, and how is it that ye have forgotten that the Lord is able to do all things according to his will, for the children of men, if it so be that they exercise faith in him? Wherefore, let us be faithful to him.

13 And if it so be that we are faithful to him, we shall obtain the land of promise; and ye shall know at some future period that the word of the Lord shall be fulfilled concerning the destruction of Jerusalem; for all things which the Lord hath spoken concerning the destruction of Jerusalem must be fulfilled.

14 For behold, the Spirit of the Lord ceaseth soon to strive with them; for behold, they have rejected the prophets, and Jeremiah have they cast into prison. And they have sought to take away the life of my father, insomuch that they have driven him out of the land.

> From verse 14, above, we learn that the Spirit of the Lord had not yet stopped trying to bring the inhabitants of Jerusalem away from wickedness and toward God. Because of the Lord's patience, it takes a lot to cause Him to withdraw His Spirit from His children, but the citizens of Jerusalem and the surrounding area are obviously pushing that limit at this time. By the way, you can read about Jeremiah's imprisonment by young King Zedekiah in Jeremiah 37:3–38:28. Zedekiah's behavior is a strong reminder that wickedness does not promote rational thought.

15 Now behold, I say unto you that if ye will return unto Jerusalem ye shall also perish with them. And now, if ye have choice, go up to the land [*go ahead and go back to Jerusalem if you want to*], and remember the words which I speak unto you, that if ye go ye will also perish [*die*]; for thus the Spirit of the Lord constraineth me [*compels me*] that I should speak.

16 And it came to pass that when I, Nephi, had spoken these words unto my brethren, they were angry with me. And it came to pass that they did lay their hands upon me, for behold, they were exceedingly wroth [*very angry*], and they did bind me with cords, for they sought to take away my life, that they might leave me in the wilderness to be devoured by wild beasts.

> We spoke earlier of the Lord's kindness in allowing each of us

to have many chances to overcome wrong thinking and wrong behaviors. We mentioned that even the commandment to return to Jerusalem again was a kindness from the Lord because it gave Laman and Lemuel a chance to "retake" the test. We pointed out that, in this sense, Laman and Lemuel had failed the first "go-back-to-Jerusalem" test and that Sam and Nephi had passed it. We had our hopes up a bit for Laman and Lemuel when they went willingly back to Jerusalem the second time, but now we have seen that their selfishness and rebellion led them down to the point of having murder in their hearts. They are failing their "retake" of the go-back-to-Jerusalem test. Not only that, but they have led and encouraged some members of Ishmael's family to join them. In contrast, Nephi's faith has continued to grow through adversity and persistent, patient obedience. We now see this faith in action as we continue this chapter.

17 But it came to pass that I prayed unto the Lord, saying: O Lord, according to my faith which is in thee, wilt thou deliver me from the hands of my brethren; yea, even give me strength that I may burst these bands with which I am bound.

18 And it came to pass that when I had said these words, behold, the bands were loosed from off my hands and feet, and I stood before my brethren, and I spake unto them again.

Because of the miracle that had just happened, we would hope that Laman and Lemuel and the angry others would be swayed toward humility and apologizing, but we are disappointed. Perhaps one of the lessons we learn from this teaching scene in the Book of Mormon record is that intentional, continued wickedness leads to deeper, unrelenting pride, which continues to damage in spite of the obvious.

19 And it came to pass that they were angry with me again, and sought to lay hands upon me; but behold, one of the daughters of Ishmael [*I hope that this is the one Nephi eventually marries*], yea, and also her mother, and one of the sons of Ishmael, did plead with my brethren, insomuch that they did soften their hearts; and they did cease striving to take away my life.

20 And it came to pass that they were sorrowful, because of their wickedness, insomuch that they did bow down before me, and did plead with me that I would forgive them of the thing that they had done against me. [*This is evidence that they are not yet beyond feeling and gives us hope that they will repent and draw close to God after all. The Lord is*

still working with them and giving them every possible chance to use their agency wisely.]

21 And it came to pass that I did frankly forgive them all that they had done, and I did exhort them that they would pray unto the Lord their God for forgiveness. And it came to pass that they did so. And after they had done praying unto the Lord we did again travel on our journey towards the tent of our father.

Nephi's complete willingness to forgive his offenders is a marvelous example for all of us. Not only does it give them an opportunity to start over as far as he is concerned, it also frees Nephi's soul, heart, and mind of the heavy burden of ill feelings and harboring bitterness and possibly hatred. Thus, it frees both his offenders and himself of damaging burdens.

22 And it came to pass that we did come down unto the tent of our father. And after I and my brethren and all the house of Ishmael had come down unto the tent of my father, they did give thanks unto the Lord their God; and they did offer sacrifice and burnt offerings unto him.

Assuming that the word "they" in "they did offer sacrifice" includes Laman and Lemuel, it would indicate that they held the priesthood. According to Joseph Fielding Smith, this would have been Melchizedek Priesthood at this time in the Book of Mormon. He taught (**bold** added for emphasis):

"The Nephites were descendants of Joseph. Lehi discovered this when reading the brass plates. He was a descendant of Manasseh, and Ishmael, who accompanied him with his family, was of the tribe of Ephraim (Alma 10:3). Therefore there were no Levites who accompanied Lehi to the Western Hemisphere. Under these conditions the **Nephites officiated by virtue of the Melchizedek Priesthood from the days of Lehi to the days of the appearance of our Savior among them**.

"It is true that Nephi 'consecrated Jacob and Joseph' that they should be priests and teachers over the land of the Nephites, but the fact that plural terms priests and teachers were used indicates that this was not a reference to the definite office in the priesthood in either case, but it was a general assignment to teach, direct, and admonish the people. Otherwise the terms priest and teacher would have been given in the singular.

"From these and numerous other passages we learn that it was by the authority of the Melchizedek Priesthood that the Nephites administered from the time they left Jerusalem until the time of the coming of

Jesus Christ." (Smith, *Answers to Gospel Questions*, 1:124–26)

FIRST NEPHI 8

In this chapter, Lehi will see the vision of the tree of life and will ask his family to come and partake of it with him. Before we proceed to this part of the Book of Mormon account, we will pause and consider a marvelous dream which Joseph Smith's father had. Have you ever wondered how the Lord prepared the Prophet Joseph Smith's parents to be the parents of a prophet? Have you ever wondered how they could be so supportive of their prophet son, in the face of such persecution and scorn?

Part of the answer certainly lies in the fact that both of Joseph's parents were given dreams and visions which specifically foreshadowed what their son would restore. It was tender and wonderful preparation for them in their role. They were prepared in ways similar to Abraham and Sarah (Isaac), Zacharias and Elizabeth (John the Baptist), even Mary and Joseph (Jesus). You can read more about the dreams and visions of Joseph Smith's parents in *History of Joseph Smith by His Mother*. For our purposes here, we will just quote Lucy Mack Smith's account of a dream which Joseph Smith Sr. had in 1811. Watch for similarities between it and Lehi's dream, then you will understand even better why Joseph Smith Sr. knew his son was indeed a prophet called of God to restore the true Church.

"In 1811, we moved from Royalton, Vermont, to the town of Lebanon, New Hampshire. Soon after arriving here, my husband received another very singular vision, which I will relate:

"'I thought,' said he, 'I was traveling in an open, desolate field, which appeared to be very barren. As I was thus traveling, the thought suddenly came into my mind that I had better stop and reflect upon what I was doing, before I went any farther. So I asked myself, "What motive can I have in traveling here, and what place can this be?" My guide, who was by my side, as before, said, "This is the desolate world; but travel on." The road was so broad and barren that I wondered why I should travel in it; for, said I to myself, "Broad is the road, and wide is the gate that leads to death, and many there be that walk therein; but narrow is the way, and strait is the gate that leads to everlasting life, and few there be that go in thereat." Traveling a short distance further, I came to a narrow path. This path I entered, and, when I had traveled a little way in it, I beheld a beautiful stream of water, which ran from the east to the west. Of this stream, I could see neither the source nor yet the mouth; but as far as my eyes could extend I could see a rope, running along the bank of it, about as high as a man could reach, and beyond me was a low, but very pleasant valley, in which stood a tree such as I had never seen before. It was exceedingly handsome, insomuch that I looked upon it with wonder and admiration. Its beautiful branches spread themselves somewhat like an umbrella, and it bore a kind of fruit, in shape much like a chestnut bur, and as white as snow, or, if possible, whiter. I gazed upon the same with considerable interest, and as I was doing so, the burs or shells commenced opening and shedding their particles, or the fruit which they contained, which was of dazzling whiteness. I drew near and began to eat of it, and I found it delicious beyond description. As I was eating, I said in my heart, "I cannot eat this alone, I must bring my wife and children, that they may partake with me." Accordingly, I went and brought my family, which consisted of a wife and seven children, and we all commenced eating and praising God for this blessing. We were exceedingly happy, insomuch that our joy could not easily be expressed. While thus engaged, I beheld a spacious building standing opposite the valley which we were in, and it appeared to reach to the very heavens. It was full of doors and windows, and they were all filled with people, who were very finely dressed. When these people observed us in the low valley, under the tree, they pointed the finger of scorn at us, and treated us with all manner of disrespect and contempt. But their contumely we utterly disregarded. I presently turned to my guide and inquired of him the meaning of the fruit that was so delicious. He told me it was the pure love of God, shed abroad in the hearts of all those who love him, and keep his commandments. He then commanded me to go and bring the rest of my children. I told him that we were all there. "No," he replied, "look yonder, you have two more, and you must bring them also." Upon raising my eyes, I saw two small children, standing some distance off. I immediately went to them, and brought them to the tree; upon which they commenced eating with the rest, and we all rejoiced together. The more we ate, the more we seemed to desire, until we even got down upon our knees and scooped it up, eating it by double handfuls. After feasting in this manner a short time, I asked my guide what was the meaning of the spacious building which I saw. He replied, "It is Babylon, it is Babylon, and it must fall. The people in the doors and windows are the inhabitants thereof, who scorn and despise the Saints of God because of their humility." I soon awoke, clapping my hands together for joy.'" (Smith, *History of Joseph Smith by His Mother*, p. 48)

This was one of at least seven dreams or visions which Joseph Smith Sr. had which were written down by his wife. Can you imagine how Father Smith felt when he read the translation of the gold plates which contained the account of Lehi's dream? What a wonderful testimony to the truthfulness of his son's work!

You will note, as we continue now with the Book of Mormon account of Lehi's dream, that there is a significant difference between Father Smith's dream and Lehi's dream, namely, all of Joseph Smith Senior's children came and partook of the fruit of the tree (in fact, during the dream, Brother and Sister Smith discovered that they were yet to have two more children, which they did), whereas, Laman and Lemuel refused Lehi's invitation to partake. We will read several verses without interruption and then go back and look at quite a bit of symbolism and teaching.

1 AND it came to pass that we had gathered together all manner of seeds of every kind, both of grain of every kind, and also of the seeds of fruit of every kind.

2 And it came to pass that while my father tarried in the wilderness he spake unto us, saying: Behold, I have dreamed a dream; or, in other words, I have seen a vision.

3 And behold, because of the thing which I have seen, I have reason to rejoice in the Lord because of Nephi and also of Sam; for I have reason to suppose that they, and also many of their seed, will be saved.

4 But behold, Laman and Lemuel, I fear exceedingly because of you; for behold, methought I saw in my dream, a dark and dreary wilderness.

5 And it came to pass that I saw a man, and he was dressed in a white robe; and he came and stood before me.

6 And it came to pass that he

FIRST NEPHI 8 39

spake unto me, and bade me follow him [*invited me to follow him*].

7 And it came to pass that as I followed him I beheld myself that I was in a dark and dreary waste.

8 And after I had traveled for the space of many hours in darkness, I began to pray unto the Lord that he would have mercy on me, according to the multitude of his tender mercies.

9 And it came to pass after I had prayed unto the Lord I beheld a large and spacious field.

10 And it came to pass that I beheld a tree, whose fruit was desirable to make one happy.

11 And it came to pass that I did go forth and partake of the fruit thereof; and I beheld that it was most sweet, above all that I ever before tasted. Yea, and I beheld that the fruit thereof was white, to exceed all the whiteness that I had ever seen.

12 And as I partook of the fruit thereof it filled my soul with exceedingly great joy; wherefore, I began to be desirous that my family should partake of it also; for I knew that it was desirable above all other fruit.

13 And as I cast my eyes round about, that perhaps I might discover my family also, I beheld a river of water; and it ran along, and it was near the tree of which I was partaking the fruit.

14 And I looked to behold from whence it came; and I saw the head thereof a little way off; and at the head thereof I beheld your mother Sariah, and Sam, and Nephi; and they stood as if they knew not whither [*where to*] they should go.

15 And it came to pass that I beckoned unto them; and I also did say unto them with a loud voice that they should come unto me, and partake of the fruit, which was desirable above all other fruit.

16 And it came to pass that they did come unto me and partake of the fruit also.

17 And it came to pass that I was desirous that Laman and Lemuel should come and partake of the fruit also; wherefore, I cast mine eyes towards the head of the river, that perhaps I might see them.

18 And it came to pass that I saw them, but they would not come unto me and partake of the fruit.

We will now go back and note several examples of symbolism in the dream so far plus point out a few other items of instruction. In order to do this, we will reread verses 1 through 18, using **bold** type and notes in parentheses along with our regular format of notes and comments.

1 AND it came to pass that we had gathered together all manner of seeds of every kind, both of grain of every kind, and also of the seeds of fruit of every kind. [*Perhaps symbolic of the fact that we need much specific preparation in order to successfully make our journey to the "promised land" or heaven.*]

2 And it came to pass that while my father tarried in the wilderness he spake unto us, saying: Behold, I have **dreamed a dream**; or, in other words, I have **seen a vision**.

> Here, the terms "dream" and "vision" seem interchangeable. There may be a message in this for us. Sometimes we can't tell the difference between whether or not we are dreaming something, under the direction and inspiration of the Holy Ghost, or actually seeing real people and objects. It is probably best not to spend too much time trying to differentiate, rather, just heed the message.

3 And behold, because of the thing which I have seen, I have reason to rejoice in the Lord because of Nephi and also of Sam; for I have reason to suppose that they, and also many of their seed, will be saved.

4 But behold, **Laman and Lemuel, I fear exceedingly because of you**; for behold, methought I saw in my dream, a dark and dreary wilderness.

> Here, we might ask a question: since Lehi saw this about Laman and Lemuel, does it mean that it has to happen? The answer is obviously "No." If we were to say "Yes," then we would be endorsing the idea of predestination. But it is certainly a warning to Laman and Lemuel that they need to change their ways. And these two rebellious sons will yet have many opportunities to change their ways. In verse 37 of this chapter, Lehi pleads with Laman and Lemuel to heed his words so that they can partake of the mercies of the Lord and not be "cast off."

5 And it came to pass that I saw a man, and he was dressed in a white robe; and he came and stood before me.

6 And it came to pass that he spake unto me, and bade me follow him [*invited me to follow him*].

7 And it came to pass that as I followed him I beheld myself

First Nephi 8

that I was in a **dark and dreary waste**.

> This could symbolize the world without the gospel of Christ. It could also be symbolic of our desperate situation in our sins and imperfections without the Atonement of Christ to redeem us. Whatever the case, as the time becomes disturbingly long for Lehi in this "darkness" (verse 8, next), he becomes acutely aware of his need for redemption and prays fervently for "the multitude of His tender mercies" made available through the Atonement.

8 And after I had traveled for **the space of many hours in darkness, I began to pray unto the Lord that he would have mercy on me, according to the multitude of his tender mercies.**

9 And it came to pass after I had prayed unto the Lord I beheld a large and spacious field.

> Verse 20 explains that the "large and spacious field" in verse 9, above, is symbolic of a world. Since the "strait and narrow path" and the "rod of iron" lead to this "large and spacious field" or "world," we can see at least two symbolic meanings for the field or world. For one thing, they can symbolize the celestial kingdom, the presence of God. Another possible meaning would be that following the "strait and narrow path" and the "rod of iron" leads us to a "large and spacious field" of new opportunities, of new starts in life because of the Savior's Atonement. This symbolism of fresh starts is taught many places in the scriptures. For instance, in Leviticus 14:7 we read of a living bird being let loose into an "open field" which symbolizes a new, wide open set of opportunities. The living bird is symbolic of a person who has been cleansed by blood (Leviticus 14:6–7.) Being cleansed by blood is symbolic of being cleansed by the Savior's Atonement. In fact, if you read Leviticus 14:1–9, you will see much Atonement symbolism.

> Verse 4 mentions cedar wood (symbolic of the cross), scarlet, and hyssop (both associated with the Savior's trial and crucifixion; in other words, they are part of symbolism) and thus represent being cleansed by the Savior's Atonement. In summary, when we qualify for the Atonement to be active in our behalf, we find newness of life and wide open opportunities for progression to celestial exaltation.

10 And it came to pass that I beheld a tree, whose fruit was desirable to make one happy.

> Here, again, there is much symbolism, this time with respect to the tree in verse 10. You have already noticed that the Lord uses much symbolism in the scriptures. Some people wish

this were not the case, because things can be harder to understand. They wish He would simply come out and say what He means. Well, symbolism can be infinitely deep, and thus allows the Holy Ghost to teach many different lessons from the same object. Such is the case with the tree in verse 10, above. In one context, the tree can symbolize the tree of life mentioned in Genesis 2:9, or the tree of life mentioned in Revelation 2:7 and in Revelation 22:2. These trees can represent nourishment from God, both in mortality as well as in eternity.

Another possible interpretation for the tree that Lehi saw is found in 1 Nephi 11:21–22. Here it seems that the tree is symbolic of the Savior. The Savior is the manifestation of the love of God. This love of the Father for us is shown by His giving His Only Begotten Son for us, that we might return to Him.

Yet another use of tree in the Book of Mormon is found in Alma 32. There, a seed is planted in faith, nourished over a period of time, and finally becomes a "tree springing up unto everlasting life" (Alma 32:41.) It yields fruit, which is symbolic of the very best that God has for us, in other words, exaltation.

11 And it came to pass that I did go forth and partake of the fruit thereof; and I beheld that it was most sweet, above all that I ever before tasted. Yea, and I beheld that the fruit thereof was white [*symbolic of purity, coming from God*], to exceed all the whiteness that I had ever seen.

12 And as I partook of the fruit thereof it filled my soul with exceedingly great joy [*symbolic, among other things, of the joy the gospel brings*]; wherefore, I began to be desirous that my family should partake of it also; for I knew that it was desirable above all other fruit [*symbolic of the fact that the things of God are the most desirable of all*].

13 And as I cast my eyes round about, that perhaps I might discover my family also, I beheld a river of water [*symbolic of the depths of hell (1 Nephi 12:16); Lehi didn't notice that the water was filthy, but Nephi noticed when he saw the same vision (Nephi 15:26–27)*]; and it ran along, and it was near the tree of which I was partaking the fruit [*symbolic of the fact that Satan puts evil and temptation just as close to the righteous as he possibly can, during our mortal lives*].

14 And I looked to behold from whence it came; and I saw the head thereof a little way off; and at the head thereof I beheld

your mother Sariah, and Sam, and Nephi; and they stood as if they knew not whither [*which direction*] they should go. [*This is a reminder that even righteous people can be confused at times as to which direction they should go. We all need the guidance of the Lord's prophets.*]

15 And it came to pass that I beckoned unto them [*motioned to come to me*]; and I also did say unto them with a loud voice that they should come unto me, and partake of the fruit, which was desirable above all other fruit [*symbolic of the love of God, manifested by His giving His Son for us. Also, a reminder that exaltation is by far the most desirable glory in which to spend eternity*].

16 And it came to pass that they did come unto me and partake of the fruit also.

17 And it came to pass that I was desirous that Laman and Lemuel should come and partake of the fruit also; wherefore, I cast mine eyes towards the head of the river, that perhaps I might see them.

18 And it came to pass that I saw them, but they would not come unto me and partake of the fruit. [*Symbolic of the fact that Laman and Lemuel refused to accept the gospel and participate actively and faithfully in it.*]

Having repeated verses 1–18 for teaching purposes, we now continue with verse 19.

19 And I beheld a rod of iron [*symbolic of the word of God; see 1 Nephi 11:25*], and it extended along the bank of the river, and led to the tree by which I stood.

20 And I also beheld a strait and narrow path, which came along by the rod of iron, even to the tree by which I stood; and it also led by the head of the fountain, unto a large and spacious field, as if it had been a world.

The phrase "strait and narrow path" in verse 20, above, is an interesting one. Note the spelling of "strait." It is not "straight." "Strait" means "narrow" or "restricted." So, in effect, we have the phrase "narrow and narrow path." It has also been suggested that the phrase can mean "narrow and narrowing" path. Perhaps the phrase itself contains an important lesson for us. It is that as the Holy Ghost reveals "line upon line" to us, the "path" gets narrower and narrower, thus leading us to exaltation.

In fact I had an interesting experience with this concept. A friend of mine had gotten way off the path for a time in his life.

Through repentance and much effort, he regained his membership in the Church and was doing very well, having served a mission with his wife and done much good.

However, one day he came to see me in my office. He expressed grave concern about his chances for gaining celestial exaltation, whereas, he had been very confident about his chances for several years now. His concern boiled down to this: He was now noticing flaws and imperfections in his daily living which he had not even noticed before this time in his life. I guess I startled him when I said, "Rejoice!"

As we chatted, I explained that the fact that he was now noticing things heretofore unnoticed by him in his life was evidence that he was now much closer to the Spirit than before. He was drawing closer and closer to God, and the "light" was shining much brighter on the path so that he was noticing and worrying about littler things in his life. It was a sign that he was doing much better! When he realized this, he paused, smiled, breathed a big sigh of relief, and left the office very happy. He has since continued to progress and serve very effectively in the Church and community. Such is the power of travel along the "narrow and narrowing" path.

Next, we will see four different groups or categories of people in Lehi's dream. The first three will have many similarities, but only one will successfully make it to salvation. The fourth group will not even get to the path. In order to study these groups, we will use **bold** to draw attention to things we want to especially consider.

<u>**Group One:**</u> (verses 21–23)

21 And I saw numberless concourses of people, many of whom were **pressing forward**, that they might **obtain the path** which led unto the tree by which I stood.

22 And it came to pass that **they did come forth, and commence in the path which led to the tree.**

So far, those in Group One want to come unto Christ. They have successfully begun to "press forward" in their lives toward that goal. In fact, they have actually entered onto the "strait and narrow path" which leads to eternal life. From 2 Nephi 31:17–18, we understand this to mean that they had been baptized into the Church. These verses explain that the "gate" which leads to entrance to the "strait and narrow path" which leads to "eternal life" is baptism. Next, sadly, these people, who had such good intentions to begin with, will be led astray and off the path.

23 And it came to pass that

there arose a **mist of darkness** [*symbolic of the "temptations of the devil" according to 1 Nephi 12:17*]; yea, even an exceedingly great mist of darkness, insomuch that **they** who had commenced in the path **did lose their way**, that they **wandered off and were lost**.

Group Two: (verses 24–28)

Those in this group start out like the ones in Group One, "pressing forward," but they make it farther along the path. These make it through the "mist of darkness" by holding on to the iron rod. Do you remember what the iron rod symbolizes? It is the "word of God" (see 1 Nephi 11:25). How do we obtain God's word? From reading and studying the scriptures and listening to the words of our living prophets. Therefore, we conclude that the people in Group Two were strengthened by the scriptures and the words of their prophets which enabled them to successfully make it through the temptations of the devil as they progressed along the "strait and narrow path." In fact, these actually make it to the tree and partake of the fruit. In other words, among other things, they actually have testimonies of the gospel.

24 And it came to pass that I beheld others **pressing forward**, and they came forth and **caught hold of the end of the rod of iron**; and **they did press forward through the mist of darkness, clinging to the rod of iron**, even until they did come forth and partake of the fruit of the tree.

One thing we are taught in the next verses is that Satan doesn't quit working on people who have reached "the tree" and partaken of its "fruit." He seems to have some especially powerful weapons designed to take them out, to destroy them. One of these is peer pressure.

25 And **after they had partaken of the fruit of the tree they did cast their eyes about** [*looked around*] **as if they were ashamed**.

26 And I also cast my eyes round about, and beheld, on the other side of the river of water [*filthiness; see 1 Nephi 15:26–27*], **a great and spacious building**; and it stood as it were **in the air**, high above the earth.

Two things. First, the righteous were separated from the proud, worldly occupants of the "great and spacious building" by filthiness. Second, the building had no foundation! It is not safe to be in! It will fall, guaranteed! (See 1 Nephi 11:36.)

27 And it was **filled with people**, both old and young, both male and female; and **their**

manner of dress was exceedingly fine [*they were materialistic and full of pride; see 1 Nephi 11:36*]; and they were in the attitude of **mocking** and **pointing their fingers towards those who had come at and were partaking of the fruit**. [*Symbolic of peer pressure.*]

28 And after they had tasted of the fruit they were ashamed, because of those that were scoffing at them; and **they fell away into forbidden paths and were lost**.

> Those people in Group One "wandered away" or "wandered off," whereas those in Group Two "fell away." Perhaps one lesson we could learn from this is that the more knowledge and testimony you have, the farther and faster you fall if you choose to break your commitments and covenants.

29 And now I, Nephi, do not speak all the words of my father.

Group Three: (verse 30 and the last part of verse 33)

> Those in this group are also "pressing forward" like those in the first two groups. These "caught hold of the end of the rod of iron" as did those in Group Two. So what are the differences between those in the third group which Lehi saw and those in the first two groups? If we learn our lesson here, from what Nephi chose to engrave for us on the small plates of Nephi, we will have some keys to successfully returning home to our Father in Heaven. We will **bold** these "keys" and make brief teaching comments in parentheses. Before we do, please note that the members in this group do not "wander off" nor do they "fall away." They remain faithful. They are successful. They obtain the prize of eternal life.

30 But, to be short in writing, behold, he saw other multitudes pressing forward; and they came and caught hold of the end of the rod of iron; and they did press their way forward, **continually** [*not just when they felt like being faithful*] holding fast to the rod of iron, until they came forth and **fell down** [*they remained humble*] and partook of the fruit of the tree. [*And, according to the last lines of verse 33, they* **continued partaking of the fruit**, *with Lehi and those of his family who remained faithful, plus, they* "**heeded . . . not**" *those who* "*did point the finger of scorn*" *at the righteous. In other words, they* **did not yield to peer pressure** *to become involved in wickedness.*]

Group Four: (verses 31–33)

> Whereas the people in the first three groups appear to be

First Nephi 8

members of the Church, those in Group Four do not even get on the "strait and narrow path." They do not seem to have definite direction, nor do they "press forward." Rather, they "feel" their way (verse 31) and "wander" (verse 32.)

31 And he also saw other multitudes **feeling their way** towards that great and spacious building.

32 And it came to pass that many were **drowned in the depths of the fountain** [*were overcome by filthiness*]; and many were lost from his view, **wandering** in strange roads [*well-used roads which led away from God*].

33 And great was the multitude that did enter into that strange building [*the great and spacious building, verse 26–27*]. And after they did enter into that building they did point the finger of scorn at me and those that were partaking of the fruit also; but **we heeded them not**. [*This is a great "short sermon" on how to deal with negative peer pressure.*]

34 These are the words of my father: For as many as heeded them [*the occupants of the great and spacious building*], had fallen away.

We might ask ourselves if we have ever entered the "great and spacious building." The answer is probably "Yes" for each of us. If we have ever said to a fellow member of the Church, "What's the matter? Can't you handle it?" when they were offended by inappropriate language, music, or perhaps a movie, then we stepped into the "great and spacious building" for a few dangerous moments. If we have ever tried to talk a friend or an acquaintance into departing from his or her higher standards for even a brief visit with us into foolish or forbidden paths, we have entered this treacherous structure. If we have ever balked at gathering for family prayer or home evening, or invited someone to join with us in skipping a Church meeting, we have entered this worldly palace and joined those who scorn the righteous. Gratefully, there is repentance, and hopefully, we will stay on the safe side of the river, by the tree, from now on.

35 And Laman and Lemuel partook not of the fruit, said my father.

36 And it came to pass after my father had spoken all the words of his dream or vision, which were many [*there is apparently much more about the dream which is not recorded here*], he said unto us, because of these things which he saw in a vision, he exceedingly feared for Laman

and Lemuel; yea, he feared lest they should be cast off from the presence of the Lord [*this is yet another opportunity for Laman and Lemuel to heed their prophet father and change their ways.*]

37 And he did exhort them then with all the feeling of a tender parent, that they would hearken to his words, that perhaps the Lord would be merciful to them, and not cast them off; yea, my father did preach unto them.

38 And after he had preached unto them, and also prophesied unto them of many things, he bade them to keep the commandments of the Lord; and he did cease speaking unto them.

> There is a bit of a message or lesson for us in the fact that Lehi "did cease speaking unto them." If we strive to listen to the Lord and His prophets, and try to hear and obey the promptings of the Holy Ghost, as did Nephi and others, there will be constant communication to us from on high. However, if we rebel and murmur constantly, as did Laman and Lemuel, there comes a time when the Spirit of the Lord will begin to withdraw from us. This is verified in 2 Nephi 26:11 wherein we are told, "For the Spirit of the Lord will not always strive with man."

FIRST NEPHI 9

In 1 Nephi 1:17, Nephi told us that he would first "make an abridgment (a summary) of the record of my father" upon the small plates, and then he would tell us of his own life. As of the end of 1 Nephi, chapter 8, he has now finished his basic summary or abridgment of his father's record. Chapter 9 is a transition between Nephi's abridgment of his father's record and the beginning of his account of his own life and proceedings which he engraved also on the small plates. In this chapter, Nephi mentions the small set of plates and the large set of plates a number of times. As mentioned in the introduction to your Book of Mormon, these are the small plates of Nephi and the large plates of Nephi. The small plates contained more of the spiritual matters and gospel teachings and less of the day-to-day history and secular doings of the people. The large plates contained more of the history of these Book of Mormon peoples.

1 AND all these things did my father see, and hear, and speak, as he dwelt in a tent, in the valley of Lemuel, and also a great many more things, which cannot be written upon these plates [*the small plates*].

2 And now, as I have spoken concerning these plates [*the small plates*], behold they are not the plates [*the large plates*] upon which I make a full account of the history of my people; for the plates [*the large plates*] upon which I make a full account of my people I have given the name of Nephi; wherefore, they are called the plates of Nephi [*the large plates*], after mine own name; and these plates [*the small plates*] also are called the plates of Nephi.

3 Nevertheless, I have received a commandment of the Lord that I should make these plates [*the small plates*], for the special purpose that there should be an account engraven of the ministry of my people [*in other words, more of the spiritual things and teachings of the prophets*].

4 Upon the other plates [*the large plates*] should be engraven an account of the reign of the kings, and the wars and contentions of my people [*in other words, the history and day-to-day happenings, political history, etc.*]; wherefore these plates [*the small plates*] are for the more part of the ministry; and the other plates [*the large plates*] are for the more part of the reign of the kings and the wars and contentions of my people.

5 Wherefore, the Lord hath commanded me to make these plates [*the small plates*] for a wise purpose in him, which purpose I know not.

6 But the Lord knoweth all things from the beginning; wherefore, he prepareth a way to accomplish all his works among the children of men; for behold, he hath all power unto the fulfilling of all his words. And thus it is. Amen.

In verse 5, above, Nephi tells us he does not know why the Lord commanded him to make the small plates and keep a separate account on them. He is a wonderful example of simple, pure faith and obedience to the commandments of God (see verse 6). Can you imagine how much extra work it would take to keep this commandment? He would have to find ore, smelt it to get the metal out, carefully pound the metal into thin enough sheets to enable engraving, and then painstakingly engrave this separate record. This would be very time-consuming! But he did it.

We now know one of the major reasons why this separate set of plates was needed. The Lord knows the future. He knew that Martin Harris would lose the 116 manuscript pages (see Doctrine and Covenants, sections 3 and 10, including the headings for each section). When Joseph Smith was once again permitted to translate the Book of Mormon plates, he was told not to go back and retranslate the portion of the gold plates he had translated while Martin Harris served as his scribe (see D&C 10:30). The lost 116 manuscript pages were the written translation from the large plates of Nephi (see D&C 10:38, including footnote 38a).

Rather than retranslating from the large plates of Nephi (in the stack of plates Joseph had been given by Moroni on the Hill Cumorah), Joseph was instructed to use the small plates of Nephi, which were also contained in the gold plates, and to translate from them to cover the same period of time dealt with in the lost 116 pages (see D&C 10:39–41). In order to summarize what we have said above, we will now quote from D&C 10:38–45, using **bold** for emphasis as well as giving a few notes in parentheses.

D&C 10:38–45

38 And now, verily I say unto you, that an account of those things that you have written [*the 116 manuscript pages*], which have gone out of your hands [*which you have lost*] is engraven upon the plates of Nephi [*the large plates of Nephi*];

39 Yea, and you remember it was said in those writings that a more particular account was given of these things upon the plates of Nephi [*the small plates of Nephi*].

40 And now, because the account which is engraven upon the plates of Nephi [*the small plates*] is more particular concerning the things which, in my wisdom, I would bring to the knowledge of the people in this account—[*the Book of Mormon*]

41 Therefore, you shall translate the engravings which are on the plates of Nephi [*the small plates*], down even till you come to the reign of king Benjamin, or until you come to that which you have translated, which you have retained [*which didn't get lost*];

The instructions in verse 41, above, are in effect saying that the first six books in the Book of Mormon, or 1 Nephi, 2 Nephi, Jacob, Enos, Jarom, and Omni, are the translation of the small plates. They cover the time down to the reign of King Benjamin, which is mentioned in The Words of Mormon and is reported in Mosiah, chapters 1 through 6. The Words of Mormon is the small book within the Book of Mormon which provides the transition from the small plates of Nephi to Mormon's abridgment of the large plates of Nephi.

42 And behold, you shall publish it [*the small plates*] as the record of Nephi; and thus I will confound those who have altered my words.

43 I will not suffer that they shall destroy my work; yea, **I will show unto them that my wisdom is greater than the cunning of the devil.**

44 Behold, they [*those who stole the 116 pages*] have only got a part, or an abridgment of the account of Nephi.

45 Behold, there are **many things engraven upon the plates of Nephi** [*the small plates*] **which do throw greater views upon my gospel** [*which teach and explain more things about the gospel*]; therefore, it is wisdom in me that you should translate this first part of the engravings of Nephi [*the small plates*], and send forth in this work [*the Book of Mormon*].

> It must be quite frustrating for the devil to see that we actually came out ahead when he engineered the theft of the 116 pages. The lost manuscript pages contained more history and secular proceedings of the Book of Mormon people; whereas, the replacement translation from the small plates teaches us more about the gospel. This situation reminds us of Satan's attempts to ruin things in the Garden of Eden. Actually, his plot blessed our lives tremendously by getting things moving so that we could enter mortality. Perhaps such failures to stop the gospel plan are alluded to in the phrase "dust shalt thou eat all the days of thy life" (Genesis 3:14; Moses 4:20). A modern translation of this phrase could be that Satan will always be eating the Savior's dust, or that the devil will always, ultimately, be left behind. At any rate, we have been greatly blessed by the loss of the 116 manuscript pages.

FIRST NEPHI 10

As Nephi now proceeds to engrave an account of his own life and ministry on the small plates, he will summarize many things his father prophesied as context and background for his own writings.

1 AND now I, Nephi, proceed to give an account upon these plates [*the small plates*] of my proceedings, and my reign and ministry; wherefore, to proceed with mine account, I must speak somewhat of the things of my father, and also of my brethren [*I will give you a context and setting for the things I will write later*].

2 For behold, it came to pass after my father had made an end of speaking the words of his dream [*as recorded in 1 Nephi 8*], and also of exhorting them to all diligence, he spake unto them concerning the Jews—

> Nephi now records some very

specific prophecies which his prophet father, Lehi, gave about the Jews and their coming captivity, about the Savior, John the Baptist, the Atonement, the crucifixion and resurrection of Christ, the scattering and gathering of Israel, and the restoration of the gospel. All these things and more are contained in the remaining twenty verses in this short chapter.

3 That after they [*the Jews*] should be [*had been*] destroyed, even that great city Jerusalem, and many be carried away captive into Babylon [*a powerful enemy nation about five hundred miles east of Jerusalem; basically, where modern-day Iraq exists today*], according to the own due time of the Lord, they [*the Jews*] should [*would*] return again, yea, even be brought back out of captivity; and after they should be brought back out of captivity they should possess again the land of their inheritance.

As you have no doubt already noticed, although the prophecies in verse 3, above, are literal, meaning they literally happened, there is also much scriptural symbolism here, which is often used elsewhere in the scriptures. For instance:

Jews can be symbolic of the Lord's covenant people.

Babylon is often symbolic of worldliness, wickedness, Satan's kingdom.

Returning from Babylon often symbolizes repentance and returning to the Lord.

Brought out of captivity symbolizes the Atonement of Christ and the gospel which leads us to the Atonement.

Possessing again the land of their inheritance is symbolic of attaining celestial exaltation, which is the "birthright" of each of us since we are the spirit children of our Heavenly Parents (see the second paragraph of "The Family: A Proclamation to the World").

4 Yea, even six hundred years from the time that my father left Jerusalem [*Lehi and his family left in 600 B.C.*], a prophet [*Christ*] would the Lord God raise up among the Jews—even a Messiah, or, in other words, a Savior of the world.

5 And he [*Lehi*] also spake concerning the prophets, how great a number had testified of these things, concerning this Messiah, of whom he had spoken, or this Redeemer of the world.

6 Wherefore, all mankind were in a lost and in a fallen state [*because of the fall of Adam*], and ever would be save they should rely on this Redeemer. [*In other*

words, without the Savior, we would all be permanently lost.]

7 And he spake also concerning a prophet [*John the Baptist*] who should [*would*] come before the Messiah, to prepare the way of the Lord—

8 Yea, even he should go forth and cry in the wilderness: Prepare ye the way of the Lord, and make his paths straight; for there standeth one [*Christ*] among you whom ye know not; and he is mightier than I [*John the Baptist*], whose shoe's latchet I am not worthy to unloose [*perhaps meaning "I am not even worthy to unbuckle His sandals in order to take them off to wash His feet"*]. And much spake [*spoke*] my father concerning this thing.

9 And my father said he [*John the Baptist*] should [*would*] baptize in Bethabara, beyond Jordan [*on the east side of the Jordan River*] and he also said he should baptize with water; even that he should baptize the Messiah with water.

10 And after he had baptized the Messiah with water, he should behold [*see*] and bear record that he had baptized the Lamb of God [*Christ*], who should take away the sins of the world [*Christ's Atonement makes exaltation available to everyone in the whole world, contingent upon personal repentance and living the gospel*].

The prophecies in the above verses are very specific, reminding us that the Lord does know the future. More such prophecies follow next.

11 And it came to pass after my father had spoken these words he spake unto my brethren concerning the gospel which should be [*would be*] preached among the Jews, and also concerning the dwindling of the Jews in unbelief [*apostasy*]. And after they had slain the Messiah [*crucified Christ*], who should come, and after he had been slain he should rise from the dead, and should make himself manifest, by the Holy Ghost, unto the Gentiles [*the non-Jews; the non-Israelites*].

12 Yea, even my father spake much concerning the Gentiles, and also concerning the house of Israel, that they should be compared like unto an olive-tree, whose branches should be broken off and should be scattered upon all the face of the earth.

Comparing the house of Israel (the tribes of Israel) to an olive tree involves interesting and significant symbolism. It is used often in scripture. We will take time here to go over some of this symbolism. We will use excerpts from the Institute of Religion *Book of Mormon Student Manual*, and use **bold** for emphasis.

"The use of the **olive tree as a symbol for the house of Israel** is an excellent example of how God uses symbolism to teach his children gospel laws and principles. For centuries the olive tree has been associated with peace. War and its grim attendants of destruction—rape of the land, siege, and death—were hardly conducive to the cultivation of **olive orchards, that require many years of careful husbandry to bring into full production**. When the dove returned to the ark, it carried an olive leaf in its beak, as though to symbolize that God was again at peace with the earth (see Genesis 8:11). The olive branch was used in ancient Greece and Rome to signify peace, and it is still used in that sense in the great seal of the United States where the American eagle is shown grasping an olive branch in its talons. The only true source of peace is Jesus Christ, the Prince of Peace. His peace comes through obedience to the laws and ordinances of the gospel. These laws and ordinances are given to the world through the house of Israel, symbolized by the olive tree. Someone once said that Israel was not chosen to be an *uplifted* people, but an *uplifting* people.

"There is further **symbolic significance in the cultivation of an olive tree**. If the green slip of an olive tree is merely planted and allowed to grow, it develops into the wild olive, a bush that grows without control into a tangle of limbs and branches producing only a small, worthless fruit (Moldenke and Moldenke, *Plants of the Bible*, p. 159). To become the productive 'tame' olive tree, the main stem of the wild tree must be cut back completely and a branch from a tame olive tree grafted into the stem of the wild one. **With careful pruning and cultivating** the tree will begin to produce its first fruit in about seven years, but it will not become fully productive for nearly fifteen years.

"In other words, **the olive tree cannot become productive by itself**; it requires grafting by the husbandman (the farmer; symbolic of God) to bring it into production. Throughout its history **Israel** has demonstrated the remarkable aptness **characterized by the symbol of the olive tree. When they gave themselves to their God for pruning and grafting the Israelites prospered and bore much fruit, but when they turned from Christ, the Master of the vineyard, and sought to become their own source of life and sustenance they became wild and unfruitful.**

"Two other characteristics of the olive tree further illustrate how it is an appropriate symbol for Israel. **First**, though requiring nearly fifteen years to come into full production, **an olive tree may produce fruit for centuries**. Some trees now growing in the Holy Land have been producing fruit abundantly for at least four hundred years. The **second** amazing quality of the tree is that **as it finally grows old and begins to die, the roots send up a number of new green shoots that, if grafted and pruned, will mature into full-grown olive trees. The root of the tree will also send up shoots after the tree is cut down**. Thus, while the tree itself may produce fruit for centuries, **the root of the tree may go on producing fruit and new trees for millennia**. It is believed that some of the ancient olive trees located in Israel today have come from trees that were ancient during Christ's mortal ministry.

"Zenos was not the only prophet to use the olive tree as a symbol for the chosen people of God. Jeremiah, foreseeing the coming destruction of the Jews by Babylonia, compared the covenant people to a green olive tree consumed by fire (see Jeremiah 11:16). The apostle Paul used a brief allegory almost identical to that of Zenos's to warn the Roman Christians against pride as they compared their favored position to that of the Jews (see Romans 11:16–24). In modern revelation, the Lord uses the parable of a vineyard and olive trees to show his will concerning the redemption of Zion (see D&C 101:43–58)." (*Book of Mormon Student Manual*, pp. 47–48).

Now, we will continue with Nephi's summary of his father's prophecies.

13 Wherefore, he said it must needs be [*it is necessary*] that we [*those journeying away from Jerusalem with Lehi at this time*] should be led with one accord into the land of promise, unto the fulfilling of the word of the Lord, that we should be scattered upon all the face of the earth. [*In other words, Nephi is telling us that he and his people are part of the fulfillment of the prophecy that Israel will be scattered throughout the world.*]

14 And after the house of Israel [*the twelve tribes of Israel*] should be scattered they should be gathered together again; or, in fine [*in summary*], after the Gentiles had received the fulness of the Gospel [*after the restoration of the gospel through the Prophet Joseph Smith*], the natural branches of the olive-tree, or the remnants of the house of Israel, should be grafted in, or come to the knowledge of

the true Messiah, their Lord and their Redeemer.

> The gathering of Israel, spoken of above, is certainly going on at an intense pace today. This gathering is both literal and spiritual. New converts as well as lifelong members are being "gathered" into the stakes of the Church wherever they live throughout the world today. However, it is not sufficient to be gathered physically. We must be gathered spiritually, in order to literally be gathered back to the presence of the Father in celestial glory and exaltation.

15 And after this manner of language did my father prophesy and speak unto my brethren, and also many more things which I do not write in this book [*the small plates*]; for I have written as many of them as were expedient for me in mine other book [*the large plates*].

16 And all these things, of which I have spoken, were done as my father dwelt in a tent, in the valley of Lemuel.

> Next, we will be taught many things by Nephi, including how to get our own testimony. We will **bold** some things for emphasis.

17 And it came to pass after I, Nephi, having **heard all the words** [*we must hear the gospel*] of my father, concerning the things which he saw in a vision, and also the things which **he spake by the power of the Holy Ghost** [*we must feel the power of the Holy Ghost bearing witness to what we have heard*], which power he received by **faith on the Son of God** [*we must have faith in Christ*]—and the Son of God was the Messiah who should come—I, Nephi, was **desirous also that I might see, and hear, and know** [*we must have a sincere, honest desire to gain a testimony*] of these things, by the power of **the Holy Ghost**, which **is the gift of God unto all those who diligently seek him** [*such a testimony is available to all*], as well in times of old as in the time that he should manifest himself unto the children of men.

18 For he is the same yesterday, today, and forever [*the plan of salvation and the requirements for exaltation have always been the same and always will be*]; and the way is prepared for all men from the foundation of the world [*the plan of salvation was prepared in premortality*], if it so be that they repent and come unto him.

19 For **he that diligently seeketh shall find** [*it requires diligence*

and time to gain a deep, abiding testimony]; and the mysteries of God [*the basics of the gospel*] shall be unfolded unto them, by the power of the Holy Ghost, as well in these times as in times of old, and as well in times of old as in times to come; wherefore, the course of the Lord is one eternal round.

> The use of the phrase "the course of the Lord is one eternal round" in verse 19, above, invites many interpretations. For instance, it can mean that God uses the same plan of salvation for all His children on all His worlds. Another interesting aspect of this phrase is that the path which leads to exaltation will always use the same principles and ordinances of the gospel for each individual who attains it.
>
> It can also mean that He always brings each group of His spirit offspring through the same "eternal round": First, "eternal" premortal life—intelligence, which was not created (D&C 93:29) and therefore was forever; second, spirit birth by heavenly parents ("The Family: A Proclamation to the World," paragraph two); third, mortality on an earth—which is not eternal, but is part of eternity; fourth, resurrection, which places his children in an eternal state of being again.
>
> The foregoing is a bit complex, so let's just summarize it by saying that "one eternal round" can mean "from eternity to mortality, then back to eternity."
>
> We are taught that we will use this same "eternal round" or plan of salvation for our spirit children when we become gods. The First Presidency made the following statement on this subject in 1916, as follows (**bold** added for emphasis):
>
> "Only **resurrected and glorified beings can become parents of spirit offspring**. Only such exalted souls have reached maturity in the appointed course of eternal life; and **the spirits born to them** in the eternal worlds **will pass in due sequence through the several stages or estates by which the glorified parents have attained exaltation**." (Smith, Lund, and Smith, 1916 First Presidency Statement, p. 942.)
>
> Next, Nephi teaches the principle of accountability and warns of the consequences of foolish choices. (**Bold** added for emphasis.)

20 Therefore remember, O man, for all thy doings thou shalt be brought into judgment.

21 Wherefore, if ye have sought to do wickedly in the days of your probation [*during your mortal lives*], then ye are found unclean before the judgment-seat [*at the final judgment*] of God;

and no unclean thing can dwell with God [*no one can dwell with God without having been made clean by the Atonement of Christ*]; wherefore, ye must be cast off forever [*you would be kept out of God's presence forever*].

22 And the Holy Ghost giveth authority that I should speak these things, and deny them not.

FIRST NEPHI 11

In the previous chapter, verse 17, Nephi told us he desired to "see, hear, and know" the things his father saw. His desire will be granted by the Lord; 1 Nephi, 11–14 provide us with a record of Nephi's vision, wherein he saw what his father saw (see 1 Nephi 14:29.) As we begin this next chapter, Nephi gives us three keys to receiving revelation. We will **bold** these for emphasis.

1 FOR it came to pass after I had **desired** to know the things that my father had seen, and **believing** that the Lord was able to make them known unto me, as I sat **pondering** in mine heart I was caught away in the Spirit of the Lord, yea, into an exceedingly high mountain, which I never had before seen, and upon which I never had before set my foot.

Many of us who desire revelation and help from the Lord do pretty well at doing the first two things Nephi mentioned above. But when it comes to "pondering," it seems that we don't do well at taking the time or making the time to do so. In our fast-paced lives, many of us are out of the habit of providing peaceful, non-pressured time for the Holy Ghost to get a word in edgewise into our minds. Thus, we miss out on much personal inspiration which we would otherwise receive.

Another thing we might note in verse 1 is the phrase "exceedingly high mountain." This is symbolic, among other things, of perspective. It is symbolic of seeing things as God sees them. If we are willing, the Lord gives us, through His Spirit, what we can call "high mountain experiences." During such times, the Lord takes our minds up "high," where we can see things from a much broader perspective. Joseph Smith had several "high mountain experiences" such as the First Vision, the visits from Moroni and other ancient prophets, the vision of the three degrees of glory (D&C 76), the revelation on celestial marriage, and many others.

The interesting thing about "high mountain experiences" in our lives is that we have to come back down to earth, so to speak, and live in a normal, everyday world with the daily tasks and challenges which are

First Nephi 11

the lot of all mortals. However, once we have been on some "high mountains," daily life can be much more meaningful and our ability to be patient and cope with trials and difficulties is much increased. We see this exemplified in the case of Joseph Smith and the Liberty Jail (see D&C 121–23). Something marvelous happens to the Prophet between the time he cries out in humble desperation at the beginning of section 121 and the ending of section 123 (see verse 17). Without once being told that the Lord would have him out of this dungeon within three weeks, Joseph's outlook changes completely.

You may wish to read D&C sections 121 through 123 in one sitting and note this change in perspective, while he still has to deal with the same dismal circumstances. You will see how the Lord takes Joseph's mind up into a "high mountain," as it were, and thus changes everything that is important.

Nephi will experience revelation and gain new perspectives while he is on this "exceedingly high mountain" which will prepare and qualify him to be a tremendous prophet and leader of his people.

It is interesting to see how "interactive" this vision is for Nephi. An active dialogue with questions and answers takes place between him and the Spirit as we will see, starting in verse 2.

We will again use some **bold** for teaching purposes.

Question:

2 And the Spirit said unto me: Behold, **what desirest thou?**

Answer:

3 And I said: I desire **to behold** [*see*] **the things which my father saw.**

Question:

4 And the Spirit said unto me: **Believest thou that thy father saw the tree of which he hath spoken?**

Answer:

5 And I said: **Yea, thou knowest that I believe all the words of my father.**

6 And when I had spoken these words, the Spirit cried with a loud voice, saying: Hosanna [*"save now"; see Bible Dictionary, p. 704*] to the Lord, the most high God; for he is God over all the earth, yea, even above all. And blessed art thou, Nephi, **because thou believest in the Son of the most high God;** wherefore, **thou shalt behold** [*see*] the things which thou hast desired.

7 And behold this thing shall be given unto thee for a sign, that after thou hast beheld the tree

which bore the fruit which thy father tasted, thou shalt also behold a man [*Christ*] descending out of heaven, and him shall ye witness [*you will see Him*]; and after ye have witnessed him ye shall bear record [*bear testimony; stand as a witness*] that it is the Son of God.

8 And it came to pass that the Spirit said unto me: Look! And I looked and beheld a tree; and it was like unto the tree which my father had seen; and the beauty thereof was far beyond, yea, exceeding of all beauty; and the whiteness thereof did exceed the whiteness of the driven snow. [*In other words, the love of God the Father—as demonstrated by His giving His Son to atone for our sins and guide us back to Him—is far beyond our ability to comprehend and is by far the most desirable thing of all!*]

9 And it came to pass after I had seen the tree, I said unto the Spirit: I behold thou hast shown unto me the tree [*symbolic of the love of God; also symbolic of Christ Himself, who is a manifestation of the love of the Father*] which is precious above all.

Question:

10 And he said unto me: **What desirest thou?**

Answer:

11 And I said unto him: **To know the interpretation thereof**—for I spake unto him as a man speaketh; for I beheld that he was in the form of a man; yet nevertheless, I knew that it was the Spirit of the Lord; and he spake unto me as a man speaketh with another.

Throughout the years, many members of the Church have asked who the "Spirit of the Lord" is in verse 11, above. Some say that it is the premortal Christ, while others believe him to be the Holy Ghost. Apostle James E. Talmage taught the following about this:

"The Holy Ghost, called also Spirit, and Spirit of the Lord, Spirit of God, Comforter, and Spirit of Truth, is not tabernacled in a body of flesh and bones, but is a personage of spirit; yet we know that the Spirit has manifested Himself in the form of a man (see 1 Nephi 11:11)." (Talmage, *Articles of Faith*, p. 38)

"That the Spirit of the Lord is capable of manifesting Himself in the form and figure of man, is indicated by the wonderful interview between the Spirit and Nephi, in which He revealed Himself to the prophet, questioned him concerning his desires and belief, instructed him in the things of God, speaking face to face with the man. 'I

First Nephi 11

spake unto him,' says Nephi, 'as a man speaketh; for I beheld that he was in the form of a man; yet nevertheless, I knew that it was the Spirit of the Lord; and he spake unto me as a man speaketh with another.'" (Talmage, *Articles of Faith*, p. 144).

12 And it came to pass that he said unto me: Look! And I looked as if to look upon him, and I saw him not; for he had gone from before my presence. *[Another "guide" will join Nephi in verse 14.]*

Next, Nephi will be shown, in effect, Matthew, Mark, Luke and John in the New Testament. We will **bold** many of the things he saw to emphasize that he was seeing what we know as the first four books of the New Testament.

13 And it came to pass that I looked and beheld *[saw]* the great city of **Jerusalem**, and also other cities. And I beheld the city of **Nazareth**; and in the city of Nazareth I beheld **a virgin** *[Mary, mother of Jesus]*, and she was exceedingly fair and white.

14 And it came to pass that I saw the heavens open; and an angel *[Nephi's guide for this portion of the vision]* came down and stood before me; and he said unto me: Nephi, what beholdest thou?

15 And I said unto him: **A virgin** *[Mary]*, **most beautiful and fair above all other virgins**. *[Mary's highly respected status is strongly emphasized in this vision. This is another witness for the fact that she was a virgin, as stated in the Bible.]*

16 And he said unto me: Knowest thou the condescension of God *[the Father]*?

The phrase "condescension of God" will be used twice in this chapter. In verse 16, above, it means that the Father is kind enough to work with us at our level of understanding. This phrase will be used again in verse 26, but this time it will refer to Jesus, the Son of God, and it will mean that Christ, a God, submitted to the trials of mortal life in order to provide salvation for us. This is explained in the *Book of Mormon Student Manual*, used in the institutes of religion of the Church, as well as at BYU and other Church schools, as follows (**bold** used for emphasis):

"In 1 Nephi 11: 26, Nephi is taught a second time about **the condescension of God**. The first time this subject was taught (verse 16) it was followed by a vision of the birth of the Son of God. This time it is followed by a vision of his ministry. Elder Bruce R. McConkie commented on the **two different senses of the phrase** in this way:

" 'The condescension of God (verse 16) (**meaning the**

Father) consists in the fact that though he is an exalted, perfected, glorified Personage, he became the personal and literal Father of a mortal Offspring born of mortal woman. And the condescension of God (verse 26) **(meaning the Son)** consists in the fact that though he himself is the Lord Omnipotent, the very Being who created the earth and all things that in it are, yet being born of mortal woman, he submitted to all the trials of mortality, suffering "temptations, and pain of body, hunger, thirst, and fatigue, even more than man can suffer, except it be unto death" (Mosiah 3:5–8), finally being put to death in a most ignominious manner.' " (McConkie, *Mormon Doctrine*, p. 155, as quoted in the 1989 edition of the *Book of Mormon Student Manual*, p. 32)

17 And I said unto him: I know that he [*the Father*] loveth his children; nevertheless, I do not know the meaning of all things [*a very wise answer by Nephi*].

18 And he said unto me: Behold, the virgin whom thou seest is the mother of the Son of God, after the manner of the flesh. [*The angel is explaining the vision and here tells Nephi that he is seeing Mary, the mortal mother of Christ.*]

19 And it came to pass that I beheld [*I saw*] that she was carried away in the Spirit; and after she had been carried away in the Spirit for the space of a time the angel spake unto me, saying: Look!

20 And I looked and beheld the virgin again, bearing a child [*Jesus*] in her arms.

21 And the angel said unto me: Behold the Lamb of God, yea, even the Son of the Eternal Father! Knowest thou the meaning of **the tree** which thy father saw?

22 And I answered him, saying: Yea [*Yes*], it **is the love of God**, which sheddeth itself abroad in the hearts of the children of men; wherefore, it is the most desirable above all things.

23 And he spake unto me, saying: Yea, and the most joyous to the soul.

Next, Nephi will be shown the Savior's mortal ministry, plus, he will be shown the interpretation of many things which his father, Lehi, saw when he was shown this vision.

24 And after he had said these words, he said unto me: Look! And I looked, and **I beheld the Son of God going forth among the children of men**; and I saw many fall down at his feet and worship him.

First Nephi 11

25 And it came to pass that I beheld that **the rod of iron**, which my father had seen, **was the word of God**, which **led to the fountain of living waters, or** to **the tree of life**; which **waters are a representation of the love of God**; and I also beheld that **the tree of life was a representation of the love of God.**

26 And the angel said unto me again: Look and behold the condescension of God [*the willingness of God the Son, Christ, to become mortal and redeem us; see note by verse 16, above*]!

27 And I looked and beheld the Redeemer of the world, of whom my father had spoken; and I also beheld the prophet [*John the Baptist*] who should [*who would*] prepare the way before him [*Jesus*]. And the Lamb of God [*Jesus*] went forth and was baptized of [*by*] him [*John the Baptist*]; and after he was baptized, I beheld the heavens open, and the Holy Ghost come down out of heaven and abide upon him [*Jesus*] in the form of a dove.

> The "form of a dove" here is symbolism. The Prophet Joseph Smith explained this symbolism as follows, as he taught of the mission of John the Baptist (**bold** added for emphasis):
>
> "First. He (John the Baptist) was entrusted with a divine mission of preparing the way before the face of the Lord. Whoever had such a trust committed to him before or since? No man. Second. He was entrusted with the important mission, and it was required at his hands, to baptize the Son of Man. Whoever had the honor of doing that? Whoever had so great a privilege and glory? Whoever led the Son of God into the waters of baptism, and had the privilege of **beholding the Holy Ghost descend in the form of a dove, or rather in the *sign* of the dove**, in witness of that administration? The sign of the dove was instituted before the creation of the world, a witness for the Holy Ghost, and the devil cannot come in the sign of a dove. **The Holy Ghost is a personage, and is in the form of a personage. It does not confine itself to the *form* of the dove, but in *sign* of the dove**. [This is not a misprint, with *the* accidentally left out; the Prophet said "in sign of the dove."] **The Holy Ghost cannot be transformed into a dove**, but the sign of a dove was given to John to signify the truth of the deed—as the dove is an emblem or token of truth and innocence." (Smith, *Teachings of the Prophet Joseph Smith*, p. 275)

28 And I beheld that he [*the Savior*] went forth ministering unto the people, in power and great glory; and the multitudes

were gathered together to hear him; and I beheld that they cast him out from among them. [*Nephi is shown that the people rejected Christ.*]

29 And I also beheld twelve others [*the Twelve Apostles in the days of Jesus*] following him. And it came to pass that they were carried away in the Spirit from before my face, and I saw them not.

30 And it came to pass that the angel spake unto me again, saying: Look! And I looked, and I beheld the heavens open again, and I saw angels descending upon the children of men; and they did minister unto them. [*From this we learn that those on the other side of the veil are very much involved in what goes on here.*]

31 And he spake unto me again, saying: Look! And I looked, and I beheld the Lamb of God going forth among the children of men. And I beheld multitudes of people who were sick, and who were afflicted with all manner of diseases, and with devils and unclean spirits; and the angel spake and showed all these things unto me. And they were healed by the power of the Lamb of God; and the devils and the unclean spirits were cast out.

The literal physical healings shown in verse 31, above, are symbolic of the power of the Savior to heal our spiritual wounds and sicknesses. He can heal "all manner of (spiritual) diseases" including the consequences of sin and foolishness. Every time we read of the physical, observable healings performed by the Master, we would do well to be reminded that the most important healing of all is the healing of the soul who is weighed down by the aftermath of sin, or who feels inadequate in a Church calling, or who mourns, etc.

Next, Nephi will see the crucifixion of the Savior in the vision.

32 And it came to pass that the angel spake unto me again, saying: Look! And I looked and beheld the Lamb of God, that he was taken by the people; yea, the Son of the everlasting God was judged of [*by*] the world; and I saw and bear record.

33 And I, Nephi, saw that he was lifted up upon the cross and slain for the sins of the world.

Next, Nephi will be shown what we know as the rest of the New Testament, beginning with Acts.

34 And after he was slain I saw the multitudes of the earth, that they were gathered together to fight against the apostles of the

Lamb; for thus were the twelve called by the angel of the Lord.

35 And the multitude of the earth was gathered together; and I beheld that they were in a **large and spacious building**, like unto the building which my father saw. And the angel of the Lord spake unto me again, saying: Behold **the world and the wisdom thereof**; yea, behold the house of Israel hath gathered together to fight against the twelve apostles of the Lamb.

36 And it came to pass that I saw and bear record, that **the great and spacious building was the pride of the world**; and it fell, and the fall thereof was exceedingly great. And the angel of the Lord spake unto me again, saying: **Thus shall be the destruction of all nations, kindreds, tongues, and people, that shall fight against the twelve apostles of the Lamb.**

FIRST NEPHI 12

Nephi's vision continues in this chapter and will continue to the end of chapter 14. In this chapter, he will basically see the whole Book of Mormon.

1 AND it came to pass that the angel said unto me: Look, and behold thy seed, and also the seed of thy brethren [*look at your descendants as well as the descendants of the others in Lehi's group*]. And I looked and beheld the land of promise [*the Americas*]; and I beheld multitudes of people, yea, even as it were in number as many as the sand of the sea. [*The Nephites and Lamanites multiplied and became very large numbers of inhabitants in the Americas.*]

> Verse 2, next, would especially represent Alma and Helaman, where we read accounts of multiple wars and terrible slaughter and destruction.

2 And it came to pass that I beheld multitudes gathered together to battle, one against the other; and I beheld wars, and rumors of wars, and great slaughters with the sword among my people.

3 And it came to pass that I beheld many generations pass away, after the manner of wars and contentions in the land; and I beheld many cities, yea, even that I did not number them.

> Just a quick comment here. Occasionally, you may run into theories that the Book of Mormon peoples represent relatively small numbers of people in scattered villages and small cities. Verses 1–3, above, do not appear to support such theories.

Next, in verses 4–10, Nephi will be shown the events of Third Nephi. In verse 4, he is shown the destruction which took place among the Book of Mormon people at the time of the Savior's crucifixion. In verse 4, he is especially seeing 3 Nephi, chapter 8, in vision.

4 And it came to pass that I saw a mist of darkness [*it was completely dark upon this land for three days after Christ was crucified; see 3 Nephi 8:19–23*] on the face of the land of promise; and I saw lightnings, and I heard thunderings, and earthquakes, and all manner of tumultuous noises; and I saw the earth and the rocks, that they rent [*were torn*]; and I saw mountains tumbling into pieces; and I saw the plains of the earth, that they were broken up; and I saw many cities that they were sunk; and I saw many that they were burned with fire; and I saw many that did tumble to the earth, because of the quaking thereof.

5 And it came to pass after I saw these things, I saw the vapor of darkness, that it passed from off the face of the earth [*after three days of total darkness*]; and behold, I saw multitudes [*who were not wicked enough to be destroyed*] who had not fallen because of the great and terrible judgments of the Lord.

Next in the vision, Nephi sees the Savior's appearance to the people in Third Nephi. Imagine how everything which he is seeing in this marvelous vision prepares and qualifies him for the responsibilities he will yet have in the future.

6 And I saw the heavens open, and the Lamb of God descending out of heaven; and he came down and showed himself unto them.

7 And I also saw and bear record that the Holy Ghost fell upon twelve others [*the Nephite Twelve Apostles*]; and they were ordained of God, and chosen.

Some members wonder whether or not to refer to the Nephite Twelve as "Apostles." We usually refer to them as the "Twelve (Nephite) Disciples" as in verse 8, below. But, it is also proper to refer to them as Apostles, since the Prophet Joseph Smith did, as recorded in History of the Church, 4:538.

8 And the angel spake unto me, saying: Behold [*see*] the Twelve Disciples of the Lamb, who are chosen to minister unto thy seed [*unto your descendants*].

Next, we are taught some things about the judgment. We discover from what Nephi was shown here that the Twelve Apostles organized by Jesus during His earthly ministry will judge the twelve tribes of

Israel. They will also judge the Twelve Nephite Disciples, who, in turn, will judge Nephi's descendants. This is rather interesting, because it seems to tell us that our judgment will involve those who have held priesthood keys and had stewardship over us throughout our lives. While we do not have much detail as to how this all works out, we do know that Jesus will be our final judge, and that He will have the final say as to our eternal placement after the Judgment Day (see John 5:22).

9 And he said unto me: Thou rememberest the Twelve Apostles of the Lamb [*in Jerusalem*]? Behold they are they who shall judge the twelve tribes of Israel; wherefore [*therefore*], the twelve ministers of thy seed [*the Twelve Nephite Disciples; see 3 Nephi 12:1, 19:4*] shall be judged of them; for ye are of the house of Israel.

10 And these twelve ministers [*the Nephite Twelve*] whom thou beholdest shall judge thy seed. And, behold, they are righteous forever; for because of their faith in the Lamb of God their garments are made white in his blood [*they will be exalted*].

Next, in verses 11–12, Nephi is shown what we will read about in Fourth Nephi, where there will be about two hundred years of peace after the Savior departs, then apostasy. In other words, falling away from the Church will take place rapidly.

11 And the angel said unto me: Look! And I looked, and beheld three generations pass away in righteousness; and their garments were white even like unto the Lamb of God. [*In other words, they were worthy of exaltation with Christ.*] And the angel said unto me: These are made white in the blood of the Lamb, because of their faith in him.

The symbolism in the phrase "made white in the blood of the Lamb" (verse 11, above) is beautiful and very significant. There is much of color symbolism in the scriptures. The color white symbolizes purity, cleansed from sin, worthiness to live in the presence of God forever, and usually means exaltation. Thus, being made white "in the blood of the Lamb" means to have been cleansed and redeemed from sin through the Atonement of Christ and made clean and worthy to live with God forever.

Just one more little bit about the color white. Once you understand what this color symbolizes in scripture, it becomes a type of "shorthand" or "one-word-says-it-all" which can take the place of much writing and explanation. For instance, in place of a longer explanation that certain people have attained celestial glory, the scriptures could simply say "they are dressed in white." An example of this is found in Revelation 7:9. A brief list of some colors and associated symbolism often used in scripture follows:

Color Symbolism Often Used in the Scriptures

white: purity; righteousness; exaltation (Example: 1 Ne. 12:10; Rev. 3:4–5)

black: evil; famine; darkness (Example: Rev. 6:5–6)

red: sins; bloodshed (Example: Rev. 6:4; D&C 133:51)

blue: heaven; godliness; remembering and keeping God's commandments (Example: Num. 15:37–40)

green: life; nature (Example: Rev. 8:7)

amber: sun; light; divine glory (Example: D&C 110:2, Rev. 1:15, Ezek. 1:4, 27; 8:2)

scarlet: royalty (Example: Dan. 5:29; Matt. 27:28–29)

silver: worth, but less than gold (Example: Ridges, *Isaiah Made Easier,* Isa. 48:10 notes)

gold: the best; exaltation (Example: Rev. 4:4)

12 And I, Nephi, also saw many of the fourth generation who passed away in righteousness.

Next, Nephi will see the terrible destruction of his descendants as described in Mormon. He will also be given more symbolic interpretations of what his father saw. We will use **bold** to highlight these interpretations.

13 And it came to pass that I saw the multitudes of the earth gathered together.

14 And the angel said unto me: Behold thy seed, and also the seed of thy brethren. [*In other words, the Nephites and the Lamanites as they gather for the final great battles depicted in Mormon.*]

15 And it came to pass that I looked and beheld the people of my seed [*the Nephites*] gathered together in multitudes against the seed of my brethren [*the Lamanites*]; and they were gathered together to battle.

16 And the angel spake unto me, saying: Behold **the fountain of filthy water** which thy father saw; yea, even **the river of which he spake; and the depths thereof are the depths of hell.**

17 And the **mists of darkness are the temptations of the devil**, which blindeth the eyes, and hardeneth the hearts of the children of men, and leadeth them away into broad roads, that they perish and are lost.

Nephi, no doubt, wants us to

First Nephi 12

learn many lessons from what he wrote for us in verse 17, above. Among these things would be that Satan attempts to "blind our eyes" so that we can't see danger, or so that we can't see nor understand spiritual truths and perspectives. He takes away wisdom and respect for those who have true wisdom. His success in such "blinding" is very evident in much of modern society.

Another warning for us from Nephi, in verse 17, is that the devil strives to harden our hearts. One definition of "hardened hearts" is lack of feeling, lack of concern about sin, lack of concern for the rights and needs of others.

Yet another warning in this verse is that Satan attempts to lead people into "broad roads." This is an interesting term. When we are on the "strait and narrow path" (1 Nephi 8:20), we have many commandments. We are blessed "with commandments not a few" (D&C 59:4), and with rules and guidelines from the Lord through the prophets. The cry of the wicked and the quest of the foolish is to do away with restrictions and rules. Thus they plunge rapidly or wobble slowly down the "broad roads" which ultimately lead to captivity, remorse, and loss of freedom. Whereas, those who voluntarily and diligently travel up the "strait and narrow" gain more and more freedom until they are among the freest people in the universe, namely, the gods.

18 And **the large and spacious building**, which thy father saw, **is vain imaginations and the pride** of the children of men. And a **great and a terrible gulf** divideth them; yea, even the word of the **justice** of the Eternal God, and the Messiah who is the Lamb of God, of whom the Holy Ghost beareth record, from the beginning of the world until this time, and from this time henceforth and forever.

The "great and terrible gulf" in verse 18, above, is a reminder that "mercy" cannot rob justice (see Alma 42:25). Those who squander opportunities to repent when mercy could have been extended to them, and thus arrive at the final judgment bar of God "filthy still" (2 Nephi 9:16), will be subject to the law of justice. They will not be deemed worthy to live in the presence of God, and will thus be out of His presence forever (see D&C 29:29, D&C 76:112, and the following quote from Spencer W. Kimball).

"After a person has been assigned to his place in the kingdom, either in the telestial, the terrestrial, or the celestial, or to his exaltation, he will never advance from his assigned glory to another glory" (Kimball, *The Miracle of Forgiveness*, pp. 243–44).

19 And while the angel spake these words, I beheld and saw that the seed of my brethren did contend against my seed, according to the word of the angel; and because of the **pride of my seed, and the temptations of the devil**, I beheld that the seed of my brethren did overpower the people of my seed [*the Lamanites destroyed the Nephite civilization (see Mormon, chapters 6 and 8)*].

20 And it came to pass that I beheld, and saw the people of the seed of my brethren that they had overcome my seed; and they went forth in multitudes upon the face of the land.

21 And I saw them gathered together in multitudes; and I saw wars and rumors of wars among them; and in wars and rumors of wars I saw many generations pass away.

> Nephi has now seen the end of the Book of Mormon and beyond in this portion of his vision.

22 And the angel said unto me: Behold these shall dwindle in unbelief.

23 And it came to pass that I beheld, after they had dwindled in unbelief they became a dark, and loathsome, and a filthy people, full of idleness and all manner of abominations.

The net result of pride and willful wickedness, described in verse 23, above, applies to any people, at any time, anywhere, regardless of race, gender, privilege, or position.

FIRST NEPHI 13

As Nephi's vision continues, he will be shown the formation of a "great and abominable church" and what we usually refer to as the "Dark Ages" along with some incredible details concerning Christopher Columbus, the Pilgrims, the destructions among the Lamanites in the Americas, the thirteen American colonies, the Revolutionary War, and God's help for the fledgling colonies as they fought for independence against Great Britain. In addition, he will be shown that the Bible would be brought by them and that many "plain and precious things" had been taken out of it. He will also be shown the establishment of the United States, the coming forth of the Book of Mormon, the joining together of the Bible and the Book of Mormon, and then a very brief view of the last days.

1 AND it came to pass that the

First Nephi 13

angel spake unto me, saying: Look! And I looked and beheld many nations and kingdoms [*by the context, we understand these to be the nations of Europe*].

2 And the angel said unto me: What beholdest thou? And I said: I behold many nations and kingdoms.

3 And he said unto me: These are the nations and kingdoms of the Gentiles.

> The word "Gentiles" as used in verse 3, above, has many different definitions, which can lead to confusion if not kept in context. In its most basic sense, it can mean "someone who is not of your group." In the scriptures, it has two general meanings, depending on context.
>
> In one sense, it came to mean people who were not of the lineage of Israel. In other scriptural contexts, it means nations which do not have the gospel, even though they may have Israelite blood (See Bible Dictionary, pp. 679–80). In the Book of Mormon, it often means people who were not from the Jerusalem area. That is what it means in verse 3, above, and it especially has reference to the nations of Europe during the Dark Ages and beyond, almost all of whom had Israelite blood.

4 And it came to pass that I saw among the nations of the Gentiles the formation of a great church.

> Here, we will be taught about the "great and abominable church." Sometimes, there is misunderstanding about this "church." In times past, many have considered this church to be a specific Christian church. If we read carefully, we will find that this is not the case, nor can it be. If it were limited to one existing church or denomination, it would leave out all others who teach or sponsor falsehood or evil, including gangs, secret combinations, nations or groups who seek the downfall of democracy, and so on.

5 And the angel said unto me: Behold the formation of a church which is most abominable above all other churches, which slayeth the saints of God, yea, and tortureth them and bindeth them down, and yoketh them with a yoke of iron, and bringeth them down into captivity.

6 And it came to pass that I beheld this great and abominable church; and I saw the devil that he was the founder of it.

> We discover in verses 5 and 6, above, that the devil is the "founder" of the "great and abominable church." This teaches us that the great and abominable church is the kingdom of the devil, no matter which front organization he may be hiding behind. This is

confirmed in 1 Nephi 14:10, wherein we are told that there are basically just two churches, one is the "church of the Lamb" and the other is the "church of the devil."

The word "church" in the phrase "church of the devil" can confuse people a bit. It sometimes makes them think it is referring to a religious organization only. It can be helpful to substitute the word "kingdom" for "church" and thus have the phrase "kingdom of the devil" meaning any groups, individuals, or organizations which fight against that which is right. The phrase "kingdom of the devil" is used in 1 Nephi 22:22.

Next, in verses 7 through 9, we run into what could be termed "Satan's big three tools." They are materialism, sexual immorality, and pride. These three major categories of temptation and sin seem to have been terribly effective in leading people astray throughout history, and are still being used by the devil today. We will use **bold** for emphasis in pointing these "big three" out.

Materialism and Sexual Immorality

7 And I also saw **gold**, and **silver**, and **silks**, and **scarlets**, and **fine-twined linen**, and **all manner of precious clothing**; and I saw **many harlots**.

8 And the angel spake unto me, saying: Behold [*look at*] the **gold**, and the **silver**, and the **silks**, and the **scarlets**, and the **fine-twined linen**, and the **precious clothing**, and the **harlots**, are the desires of this great and abominable church.

Pride

9 And also **for the praise of the world** do they destroy the saints of God, and bring them down into captivity.

10 And it came to pass that I looked and beheld many waters [*oceans*]; and they divided the Gentiles [*especially those in Britain and Europe*] from the seed of my brethren [*from the Lamanites in the Americas*].

11 And it came to pass that the angel said unto me: Behold the wrath of God is upon the seed of thy brethren [*the anger of the Lord is upon the Lamanites*].

12 And I looked and beheld a man [*Christopher Columbus*] among the Gentiles [*in Europe*], who was separated from the seed of my brethren [*in the Americas*] by the many waters [*oceans*]; and I beheld the Spirit of God, that it came down and wrought upon [*inspired and worked upon*] the man; and he went forth upon the many waters [*Columbus sailed*

First Nephi 13

out upon the ocean], even unto the seed of my brethren, who were in the promised land.

Elder Mark E. Peterson of the Quorum of the Twelve Apostles wrote that Christopher Columbus felt that he was inspired to make his journey. Elder Peterson explained:

"Columbus believed he could reach 'the Indies' by sailing westward. Although there were some people who still thought the world was flat, Columbus did not, and he was anxious to make his journey. But it was more than an urge for adventure that impelled the discoverer to undertake what he called 'his enterprise.'

"Go to any public library, read almost any detailed biography of the discoverer [*Columbus*], and it becomes immediately clear that he felt himself an inspired man, sent of heaven to make the voyage. For example, *Columbus, Don Quixote of the Seas*, written in German by Jacob Wassermann and translated into English by Eric Sutton, tells the story very well [*quoting Columbus*]:

"'From my first youth onward, I was a seaman and have so continued until this day. . . . Wherever on the earth a ship has been, I have been. I have spoken and treated with learned men, priests, and laymen, Latins and Greeks, Jews and Moors, and with many men of other faiths. The Lord was well disposed to my desire, and He bestowed upon me courage and understanding; knowledge of seafaring He gave me in abundance, of astrology as much as was needed, and of geometry and astronomy likewise. Further, He gave me joy and cunning in drawing maps and thereon cities, mountains, rivers, islands, and harbours, each one in its place. I have seen and truly I have studied all books—cosmographies, histories, chronicles, and philosophies, and other arts, for which our Lord unlocked my mind, sent me upon the sea, and gave me fire for the deed. Those who heard of my emprise called it foolish, mocked me, and laughed. But who can doubt but that the Holy Ghost inspired me?'" (Petersen, *The Great Prologue*, pp. 25–26).

Next, Nephi sees the Pilgrims fleeing oppression and coming to America.

13 And it came to pass that I beheld the Spirit of God, that it wrought upon other Gentiles [*the Pilgrims*]; and they went forth out of captivity, upon the many waters.

14 And it came to pass that I beheld many multitudes of the Gentiles [*early colonists*] upon the land of promise; and I beheld the wrath of God, that it was upon the seed of my brethren

[*the Lamanites in the Americas*]; and they were scattered before the Gentiles and were smitten.

In verse 14, above, Nephi sees devastation among the Lamanites as foreign explorers and colonists come to the Americas and begin to spread out among the Indians. The following quote from the old *Book of Mormon Student Manual*, page 35, (1982 edition, used at BYU and in the Institutes of Religion plus other Church schools) gives a summary of ways in which the Indians were "scattered before the Gentiles and were smitten" (**bold** added for emphasis):

"The fulfillment of Nephi's prophecy concerning the scattering of the seed of his brethren is so vast a topic as to fill volumes and can be touched on here only briefly. It is one of the most tragic stories of history, equaling in many ways the persecution and suffering of the Jewish people through the centuries (see 1 Nephi 19:13–15). From the time Columbus landed in the West Indies, the destruction and driving of the Indian people began. The extent of this destruction has only recently started coming to full light.

"For example, Wilbur R. Jacobs, a noted historian, refutes the earlier projections made by European and American scholars of the Indian population **at the time Columbus arrived in the Western Hemisphere** in 1492. Estimates used to place the **Indian population** of North America at about a million, and in both North and South America at no more than 8 million. However, according to Jacobs, modern projections which are widely accepted today place the total at **90 million** for the whole of the Western Hemisphere and nearly **10 million in North America alone** (Jacobs, "The Indian and the Frontier in American History—A Need for Revision," p. 45).

"When this total of **10 million Indians living in North America is compared with the estimated 235,000 who were alive at the turn of the twentieth century**, one begins to glimpse the scope of the tragedy.

"What happened to all those Indians? Cook and Dobyns, researchers in the spread of **epidemic diseases among Indians**, argue convincingly that millions of Indians were killed off by catastrophic disease frontiers in the form of epidemics of **smallpox, bubonic plague, typhus, influenza, malaria, measles, yellow fever, and other diseases**. (Besides bringing Old World strains of virus and bacteria, Europeans brought weeds, plants, rats, insects, domestic animals, liquor, and a new technology to alter Indian life and the ecological balance wheel.) **Smallpox**, caused by an airborne virus, was and is about the most deadly of the contagious diseases. Virulent strains, transmitted by air, by clothing, blankets, or by slight contact (even by an immune individual), **snuffed out whole tribes**, often leaving only a handful of survivors. Although some kinds of epidemic diseases might be reduced to a mild virulence among Indians (as among whites) after generations of exposure, **smallpox was undoubtedly the Indians' worst killer** because it returned time and again to attack surviving generations of Indians to kill them off too." (See Jacobs, *The Indian*, p. 46.)

"Nor was the decimation by disease the only tragedy to befall the descendants of Lehi. The Indians as described by Columbus were 'gentle beings, souls of hospitality, curious and merry, truthful and faithful, walking in beauty and possessors of a spiritual religion' (Collier, *The Indians of the Americas*, pp. 97–98). They were not prepared for the ruthless, predatory nature of the white men who came in search of gold and converts. 'The situation was as if a mysterious stranger, announcing himself with words of love, welcomed with delight as a guest, embraced as a friend, given the run of the house and taken into the family's bosom, had suddenly revealed himself as no man at all but a devouring werewolf' (Collier, *The Indians*, p. 97). Immediate exploitation of the Indians as a cheap source of slave labor took place. **Thousands were shipped to Europe** and thousands of Europeans came to America to received a grant of land with accompanying **unpaid, forced, Indian labor** for life." (Collier, *The Indians*, p. 98)

"But in the West Indies it was not decimation that befell the Indians the peoples whom Columbus had found to be gentle, merry and walking in beauty. It was annihilation. Since the supply was supposed to be unlimited in the beginning, these **chattel slaves** (Indians) **were worked to death**. So terrible was their life that they were driven to **mass suicide**, to mass **infanticide**, to mass **abstinence from sexual life** in order that children should not be born into horror. **Lethal epidemics** followed upon the will to die. The **murders and desolations** exceeded those of the most pitiless tyrants of earlier history; nor have they been surpassed since." (Collier, *The Indians*, p. 98)

Collier notes that "**the Indian population of Haiti and Santo Domingo, estimated to be between two and three hundred thousand when Columbus arrived, had plummeted to less than five hundred natives surviving in 1548, only fifty-six years later!**" (Collier, *The Indians*, p. 99)

That story was repeated numerous times at the hands of men like Cortez, Pizzaro, and DeSoto, in Peru, Colombia, Mexico, and the United States. The scenes viewed by Nephi six hundred years before Christ's birth were fulfilled with horrible reality. As one author put it:

"Here was a race in process of being engulfed in an irresistible flood of peoples of an utterly different culture. Dislocated from their accustomed seats, transplanted again and again, treated by whites as hostile encumbrances of the fertile earth to be brushed aside or destroyed, bewildered by a type of economy for which they were unprepared, decimated by disease and vices to which they had built up no resistance, repeatedly seeing solemn treaties violated, subject to shifting governmental policies, preyed upon by incompetent and greedy officials, and at times demoralized by an excess of well intentioned but ill directed paternalistic kindness, it is a wonder that the Indians survived." (Latourette, *A History of the Expansion of Christianity, The Great Century*, 4:323)

15 And I beheld the Spirit of the Lord, that it was upon the Gentiles [*the colonists*], and they did prosper and obtain the land for their inheritance; and I beheld that they were white, and exceedingly fair and beautiful, like unto my people [*the Nephites*] before they were slain.

16 And it came to pass that I, Nephi, beheld that the Gentiles [*who became the thirteen colonies and eventually became the United States*] who had gone forth out of captivity did humble themselves before the Lord; and the power of the Lord was with them.

Next, the prophet Nephi sees the Revolutionary War in his vision. He sees the hand of God helping the small, poorly equipped and undertrained bands of colonist under the leadership of George Washington. He is shown their triumph over vastly better trained and equipped armies of the British.

17 And I beheld that their mother Gentiles [*Great Britain*] were gathered together upon the waters, and upon the land also [*Great Britain sent navies and armies*], to battle against them [*the colonists in North America*].

18 And I beheld that the power of God was with them, and also that the wrath of God was upon all those that were gathered together against them to battle.

There are numerous accounts of the power of God exercised in behalf of George Washington and his soldiers. Time and time again, his ragged and struggling fighters were saved against all odds. In a fascinating article in the October 1987 *Ensign* entitled "Delivered by the Power of God," Jonathan A. Dibble gives examples of this power. One excerpt from this article follows:

"The British soon withdrew from Boston and sailed toward New York. Washington, anticipating this move, marched on New York. There, several events led to another miraculous rescue of the American soldiers. Washington split his command and landed most of his troops on Long Island's Brooklyn Heights. He had only ten thousand troops to guard a fifteen-mile front, while General Howe embarked approximately fifteen thousand British and Hessian soldiers at Gravesend Bay, Long Island. He left four thousand soldiers behind on Staten Island as reinforcements. . . . The British, by sailing up the East River, could land troops behind Washington and surround his army. The prospect for the Americans was serious. If Washington were to lose ten thousand men at the outset of the war, the Declaration of Independence would most likely not gain the public support to fuel the fires of freedom.

"However, once again the elements intervened. On 26 August 1776, Howe's reinforcements (the British) were delayed by a strong northeast wind and an ebbing tide that 'compelled the fleet to drop down the bay and come to anchor.' At nine o'clock the next morning, the Americans could hear the British cannons in the American rear. In a brilliant night march, the British General Henry Clinton had slipped by the east side of the Americans and had captured eight hundred prisoners, including Generals John Sullivan and William Stirling.

"At this point, Washington, instead of retreating across the East River, reinforced the American positions on Brooklyn Heights and waited for Howe's assault. Seeing the entrenched American troops, British General Howe decided to delay his attack until the fleet had entered the East River. But the British ships were held back again by another strong northeast wind. Then torrents of rain fell, further hindering the fleet in the East River and subduing the efforts of the British troops on land. Howe began to raise siege works along Washington's lines when, according to historian Henry B. Carrington, 'The rain (became) so incessant, and accompanied by a wind so violent, that the British troops kept within their tents, and their works made slow progress.'

"Finally, on the night of 29 August 1776, Washington, recognizing the opportunity to make a tactical retreat, ordered his troops across the East River. The first unit embarked at ten o'clock. But at midnight, the wind changed. Just as the British advance had earlier been halted by the elements, this time the Americans' retreat was threatened with disaster. Sloops and other sailing craft could not sail, and there were too few rowboats to complete the evacuation in one night. According to Carrington, 'the wind and tide were so violent that even the seamen soldiers of Massachusetts could not spread a close reefed sail upon a single vessel; and the larger vessels, upon which so much depended, would have been swept to the ocean if once entrusted to the current.'

"Washington was urged to abandon the evacuation; but then, miraculously, the wind abruptly shifted, allowing the Americans to cross the river in the predawn hours. Nine thousand men were moved in that retreat, and historian Bart McDowell records that after dawn, as the last of the army sailed away, one young captain noted that the boats moved under 'the friendly cover of a thick fog,' which 'increased the danger of panic, but also prevented discovery.' Historian Christopher Ward points out that 'freakish Nature (had) again favored the Americans.' Washington 'had snatched a beaten army from the very jaws of a victorious force, and practically under the nose of the greatest armada ever seen in American waters'" (Dibble, " 'Delivered by the Power of God': The American Revolution and Nephi's Prophecy," pp. 45–52).

19 And I, Nephi, beheld that the Gentiles that had gone out of captivity [*the colonists*] were delivered by the power of God out of the hands of all other nations.

20 And it came to pass that I, Nephi, beheld that they did prosper in the land; and I beheld a book [*the Bible*], and it was carried forth among them. [*The Christian immigrants brought the Bible with them from the "old countries."*]

21 And the angel said unto me: Knowest thou the meaning of the book?

22 And I said unto him: I know not.

23 And he said: Behold it [*the Bible*] proceedeth out of the mouth of a Jew [*the Bible comes to us from the Jews*]. And I, Nephi, beheld it [*saw the Bible*]; and he said unto me: The book that thou beholdest [*which you are seeing*] is a record of the Jews, which contains the covenants of the Lord, which he hath made unto the house of Israel; and it also containeth many of the prophecies of the holy prophets; and it is a record like unto the engravings which are upon the plates of brass, save there are not so many; nevertheless, they contain the covenants of the Lord, which he hath made unto the house of Israel; wherefore, they are of great worth unto the Gentiles.

We learn from verse 23, above, that the brass plates contained more Old Testament writings than our current Old Testament. Next, Nephi will be shown that much was taken out of the Bible before we got it.

24 And the angel of the Lord said unto me: Thou hast beheld [*you have seen*] that the book [*the Bible*] proceeded forth from the mouth of a Jew; and when it proceeded forth from the mouth of a Jew it contained the fulness of the gospel of the Lord, of whom the twelve apostles bear record; and they bear record according to the truth which is in the Lamb of God.

In other words, the original sermons and teachings from which the Bible was eventually compiled, contained the fulness of the gospel of Jesus Christ. We will use **bold** to emphasize some things in the next few verses.

25 Wherefore, these things [*the original writings and teachings of the Bible*] go forth from the Jews in purity unto the Gentiles, according to the truth which is in God.

26 And after they go forth by the hand of the twelve apostles of the Lamb [*Christ*], from the Jews unto the Gentiles [*non-Jews*], thou seest the formation of that great and abominable church [*the church of the devil; see 1 Nephi 14:10*], which is most abominable above all other churches; for behold, **they have taken away from the gospel of the Lamb many parts which are plain and most precious**; and **also many covenants** of the Lord have they taken away.

You may have noticed that covenants are only required to enter the celestial kingdom. Covenants are not required for entrance into terrestrial or telestial glory. Thus, by taking away priesthood and covenants, Satan has done major damage.

27 And all this have they done that they might pervert the right ways of the Lord, that they might blind the eyes and harden the hearts of the children of men.

28 Wherefore, thou seest that after the book [*the Bible*] hath gone forth through the hands of the great and abominable church, that there are many plain and precious things taken away from the book, which is the book of the Lamb of God.

29 And **after these plain and precious things were taken away it goeth forth unto all the nations of the Gentiles**; and after it goeth forth unto all nations of the Gentiles, yea, even

across the many waters which thou hast seen with the Gentiles which have gone forth out of captivity, thou seest—**because of the many plain and precious things which have been taken out of the book**, which were plain unto the understanding of the children of men, according to the plainness which is in the Lamb of God—because of these things which are taken away out of the gospel of the Lamb, an exceedingly great **many** do **stumble**, yea, insomuch that **Satan hath great power over them.** [*Ignorance of gospel truths and covenants is a terrible disadvantage. This is one of the reasons that the Book of Mormon and modern scriptures are so precious. They restore these "plain and precious things" to us.*]

> We owe a great debt of gratitude to the Catholic monks and priests and others of long ago who meticulously preserved the Bible for us in its present form. It has gone to all the world basically in the form in which they preserved it, as attested by ancient manuscripts in museums and archives today. They took great pains to preserve it in the form in which they received it from previous generations.
>
> Unfortunately, some people today blame them for significantly altering the Bible. But verse 29, above, tells us that the "plain and precious things" were taken out before the Bible went "forth unto all the nations of the Gentiles." We might do well to tell a Catholic friend "Thanks!" for the great gift they have given the world. Next, Nephi will be taught about the divine help received by the United States.

30 Nevertheless, thou beholdest that the Gentiles who have gone forth out of captivity [*the early colonists in the new world who became the United States*], and have been lifted up by the power of God above all other nations, upon the face of the land which is choice above all other lands, which is the land that the Lord God hath covenanted with thy father that his seed should have for the land of their inheritance; wherefore, thou seest that the Lord God will not suffer that the Gentiles will utterly destroy the mixture of thy seed, which are among thy brethren. [*Nephi's surviving descendants, who will have intermixed with the Lamanites, will not be completely destroyed by the influx of immigrants from across the oceans.*]

31 Neither will he suffer [*permit*] that the Gentiles shall destroy the seed of thy brethren [*the Lamanites*].

Next, the stage will be set in

First Nephi 13

Nephi's mind for him to be shown the restoration of the gospel through Joseph Smith.

32 Neither will the Lord God suffer [*allow*] that the Gentiles shall forever remain in that awful state of blindness, which thou beholdest they are in, because of the plain and most precious parts of the gospel of the Lamb which have been kept back by that abominable church, whose formation thou hast seen.

33 Wherefore saith the Lamb of God [*Christ*]: I will be merciful unto the Gentiles, unto the visiting of the remnant of the house of Israel [*Lehi's descendants, in other words, the Lamanites; see verse 34*] in great judgment.

> "Visited with great judgment" is a scriptural term which basically means to finally reap the consequences of continued rejection of God's commandments and teachings.

34 And it came to pass that the angel of the Lord spake unto me, saying: Behold, saith the Lamb of God, after I have visited the remnant of the house of Israel—and this remnant of whom I speak is the seed of thy father [*the Indians in the Americas*]—wherefore, after I have visited them in judgment, and smitten them by the hand of the Gentiles, and after the Gentiles do stumble exceedingly, because of the most plain and precious parts of the gospel of the Lamb which have been kept back by that abominable church, which is the mother of harlots, saith the Lamb—I will be merciful unto the Gentiles in that day, insomuch that I will bring forth unto them, in mine own power, much of my gospel, which shall be plain and precious, saith the Lamb. [*In other words, God will restore His true Church to the earth. This is the Restoration which began with the Prophet Joseph Smith.*]

> The phrase "mother of harlots" in verse 34 above, is very typical of near eastern languages. "Mother" can mean "the source of" or "the leader of." Perhaps a bit of explanation of the word "harlot" could be helpful, too. A synonym would be the verb "prostitute" which means to badly misuse that which is holy and pure. Thus, the term "mother of harlots" is a very accurate description of the devil and his evil work.

35 For, behold, saith the Lamb: I will manifest myself unto thy seed [*this would be the visit of the Resurrected Lord as recorded in Third Nephi*], that they shall write many things which I shall minister unto them, which shall be plain and precious; and after

thy seed shall be destroyed [*as recorded in Fourth Nephi*], and dwindle in unbelief, and also the seed of thy brethren, behold, these things shall be hid up [*Moroni hid the records in the Hill Cumorah*], to come forth unto the Gentiles [*through Joseph Smith to all of us*], by the gift and power of the Lamb.

36 And in them [*the plates, including those from which the Book of Mormon was translated*] shall be written my gospel, saith the Lamb, and my rock and my salvation.

37 And blessed are they [*including all faithful Church members today*] who shall seek to bring forth my Zion at that day [*in the last days*], for they shall have the gift and the power of the Holy Ghost; and if they endure unto the end they shall be lifted up [*exalted*] at the last day [*on Judgment Day*], and shall be saved in the everlasting kingdom of the Lamb [*in the celestial kingdom*]; and whoso shall publish peace, yea, tidings of great joy, how beautiful upon the mountains shall they be.

> Next, Nephi will be shown how the restoration of the true gospel of Jesus Christ will take place in the last days.

38 And it came to pass that I beheld [*saw*] the remnant of the seed of my brethren [*the Lamanites*], and also the book [*the Bible*] of the Lamb of God, which had proceeded forth from the mouth of the Jew, that it came forth from the Gentiles [*the colonists, Pilgrims, missionaries, immigrants, etc., who came to the Americas*] unto the remnant of the seed of my brethren [*the Lamanites*].

39 And after it [*the Bible*] had come forth unto them I beheld other books [*such as the Book of Mormon, Doctrine and Covenants, and the Pearl of Great Price*], which came forth by the power of the Lamb, from the Gentiles [*Joseph Smith and the members of the Church, including us*] unto them [*the Lamanites*], unto the convincing of the Gentiles [*generally speaking, non-members everywhere*] and the remnant of the seed of my brethren [*specifically speaking of the Lamanites*], and also the Jews [*this part of the vision has not yet been fulfilled, except for isolated, wonderful cases here and there*] who were scattered upon all the face of the earth, that the records of the prophets [*contained in the Bible*] and of the twelve apostles of the Lamb [*contained in the New Testament*] are true.

The Book of Mormon plus the "other books" referred to in verse 39, above, bear witness of the Bible. This is particularly needed in our day when so many people no longer consider the Bible to contain the word of God. Rather, they have "demoted it" to a position of simply being cultural literature.

Perhaps you remember when the statement "Another Testament of Jesus Christ" was added to the title of the Book of Mormon. Thus, the Book of Mormon and the other standard works, as well as the teachings of modern prophets and apostles all sustain the Bible as containing the word of God, as seen by Nephi in this vision.

40 And the angel spake unto me, saying: These last records [*the Book of Mormon plus the "other books" in verse 39*] which thou hast seen among the Gentiles, shall establish the truth of the first [*will sustain and support the Bible as having truths from God in it*], which are of the twelve apostles of the Lamb, and shall make known the plain and precious things which have been taken away from them [*will restore the teachings, doctrines, and covenants which were taken out of the Bible*]; and shall make known to all kindreds, tongues, and people [*everyone on earth*], that the Lamb of God [*Christ*] is the Son of the Eternal Father, and the Savior of the world; and that all men must come unto him, or they cannot be saved.

From such small beginnings, in upstate New York on April 6, 1830, we are witnessing the fulfillment of the prophecy in verse 40, above, that this gospel will go to all the world. In fact, in the October General Conference of the Church of 1995, President Gordon B. Hinckley told members that early in 1996 there would be more members of the Church outside the United States than in it. This has now come to pass. Thus, we are privileged to witness the fulfilling of ancient and modern prophecies on every side. What an exciting time to be alive!

In verse 41, next, you will see it emphasized again that there is no other way to be saved, other than coming unto Christ. There is only one path which leads to salvation and exaltation in celestial glory. Many other churches can lead to terrestrial glory, but only one can lead to celestial.

41 And they must come [*all people must come to Christ, as stated in verse 40*] according to the words which shall be established by the mouth of the Lamb; and the words of the Lamb shall be made known in the records of thy seed [*the Book of Mormon*], as well as in the records of the

twelve apostles of the Lamb [*the Bible*]; wherefore they both shall be established in one [*the Bible and the Book of Mormon will come together, united as witnesses for Christ; see also Ezekiel 37:16–17*]; for there is one God and one Shepherd [*Christ*] over all the earth.

> Next, Nephi will be taught that Christ will come to earth and establish His gospel among the Jews and then among the Gentiles (especially through the Apostle Paul). This happened in New Testament times. Nephi is then shown that in the last days, it will be in reverse order. That is, Jesus will manifest Himself first to the Gentiles (through Joseph Smith and the Restoration), and lastly, there will be a large-scale conversion among the Jews.

42 And the time cometh [*in about six hundred years from when Nephi is seeing this vision*] that he [*Christ*] shall manifest himself unto all nations, both unto the Jews and also unto the Gentiles [*New Testament times*]; and after he has manifested himself unto the Jews and also unto the Gentiles, then [*in the last days*] he shall manifest himself unto the Gentiles [*non-Jews*] and also unto the Jews, and the last [*Gentiles who received the gospel "last" in the New Testament, after the Jews*] shall be first, and the first [*the Jews, who were given the gospel first in the New Testament ministry of the Savior*] shall be last [*to receive the gospel in the last days*].

FIRST NEPHI 14

This chapter is the last chapter of Nephi's vision, wherein he was shown the things which his father, Lehi, saw. In it, he will be shown things concerning the latter days, including the day in which we now live. The angel, mentioned in chapter 13, verse 40, is still directing this vision for Nephi and explaining things to him, which he is seeing and feeling.

In the next several verses, the main issue is the significance of having God on your side through personal righteousness, even though living in a wicked world. This is a most crucial message for each of us.

1 AND it shall come to pass, that if the Gentiles [*the people to whom the restoration of the gospel comes first, in the last days*] shall hearken unto the Lamb of God in that day [*the last days*] that he shall manifest himself unto them in word, and also in power, in very deed, unto the taking away of their stumbling

blocks—[*the stumbling blocks mentioned in 1 Nephi 13:26–29*]

2 And harden not their hearts against the Lamb of God, [*in other words, if they accept and live the gospel faithfully*] they shall be numbered among the seed of thy father [*they will be considered worthy and righteous like Nephi and other righteous descendants of Lehi were*]; yea, they shall be numbered among the house of Israel [*a scriptural phrase for saying that they will receive all the blessings of Abraham, Isaac, and Jacob, who have already become gods (see D&C 132:37); in other words, this is a way of saying they will receive exaltation*]; and they shall be a blessed people upon the promised land forever [*symbolic of attaining heaven, the celestial glory, and living in the presence of the Father and Christ forever*]; they shall be no more brought down into captivity [*Satan will not succeed against them*]; and the house of Israel shall no more be confounded [*confused, stopped, led astray*].

3 And that great pit [*Satan's trap for us; hell; outer darkness*], which hath been digged for them by that great and abominable church [*the church of the devil; everything Satan tries to do to trap and destroy us; 1 Nephi 14:10*], which was founded by the devil and his children [*his followers*], that he might lead away the souls of men down to hell—yea, that great pit which hath been digged for the destruction of men shall be filled by those who digged it [*the wicked end up destroying themselves; see Mormon 4:5*], unto their utter destruction, saith the Lamb of God; not the destruction of the soul, save it be the casting of it into that hell which hath no end.

"Not the destruction of the soul" in verse 3, above, is a very important doctrinal statement. Nobody can or will ever cease to exist. I had a student once who asked me if I knew of a sin she could commit which would cause her to cease to exist completely. She explained that she knew that after we die, and our mortal body eventually dissolves away, that we still continue to exist until resurrection as spirit beings. She wanted her spirit and intelligence also to cease to exist. I gently explained that this was impossible. Then with the help of her good bishop, problems were resolved and life became worthwhile again. The point here is that we are eternal beings already and that the "destruction of the soul," verse 3, above, means total captivity of the soul by the devil, and being under such captivity forever (see Alma 34:35). This "forever" captivity would only apply to sons of perdition, since all others are eventually out of Satan's reach (see the vision of the three degrees of glory and sons of perdition—outer darkness—in Doctrine and Covenants, section 76).

4 For behold, this is according to the captivity of the devil, and also according to the justice of God [*the law of justice*], upon all those who will [*want to, desire to*] work wickedness and abomination [*terrible, blatant, wide open wickedness*] before him.

It is interesting that, according to verse 4, above, self-destruction (unrepented of personal wickedness) follows rules too.

The prophecy in verse 5, next, is what can be termed a "conditional prophecy," meaning that there is an "if—then" relationship involved. In other words, "If they do or do not . . . whatever the topic is . . . then thus and such will or will not happen." It is the type of prophecy which reminds us that we have agency, and that by how we use our agency, we are determining our future. We will **bold** and underline for emphasis and teaching purposes.

5 And it came to pass that the angel spake unto me, Nephi, saying: Thou hast beheld that **if** the Gentiles **repent** it shall be **well with them**; and thou also knowest concerning the covenants of the Lord unto the house of Israel; and thou also hast heard that whoso **repenteth not** must **perish**.

6 Therefore, wo be unto the Gentiles **if** it so be that they **harden their hearts** against the Lamb of God.

7 For the time cometh, saith the Lamb of God, that I will work a great and a marvelous work among the children of men; a work which shall be everlasting, either on the one hand or on the other—**either** to the **convincing of them unto peace and life eternal, or** unto the **deliverance of them to the hardness of their hearts and the blindness of their minds** unto their being brought down into **captivity**, and also into **destruction**, both temporally [*being killed, destroyed literally here in mortality*] and spiritually [*as far as personal spirituality and righteousness are concerned*], according to the captivity of the devil, of which I have spoken.

The above verses are clear reminders of the role which our agency plays in our eventual "placement" for eternity. Our choices have everlasting consequences. In effect, we are now, during our "University of Earth" experience, making our final decisions for our eternal

First Nephi 14

placement. We prepared for eons of time in premortality for this final test, and we are now taking it.

8 And it came to pass that when the angel had spoken these words, he said unto me: Rememberest thou the covenants of the Father unto the house of Israel? [*By the way, you can review these covenants by reading Abraham 2:9–11, in your Pearl of Great Price.*] I said unto him, Yea [*Yes*].

9 And it came to pass that he [*the angel*] said unto me: Look, and behold [*see*] that great and abominable church, which is the mother of abominations [*which produces such terrible corruption and wickedness*], whose founder is the devil.

10 And he said unto me: Behold there are save two churches only; the one is the church of the Lamb of God, and the other is the church of the devil; wherefore, whoso belongeth not to the church of the Lamb of God belongeth to that great church, which is the mother of abominations; and she is the whore of all the earth.

Verse 10, above, is filled with very strong, basic doctrine. Ultimately, there are just two positions you can take. Either you are with God or with the devil. Many people are uncomfortable with boiling it down to such simple terms. Indeed, part of Satan's cunning deception is that there is lots of middle ground and that we can put off making decisions as to loyalty to God or the devil for a future time.

Furthermore, there are just two "churches." The Church of Jesus Christ of Latter-day Saints stands alone as the one true Church and stands alone in glory and power to make exaltation available to all who will come unto Christ. All influences which lead people away from the commitments and covenants available in the true Church are part of the other "church," or the "kingdom of the devil" as it is referred to in 1 Nephi 22:22.

We must be careful not to be "down" on all Christian and non-Christian churches as a result of our reading of verse 10, above. Indeed, D&C 10:52 reminds us not to "bash" other churches, rather to understand that our church fills in the gaps in the doctrines and teachings of others and thus builds them up and completes what they have started.

Next, in verse 11, strong language is used to describe Satan's kingdom and power in the last days. The term "whore" is a word which means "one who takes that which is pure and holy and good and converts it to uses which degrade, make filthy, and destroy." The image of the "whore" (Satan and his evil followers) sitting upon the "many waters" reminds us that filthy water, for instance in the case of a devastating flood in one's basement, tries to get into everything. Thus, Satan, in the last days, will be very powerful and will be trying to "get into" every aspect of our lives.

11 And it came to pass that I looked and beheld the whore of all the earth [*Satan's kingdom in the last days*], and she sat upon many waters [*symbolic of ability to get into every aspect of society*]; and she had dominion [*great power*] over all the earth, among all nations, kindreds, tongues, and people.

Next, Nephi sees that, in the last days, after the restoration of the gospel through Joseph Smith, the members of the Church, though relatively small in number, have influence throughout the world.

12 And it came to pass that I beheld the church of the Lamb of God [*the true Church*], and its numbers were few, because of the wickedness and abominations of the whore who sat upon many waters [*because of Satan's power and dominion*]; nevertheless, I beheld that the church of the Lamb, who were the saints of God, were also upon all the face of the earth; and their dominions upon the face of the earth were small, because of the wickedness of the great whore whom I saw.

13 And it came to pass that I beheld that the great mother of abominations [*Satan and his evil followers*] did gather together multitudes upon the face of all the earth, among all the nations of the Gentiles, to fight against the Lamb of God. [*Satan will have many "allies" in the last days, as he wages war against the spread of the true gospel of Christ.*]

Verse 14, next, is very comforting and reassuring. It reminds us that we are definitely not alone. (**Bold** added for emphasis.)

14 And it came to pass that I, Nephi, beheld the power of the Lamb of God, that it descended upon the saints of the church of the Lamb, and upon the covenant people of the Lord, who were scattered upon all the face of the earth; and they were **armed with righteousness** and with the **power of God in great glory**.

Next, Nephi sees the "wars and rumors of war" which are one of the prominent signs of the times, signaling that the Second Coming of the Savior is not far off.

15 And it came to pass that I beheld that the wrath of God was poured out upon that great and abominable church, insomuch that there were wars and rumors of wars among all the nations and kindreds of the earth.

16 And as there began to be wars and rumors of wars among all the nations which belonged to the mother of abominations [*which adhere to Satan's goals and personal standards*], the angel spake unto me, saying [*the angel will now emphasize and explain key concepts and teachings in this vision for Nephi*]: Behold, the wrath of God is upon the mother of harlots [*the wicked; Satan's kingdom*]; and behold, thou seest all these things.

> As stated above, the angel is now reviewing key elements of the vision, leading up to the restoration of the true Church in the last days.

17 And when the day cometh that the wrath of God is poured out upon the mother of harlots, which is the great and abominable church of all the earth, whose founder is the devil, then, at that day, the work of the Father shall commence, in preparing the way for the fulfilling of his covenants, which he hath made to his people who are of the house of Israel. [*In other words, when the time arrives, as depicted in the vision, the gospel will be restored, and the long-prophesied gathering of Israel will begin. Nephi is seeing our day.*]

18 And it came to pass that the angel spake unto me, saying: Look!

19 And I looked and beheld a man [*John, the Beloved Apostle, who wrote the book of Revelation in our Bible; see verse 27 in this chapter*], and he was dressed in a white robe.

> Just a reminder of scriptural symbolism. John is dressed in white, symbolizing purity and worthiness to be in the presence of God. He is dressed in a robe, symbolizing that he has made and kept covenants, and is thus worthy of exaltation, godhood.

20 And the angel said unto me: Behold one of the twelve apostles of the Lamb.

21 Behold, he shall see and write the remainder of these things [*the next things you, Nephi, will see in this vision*]; yea, and also many things which have been.

22 And he shall also write concerning the end of the world.

23 Wherefore, the things which he shall write are just and true; and behold they are written in the book [*the Bible*] which thou beheld

proceeding out of the mouth of the Jew; and at the time they proceeded out of the mouth of the Jew, or, at the time the book proceeded out of the mouth of the Jew, the things which were written were plain and pure, and most precious and easy to the understanding of all men. [*In other words, when the book of Revelation was first written, it was clear and easy to understand.*]

24 And behold, the things which this apostle of the Lamb shall write are many things which thou hast seen; and behold, the remainder shalt thou see.

25 But the things which thou shalt see hereafter thou shalt not write; for the Lord God hath ordained the apostle of the Lamb of God that he should write them.

> This is a most fascinating instruction given to Nephi. He will now see many more things leading up to the end of the earth. But it is not his stewardship to write them. It is the stewardship of the Apostle John, who lived almost seven hundred years after Nephi, seeing the same things Nephi will now see. John is the one who is to write these things for us to read. These writings of John are written in the Bible in the book of Revelation.
>
> Unfortunately for many people, the book of Revelation is a very difficult book to understand. However, for those who pay the price to study and understand it, it becomes a most beautiful book and a wonderful doctrinal review of the plan of salvation, containing several doctrines which have been left out or intentionally taken out of other books in the Bible. You may wish to get additional help understanding the book of Revelation by reading through the notes on it given in *The New Testament Made Easier, Part 2*, by David J. Ridges, published by Cedar Fort, Inc., 2003.

26 And also others who have been, to them hath he shown all things, and they have written them; and they are sealed up to come forth in their purity, according to the truth which is in the Lamb, in the own due time of the Lord, unto the house of Israel.

> Verse 26, above, informs us that there are yet other sealed records, which someday will be made available to the people of the Lord by the power of God. This must have been a fascinating verse for Joseph Smith, to realize that others would also be involved someday in bringing ancient records to light.

27 And I, Nephi, heard and bear record, that the name of the apostle of the Lamb was John, according to the word of the angel.

John, mentioned above, was the apostle who wrote the Gospel of John, plus 1 John, 2 John, 3 John, and the book of Revelation. He was the one who served in the First Presidency of the Church after the Savior's ascension into heaven. It was this presidency—Peter, James, and John—who restored the Melchizedek Priesthood to Joseph Smith and Oliver Cowdery (see D&C 27:12).

Next, Nephi brings his recording of his vision to a close, reminding us that he is simply following the instructions of the angel not to write the rest of what he saw in the vision.

28 And behold, I, Nephi, am forbidden that I should write the remainder of the things which I saw and heard; wherefore the things which I have written sufficeth me; and I have written but a small part of the things which I saw. [*It will be interesting to someday be with Nephi when he has time and is permitted to tell us the rest of what he saw.*]

29 And I bear record [*I bear testimony*] that I saw the things which my father saw, and the angel of the Lord did make them known unto me.

30 And now I make an end of speaking concerning the things which I saw while I was carried away in the spirit; and if all the things which I saw are not written [*perhaps he is saying, "I don't have time, energy, or enough room on these plates to record everything I am permitted to write, and so. . . ."*], the things which I have written are true. And thus it is. Amen.

This is the end of Nephi's vision.

FIRST NEPHI 15

Nephi has now had a marvelous "high mountain" experience. He has seen what will happen to his descendants and what will happen to the descendants of his brethren. He has been shown what we know as the New Testament, the discovery and colonization of America, the Revolutionary War, the establishment of the United States of America, the restoration of the gospel, the coming forth of the book of Mormon, and the last days, plus everything which John the Revelator saw. No doubt he is now anxious to share his witness and testimony of these things which his father saw with the others back at camp. As he approaches, however, he sees his brothers arguing. What a letdown! We will now listen to him as he recounts this part of his history.

1 AND it came to pass that after I, Nephi, had been carried away in the spirit, and seen all these things, I returned to the tent of my father.

2 And it came to pass that I beheld my brethren, and they were disputing one with another concerning the things which my father had spoken unto them.

3 For he truly spake many great things unto them, which were hard to be understood, save a man should inquire of the Lord; and they being hard in their hearts, therefore they did not look unto the Lord as they ought.

> We are reminded by Nephi in the previous verse that the things of God are hard to understand unless we turn to the Lord for help. This is a most important lesson for all of us.
>
> Next, we will see Nephi almost overcome with grief. Knowing that Nephi was inspired as to what to include in the special record contained on the small plates, we can perhaps take comfort in this message from the Lord that even great and highly capable people can have times of depression and sorrow.

4 And now I, Nephi, was grieved because of the hardness of their hearts, and also, because of the things which I had seen [*remember that he had seen the downfall of his own people*], and knew they must unavoidably come to pass because of the great wickedness of the children of men.

> The phrase "children of men" as used in verse 4, above, is a term that is used often in the scriptures. It means "people here on earth."

5 And it came to pass that I was overcome because of my afflictions, for I considered that mine afflictions were great above all, because of the destruction of my people, for I had beheld their fall.

> Next, we will watch Nephi try to help his brethren understand the things of God. When we get to verse 11, we will be given a formula for getting help and counsel from God. It is also a formula for getting a personal testimony.

6 And it came to pass that after I had received strength I spake unto my brethren, desiring to know of them the cause of their disputations [*the cause of their arguing among themselves*].

7 And they said: Behold, we cannot understand the words which our father hath spoken concerning the natural branches of the olive-tree, and also concerning the Gentiles.

8 And I said unto them: Have ye inquired of the Lord?

9 And they said unto me: We have not; for the Lord maketh no such thing known unto us. [*It may be that there is a touch of sarcasm in their response, in effect saying, "The Lord doesn't talk to us like he does to you, holy little brother."*]

Next, we will use **bold** to emphasize Nephi's teachings about things which can prevent our being sensitive to the Holy Ghost and thus coming to understand the things of God.

10 Behold, I said unto them: How is it that **ye do not keep the commandments of the Lord** [*a major cause of not being sensitive to the Spirit of the Lord*]? How is it that ye will perish [*be destroyed spiritually, in other words, as far as spiritual things are concerned*], because of **the hardness of your hearts**?

11 [*Here is the formula for receiving help from the Spirit to understand the things of God which we mentioned in the note after verse 5, above. We will use bold for emphasis and teaching purposes.*] Do ye not remember the things which the Lord hath said?—**If** ye will **not harden your hearts**, and **ask me in faith, believing that ye shall receive**, with **diligence in keeping my commandments**, surely **these things shall be made known unto you**.

Next, Nephi will teach and explain to his brethren the use of the olive-tree symbolism which was shown to Father Lehi. You may wish to review the notes given in 1 Nephi 10 regarding the olive tree. It deals with the gathering of Israel in the last days, and we have the privilege of watching the fulfillment of this prophecy as it continues to gain momentum in our day. It is a powerful testimony of the truth of the book of Mormon.

12 Behold, I say unto you, that the house of Israel was compared unto an olive-tree, by the Spirit of the Lord which was in our father; and behold are we not broken off from the house of Israel [*symbolizing being scattered away from the rest of Israel*], and are we not a branch of the house of Israel [*don't we belong to Israel*]?

13 And now, the thing which our father meaneth concerning the grafting in [*being reattached to the main tree*] of the natural branches through the fulness of the Gentiles [*through the fulness of the gospel being restored among the Gentiles—Joseph Smith and the Restoration*], is, that in the latter days [*in the last days, before the Second*

Coming], when our seed [*posterity*] shall have dwindled in unbelief [*will have gone into apostasy, fallen away from the gospel of Christ*], yea, for the space of many years, and many generations after the Messiah shall be manifested in body unto the children of men [*many generations after the mortal ministry of the Savior*], then shall the fulness of the gospel of the Messiah come unto the Gentiles [*the gospel and the true Church will be restored again, this time to the Gentiles, meaning Joseph Smith and the Restoration*], and from the Gentiles unto the remnant of our seed [*and the Lamanites will receive it from the members of the restored church*]—

> It is vital that we know "who we are." We must understand that we are children of God, that we have within us the potential to become like Him, to become gods. Knowing this is vital to our self-worth and to our developing righteous behaviors and deep internal commitment to the principles of Christ's gospel. Next, Nephi will prophesy that this blessing of knowing who they are will be restored to the Lamanites in the last days.

Elder Spencer W. Kimball, of the Quorum of the Twelve Apostles, emphasized this fact as follows:

"Of immense importance to this work of gathering the scattered branches of the house of Israel is the work of carrying the blessings of the restored gospel of Jesus Christ to the Lamanites, for the Lord's work in these latter days can in no wise be complete until these children of great promise are brought back into the fold. The Lord said through his prophet Lehi, 'Behold, I say unto you, Yea; they shall be remembered again among the house of Israel; they shall be grafted in, being a natural branch of the olive-tree, into the true olive-tree.' (1 Ne. 15:16.) We are witnesses to these events.

"For a thousand years after the closing of the Book of Mormon record, these people wandered in spiritual darkness and were scattered upon the American continents and the isles of the sea. They lost their written language, their high culture, and, worst of all, their knowledge of the living God and his work. Faith was replaced by fear, rich language by crippled dialects, and an understanding of God and his ways by idolatry. . . . Only the most brazen soul could fail to weep when contemplating the fall of this people, and yet it was the decree of the Lord that the Lamanites should be preserved in the land, that this remnant of Joseph should again come into their promised inheritance.

"The Lord's promises with regard to the Lamanites began

to be fulfilled with the coming forth of the Book of Mormon in this dispensation (see Ether 4:17).

"Truly our paths have met once more—we a mixed remnant of Israel, principally Ephraim, even referred to as gentiles, now come forth out of captivity (see, e.g., 1 Ne. 13:19, 39), . . . now only through the grace of Almighty God restored to the blessings of the gospel, that we in turn might be a blessing to the nations of the earth; and the Lamanites, also a people of disobedience now returned to the fold.

"The Lamanites must rise again in dignity and strength to fully join their brethren and sisters of the household of God in carrying forth his work in preparation for that day when the Lord Jesus Christ will return to lead his people" (Kimball, "Our Paths Have Met Again," pp. 4–5, 7).

14 And at that day [*after the gospel has been restored among the Gentiles in the last days*] shall the remnant of our seed [*the Lamanites*] know that they are of the house of Israel, and that they are the covenant people of the Lord; and then shall they know and come to the knowledge of their forefathers, and also to the knowledge of the gospel of their Redeemer, which was ministered unto their fathers by him; wherefore, they shall come to the knowledge of their Redeemer and the very points of his doctrine, **that they may know how to come unto him** and be saved.

The message at the end of verse 14, above is most important. It is not enough for people to want to be saved. They must know how to be saved. Perhaps many other Christian as well as non-Christian churches and individuals disagree with us on this. But that is most likely because they do not know what it is to "be saved." They don't realize nor do they accept the fact that, almost always in the scriptures, "being saved" means to become like God, and to become gods ourselves.

Thus, with their understanding limited by lack of knowledge ("points of his doctrine," verse 14, above), they believe that to be "saved" one needs but to be good. This, in fact, is true in reference to obtaining terrestrial glory (see D&C 76:75). But in order to be "saved" in celestial exaltation, we need knowledge of the gospel. We need "points" of doctrine. We need priesthood authority and ordinances so that we can make and keep covenants. It is impossible for us to be saved in ignorance of the gospel (see D&C 131:6).

15 And then at that day will they [*the Lamanites*] not rejoice and give praise unto their everlasting God, their rock and their

salvation? Yea, at that day, will they not receive the strength and nourishment from the true vine [*Christ; see John 15:1*]? Yea, will they not come unto the true fold [*the true Church; ultimately, celestial exaltation*] of God?

16 Behold, I say unto you, Yea; they shall be remembered again among the house of Israel; they shall be grafted in [*gathered in and reattached to the "olive tree," to the "true vine"*], being a natural branch of the olive-tree [*being blood line descendants of Israel—Abraham, Isaac, and Jacob*], into the true olive-tree.

17 And this is what our father meaneth; and he meaneth that it will not come to pass until after they are scattered by the Gentiles; and he meaneth that it shall come by way of the Gentiles [*it will come to the Lamanites through the church that Joseph Smith will establish among the Gentiles (non-Jews)*], that the Lord may show his power unto the Gentiles, for the very cause that he shall be rejected of [*by*] the Jews, or of the house of Israel.

There may still be some confusion as to the difference between the words "Jews" and "Gentiles" as used in the Book of Mormon. A brief review may help. "Jews" in the Book of Mormon may have come from any or many of the tribes of Israel in the Holy Land. The point is that they were "geographically" from the Holy Land in relatively recent times. In the Book of Mormon usage, "Gentiles" are all of the people in the world who don't come from the Holy Land. Many of the Gentiles have the blood of Israel in them, but are not "geographically" from the Holy Land in relatively recent times. Even today, the term 'Jew" basically refers to non-Arabic citizens of Israel, plus people elsewhere in the world whose ancestors came from the Holy Land in relatively modern times. Most "Jews" have blood from many of the twelve tribes of Israel in their veins.

Also, just a quick note about the term "house of Israel." It means the descendants of Abraham, Isaac and Jacob, or, "the covenant people." Abraham and Sarah had Isaac. Isaac and Rebekah had Jacob. Jacob and his wives had twelve sons. Jacob's name was changed to "Israel." Thus, we have the "house of Israel" or "the family of Israel." The blessings of the gospel and priesthood covenants come to all the world through this lineage. In summary, we have Abraham, Isaac, and Jacob. God covenanted with Abraham and renewed it with Isaac and with Jacob that through them, all the world would be blessed (see Genesis 12:1–3, 17:4–8, Abraham 2:9–11; Genesis 26:2–

5; Genesis 32:24–30.) Jacob's name was changed to Israel (Genesis 32:28) which means "one who has power with God." Israel had twelve sons, through whom the blood of Abraham and Isaac was perpetuated and multiplied out upon the face of the earth as they married and their children married, and so on. It is the responsibility of Israel to carry the gospel and the blessings of the priesthood to all the world in our day.

That is one key reason the designation of lineage in your patriarchal blessing is so important. It reminds you of your responsibilities as a missionary all of your life. It also reminds you that you have the potential to become a god. Abraham, Isaac, and Jacob (and their wives) have all become gods already (see D&C 132:37).

18 Wherefore, our father hath not spoken of our seed [*posterity*] alone, but also of all the house of Israel [*all of the descendants of Abraham, Isaac, and Jacob*], pointing to the covenant which should be fulfilled in the latter days; which covenant the Lord made to our father Abraham, saying: In thy seed shall all the kindreds [*people*] of the earth be blessed.

19 And it came to pass that I, Nephi, spake much unto them concerning these things; yea, I spake unto them concerning the restoration of the Jews in the latter days. [*The Jews will be gathered back to the Holy Land and become a nation. This has happened and is continuing to happen in our day. It is one of the signs of the times which will take place before the Second Coming. There is another "gathering" of the Jews which must yet take place. It is the gathering of them to Christ and to the true Church. Except for a few isolated cases, this appears to be a future occurrence.*]

20 And I did rehearse unto them the words of Isaiah, who spake concerning the restoration of the Jews, or of the house of Israel [*here, the term "Jews" is expanded to mean all the house of Israel, which would include all of us*]; and after they were restored they should no more be confounded [*confused; stopped in progressing toward celestial exaltation*], neither should they be scattered again. [*The Church will never go into apostasy again, after the Restoration through Joseph Smith. This is also in Daniel 2:35, 44–45.*] And it came to pass that I did speak many words unto my brethren, that they were pacified and did humble themselves before the Lord. [*This gives us hope, once again, for Laman and*

Lemuel and the others in the family who have been rebellious.]

It is quite encouraging at this point to see these rebellious members of the group begin to ask sincere, intelligent questions. It must have done Nephi's heart good to see this happening. In fact, a very helpful question and answer session begins now, which will help us too. We will use **bold** for purposes of emphasis and teaching.

<u>Question:</u>

21 And it came to pass that they did speak unto me again, saying: **What meaneth this thing which our father saw in a dream? What meaneth the tree which he saw?**

<u>Answer:</u>

22 And I said unto them: **It was a representation of the tree of life.**

<u>Question</u>:

23 And they said unto me: **What meaneth the rod of iron which our father saw, that led to the tree?**

<u>Answer:</u>

24 And I said unto them that **it was the word of God; and whoso would hearken unto the word of God, and would hold fast unto it, they would never perish** [*this is a tremendous promise!*]; **neither could the temptations and the fiery darts of the adversary overpower them unto blindness, to lead them away to destruction.**

25 Wherefore, I, Nephi, did exhort [*strongly urge*] them to give heed unto the word of the Lord; yea, I did exhort them with all the energies of my soul, and with all the faculty which I possessed, that they would give heed to [*pay careful attention to*] the word of God and remember to keep his commandments always in all things.

<u>Question:</u>

26 And they said unto me: **What meaneth the river of water which our father saw?**

<u>Answer:</u>

27 And I said unto them that **the water which my father saw was filthiness**; and so much was his mind swallowed up in other things that he beheld not the filthiness of the water.

28 And I said unto them that **it was an awful gulf, which separated the wicked from the tree of life, and also from the saints of God.**

29 And I said unto them that **it was a representation of that**

First Nephi 15

awful hell, which the angel said unto me was prepared for the wicked.

30 And I said unto them that our father also saw that **the justice of God did also divide the wicked from the righteous; and the brightness thereof was like unto the brightness of a flaming fire, which ascendeth up unto God forever and ever, and hath no end.**

Question:

31 And they said unto me: **Doth this thing mean the torment of the body in the days of probation** [*during our life on earth*]**, or doth it mean the final state of the soul after the death of the temporal body** [*the physical body*]**, or doth it speak of the things which are temporal** [*things which pertain to this mortal life*]**?**

Answer:

32 And it came to pass that I said unto them that **it was a representation of things both temporal and spiritual; for the day should come that they must be judged of their works, yea, even the works which were done by the temporal body in their days of probation.** [*In other words, we will all face Christ to answer for our choices during this testing period on earth.*]

It is important to keep the scriptures in context, and to consider major doctrines such as agency and judgment in the overall context of the scriptures and the words of modern prophets. In the above verses, Nephi has been talking to and answering questions for individuals who have had many obvious witnesses that there is a God and that Lehi and Nephi are teaching truth. They will yet have many more such witnesses that they are on the errand of God. If and when they reject the gospel, it will be against knowledge. Thus, how they choose to spend the "days of their probation," in other words, their mortal lives, will constitute their final judgment. Nephi is clearly teaching this to them.

However, we know that many in this life do not get such a complete set of clear chances to understand and obey the laws of God. God is completely fair. Thus, for such individuals, the completion of their opportunities to understand and accept the gospel laws and covenants will come in the spirit world mission field, as taught in D&C 138.

We would do well not to judge one another as to who has and who has not had a complete set of fair chances here on earth, or during the days of their mortal or temporal probation or testing. However, we would no doubt do well to consider our temporal or mortal days to be the determining factor as to whether or not we will be allowed to continue progressing toward exaltation after we die.

We know from D&C 76:74 and 79 that those who do receive a complete set of fair chances to accept and live the gospel here during their mortal lives, and who do not live accordingly, will be limited to the terrestrial kingdom as far as how high they can go after the final Judgment Day.

33 Wherefore, **if they should die in their wickedness they must be cast off also, as to the things which are spiritual, which are pertaining to righteousness; wherefore, they must be brought to stand before God** [*final Judgment Day*], **to be judged of their works; and if their works have been filthiness they must needs be filthy; and if they be filthy it must needs be** [*it has to be*] **that they cannot dwell in the kingdom of God; if so, the kingdom of God must be** [*would become*] **filthy also.**

Next, Nephi continues explaining the logic and reasoning behind the fact that unworthy people cannot return to live forever with God. His brethren asked sincere questions, and he is an excellent teacher as he gives them a chance to understand.

34 But behold, I say unto you, the kingdom of God is not filthy, and there cannot any unclean thing enter into the kingdom of God; wherefore [*therefore*] there must needs be a place of filthiness prepared for that which is filthy.

35 And there is a place prepared, yea, even that awful hell of which I have spoken, and the devil is the preparator [*the preparer*] of it; wherefore the final state of the souls of men is to dwell in the kingdom of God, or to be cast out because of that justice [*the law of justice*] of which I have spoken.

36 Wherefore [*this is why*], the wicked are rejected [*ultimately separated*] from the righteous, and also from that tree of life, whose fruit is most precious and most desirable above all other fruits; yea, and it [*exaltation; see D&C 14:7*] is the greatest of all the gifts of God. And thus I spake unto my brethren. Amen.

FIRST NEPHI 16

As mentioned in the previous chapter, Nephi's brethren have sincerely asked some insightful and searching questions in order to understand what Lehi taught them. Although they were apparently sincere, the answers to their questions are in stark contrast to their lifestyles up to now. Therefore, these answers about personal accountability, final judgment, filthiness, the requirements to be in the presence of God forever, etc., are quite hard for them to accept. It often requires time and patience to implement gospel standards of behavior into daily living when previous attitudes and goals have been much less than righteous. And unless one is diligent and willing to persevere, resolve is in danger of collapsing and people commonly revert back to previous attitudes and lifestyles.

Next, Nephi's brethren express their concern that what they have heard is hard. But tough stains generally can't be taken out by gentle soap. This is a lesson clearly taught now by Nephi, and his hopes are raised again by his brethren's responses. We will again use **bold** for emphasis and for teaching purposes.

1 AND now it came to pass that after I, Nephi, had made an end of speaking to my brethren, behold they said unto me: Thou hast declared unto us **hard things, more than we are able to bear.**

2 And it came to pass that I said unto them that I knew that I had spoken hard things against the wicked, according to the truth; and **the righteous have I justified** [*I have shown that righteousness will pay off eternally*]**,** and testified that they should be lifted up [*exalted*] at the last day [*on Judgment Day*]; wherefore, **the guilty taketh the truth to be hard, for it cutteth them to the very center.**

3 And now my brethren, **if ye were righteous** and were **willing to hearken to the truth**, and give **heed** unto **it**, that ye might **walk uprightly** before God, **then ye would not murmur because of the truth**, and say: Thou speakest hard things against us.

4 And it came to pass that I, Nephi, did exhort [*teach and urge*] my brethren, with all diligence, to keep the commandments of the Lord.

5 And it came to pass that **they did humble themselves before the Lord**; insomuch that **I had joy and great hopes of them**, that they would walk in the paths of righteousness.

6 Now, all these things were said and done as my father dwelt in a tent in the valley which he called Lemuel.

7 And it came to pass that I, Nephi, took one of the daughters of Ishmael to wife; and also, my

brethren took of the daughters of Ishmael to wife; and also Zoram took the eldest daughter of Ishmael to wife. [*This must have been quite a ceremony, and quite a time of celebrating and rejoicing!*]

Next, Nephi makes quite a statement about his father, which could be comforting to other parents whose children have not all followed the strait and narrow path.

8 And thus my father had fulfilled all the commandments of the Lord which had been given unto him. And also, I, Nephi, had been blessed of the Lord exceedingly.

It appears that Lehi and his little group of travelers have been camped in the Valley of Lemuel (see 1 Nephi 2:6, 14; 16:6) for some time. Lehi and Sariah waited there while their sons went back to get the brass plates. They remained there while the brothers went back to Jerusalem to get Ishmael and his family to join them so that they could have wives and families. They were camped in this valley when Lehi had his dream of the tree of life, and while Nephi had his "high mountain" experience wherein he saw all the things his father saw.

We don't know how much of the eight years they spent in the wilderness had already passed when the Lord commanded Lehi to continue their journey into the wilderness. Whatever the case, they will now continue their journey and will eventually arrive at the ocean where they will build a ship and cross the waters to the promised land.

Many familiar scenes for those who have read and studied the Book of Mormon will take place next. Lehi will be given the Liahona. Nephi will break his bow. Ishmael will die and there will be a rebellion among some in the group. Laman will plot with others to take Lehi's life and also to kill Nephi. These rebellious members of the group will have yet another chance to repent and change their attitudes and the direction of their lives when the Lord speaks directly to them and severely scolds them.

9 And it came to pass that the voice of the Lord spake unto my father by night, and commanded him that on the morrow he should take his journey into the wilderness.

10 And it came to pass that as my father arose in the morning, and went forth to the tent door, to his great astonishment he beheld upon the ground a round ball of curious workmanship [*the Liahona; see Alma 37:38*]; and it was of fine brass. And within the ball were two spindles; and the one pointed the way whither we

should go into the wilderness.

> From time to time, the Lord has provided his prophets with physical devices to assist and direct them and their people. We know that there was more than one Urim and Thummim (see Bible Dictionary, pp. 786–87.) Here, Lehi is given a marvelous device of very fine workmanship to assist him and his people as they travel through a dangerous wilderness.

> Some symbolism here is quite obvious. Among other things, this earth can be a rather dangerous "wilderness" with the traps and decoys set up by the devil and his evil followers. We need constant guidance as we journey through life. We receive it through the scriptures and the counsel and teachings of our modern prophets and apostles, as well as from our local leaders. It might even be suggested that we have our "Liahonas" in the form of electronic access to the words and teachings of the Brethren. We can look to their counsels, electronically sort through and access many of their messages on specific topics, and so forth.

11 And it came to pass that we did gather together whatsoever things we should carry into the wilderness, and all the remainder of our provisions which the Lord had given unto us; and we did take seed of every kind that we might carry into the wilderness.

12 And it came to pass that we did take our tents and depart into the wilderness, across the river Laman.

13 And it came to pass that we traveled for the space of four days, nearly a south-southeast direction, and we did pitch our tents again; and we did call the name of the place Shazer.

14 And it came to pass that we did take our bows and our arrows, and go forth into the wilderness to slay food for our families; and after we had slain food for our families we did return again to our families in the wilderness, to the place of Shazer. And we did go forth again in the wilderness, following the same direction, keeping in the most fertile parts of the wilderness, which were in the borders near the Red Sea.

15 And it came to pass that we did travel for the space of many days, slaying food by the way, with our bows and our arrows and our stones and our slings.

16 And we did follow the directions of the ball, which led us in the more fertile parts of the wilderness.

> Since Nephi tells us, in verse 28 of this chapter, that the pointers in the Liahona worked "according to the faith and diligence and

heed which we did give unto them," and since, according to verse 16 above, the "ball" was functioning to guide them, we are probably safe to think that, at this point, most, and hopefully all members of the company of travelers, were exercising faith and obedience, and thus, the Liahona worked for them.

17 And after we had traveled for the space of many days, we did pitch our tents for the space of a time, that we might again rest ourselves and obtain food for our families.

> Perhaps you have noticed that things seem to go quite well as long as they are busy traveling. It seems to be when they have stopped and have extra time on their hands that those with a tendency to rebel do so.
>
> It is during these rest stops that Laman and Lemuel and the sons of Ishmael murmur against Nephi. It is when they again stop for a while (verse 33) and Ishmael dies, that vicious rebellion flares up again. As they again take their journey (1 Nephi 17:1) and are kept busy with the work of traveling, they go without murmuring (chapter 17, verse 2, but when they finally reach the ocean where they stop for a while, rebellion breaks out again (1 Nephi 17:17–20).
>
> Surely, there is a lesson in this for us. There is truth in the old saying, "An idle mind is the devil's workshop."
>
> Next, Nephi will break his bow. It is sad that his brethren seem anxious to blame him for all their woes, when they themselves perhaps have not unstrung their own bows when they might have in order to preserve the spring in them. Whatever the case, it seems to be Satan's way to find someone else to blame for one's own inappropriate and sinful behavior.

18 And it came to pass that as I, Nephi, went forth to slay food, behold, I did break my bow, which was made of fine steel; and after I did break my bow, behold, my brethren were angry with me because of the loss of my bow, for we did obtain no food.

> For many years, critics of the Book of Mormon found fault with the idea that Nephi could have a bow made of "fine steel." They claimed that there was no such thing at the time period claimed by the Book of Mormon for Nephi's journeying. Hugh Nibley had a word for such critics. A quote from his writings follows:
>
> "Through the years critics of the Book of Mormon have constantly called attention to the mention of steel in that book as a gross anachronism (something which was way ahead

of its time). But now we are being reminded that one cannot be dogmatic in dating the appearance of steel since there is more than one kind of steel with 'a whole series of variants in the combination of iron and steel components' in ancient times; and when a particularly fine combination was hit upon it would be kept secret in 'individual workshops' and 'passed on from father to son for many generations.' Hence it is not too surprising to learn that 'even in early European times' there is evidence for the production of steel 'of very high quality' and extreme hardness. Further east steel is attested even earlier" (Nibley, *Since Cumorah: The Book of Mormon in the Modern World*, p. 254).

19 And it came to pass that we did return without food to our families, and being much fatigued, because of their journeying, they did suffer much for the want of food.

20 And it came to pass that Laman and Lemuel and the sons of Ishmael did begin to murmur exceedingly, because of their sufferings and afflictions in the wilderness; and also my father began to murmur against the Lord his God; yea, and they were all exceedingly sorrowful, even that they did murmur against the Lord.

We have almost come to expect that Laman and Lemuel along with the sons of Ishmael will start to complain and become ugly when things become difficult. But to see Lehi also "murmur against the Lord his God" catches us off guard and can be very disappointing.

However, when we recall from 1 Nephi 1:20 that one of the purposes Nephi stated for writing the things he did was to show us "the tender mercies of the Lord," then we begin to see that perhaps one of the reasons he mentioned this especially difficult time for his father was to show us the kindness of the Lord even to those who definitely know better than to murmur.

21 Now it came to pass that I, Nephi, having been afflicted with my brethren because of the loss of my bow, and their bows having lost their springs [*probably because they neglected to unstring them when they were not in use*], it began to be exceedingly difficult, yea, insomuch that we could obtain no food.

22 And it came to pass that I, Nephi, did speak much unto my brethren, because they had hardened their hearts again, even unto complaining against the Lord their God.

23 And it came to pass that I, Nephi, did make out of wood a

bow, and out of a straight stick, an arrow; wherefore, I did arm myself with a bow and an arrow, with a sling and with stones. And I said unto my father: Whither shall I go to obtain food?

> I had an interesting experience concerning the wood bow and the wooden arrow which Nephi made as mentioned above. Some years ago a good friend called me one evening and said, "Dave, do you know how true the Book of Mormon is?" I said, "Yes, I think I do." To which he responded, "Yes, but do you know *how* true?" I began to wonder where this was going, so I said, "Tell me. How true is it?" That was the response he had been waiting for.
>
> He asked, "Do you know why Nephi made an arrow out of a stick to use with the wood bow he had just made? Why didn't he simply use one of the arrows he had for his steel bow, which he broke?" I replied that I hadn't ever even thought about that. He went on to say that he had become interested in archery, and upon reading this part of the Book of Mormon again, it occurred to him that the steel bow would use relatively short arrows, but the wooden bow would bend back much farther than a steel bow, thus, the wood bow would require considerably longer arrows.
>
> He concluded our telephone conversation by expressing his testimony that Joseph Smith could not possibly have made the Book of Mormon up and that this passage about needing a new arrow for the wood bow was another testimony to the divine calling of the Prophet. He felt that there was no way that Joseph Smith could have even known about such things from practical experience in his day, in order to fabricate such an account.
>
> I thanked my friend for sharing this information with me, and now I, too, marvel even more at the truthfulness of the Book of Mormon each time I read this account of Nephi's broken steel bow.
>
> In verse 23, above, we find a major lesson, namely, that we should honor parents, even though they may not always live up to our hopes and expectations. The effect on Lehi when his son, Nephi, still honored him, despite his negative response to the hardships they were suffering, must have been extremely humbling, yet at the same time, redeeming.

24 And it came to pass that he did inquire of the Lord, for they had humbled themselves because of my words; for I did say many things unto them in the energy of my soul.

25 And it came to pass that the voice of the Lord came unto my father; and he was truly chastened

[*scolded*] because of his murmuring against the Lord, insomuch that he was brought down into the depths of sorrow.

There is a name for the kind of sorrow experienced by Lehi here. It is called "godly sorrow" and is the type of sorrow that causes deep change toward more personal righteousness and deeper strength in following God's commandments. The Apostle Paul spoke of this "godly sorrow" in 2 Corinthians 7:8–11. We will now take a moment to review Paul's teachings on this subject. We will include some teaching notes along with it.

2 Corinthians 7:8–11

8 For though I made you sorry with a letter [*even though I caused you sorrow when I scolded you in my last letter to you—First Corinthians*], I do not repent [*I don't take back what I said because you needed it*], though I did repent [*though I did regret hurting your feelings*]: for I perceive that the same epistle [*that letter*] hath made you sorry, though *it were* but for a season [*even though you got over it after a while*].

9 Now I rejoice, not that ye were made sorry [*not because I caused you pain*], but that ye sorrowed to repentance [*but because you actually repented because of what I said to you*]: for ye were made sorry after a godly manner [*my letter caused you to have "godly sorrow" so that you truly repented*], that ye might receive damage by us in nothing [*so that, as it ultimately turned out, we did not hurt you in any way*].

Paul now defines "godly sorrow" which is a vital part of truly repenting.

10 For godly sorrow worketh repentance [*causes us to repent*] to salvation [*and thus obtain exaltation*] not to be repented of [*and leaves us with no regrets*]: but the sorrow of the world [*being sorry you got caught, or sorry because you are embarrassed, or sorry that your opportunity to continue committing that sin has been taken away, etc.*] worketh death [*leads to spiritual death*].

Now, Paul describes some components of "godly sorrow" which make it so effective in cleansing us from sin and leading to our truly changing and becoming more righteous.

11 For behold this selfsame thing [*this godly sorrow, the very thing I'm teaching you about, namely*], that ye sorrowed [*were sorry for sins*] after a godly sort [*in the way God wants you to be*], what carefulness [*sincerity, anxiety*] it wrought [*caused*] in you, yea, what clearing of yourselves [*eagerness to become clear of the sin*], yea, what indignation [*irritation, anger at yourself for committing the sin*], yea, what fear [*alarm*], yea, what

vehement desire [*strong desire to change*], yea, what zeal [*enthusiasm to change*], yea, what revenge [*punishment; suffering whatever is necessary to make permanent change*]! In all things ye have approved yourselves to be clear in this matter [*in everything you have done you have demonstrated that you understand godly sorrow*].

26 And it came to pass that the voice of the Lord said unto him [*Lehi*]: Look upon the ball, and behold the things which are written.

27 And it came to pass that when my father beheld the things which were written upon the ball, he did fear and tremble exceedingly, and also my brethren and the sons of Ishmael and our wives.

> There are some strong parallels between how the Liahona worked for Lehi's company and how the Holy Ghost works for us. It has much to do with the "faith and diligence and heed" which we give to it.

28 And it came to pass that I, Nephi, beheld the pointers which were in the ball, that they did work according to the faith and diligence and heed which we did give unto them.

29 And there was also written upon them a new writing, which was plain to be read, which did give us understanding concerning the ways of the Lord; [*The Lord is constantly striving to teach us if we will listen.*] and it was written and changed from time to time, according to the faith and diligence which we gave unto it. And thus we see that by small means the Lord can bring about great things.

> There is much to learn from verse 29, above. For one thing, the value of obedience as a prerequisite for additional knowledge and revelation is taught. Nephi said that the things on the pointers were plain and were changed from time to time depending on his family's obedience to them.

> One of the most basic principles for personal progress taught in the scriptures is that faith obedience precedes additional revelation.

> A great example of how faithful, diligent obedience can lead to additional light and understanding is found in Moses 5:5–11. We will consider these verses here. Watch as Adam and Eve receive much additional light and knowledge because of simple faith obedience (**bold** added for emphasis):

First Nephi 16

Pearl of Great Price: Moses 5:5–11

5 And he gave unto them commandments, that they should worship the Lord their God, and should offer the firstlings of their flocks, for an offering unto the Lord. And **Adam was obedient** unto the commandments of the Lord.

6 And after many days an angel of the Lord appeared unto Adam, saying: **Why dost thou offer sacrifices unto the Lord?** And Adam said unto him: **I know not, save the Lord commanded me** [*an example of pure, faith obedience*].

Watch, now, as the angel teaches Adam and gives him much additional knowledge and light as a result of his faithful obedience. We will continue to use **bold** for teaching emphasis.

7 And then the angel spake, saying: This thing [*offering sacrifice*] is a similitude of [*is symbolic of*] the sacrifice of the Only Begotten of the Father [*Christ*], which is full of grace [*ability and desire to help us*] and truth.

8 Wherefore [*this is the reason that*], thou shalt **do all that thou doest in the name of the Son**, and **thou shalt repent** and **call upon God in the name of the Son forevermore**.

9 And in that day **the Holy Ghost fell upon Adam**, which beareth record of the Father and the Son, saying [*bearing testimony of Christ*]: I am the Only Begotten of the Father from the beginning, henceforth and forever, that as thou hast fallen **thou mayest be redeemed, and all mankind, even as many as will** [*all those who desire it*].

Now watch as both Adam and Eve summarize the tremendous insights and testimony they have received from the angel and from the Holy Ghost, all because of their simple faith obedience.

10 And in that day **Adam** blessed God and **was filled** [*with the Holy Ghost*], and **began to prophesy** concerning all the families of the earth, saying: Blessed be the name of God, for **because of my transgression my eyes are opened, and in this life I shall have joy**, and again in the flesh I shall see God.

11 And **Eve**, his wife, heard all these things and **was glad**, saying: **Were it not for our transgression we never should have had seed** [*children*], and **never should have known good and evil**, and the **joy** of our redemption, and the eternal life which God giveth unto all **the obedient**.

In summary, the basic principle is this: First, we obey, with faith in God and Christ. Then we receive more light and knowledge. If we then obey that, we receive more.

If we obey that, we receive yet more, and on and on until, someday, we get to the point that we "shall comprehend even God" (D&C 88:49).

Thus, in this portion of the Book of Mormon, Nephi is teaching us the power and potential of simple faith obedience.

30 And it came to pass that I, Nephi, did go forth up into the top of the mountain, according to the directions which were given upon the ball.

31 And it came to pass that I did slay wild beasts, insomuch that I did obtain food for our families.

32 And it came to pass that I did return to our tents, bearing the beasts which I had slain; and now when they beheld that I had obtained food, how great was their joy! And it came to pass that they did humble themselves before the Lord, and did give thanks unto him. [*Here, again, they humble themselves, and Nephi's hopes for them are raised.*]

33 And it came to pass that we did again take our journey, traveling nearly the same course as in the beginning; and after we had traveled for the space of many days we did pitch our tents again, that we might tarry [*stop; stay in the same place*] for the space of a time.

Perhaps, by now, it makes you a bit nervous when they stop traveling and thus have time on their hands. Sure enough, there will be trouble, and this time things will get extremely ugly. And this time, Nephi specifically mentions the murmuring of some of the women in the group. It is sometimes said that Satan often has a rather easy time of it when it comes to getting men to turn to evil and wickedness. But as long as women remain true to gospel principles, society remains relatively stable. But when the devil succeeds in getting women to succumb also to evil, watch out!

We will use **bold** to emphasize things in the next verses.

34 And it came to pass that **Ishmael died**, and was buried in the place which was called Nahom.

35 And it came to pass that **the daughters of Ishmael did mourn exceedingly, because of** the **loss of their father**, and because of their **afflictions in the wilderness;** and **they did murmur against my father**, because he had brought them out of the land of Jerusalem, saying: Our father is dead; yea, and we have wandered much in the wilderness, and we have suffered much affliction, hunger, thirst, and fatigue; and after all these sufferings we must perish in the wilderness with hunger.

36 And **thus they did murmur against my father, and also against me**; and they were **desirous to return again to Jerusalem**. [*Remember that several prophets had already prophesied that Jerusalem would be destroyed. Therefore, in expressing a desire to return to Jerusalem, they were overtly expressing lack of faith and openly rebelling.*]

We have already seen the mercies and patience of God many times so far with respect to rebellious members of Lehi's company. We appreciate this because we need it ourselves. As stated previously, Laman and Lemuel as well as the sons of Ishmael have had many chances up to now to know of God, to gain wisdom and personal testimonies, and to be faithful and obedient to principles which lead to exaltation. Our hopes for them have been raised several times, but now we will see why the scriptures constantly counsel us to "endure to the end."

Satan seems to work hard to mold people into being "fair weather friends." Fair weather friends are those who are loyal when things go well and their immediate needs and self-centered desires are being met. But as soon as the obvious "rewards" slow down or stop coming for a while, they withdraw their loyalty.

These brothers and brothers-in-law do not seem to want to endure to the next hour, let alone "endure to the end." One of Lucifer's traps is to condition people to expect instant gratification, with instant rewards. He thus weakens their resolve to be faithful between obvious rewards for good behavior.

Another lesson we might learn from what happens next is that when individuals and groups rebel time and again against obvious truth and righteousness, they seem to need to get more vicious to sustain their rebellion and blindness. In short, they become more like the devil.

37 And Laman said unto Lemuel and also unto the sons of Ishmael: Behold, let us slay our father, and also our brother Nephi, who has taken it upon him to be our ruler and our teacher, who are his elder brethren. [*Pride is gaining a stranglehold on these men now.*]

38 Now, he says that the Lord has talked with him, and also that angels have ministered unto him. But behold, we know that he lies unto us; and he tells us these things, and he worketh many things by his cunning arts, that he may deceive our eyes, thinking, perhaps, that he may lead us away into some strange wilderness; and after he has led us away,

he has thought to make himself a king and a ruler over us, that he may do with us according to his will and pleasure. And after this manner did my brother Laman stir up their hearts to anger.

> Laman's behavior is becoming more like Satan's. He is now telling bold-faced lies in order to stir up his allies against Lehi and Nephi. We are inclined to recoil from him and say, "Wait a minute, he knows better than that!" And indeed he does. Or, perhaps we must begin to say, "And indeed he did." In other words, what we are probably beginning to see is one of the ultimate deceptions of the Adversary in action. He toys with us until we begin to believe our own lies. This happened to Korihor (see Alma 30:53). We begin to demonstrate the fact that wickedness does not promote rational thought. Reality and truth are distorted in our minds to the point that we don't think like righteous people do. This is one of the reasons that wickedness is so dangerous to our souls. It destroys our ability to think like God thinks. If we find ourselves on the path of rebellion against light and truth, at all, we would do well to turn around immediately, and flee in the opposite direction.
>
> Next, Laman and his allies will be given yet another chance to repent and act in accordance with gospel principles. This is another reminder to us of the unfathomable patience and love of a kind Father and a Savior who have infinite love. You may notice that as Laman and Lemuel and their confederates become more hardened and insensitive, the methods of the Lord, as He tries to reach them, while still respecting their agency, necessarily become stronger and tougher.

39 And it came to pass that the Lord was with us, yea, even the voice of the Lord came and did speak many words unto them, and did chasten [*scold*] them exceedingly; and after they were chastened by the voice of the Lord they did turn away their anger, and did repent of their sins, insomuch that the Lord did bless us again with food, that we did not perish. [*They respond positively to this stronger approach by a loving God, and our hopes for them are once again raised.*]

FIRST NEPHI 17

As we begin chapter 17, we note that the company of emigrants is again underway, and traveling nearly eastward. Most Book of Mormon scholars tend to believe that at this point Lehi and his people are traveling eastward along the bottom of the Saudi Arabian Peninsula. Once again,

First Nephi 17

we see that repentance plus being kept busy with daily travel seems to promote well being and harmony among the group. In fact, as Nephi points out in verse two, the blessings of the Lord are poured out generously and they continue the journey without murmuring.

There is a major message for us here. According to verses 1 and 2, there are still plenty of hardships. Yet, with the help and blessings of the Lord, their burdens seem light and thus, in effect, they are light. This is similar to Alma's colony of righteous Saints as mentioned in Mosiah 24:14–15. Likewise with us. You have no doubt met faithful members who are going through severe trials and who carry heavy burdens, yet are cheerful and happy. This is a direct blessing from the Lord.

1 AND it came to pass that we did again take our journey in the wilderness; and we did travel nearly eastward from that time forth. And we did travel and wade through much affliction in the wilderness; and our women did bear children in the wilderness.

2 And so great were the blessings of the Lord upon us, that while we did live upon raw meat in the wilderness, our women did give plenty of suck for their children, and were strong, yea, even like unto the men; and they began to bear their journeyings without murmurings.

3 And thus we see that the commandments of God must be fulfilled. And if it so be that the children of men keep the commandments of God he doth nourish them, and strengthen them, and provide means whereby they can accomplish the thing which he has commanded them; wherefore, he did provide means for us while we did sojourn in the wilderness.

4 And we did sojourn for the space of many years, yea, even eight years in the wilderness.

Next, they finally arrive at the ocean.

5 And we did come to the land which we called Bountiful, because of its much fruit and also wild honey; and all these things were prepared of the Lord that we might not perish. And we beheld the sea, which we called Irreantum, which, being interpreted, is many waters.

6 And it came to pass that we did pitch our tents by the seashore; and notwithstanding we had suffered many afflictions

and much difficulty, yea, even so much that we cannot write them all, we were exceedingly rejoiced when we came to the seashore; and we called the place Bountiful, because of its much fruit.

> We again learn much about attitude and simple obedience from Nephi here. Watch his reaction as the Lord asks him to build a ship.

7 And it came to pass that after I, Nephi, had been in the land of Bountiful for the space of many days, the voice of the Lord came unto me, saying: Arise, and get thee into the mountain. And it came to pass that I arose and went up into the mountain, and cried unto the Lord.

> Just a quick comment about some possible symbolism in going up into a mountain to commune with the Lord. It requires effort to climb up a mountain. Similarly, it requires effort for us to live worthy of inspiration and guidance from God. Symbolically, climbing up into a mountain could also represent drawing closer to heaven, or closer to God.

8 And it came to pass that the Lord spake unto me, saying: Thou shalt construct a ship, after the manner which I shall show thee, that I may carry thy people across these waters.

9 And I said: Lord, whither shall I go that I may find ore to molten, that I may make tools to construct the ship after the manner which thou hast shown unto me?

10 And it came to pass that the Lord told me whither I should go to find ore, that I might make tools.

> We can learn much from Nephi's reaction to the commandment to build a ship. Think of how much work it would take to make a bellows of animal skins to blow on the fire to get it hot enough to melt ore in order to have metal with which to make tools for constructing the ship.
>
> First, Nephi would have to go hunting. After a successful hunt, he would have to skin the animal or animals, tan the hides, cut them out, and sew the parts together to form a bellows. Then he would have to dig the ore which the Lord told him about, gather fuel, build a fire, melt the ore, and form the molten metal into tools. All this he did without one complaint. He is earning his exaltation!

11 And it came to pass that I, Nephi, did make a bellows wherewith to blow the fire, of the skins of beasts; and after I had made a bellows, that I might have wherewith to blow the fire, I did smite two stones together that I might make fire.

12 For the Lord had not hitherto suffered that we should make much fire, as we journeyed in the wilderness; for he said: I will make thy food become sweet, that ye cook it not;

13 And I will also be your light in the wilderness; and I will prepare the way before you, if it so be that ye shall keep my commandments; wherefore, inasmuch as ye shall keep my commandments ye shall be led towards the promised land [*also symbolic of heaven*]; and ye shall know that it is by me that ye are led.

14 Yea, and the Lord said also that: After ye have arrived in the promised land, ye shall know that I, the Lord, am God; and that I, the Lord, did deliver you from destruction; yea, that I did bring you out of the land of Jerusalem.

There is much symbolic teaching in verse 14, above. Right now, as we journey through our mortal lives, we do much on faith. But when we actually arrive in heaven (the "promised land") we will then know positively that the Lord is God, that He exists, and we will become aware of the many times He intervened in our lives while here on earth. We will know that He delivered us from spiritual destruction and bondage through the Atonement of Christ. We will know that He brought us out of the world and worldliness and into heaven.

15 Wherefore, I, Nephi, did strive to keep the commandments of the Lord, and I did exhort my brethren to faithfulness and diligence.

16 And it came to pass that I did make tools of the ore which I did molten [*melt*] out of the rock [*ore*].

Sadly, in the next verses we will be given keen insights into some of Satan's methodology for discouraging the righteous. As usual, we will use **bold** for emphasis and teaching. (Imagine what Noah and Nephi would have to say to each other as they chatted about how they were mocked when they set out to build their ships!)

17 And when my brethren saw that I was about to build a ship, they began to murmur against me, saying: **Our brother is a fool**, for he thinketh that he can build a ship; yea, and he also thinketh that he can cross these great waters.

18 And thus my brethren **did complain against me**, and were desirous that they might not labor, for they **did not believe that I could build a ship; neither would they believe that I was instructed of the Lord.**

The attitude of Nephi's brethren caused Nephi much sadness. And, as is usually the case with others who mock the righteous, they took great pleasure in the sorrow they were causing him. This is similar to Satan's behavior when he causes the destruction of the Lord's children. An example of this is found in 3 Nephi 9:1–2 as follows (**bold** added for emphasis): "And it came to pass that there was a voice heard among all the inhabitants of the earth, upon all the face of this land, crying: Wo, wo, wo unto this people; wo unto the inhabitants of the whole earth except they shall repent; for **the devil laugheth, and his angels rejoice, because of the slain of the fair sons and daughters of my people**; and it is because of their iniquity and abominations that they are fallen!"

19 And now it came to pass that I, Nephi, was exceedingly sorrowful because of the hardness of their hearts; and now **when they saw that I began to be sorrowful they were glad in their hearts, insomuch that they did rejoice over me**, saying: We knew that ye could not construct a ship, for we knew that ye were lacking in judgment; wherefore, thou canst not accomplish so great a work.

Satan's way is to blame others for our own shortcomings and follies. Next, Laman and Lemuel and the others try to lay the guilt for all their troubles on Lehi. They seem to have very quickly forgotten that when they themselves were faithful and obedient, they were blessed abundantly, even to the point that their women and children prospered and life was very good (see verse 2, above).

20 And **thou art like unto our father, led away by the foolish imaginations of his heart**; yea, he hath led us out of the land of Jerusalem, and we have wandered in the wilderness for these many years; and **our women have toiled, being big with child; and they have borne children in the wilderness and suffered all things, save it were death**; and **it would have been better that they had died** before they came out of Jerusalem than to have suffered these afflictions.

21 Behold, these many years we have suffered in the wilderness, which time we might have enjoyed our possessions and the land of our inheritance; yea, and we might have been happy.

It is somewhat shocking to see how far off the mark these rebellious men have gone and how quickly they reverted back to old spiritual blindness and irrational thought. In fact, you may have already noticed that they have not only reverted back, but they have sunk to new lows in lack of reason and lack of awareness of things as they really are. It is once again profoundly evident that wickedness does not promote rational thought!

In the next verse, they think back on Jerusalem and praise its inhabitants as righteous, God-fearing citizens and keepers of the commandments given by the Lord through Moses (remember that they were actually ripe in iniquity and ready for destruction). Nephi now teaches us a lesson in how quickly Satan can warp and corrupt the senses and sensibilities of willing students of wickedness. In a sad and rather startling way, Laman, Lemuel, and the others bear testimony that wickedness is actually righteousness. We fear that they believe their own lies.

22 And **we know** that **the people who were in the land of Jerusalem were a righteous people**; for **they kept the statutes and judgments of the Lord, and all his commandments**, according to the law of Moses; wherefore, **we know** that **they are a righteous people**; and our father hath judged them, and hath led us away because we would hearken unto his words; yea, and our brother is like unto him. And after this manner of language did my brethren murmur and complain against us.

Next, an inspired Nephi will skillfully teach his wayward and rebellious brethren, using scriptures familiar to them. And when he has finished, the Lord will add His testimony in ways which they cannot possibly miss. And once again, they will humble themselves and then will immediately begin helping Nephi build the ship.

There is a major message here, being repeated over and over. It is this: The Lord loves us. He loves to bless us. He even loves stinkers! And He gives them chance after chance after chance. Even when they rebel and reject Him and His messengers, He gives them additional opportunities to repent and return to Him. This is clearly taught elsewhere in the scriptures also. For example, in **Ezekiel 18:21–32**, we read (**bold** added for emphasis):

21 But **if the wicked will turn from all his sins that he hath committed, and keep all my statutes, and do that which is lawful and right, he shall surely live** [*he will be saved in heaven*] he shall not die [*spiritually*].

22 **All his transgressions that he hath committed, they shall not be mentioned unto him**: [*Compare with D&C 58:42–43.*] in his righteousness that he hath done he shall live.

23 **Have I any pleasure at all that the wicked should die?** saith the Lord GOD: *and* not that he should return from his ways, and live?

24 But when the righteous turneth away from his righteousness, and committeth iniquity, *and* doeth according to all the abominations that the wicked *man* doeth, shall he live? All his righteousness that he hath done shall not be mentioned: in his trespass that he hath trespassed, and in his sin that he hath sinned, in them shall he die.

25 Yet ye say, The way of the Lord is not equal. Hear now, O house of Israel; Is not my way equal? are not your ways unequal?

26 When a righteous *man* turneth away from his righteousness, and committeth iniquity, and dieth in them; for his iniquity that he hath done shall he die.

27 **Again, when the wicked *man* turneth away from his wickedness that he hath committed, and doeth that which is lawful and right, he shall save his soul alive.**

28 **Because he considereth** [*considers his ways and repents*], **and turneth away from all his transgressions** that he hath committed, he shall surely live, he shall not die.

29 Yet saith the house of Israel, The way of the Lord is not equal. O house of Israel, are not my ways equal? are not your ways unequal?

30 Therefore I will judge you, O house of Israel, every one according to his ways, saith the Lord GOD. **Repent, and turn *yourselves* from all your transgressions; so iniquity shall not be your ruin.**

31 Cast away from you all your transgressions, whereby ye have transgressed; and **make you a new heart and a new spirit**: for why will ye die, O house of Israel?

32 For **I have no pleasure in the death of him that dieth, saith the Lord GOD: wherefore turn *yourselves*, and live ye.**

So, now we will watch and learn as Nephi teaches his spiritually needy brethren from the scriptures. He will emphasize past blessings from the Lord and the importance of using those blessings as a basis for being loyal to the Lord now. There is much symbolism in the literal events Nephi uses to teach his people. We will point some of that out as we go along.

23 And it came to pass that I, Nephi, spake unto them, saying: Do ye believe that our fathers [*ancestors*], who were the children of Israel, would have been

led away out of the hands of the Egyptians if they had not hearkened unto the words of the Lord? [*Symbolism: Do you think we would be rescued from the bondage of sin if we did not listen to the Lord?*]

24 Yea, do ye suppose that they would have been led out of bondage, if the Lord had not commanded Moses that he should lead them out of bondage? [*Symbolism: Do you think we would be led out from being slaves to sin if we refuse to listen to our current prophets?*]

25 Now ye know that the children of Israel were in bondage; and ye know that they were laden with tasks, which were grievous to be borne; wherefore, ye know that it must needs be a good thing for them, that they should be brought out of bondage. [*Symbolism: You know that sin is a terrible taskmaster or slave driver. You know that sin places heavy burdens upon you. So, you know that it is very good to be rescued from sin by the Lord.*]

26 Now ye know that Moses was commanded of the Lord to do that great work; and ye know that by his word the waters of the Red Sea were divided hither and thither, and they passed through on dry ground. [*Symbolism: Our prophets are guided and directed by the Lord, so if we follow them faithfully, we can get through our difficulties and escape the forces of evil also.*]

Just a quick comment about Bible critics who claim that the Red Sea did not really part. Rather, they say that Moses led the children of Israel through a "Reed Sea" (a very shallow marsh land that, luckily, had dried up because of constant dry winds. The critics are wrong, and the Book of Mormon comes to the rescue. This is another example of where the Book of Mormon substantiates the Bible. This would be just a bit of the fulfillment of the prophecy of Ezekiel wherein he saw the day when the Bible and Book of Mormon would come together and "become one in thine hand" (see Ezekiel 37:16–20).

27 But ye know that the Egyptians were drowned in the Red Sea, who were the armies of Pharaoh. [*Symbolism: The day will come when the wicked who persecute the work of the Lord, who refuse to repent, will be destroyed.*]

28 And ye also know that they were fed with manna in the wilderness. [*Symbolism: The Lord sustains His people with blessings from above.*]

29 Yea, and ye also know that Moses, by his word according to the power of God which was in him, smote the rock, and there came forth water, that the children of Israel might quench their thirst. [*Symbolism: Our thirst for the things of God is quenched by the "living water" which comes from Christ and His Atonement; see John 4:10, 14*].

30 And notwithstanding they being led, the Lord their God, their Redeemer, going before them, leading them by day and giving light unto them by night, and doing all things for them which were expedient for man to receive, they hardened their hearts and blinded their minds, and reviled against Moses and against the true and living God. [*Symbolism: Even though God does everything possible to bless His children, some of them still rebel.*]

> Verse 30, above, is especially relevant to Laman and Lemuel and their cohorts in rebellion. It is a strong hint from Nephi that they are being just like the foolish children of Israel who, in the face of such obvious help and witnesses from God, still rebelled against their prophet leader as well as God.

31 And it came to pass that according to his word he did destroy them; and according to his word he did lead them; and according to his word he did do all things for them; and there was not any thing done save it were by his word.

32 And after they had crossed the river Jordan he did make them mighty unto the driving out of the children of the land, yea, unto the scattering them to destruction.

> Symbolism: One can find much symbolism in the crossing of the Jordan River into the promised land. For instance, we must pass through the "water" (baptism) to gain entrance into the "promised land" (celestial kingdom). Priesthood holders (the priests who carried the ark of the covenant; see Joshua 3:6) enabled the children of Israel to pass through the water (priesthood holders baptize us). Through the help of God, we can drive all "enemies" such as sin, bad habits, etc., out of our lives.

33 And now, do ye suppose that the children of this land [*the inhabitants of Palestine—Canaan—when Joshua led the children of Israel into it*], who were in the land of promise, who were driven out by our fathers, do ye suppose that they were righteous? Behold, I say unto you, Nay.

34 Do ye suppose that our fathers would have been more choice than they if they had

been righteous? I say unto you, Nay. [*Symbolism: It is true that righteousness puts all people, regardless of race or other factors, on an equal footing with God as far as eternal blessings are concerned.*]

35 Behold, the Lord esteemeth all flesh in one; he that is righteous is favored of God. But behold, this people had rejected every word of God, and they were ripe in iniquity; and the fulness of the wrath of God was upon them; and the Lord did curse the land against them, and bless it unto our fathers [*ancestors*]; yea, he did curse it against them unto their destruction, and he did bless it unto our fathers unto their obtaining power over it.

36 Behold, the Lord hath created the earth that it should be inhabited; and he hath created his children that they should possess it. [*Message: The purpose of this earth is to be a place where people can grow and develop, not to be a place where they come to be destroyed. Hint to Laman and Lemuel: If you get yourselves destroyed because of wickedness, you are wasting the purposes for being sent to earth.*]

37 And he raiseth up a righteous nation, and destroyeth the nations of the wicked.

38 And he leadeth away the righteous into precious lands, and the wicked he destroyeth, and curseth the land unto them for their sakes. [*Message: God manages things here on earth depending on how people use their agency.*]

39 He ruleth high in the heavens, for it is his throne, and this earth is his footstool. [*Symbolism: We are all subordinate to God. He has power over all things—including shipbuilding . . . hint, hint.*]

40 And he loveth those who will have him to be their God. Behold, he loved our fathers, and he covenanted with them, yea, even Abraham, Isaac, and Jacob; and he remembered the covenants which he had made; wherefore, he did bring them out of the land of Egypt.

> The word "loveth," as used in the context of verse 40, above, as well as numerous other scripture references, means, in effect, "is able to bless."

41 And he did straiten [*discipline; punish*] them in the wilderness with his rod; for they hardened their hearts, even as ye have; and the Lord straitened them because of their iniquity [*wickedness*]. He sent fiery flying serpents among them; and after they were bitten he prepared a way that they might

be healed; and the labor which they had to perform was to look; and because of the simpleness of the way, or the easiness of it, there were many who perished. [*Symbolism: The gospel way of life is actually the simplest way. Many consider it to be too simplistic or even simple-minded to believe in God and the Atonement of Christ, personal accountability, life after death, etc. Therefore, they refuse the gospel in their lives.*]

42 And they did harden their hearts from time to time, and they did revile against [*criticize; rebel against*] Moses, and also against God; nevertheless, ye know that they were led forth by his matchless power into the land of promise.

43 And now, after all these things, the time has come that they [*the Jews, meaning the descendants of the children of Israel who dwell in the Jerusalem area at the time of Lehi*] have become wicked, yea, nearly unto ripeness [*about ready for destruction*]; and I know not but they are at this day about to be destroyed; for I know that the day must surely come that they must be destroyed, save [*except for*] a few only, who shall be led away into captivity.

44 Wherefore [*this is the reason that*], the Lord commanded my father that he should depart into the wilderness; and the Jews also sought to take away his life; yea, and ye also have sought to take away his life; wherefore, ye are murderers in your hearts and ye are like unto them.

This is strong language and helps explain why Nephi's rebellious brothers and the rebellious others are so insensitive to the Spirit. We are now coming to one of the more famous verses in the Book of Mormon, verse 45. It clearly explains that they have had marvelous manifestations which should have strengthened their testimonies and made them firm in the gospel. It explains what is wrong with them now and it tells why the Lord has to "turn up the volume" in order to try to retrieve some of His wayward children here on earth.

We will **bold** some of Nephi's words and phrases which seem to indicate that the accountability level of Laman, Lemuel, and the sons of Ishmael is increasing.

45 Ye are swift to do iniquity but slow to remember the Lord your God. **Ye have seen an angel**, and **he spake unto you**; yea, **ye have heard his voice from time to time**; and **he hath spoken unto you in a still small voice**, but ye

were past feeling, that ye could not feel his words; wherefore, **he has spoken unto you like unto the voice of thunder,** which **did cause the earth to shake** as if it were to divide asunder.

46 And **ye** also **know** that by the power of his almighty word he can cause the earth that it shall pass away; yea, and **ye know** that by his word he can cause the rough places to be made smooth, and smooth places shall be broken up. O, then, why is it, that ye can be so hard in your hearts?

47 Behold, my soul is rent [*torn*] with anguish because of you, and my heart is pained; I fear lest ye shall be cast off forever. Behold, I am full of the Spirit of God, insomuch that my frame has no strength.

> Perhaps you've noticed that when the Spirit of the Lord is upon you, you have strong feelings of compassion and love for others. Thus, we understand somewhat why Nephi can care so strongly for his brethren, verse 47, above, in spite of such hateful treatment at their hands.

48 And now it came to pass that when I had spoken these words they were angry with me, and were desirous to throw me into the depths of the sea; and as they came forth to lay their hands upon me I spake unto them, saying: In the name of the Almighty God, I command you that ye touch me not, for I am filled with the power of God, even unto the consuming of my flesh; and whoso shall lay his hands upon me shall wither even as a dried reed; and he shall be as naught [*nothing*] before the power of God, for God shall smite him.

49 And it came to pass that I, Nephi, said unto them that they should murmur no more against their father; neither should they withhold their labor from me, for God had commanded me that I should build a ship.

50 And I said unto them: If God had commanded me to do all things I could do them. If he should command me that I should say unto this water, be thou earth, it should be earth; and if I should say it, it would be done.

51 And now, if the Lord has such great power, and has wrought so many miracles among the children of men, how is it that he cannot instruct me, that I should build a ship?

52 And it came to pass that I, Nephi, said many things unto my brethren, insomuch that they were confounded and could not

contend against me; neither durst they lay their hands upon me nor touch me with their fingers, even for the space of many days. Now they durst not do this lest they should wither before me, so powerful was the Spirit of God; and thus it had wrought upon them.

> The gentle approach of the "still small voice" could not humble them. But the threat of physical destruction does. In many ways, such is the case in our day (see D&C 88:88–90). We understand this to be the root cause of so many natural disasters and upheavals in nature in the last days. It is a final attempt by the Lord to get people's attention so that they can repent. Otherwise, they will be destroyed by the final wars, etc. or at the actual Second Coming.
>
> Next, we see yet another opportunity given by a loving God for these rebellious ones to repent. While some may look at it as rather harsh, in the eternal scheme of things it is a wonderful kindness. (**Bold** used for emphasis.)

53 And it came to pass that the Lord said unto me: Stretch forth thine hand again unto thy brethren, and they shall not wither before thee, but I will shock them, saith the Lord, and **this will I do, that <u>they may know</u> that I am the Lord their God.**

54 And it came to pass that I stretched forth my hand unto my brethren, and they did not wither before me; but the Lord did shake them, even according to the word which he had spoken.

55 And **now**, they said: **We know of a surety** that the Lord is with thee, for **we know** that it is the power of the Lord that has shaken us. And they fell down before me, and were about to worship me, but I would not suffer them [*allow them to do so*], saying: I am thy brother, yea, even thy younger brother; wherefore, worship the Lord thy God, and honor thy father and thy mother, that thy days may be long in the land which the Lord thy God shall give thee.

FIRST NEPHI 18

The work of building the ship now progresses rapidly, because they are working in harmony, as directed by the Lord as He communicates with Nephi from time to time. They are all busy, and things go well. There is perhaps some interesting and important symbolism, even in the construction of the ship. Notice that their goal is to cross the waters to get to the promised land. Again, water can symbolize baptism, and the promised land can symbolize heaven. The ship can symbolize the help of God to get us back to heaven. Without His help (the ship), we cannot make it. The fact that this ship is not "after the manner of men" (verse 2), could symbolize that we can't get to the promised land by living the common lifestyle of the "natural man" (Mosiah 3:19). Finally, the fact that Nephi "did pray oft" (verse 3) can remind us of the need for constant prayer and communication with God throughout our lives. We will use **bold** just a bit to emphasize what was said in this note.

1 AND it came to pass that **they did worship the Lord, and did go forth with me**; and we did work timbers of curious [*usually means "skillful" or "fine"*] workmanship. And **the Lord did show me** from time to time after what manner I should work the timbers of the ship.

2 Now I, Nephi, did **not** work the timbers after the manner which was learned by men [*not according to men's knowledge*], neither did I build the ship **after the manner of men**; but I did build it after the manner which the Lord had shown unto me; wherefore, it was not after the manner of men.

3 And **I, Nephi, did go into the mount oft, and I did pray oft unto the Lord**; wherefore the Lord showed unto me great things. [*Symbolism: When we communicate with the Lord, we are shown great things of the gospel and eternal life, by the Holy Ghost.*]

4 And it came to pass that after I had finished the ship, according to the word of the Lord, my brethren beheld that it was good, and that the workmanship thereof was exceedingly fine; wherefore, **they did humble themselves again** before the Lord.

5 And it came to pass that the voice of the Lord came unto my father, that we should arise and go down into the ship.

6 And it came to pass that on the morrow, after we had prepared all things, much fruits and meat from the wilderness, and honey in abundance, and provisions according to that which the Lord had commanded us, we did go down into the ship, with all our loading and our seeds, and whatsoever thing we had brought with us, every one according to his age; wherefore, we did all go down into the ship, with our wives and our children.

Next, Nephi tells us more about his parents' family. In addition to these two more sons, we are told also that Lehi and Sariah had daughters (see 2 Nephi 5:6).

7 And now, my father had begat [*fathered*] two sons in the wilderness [*during the eight years in the wilderness*]; the elder was called Jacob and the younger Joseph.

8 And it came to pass after we had all gone down into the ship, and had taken with us our provisions and things which had been commanded us, we did put forth into the sea and were driven forth before the wind towards the promised land. [*Perhaps "wind" in this verse could symbolize the help of the Lord. You can't see it but you can feel it. And if you use your agency to steer your life in the direction the wind is gently blowing you, you will end up in the "promised land."*]

Perhaps you are already getting a little bit apprehensive because, while they are aboard the ship, they have spare time on their hands. Perhaps one of our most difficult tests in this life is what we do with spare time.

9 And after we had been driven forth before the wind for the space of many days, behold, my brethren and the sons of Ishmael and also their wives began to make themselves merry [*we assume that the word "merry," as used here, means "boisterous, loud, and inappropriate"*], insomuch that they began to dance, and to sing, and to speak with much rudeness, yea, even that they did forget by what power they had been brought thither; yea, they were lifted up unto exceeding rudeness. [*"Rudeness" and its accompanying crudeness are offensive to the Spirit. Unfortunately, our society and, in fact, the whole world have become and are continuing to become more rude and more crude as Satan plies his incessant wiles in an increased frenzy in the last days. We would do well to avoid these preliminary insensitivities which lead to grosser sins.*]

The singing and dancing mentioned in verse 9, above, had to be inappropriate singing and dancing of some sort, since the Lord obviously approves of appropriate music and dancing. In D&C 136:28, He said: "If thou art merry, praise the Lord with singing, with music, with dancing, and with a prayer of praise and thanksgiving."

10 And I, Nephi, began to fear exceedingly lest the Lord should be angry with us, and smite us because of our iniquity, that we should be swallowed up in the depths of the sea; wherefore, I, Nephi, began to speak to

First Nephi 18

them with much soberness; but behold they were angry with me, saying: We will not that our younger brother shall be a ruler over us.

11 And it came to pass that Laman and Lemuel did take me and bind me with cords, and they did treat me with much harshness; nevertheless, the Lord did suffer [*allow*] it that he might show forth his power, unto the fulfilling of his word which he had spoken concerning the wicked.

> This (verse 11, above) is a very important explanation of some of the suffering which the righteous suffer at the hands of the wicked. Although the righteous often suffer much because of the evil acts of the wicked, they will be fine in eternity, which is what ultimately counts; whereas, the wicked will not "be fine" in the eternities, unless they repent. If the Lord were to stop every cruel act performed against the righteous, soon there would be no real agency, and mortal life as a testing ground would be rendered nonfunctional.

12 And it came to pass that after they had bound me insomuch that I could not move, the compass [*the Liahona; symbolic of the Holy Ghost; compare with 1 Nephi 16:28*], which had been prepared of the Lord, did cease to work.

13 Wherefore, they knew not whither they should steer the ship, insomuch that there arose a great storm, yea, a great and terrible tempest, and we were driven back upon the waters for the space of three days [*symbolic of the fact that when we cease to follow the Spirit, we lose ground*]; and they began to be frightened exceedingly lest they should be drowned in the sea; nevertheless they did not loose me.

14 And on the fourth day, which we had been driven back, the tempest began to be exceedingly sore [*very bad*].

15 And it came to pass that we were about to be swallowed up in the depths of the sea. And after we had been driven back upon the waters for the space of four days, my brethren began to see that the judgments of God were upon them, and that they must perish save that they should [*unless they would*] repent of their iniquities; wherefore, they came unto me, and loosed the bands which were upon my wrists, and behold they had swollen exceedingly; and also mine ankles were much swollen, and great was the soreness thereof.

Nephi is a great example of

what perspective and closeness to the Lord can do for a person under extreme trial and tribulation. Such sufferings and hardships are but a "moment in eternity"; yet while going through them, they are "an eternal moment." But with the help of the Lord, they can be "endured well" (D&C 121:8). Next, Nephi gives clear counsel as to how to endure well. (**Bold** added for emphasis.)

16 Nevertheless, **I did look unto my God, and I did praise him all the day long; and I did not murmur against the Lord because of mine afflictions.**

17 Now my father, Lehi, had said many things unto them, and also unto the sons of Ishmael; but, behold, they did breathe out much threatenings against anyone that should speak for me; and my parents being stricken in years [*being elderly*], and having suffered much grief because of their children, they were brought down, yea, even upon their sickbeds. [*The behavior of Laman and Lemuel and the sons of Ishmael almost killed Lehi and Sariah.*]

18 Because of their grief and much sorrow, and the iniquity of my brethren, they were brought near even to be carried out of this time to meet their God; yea, their grey hairs were about to be brought down to lie low in the dust; yea, even they were near to be cast with sorrow into a watery grave.

The wording in verse 18, above, is typical of near eastern language. Again, an internal evidence that the Book of Mormon account began in a near eastern setting.

19 And Jacob and Joseph also, being young [*neither could have been more than eight years of age*], having need of much nourishment, were grieved because of the afflictions of their mother; and also my wife with her tears and prayers, and also my children [*Nephi now has his own family*], did not soften the hearts of my brethren that they would loose me.

20 And there was nothing save it were the power of God, which threatened them with destruction, could soften their hearts; wherefore, when they saw that they were about to be swallowed up in the depths of the sea they repented of the thing which they had done, insomuch that they loosed me.

Once again, Laman and Lemuel and their rebellious in-laws repented, but only when their own lives were threatened. They seem to be continuing on a downward spiral. Every time they rebel against an earlier "testimony building experience," it seems to require a more powerful and more personally threatening experience to bring them to their senses. Even in the raging tempest, the love of God was manifest to them, because it was given them to invite them to repent and have a happy, pleasant eternity.

21 And it came to pass after they had loosed me, behold, I took the compass, and it did work whither I desired it. And it came to pass that I prayed unto the Lord; and after I had prayed the winds did cease, and the storm did cease, and **there was a great calm**. [*Symbolic of what happens in our lives when we turn away from evil and return to God.*]

22 And it came to pass that I, Nephi, did guide the ship, that we sailed again towards the promised land.

23 And it came to pass that after we had sailed for the space of many days we did arrive at the promised land; and we went forth upon the land, and did pitch our tents; and we did call it the promised land.

24 And it came to pass that we did begin to till the earth, and we began to plant seeds; yea, we did put all our seeds into the earth, which we had brought from the land of Jerusalem. And it came to pass that they did grow exceedingly; wherefore, we were blessed in abundance.

25 And it came to pass that we did find upon the land of promise, as we journeyed in the wilderness, that there were beasts in the forests of every kind, both the cow and the ox, and the ass and the horse, and the goat and the wild goat, and all manner of wild animals, which were for the use of men. And we did find all manner of ore, both of gold, and of silver, and of copper.

Critics of Joseph Smith and the Book of Mormon have ridiculed the idea that there were horses in the New World. However, solid evidence has since surfaced that horses were indeed in America before Columbus arrived.

The following quote from page 19 of the 1996 *Book of Mormon Student Manual*, used at BYU and in the Institutes of Religion, eliminates the criticism. It reads as follows: "If Joseph Smith had been writing the Book of Mormon instead of translating it from ancient records, he would have been very foolish to have included references to horses on the American continent in Book of Mormon times (1 Nephi 18:25; Enos 21). In 1830, nearly all the historians and scholars were convinced there had been no horses on the American continent before the coming of Columbus. After the Book of Mormon was published, however, archaeological discoveries were made that clearly indicate that horses were in the Americas before Columbus arrived. In the asphalt deposits of Rancho LaBrea in southern California, numerous fossil remains of horses have been found that antedate (predate) Book of Mormon times. Although these discoveries do not absolutely prove horses were in the Americas in the time period covered by the Book of Mormon (about 2600 B.C. to A.D. 421), they do prove horses were there before Columbus" (Ludlow, *A Companion to Your Study of the Book of Mormon*, p. 117).

FIRST NEPHI 19

Nephi will pause here and explain again that he has been commanded to make two sets of records, or plates. As explained in 1 Nephi, chapters 6 and 9, these two sets are referred to as the large plates of Nephi and the small plates of Nephi.

Also, among many other things in this chapter, he will explain why the words of Isaiah are so important and valuable.

1 AND it came to pass that the Lord commanded me, wherefore I did make plates of ore [*the large plates of Nephi*] that I might engraven upon them the record of my people. And upon the plates which I made [*the large plates*] I did engraven the record of my father, and also our journeyings in the wilderness, and the prophecies of my father; and also many of mine own prophecies have I engraven upon them.

2 And I knew not at the time when I made them [*the large plates*] that I should be commanded of the Lord to make these plates [*the small plates of Nephi*]; wherefore, the record of my father, and the genealogy of his fathers, and the more part of all our proceedings in the wilderness are engraven upon those first plates [*the large plates*] of which I have spoken; wherefore, the things which transpired before I made these plates [*the small plates*] are, of a truth, more particularly made mention upon the first plates [*the large plates*].

Next, in verse 3, we will find that the loss of the 116 manuscript pages by Martin Harris actually worked to our benefit, because the replacement translation came from the small plates of Nephi which contained more spiritual things compared to the large plates of Nephi from which the 116 pages were translated. We will use **bold** to emphasize this.

3 And after I had made these plates [*the small plates*] by way of commandment, I, Nephi, received a commandment that **the ministry and the prophecies, the more plain and precious parts of them, should be written upon these plates;** and that the things which were written should be kept **for the instruction of my people**, who should possess the land, and **also for other wise purposes** [*including replacing the lost 116 pages of translation previously referred to*], which purposes are known unto the Lord.

4 Wherefore, I, Nephi, did make a record upon **the other plates** [*the large plates*], which gives an account, or which gives **a greater account of the wars and contentions and destructions of my people**. And this have I done, and commanded my people what they should do after I was gone; and that these plates [*the small plates*] should be handed down from one generation to another, or from one prophet to another, until further commandments of the Lord.

5 And an account of my making these plates [*the small plates*] shall be given hereafter [*in 2 Nephi 5:28–33*]; and then, behold, I proceed according to that which I have spoken; and this I do that **the more sacred things may be kept** [*on the small plates*] for the knowledge of my people.

6 Nevertheless, I do not write anything upon plates save [*unless*] it be that I think it be sacred. And now, if I do err, even did they err of old; not that I would excuse myself because of other men, but because of the weakness which is in me, according to the flesh, I would excuse myself.

7 For the things which some men esteem to be of great worth, both to the body and soul, others set at naught [*toss aside*] and trample under their feet. Yea, even the very God of Israel [*Christ; see verse 8*] do men trample under their feet; I say, trample under their feet but I would speak in other words—they set him at naught, and hearken not to the voice of his counsels.

> In verse 7, above, we get a rather strong definition of what it means to ignore the teachings and counsels of the Savior. When we do this, we are, in effect, "walking" on Him!

8 And behold he cometh, according to the words of the angel, in six hundred years from the time my father left Jerusalem. [*This is*

how we calculate that Lehi left Jerusalem about 600 B.C.]

9 And the world, because of their iniquity [*wickedness*], shall judge him [*Christ*] to be a thing of naught [*a person of no value*]; wherefore they scourge [*whip*] him [*Matthew 27:26*], and he suffereth [*allows*] it; and they smite him [*Matthew 27:30; Luke 22:63–64*], and he suffereth it. Yea, they spit upon him [*Matthew 27:30*], and he suffereth it, because of his loving kindness and his long-suffering [*patience*] towards the children of men.

> In verse 10, next, we have one of the clearest explanations ever given in scripture of the fact that Jesus Christ is the God of the Old Testament. (**Bold** used for emphasis.)

10 And **the God of our fathers** [*ancestors*], who were led out of Egypt, out of bondage, and also were **preserved in the wilderness by him**, yea, **the God of Abraham, and of Isaac, and the God of Jacob, yieldeth himself**, according to the words of the angel, as a man, **into the hands of wicked men, to be lifted up** [*on the cross*], according to the words of Zenock, and to be **crucified**, according to the words of Neum, and to be **buried in a sepulchre** [*tomb*], according to the words of Zenos, which he spake concerning the three days of darkness, which should be a sign given of his death unto those who should inhabit the isles of the sea, more especially given unto those who are of the house of Israel.

> You probably noticed three prophets spoken of in verse 10, whose names are not mentioned anywhere else other than the Book of Mormon. They are Zenock, Neum, and Zenos. They were apparently Old Testament prophets, whose writings have been left out of or lost from the Bible.
>
> The Bible Dictionary, pages 725–26, under **Lost Books**, explains that many books of scripture are not contained in our current Bible. In other words, the Bible is not complete. Bible Dictionary, page 726, says the following about these three prophets mentioned in the Book of Mormon:
>
> "The Book of Mormon makes reference to writings of O.T. times and connection that are not found in the Bible, the Book of Mormon, or in any other known source. These writings are of Zenock, Zenos, and Neum (1 Nephi 19:10; Alma 33:13–17)."
>
> Someday, no doubt, if not here, then in the next life, we will be privileged to read the word of these three prophets as mentioned in verse 10. By the way,

First Nephi 19

we do have another writing of Zenos. It is quoted by Jacob in Jacob chapter 5, which is the allegory of the tame and wild olive trees.

Also, a phrase is used in verse 10 which we need to understand as we study the Book of Mormon. The phrase is "isles of the sea." Most of us probably think of relatively small islands in the ocean when we read this phrase. That is not what the phrase means in the Book of Mormon. It means all continents and land masses outside of the lands reachable on the common trade routes from Israel. A quote from *The Book of Mormon Student Manual*, 1982 edition, p. 55, explains this as follows:

"According to a quotation by Reynolds and Sjodahl, 'Sir Isaac Newton observes that to the Hebrews the continents of Asia and Africa were "the earth," because they had access to them by land, while the parts of the earth to which they sailed over the sea were "the isles of the sea."' (Reynolds and Sjodahl, *Commentary on The Book of Mormon*, 1:214)

"Thus, Nephi not only refers to the isles of the sea as the location of other remnants of the house of Israel, but he also indicates that he and his people were then living upon an 'isle of the sea' when he quite clearly is referring to the great land mass known as the American continent (2 Nephi 10:20–21).

The following quotation is of interest:

"'The Indians almost universally believed the dry land they knew to be a part of a great island, everywhere surrounded by wide waters whose limits were unknown. Many tribes had vague myths of a journey from beyond this sea; many placed beyond it the home of the sun and of light, and the happy hunting grounds of departed souls' (Brinton, *Library of Aboriginal American Literature,* 5:134; Reynolds and Sjodahl, *Commentary on The Book of Mormon,* 1:319)." (Ludlow, *A Companion to Your Study of the Book of Mormon*, p. 121; *Book of Mormon Student Manual,* 1982, p. 55.)

Next, Nephi quotes one of the prophets (possibly Zenos, but we don't know for sure) as he describes the conditions on the American continent at the time of the Savior's crucifixion and resurrection. It is significant to note that the more righteous at the time will hear the Savior personally, whereas the others will meet with destruction because of their wickedness. We will **bold** things in the next two verses which emphasize this difference.

11 For thus spake the prophet: The Lord God surely shall visit all the house of Israel at that day, **some with his voice, because of their righteousness, unto their great joy and salvation,**

and **others with the thunderings and the lightnings of his power, by tempest, by fire, and by smoke, and vapor of darkness, and by the opening of the earth, and by mountains which shall be carried up.**

12 And all these things must surely come, saith the prophet Zenos. And **the rocks of the earth must rend** [*be torn apart*]; and because of the groanings of the earth, many of the kings of the isles of the sea shall be wrought upon [*influenced*] by the Spirit of God, to exclaim: The God of nature suffers.

> The prophecy continues and gives prophetic details concerning the Jews, after they crucify Christ.

13 And as for those who are at Jerusalem, saith the prophet, they shall be scourged [*beaten; badly treated*] by all people, because they crucify the God of Israel [*Christ*], and turn their hearts aside, rejecting signs and wonders [*including the miracles performed by the Savior*], and the power and glory of the God of Israel.

14 And because they turn their hearts aside [*because they refuse to believe in Christ and His gospel*], saith the prophet, and have despised the Holy One of Israel [*Christ*], they shall wander in the flesh [*they will wander here and there on the earth*], and perish [*die*], and become a hiss and a byword [*and become a cuss word; become looked down upon*], and be hated among all nations.

15 Nevertheless, when that day cometh, saith the prophet, that they no more turn aside their hearts against the Holy One of Israel [*when they repent and come unto Christ*], then will he remember [*be able to keep*] the covenants which he made to their fathers [*ancestors*].

> Here, Nephi is teaching us about the gathering of Israel when the gospel is restored in the last days. The gospel will go to all the earth in the last days.

16 Yea, then will he remember [*bring His gospel and its covenants to*] the isles of the sea [*the other lands of the earth, including the Americas*]; yea, and all the people who are of the house of Israel, will I gather in, saith the Lord, according to the words of the prophet Zenos, from the four quarters of the earth [*from all the earth*].

17 Yea, and all the earth [*all people*] shall see the salvation of the Lord, saith the prophet; every nation, kindred, tongue and people shall be blessed.

It is important to keep in mind, as we speak of the gathering of Israel in the last days, that we must all be "gathered" spiritually. In other words, while there are many physical "gatherings" to various lands, such as the Jews being gathered back to the Holy Land, all who desire salvation in celestial exaltation must allow themselves to be "gathered" to the Savior and His Father.

18 And I, Nephi, have written these things unto my people, that perhaps I might persuade them that they would remember the Lord their Redeemer.

19 Wherefore [*this is the reason*], I speak unto all the house of Israel, if it so be that they should obtain these things [*my writings; the scriptures*].

20 For behold, I have workings in the spirit [*I have great cause for concern in my mind and soul*], which doth weary me even that all my joints are weak [*this is a very near eastern phrase—another internal testimony that the Book of Mormon is of ancient origins*], for those who are at Jerusalem; for had not the Lord been merciful, to show unto me concerning them, even as he had prophets of old, I should have perished also.

21 And he surely did show unto the prophets of old all things concerning them; and also he did show unto many concerning us; wherefore, it must needs be [*it is very important*] that we know concerning them for they are written upon the plates of brass.

At this point, Nephi explains to us why it was so important that he and his people had access to the scriptures written upon the brass plates. We will use **bold** for emphasis.

22 Now it came to pass that I, Nephi, did teach my brethren these things [*about the gathering of Israel spoken of in the previous verses*]; and it came to pass that I did read many things to them, which were engraven upon the plates of brass, that they might know concerning the doings of the Lord in other lands, among people of old.

23 And I did read many things unto them which were written in the books of Moses [*the first five books of the Old Testament, written by Moses, namely, Genesis, Exodus, Leviticus, Numbers, and Deuteronomy*]; but that I might more fully persuade them to believe in the Lord their Redeemer I did read unto them that which was written by the prophet Isaiah; for I did liken all scriptures unto us, that it might be for our profit and learning.

Above, in verse 23, we find a great key to understanding and applying the scriptures in our lives. We must "liken all scriptures unto us." We need to develop the ability to see applications in the scriptures which would parallel conditions or situations in our own lives. Then the scriptures come to life.

For instance, Nephi's brothers badly mistreat him, yet he then "frankly" forgives them (1 Nephi 7:21). It is probable that each of us has encountered, or yet will encounter, situations in which people treat us badly. If we are successful in "likening the scriptures unto us," we will frankly forgive too. We will thus free ourselves from the bondage of bitterness and hatred.

We will now repeat verse 23 again so that it flows into verse 24. There is a very important reason for doing so. It is that Nephi will now point out why it is so important for us to understand the words of Isaiah. He will give us two major reasons for studying Isaiah's writings.

23 And I did read many things unto them which were written in the books of Moses [*the first five books of the Old Testament, written by Moses, namely, Genesis, Exodus, Leviticus, Numbers, and Deuteronomy*]; but **that I might more fully persuade them to believe in the Lord their Redeemer** I did read unto them that which was written by the prophet Isaiah; for I did liken all scriptures unto us, that it might be for our profit and learning.

24 Wherefore I spake unto them, saying: Hear ye the words of the prophet, ye who are a remnant of the house of Israel, a branch who have been broken off; hear ye the words of the prophet, which were written unto all the house of Israel, and liken them unto yourselves, **that ye may have hope** as well as your brethren from whom ye have been broken off; for after this manner has the prophet written.

Just a few more thoughts and comments about understanding Isaiah before we go to the next two chapters of First Nephi. For many members of the Church, Isaiah is difficult to understand. Just knowing what Nephi said in verses 23 and 24, above, is motivation for a renewed effort at understanding Isaiah's writings. If we succeed, we will have a stronger understanding and testimony of Christ as our Redeemer. This, in turn, will give us wonderful "hope" that we will have a pleasant judgment day. The word "hope," as used in the Book of Mormon, is not the same as in common English usage today. In the Book of Mormon, "hope" means "assurance" (see Alma 57:11). Thus, in 2 Nephi 31:20,

Nephi speaks of "steadfastness in Christ" which brings "a perfect brightness of hope" which leads to eternal life (exaltation). There is nothing "wishy-washy" or "maybe-ish" about this type of hope.

Isaiah, then, when adequately understood, bears witness of Christ. As this witness is confirmed into our souls by the Holy Ghost, we can be strengthened to the point in our attitudes and behaviors that we can plan on eternal life. This planning on eternal life is not arrogant. It is not prideful, nor is it unwise. It is simply the true state of the humble followers of Christ. It is the "<u>perfect</u> (or complete) brightness of hope" to which we are invited by Isaiah.

If you will pay the price to study the next two chapters and accompanying notes carefully and prayerfully, you will begin to understand Isaiah. You will see that he uses rich symbolism. You will see that he paints pictures with words. We will use many notes within the verses to help you get the feel for Isaiah's writing style and message. Be aware that the Savior quoted Isaiah more than He quoted any other prophet. In fact, in 3 Nephi 23:1, Jesus commanded His people to study Isaiah. He said, "Ye ought to search these things (Isaiah's writings). Yea, a commandment I give unto you that ye search these things diligently; for great are the words of Isaiah."

One last suggestion before we get into these next two chapters. Nephi said that his people had difficulty understanding Isaiah because **"they know not concerning the manner of prophesying among the Jews"** (see 2 Nephi 25:1). This can make it difficult for us also. It may help to note a few characteristics of Isaiah's "manner of prophesying." For instance:

Isaiah uses much symbolism. He uses many phrases peculiar to his time and people. These are known as idioms.

<u>Example:</u>

"Thy neck is an iron sinew, and thy brow brass" (1 Nephi 20:4). This is, in effect, saying, "You have iron in your neck and you are thick-skulled." In other words, you are not humble; you won't bow your heads in humility before God, and it is hard to get anything into your heads.

Isaiah deliberately repeats for emphasis. Because of this writing and teaching technique, some people begin to think they have missed something, because they don't believe that Isaiah would constantly repeat things.

<u>Example:</u>

"Go ye forth of Babylon, flee ye from the Chaldeans (the inhabitants of southern Babylon)" (1 Nephi 20:20). In other words, flee evil!

Example:

Isaiah repeats the same concept in two different ways in the following: "The Lord hath called me from the womb; from the bowels of my mother hath he made mention of my name" (1 Nephi 21:1). In other words, Israel was foreordained to be God's covenant people.

Many of the things Isaiah teaches can have more than one meaning and more than one fulfillment. Therefore, it is usually unwise to limit what he teaches to only one specific meaning, unless the context warrants it.

Example:

"And they thirsted not; he led them through the deserts; he caused the waters to flow out of the rock for them; he clave the rock also and the waters gushed out" (1 Nephi 20:21). While the Lord literally led the children of Israel through the wilderness and literally caused water to flow out of the rock to quench their thirst and save their lives, there is much symbolic meaning also. For instance, He leads us through the wilderness of sin and wickedness. He provides "living water" (John 4:10) and quenches our spiritual thirst eternally.

FIRST NEPHI 20

Every verse in this chapter reads differently than in Isaiah, chapter 48, in the Bible. Nephi lived just one hundred years after Isaiah, which puts him much closer to the original records containing Isaiah's writings, including the brass plates. Nephi was also a prophet of God and, thus, could be inspired to make certain that his rendition of Isaiah's writings was correct. Also remember that Nephi's main reason for teaching Isaiah to his people as well as Laman, Lemuel, and the others, is to give them hope, not to condemn them (see 1 Nephi 19:23–24). We would do well to keep this major message of Isaiah in mind also, rather than seeing him only as a dismal prophet of doom as so many people do.

1 Hearken and hear this, O house of Jacob [*Jacob's children; in other words, the twelve tribes of Israel*], who are called by the name of Israel [*Jacob*], and are come forth out of the waters of Judah, or out of the waters of baptism [*who are my covenant people*], who swear [*make covenants*] by the name of the Lord [*just as we, today, make covenants in the name of Jesus Christ*], and make mention of [*pray to and talk about*] the God of Israel, yet they swear [*make covenants*] not in truth nor in righteousness [*the problem is that they claim to be the*

First Nephi 20

Lord's people but break covenants, don't live the gospel].

2 Nevertheless, they call themselves of the holy city [*claim to be the Lord's people*], but they do not stay themselves [*do not rely*] upon the God of Israel, who is the Lord of Hosts [*the God of all*]; yea, the Lord of Hosts is his name.

> In the next several verses, Isaiah reminds Israel that there is no lack of obvious evidence that the true God exists.

3 Behold, I [*the Lord*] have declared the former things [*prophecies*] from the beginning [*so you would have plenty of evidence that I exist*]; and they [*prophecies*] went forth out of my mouth [*through the prophets*], and I showed [*fulfilled*] them. I did show them suddenly [*when you did not expect them to take place, so you can know I really am your God, and your idols are false; see Isaiah 42:9*].

> Next, the Lord tells His covenant people that they are prideful and stubborn.

4 And I [*the Lord*] did it [*gave and fulfilled prophecies*] because I knew that thou art obstinate [*prideful, stubborn*], and thy neck is an iron sinew [*your necks are as if they have iron in them; you are not humble, won't bend your neck in humility*], and thy brow brass [*thick-headed; it is hard to get anything through your thick skulls*];

> Next, through Isaiah, the Lord tells covenant Israel that from the very beginning He has placed obvious evidence that He exists in the form of prophecies of the future. He has then fulfilled these prophecies so that His people have every chance of gaining and keeping testimonies of His existence and love and concern for them. This is similar to the prophecies of the last days, or signs of the times, which are being fulfilled all around us now.

5 And I have even from the beginning declared to thee [*prophesied things*]; before it [*the prophesied events*] came to pass I showed them thee [*I prophesied them to you*]; and I showed them for fear lest thou shouldst say—mine idol hath done them, and my graven image, and my molten image hath commanded them [*I have shown you my power via prophecies, so you couldn't claim your idols have power*].

6 Thou hast seen and heard all this [*all this obvious evidence that I exist*]; and will ye not declare [*acknowledge*]

them? And that I have showed thee new things [*things you couldn't possibly have known in advance*] from this time, even hidden things, and thou didst not know them [*didn't pay attention; didn't acknowledge them*].

7 They are created now [*the prophesied events are taking place now*], and not from the beginning [*you couldn't have guessed they were going to happen back then when the prophecies were given*], even before the day when thou heardest them not [*back then when there was no clue that the prophesied events would take place*] they were declared unto thee [*I told you in advance*], lest thou shouldst say—Behold I knew them.

8 Yea, and thou heardest not [*you ignored the prophecies*]; yea, thou knewest not [*you would not acknowledge them*]; yea, from that time thine ear was not opened [*you refused to listen*]; for I knew that thou wouldst deal very treacherously, and wast called a transgressor from the womb [*I've had trouble with you Israelites right from the start!*].

Next, the Lord reminds all of us that if it were not for His mercy, Israel would have been cut off long ago.

9 Nevertheless, for my name's sake [*I, the Lord, have a reputation of being merciful to uphold*] will I defer mine anger, and for my praise [*the German Bible, Martin Luther edition: glory, honor; reputation*] will I refrain from thee, that I cut thee not off [*I'll not destroy you completely*].

10 For, behold, I [*the Lord*] have refined thee [*Israel*], I have chosen thee [*German: I will make you*] in the furnace of affliction [*I will purify you in the refiner's fire*].

"The refiner's fire" calls up the image of a skillful craftsman carefully applying fire to the ore in order to remove all the impurities and thus produce pure gold.

Next, in verse 11, we are reminded that the Lord doesn't help us only because it is His calling as the Redeemer and Savior. Rather, He helps us and works patiently with us because He loves us.

11 For mine own sake [*because I love you; see verse 14*], yea, for mine own sake [*because I want to*] will I do this [*refine and purify you in the furnace of affliction*], for I will not suffer [*allow*] my name to be polluted [*German:*

First Nephi 20

lest my name be slandered for not keeping my promises to Israel], and I will not give my glory unto another [*I will remain true to you; see Jeremiah 3:14. By the way, this can be good advice for marriage partners*].

The main theme of verses 12–17 is that Israel is called and foreordained to serve.

12 Hearken unto me, O Jacob, and Israel my called [*you have a calling; see Abr. 2:9–11*], for I am he [*Christ*]; I am the first, and I am also the last [*I am your Savior; Jesus was there at the creation and will be there at final judgment*].

13 Mine hand hath also laid the foundation of the earth [*I am the Creator*], and my right hand [*covenant hand; hand of power*] hath spanned the heavens [*spread out; created the skies*]. I call unto them [*Israel in verses 12 and 14*] and they stand up together [*let them, Israel, all stand up and listen; this goes with the first part of verse 14*].

14 All ye, assemble yourselves, and hear; who among them [*perhaps referring to Israel's idols; see verse 5*] hath declared these things [*prophecies; see verses 3, 6, etc.*] unto them [*Israel*]? The Lord hath loved him [*Israel*]; yea, and he [*the Lord*] will fulfill his word which he hath declared by them [*the prophets*]; and he will do his pleasure on Babylon, and his arm [*symbolic of power*] shall come upon the Chaldeans [*southern Babylon; Babylon will eventually be destroyed, just as has been prophesied*].

15 Also, saith the Lord; I the Lord, yea, I have spoken; yea, I have called him [*Israel*] to declare [*Israel has a job to do*], I have brought him, and he shall make his way prosperous [*God will help; could also mean that Heavenly Father called Christ to prophesy; also that Christ called Isaiah to prophesy*].

Verse 15, above, is an example of where Isaiah's writing can have more than one meaning.

16 Come ye [*Israel*] near unto me; I have not spoken in secret [*I have been very open about the gospel, etc.*]; from the beginning, from the time that it was declared have I spoken; and the Lord God, and his Spirit, hath sent me [*the Father sent Christ; or perhaps this means that Christ sent Isaiah*].

17 And thus saith the Lord, thy Redeemer [*Christ*], the Holy One of Israel; I have sent him [*Israel; see verses 12 and 19; or, dualistically, this could refer to*

Isaiah], the Lord thy God who teacheth thee to profit [*German: for your profit, benefit*], who leadeth thee by the way thou shouldst go, hath done it.

18 O that thou hadst hearkened to my commandments [*can apply directly to Laman and Lemuel; no doubt this is one reason Nephi is quoting Isaiah to them*]—then had thy peace been as a river [*you could have had peace flowing constantly into your lives*], and thy righteousness as the waves of the sea [*steady, constant*].

> Next, Isaiah says, in effect, that Israel has the potential to become a truly large and great nation, if they would just make and keep covenants with God. As it is, though, Isaiah goes into what can be termed "future perfect tense" wherein he treats the future as if it has already happened and prophetically tells the Israelites that they could have become a great nation, if only. . . .

19 Thy [*Israel's*] seed [*posterity*] also had been [*would have been*] as the sand; the offspring of thy bowels [*your descendants*] like the gravel [*grains of sand*] thereof; his [*Israel's*] name should not [*would not*] have been cut off nor destroyed from before me [*Israel could have had it very good, and could have avoided such great destruction*].

20 Go ye forth of Babylon [*flee wickedness; stop being wicked*], flee ye from the Chaldeans [*wickedness; Chaldeans were residents of southern Babylon*], with a voice of singing [*be happy about being righteous*] declare ye, tell this, utter to the end of the earth; say ye: The Lord hath redeemed his servant Jacob [*Israel can be saved—including Laman and Lemuel—if they will repent*].

> "Babylon," as used in verse 20, above, is very symbolic. Anciently, it was an actual country and city, basically where Iraq is today. Isaiah as well as many other prophets use Babylon to symbolize wickedness and to represent Satan's kingdom. The imagery is fascinating, because Babylon was a fearsome enemy of Israel.
>
> The huge city of Babylon was so enormous that it took 56 miles of walls to surround and protect it. The walls were 335 feet high and 85 feet wide (see Bible Dictionary, page 618). It was a center of wickedness, and thus in many scriptures it came to symbolize general wickedness and the devil's domain.
>
> In fact, part of the imagery of Babylon is that it seemed indestructible, just as Satan's kingdom and domain on earth

seems powerful and indestructible. However, Babylon fell in 538 B.C. and was never rebuilt, just as Satan's kingdom will eventually fall, and never be rebuilt as he and his evil followers are cast into outer darkness (see D&C 1:16; 88:111–15).

21 And they thirsted not; he led them through the deserts; he caused the waters to flow out of the rock for them; he clave the rock also and the waters gushed out [*just look what the Lord can do for those who trust in him!*].

22 And notwithstanding [*even though*] he hath done all this, and greater also, there is no peace, saith the Lord, unto the wicked [*a major message for Laman and Lemuel and all of us*].

FIRST NEPHI 21

Isaiah continues his prophecy about the Messiah and of the gathering of Israel in the last days. The prophecy includes the fact that the governments of many nations will assist in this gathering. In the last days, Israel will finally do the work she was originally called to do but failed to accomplish.

This particular chapter contains one of my personal favorite verses, verse 16, which contains beautiful Atonement symbolism.

Beginning with verse 1, we will be taught about the foreordination of covenant Israel and the responsibilities we have as the Lord's chosen people. Remember that "chosen" includes the concept that we are chosen to carry whatever burdens are necessary in order to spread the gospel and the priesthood throughout the earth.

Isaiah sets the stage for this prophecy by having us think of Israel as a person who is thinking about her past and feels like she has been a failure as far as her calling and mission from the Lord is concerned. Then she is startled by her success in the last days. Note that Isaiah says the same thing twice in a row, using different words, several times in this chapter. In verse 1, for example, he says "Listen, O isles unto me; and hearken . . ." As previously mentioned in this study guide, this was typical repetition for emphasis in biblical culture.

1 And again: Hearken, O ye house of Israel, all ye that are broken off and are driven out [*scattered; Isaiah is speaking prophetically to scattered Israel*] because of the wickedness of the pastors [*leaders and teachers*] of my people; yea, all ye that are broken off,

that are scattered abroad, who are of my people, O house of Israel. Listen, O isles [*faraway nations and lands, including those across the sea*], unto me [*Israel; see verse 3*], and hearken ye people from far; the Lord hath called me [*Israel*] from the womb [*foreordination*]; from the bowels of my mother hath he [*the Lord*] made mention of my name [*Israel has had a job to do since the beginning*].

2 And he hath made my mouth like a sharp sword [*Israel is to spread the gospel, which is hard on the wicked, but enables the righteous to cut through falsehood*]; in the shadow [*shade; protection*] of his hand hath he hid me, and made me a polished shaft [*an effective servant of the Lord, such as Joseph Smith, Isaiah, or any faithful Israelite*]; in his quiver hath he hid me;

3 And said unto me [*Israel*]: Thou art my servant, O Israel, in whom I will be glorified [*Israel will yet fulfill its stewardship*].

In verses 4–12 and beyond, Isaiah portrays the loneliness of Israel waiting for the Restoration. It is almost as if Isaiah were writing a stage play with one lone character on the stage, representing Israel, speaking in a sad, lonely, remorseful voice and recounting the missed and seemingly lost opportunities to fulfill her mission and God-given destiny.

4 Then I [*Israel*] said, I have labored in vain [*I haven't been a very good servant; I have wasted my efforts*], I have spent my strength for naught [*for nothing*] and in vain [*in false religions and riotous living*]; surely my judgment is with the Lord, and my work with my God [*in other words, my fate rests with the Lord; it is up to God what He wants to do with me now that I have failed Him*].

5 And now, saith the Lord—that formed me from the womb [*who foreordained me*] that I [*especially Ephraim*] should be his servant, to bring Jacob again to him—though Israel be not gathered, yet shall I be glorious in the eyes of the Lord [*if I do my best, I'll be okay, even if people reject my message*], and my God shall be my strength.

Next, in this "drama," the Lord, in effect, tells Israel that it is too easy of a calling to merely work at bringing scattered Israel back to God. Israel needs to have something more challenging to do, namely, to bring the gospel to all peoples of the earth.

6 And he [*the Lord*] said: It is a light thing [*German: not enough*] that thou [*Israel*] shouldst be my

First Nephi 21

servant to raise up [*restore the gospel to*] the tribes of Jacob, and to restore the preserved [*remnant*] of Israel [*the job of the Church today*]. I will also give thee for [*another assignment, namely to be*] a light to the Gentiles [*quite a prophecy in Isaiah's day when almost any nation that wanted to could walk all over Israel*], that thou mayest be my salvation unto the ends of the earth [*bring the gospel to everyone on earth*].

Abraham 2:9–11 clearly teaches this responsibility which Israel has, to bring the gospel and the priesthood blessings to all the earth. In fact, in your patriarchal blessing, your lineage is declared. This is a most important part of your blessing because it reminds you of your sacred duty to help bring the gospel to all the world throughout your life.

Next, Isaiah prophesies that the day will come when Israel will become a powerful force in the world, whereas, in the past, Israel was walked on almost at will by nation after nation.

7 Thus saith the Lord, the Redeemer of Israel [*Christ*], his [*Israel's*] Holy One, to him [*Israel*] whom man despiseth, to him whom the nation abhorreth [*German: to the nation abhorred by others*], to servant of rulers [*for much of past history, Israel has been servants and slaves to many nations*]: Kings shall see and arise [*out of respect for Israel*], princes [*leaders of nations*] also shall worship, because of the Lord that is faithful [*because the Lord will keep His promises to you*].

8 Thus saith the Lord: In an acceptable time [*when the time is right, beginning with the Restoration and Joseph Smith*] have I heard thee [*I will have answered your cries for help*], O isles of the sea [*far continents beyond Asia and Africa, such as America, etc.*], and in a day of salvation have I helped thee; and I will preserve thee, and give thee my servant [*prophets, including Joseph Smith*] for a covenant of the people, to establish the earth [*to reestablish the gospel upon the earth*], to cause to inherit the desolate heritages [*to restore Israel to the lands of her inheritance. In other words, the gathering will take place; see verse 19*];

9 That thou mayest say to the prisoners [*the living and the dead in spiritual darkness*]: Go forth [*go free from spiritual bondage*]; to them that sit in darkness: Show yourselves [*come out of prison*]. They shall feed

in the ways [*their "Shepherd," Christ, will lead them to the gospel path*], and their pastures shall be in all high places [*they will partake of the best, the highest, the gospel of Christ*].

10 They shall not hunger nor thirst [*for the true gospel any more, because they will have it*], neither shall the heat nor the sun smite them; for he that hath mercy on them shall lead them, even by the springs of water [*symbolic of living water; see John 4:10*] shall he guide them [*benefits of accepting and living the gospel*].

> As mentioned at the beginning of chapter 20, Isaiah is very thorough. He repeats, then repeats the message, and then repeats it again, and yet again. In these verses, we are seeing this method employed by Isaiah to emphasize the wonderful benefits of the restored gospel and following Christ to the "high places" where the best "pasture" is to be found, namely, eternal exaltation.

11 And I will make all my mountains [*"mountains" are often symbolic of temples*] a way [*a means of arriving at a destination*], and my highways shall be exalted [*I will prepare "gospel highways" in all parts of the world, through the restoration of the gospel and the gathering in the last days, which will lead the faithful Saints to exaltation*].

12 And then [*in the days of gathering*], O house of Israel, behold, these [*Israel*] shall come from far; and lo, these from the north and from the west; and these from the land of Sinim [*Strong's Exhaustive Bible Concordance says this might refer to inhabitants of southern China; see also Smith's Bible Dictionary, under "Sinim"*].

13 Sing, O heavens; and be joyful, O earth; for the feet of those who are in the east shall be established; and break forth into singing, O mountains; for they shall be smitten no more; for the Lord hath comforted his people [*speaking prophetically of the future, as if it has already happened*], and will have mercy upon his afflicted [*the Lord will eventually redeem Israel*].

> Remember, after verse 3, above, we suggested that verses 4–12 (and beyond) could be like a stage play, with Israel as the sole actor or actress, lamenting her failure to do what the Lord called her to do. In verse 14, next, Israel in effect brushes off the prophetic encouragement given in verse 13.

14 But, behold, Zion [*Israel*] hath said: The Lord hath forsaken

First Nephi 21

me, and my Lord hath forgotten me [*wicked Israel's complaint*]—but he will show that he hath not.

15 For can a woman forget her sucking [*nursing*] child, that she should not have compassion on the son of her womb? Yea, they may forget [*yes, even that happens among mortals*], yet will I not forget thee, O house of Israel [*a promise! I will keep my promise to restore the gospel and to gather Israel again*].

> Verse 16, next, contains some of the most beautiful Atonement symbolism in scripture. Just as a workman's hands bear witness of his work, such as a carpenter with callouses and blisters, so shall the nail prints in the Savior's hands bear witness of His work for us.

16 Behold, I have graven thee upon the palms of my hands [*each of us is "engraved" upon the Savior's hands where the nails pierced His flesh; in other words, the wounds on the palms of His hands bear witness of His work for us*]; thy walls are continually before me [*"walls" would represent a person's house; in other words, I know where you live and always know what help you need*].

> Next, Isaiah prophesies that things will be turned around in the last days such that the enemies of Israel, who once distressed her, will now flee from her.

17 Thy children shall make haste against thy destroyers [*your descendants will finally gain the upper hand against your enemies*]; and they that made thee waste shall go forth of thee [*will flee from you, the tables will be turned in the last days*].

18 Lift up thine eyes [*let me show you—complaining Israel in verse 14—the future*] round about and behold; all these [*righteous, faithful descendants in the last days*] gather themselves together [*You thought you were going to be wiped out completely, but look at all your descendants in the future!*], and they shall come to thee. And as I live [*the most serious and solemn promise in Hebrew culture*], saith the Lord, thou shalt surely clothe thee with them all, as with an ornament, and bind them on even as a bride [*a bride puts on her finest clothing for the occasion; Israel will have her finest descendants in the last days*].

19 For thy waste and thy desolate places, and the land of thy destruction [*you've been trodden down for centuries*], shall even now be too narrow by

reason of the inhabitants [*you will have so many descendants you'll seem to be running out of room; latter-day gathering of Israel*]; and they [*your former enemies*] that swallowed thee up shall be far away.

20 The children [*converts to the true gospel*] whom thou shalt have, after thou hast lost the first [*via apostasy, war, etc.*], shall again in thine ears say: The place is too strait for me [*there's not enough room for us all*]; give place to me that I may dwell.

> The fulfillment of the above prophecy that, in the last days, there will be a great increase in faithful members of the Church is very apparent in our day. Just consider the vast building program of the Church as we build temples and chapels to try to keep up with the increase.

21 Then [*in the last days*] shalt thou [*Israel*] say in thine heart: Who hath begotten me these [*where in the world did all these Israelites come from?*], seeing I have lost my children, and am desolate, a captive, and removing to and fro [*scattered*]? And who hath brought up these? Behold, I was left alone [*I thought I was finished off, done for*]; these, where have they been?

I hope you are beginning to appreciate Isaiah's inspired ability to create pictures and feelings, indeed drama, with words as he teaches. Perhaps you have now felt Israel's discouragement and maybe even caught a slight touch of self-pity on her part as Isaiah has portrayed her in this chapter. Isaiah thus skillfully set the stage for her astonishment at the fulfillment of the Lord's promises to her in the last days. This could be symbolic of skeptics in all ages of the world who are bound to be caught off guard as the prophesied miracles of gathering take place.

Next, the Lord answers Israel's question, "Where did all these come from?" He tells us how He will accomplish this great gathering of Israel in the last days.

22 Thus saith the Lord God: Behold, I will lift up mine hand [*I will signal*] to the Gentiles, and set up my standard [*the Church, true gospel of Christ*] to the people; and they [*the Gentiles*] shall bring thy sons in their arms, and thy daughters shall be carried upon their shoulders [*Gentile nations will help gather Israel*].

23 And kings shall be thy nursing fathers, and their queens thy nursing mothers [*example: Great Britain was very influential in establishing a homeland for the Jews in Palestine, after World War I, and helped sponsor the establishment of the Nation*

of Israel, in the United Nations in 1948]; they [*the leaders of nations*] shall bow down to thee with their face towards the earth, and lick up the dust of thy feet [*the tables will be turned in the last days*]; and thou shalt know that I am the Lord; for they shall not be ashamed that wait for [*trust in*] me.

> Just a bit more about the fulfillment of the marvelous prophecy in verse 23, above. In 1830, when the Church was officially organized, the Jewish population in the Holy Land was about seven thousand. Now, it is over three million! Next, in verse 24, Isaiah portrays Israel as asking, in effect, "How could we, who have virtually always been victims (prey) of such powerful enemies, ever be rescued from them and set free?" The Lord will answer their question in verse 25.

24 For shall the prey [*Israel*] be taken from the mighty [*powerful enemies*], or the lawful [*the Lord's covenant people*] captives delivered [*be set free*]?

25 But thus saith the Lord, even the captives [*Israel*] of the mighty [*powerful enemies*] shall be taken away [*rescued*], and the prey [*victims*] of the terrible [*tyrants*] shall be delivered [*set free*]; for I [*the Lord*] will contend with him that contendeth with thee [*Israel*], and I will save thy children [*the answer to Israel's question in verse 24 is that the Lord will rescue them and set them free*].

26 And I will feed them [*Israel's enemies*] that oppress thee with their own flesh; they shall be drunken [*out of control*] with their own blood as with sweet wine [*your enemies will turn against each other and destroy themselves; compare with Mormon 4:5*]; and all flesh shall know that I, the Lord, am thy Savior and thy Redeemer, the Mighty One of Jacob.

FIRST NEPHI 22

One of the greatest blessings of having the Book of Mormon is that Nephi explains many chapters of Isaiah for us. This gives us a great advantage over all other people on earth as far as understanding Isaiah is concerned. In this case, Nephi will explain what Isaiah said in 1 Nephi, chapters 20–21. Having Nephi as our teacher will greatly increase our ability to understand other chapters of Isaiah also.

By the way, since the brass plates were likely produced approximately one hundred years (or less) after Isaiah lived, the writings of

Isaiah on the plates would be a much more original source than the earliest manuscripts for the Bible. In fact, the brass plates even had three verses which our Bible doesn't have. These three verses appear as 1 Nephi 22:15–17. Nephi quotes them as he explains this segment of Isaiah.

As we continue now, Nephi's brethren will ask good questions about understanding Isaiah. Nephi's answers will be helpful to us too. We will use **bold** occasionally for teaching purposes.

1 AND now it came to pass that after I, Nephi, had read these things [*some of Isaiah's writings*] which were engraven upon the plates of brass, my brethren came unto me and said unto me: [*Question:*] **What meaneth these things which ye have read?** [*Question:*] Behold, **are they to be understood according to things which are spiritual, which shall come to pass according to the spirit and not the flesh** [*are they spiritual or literal*]?

2 And I, Nephi, said unto them: Behold they were manifest unto the prophet by the voice of the Spirit; for by the Spirit are all things made known unto the prophets, which shall come upon the children of men according to the flesh [*during mortality*].

3 Wherefore, [*Answer:*] **the things of which I have read are things pertaining to things both temporal and spiritual** [*they are things which will literally happen to the house of Israel, as well as things with spiritual meanings also*]; for it appears that **the house of Israel** [*the descendants of Abraham, Isaac, and Jacob*], sooner or later, **will be scattered upon all the face of the earth**, and also among all nations.

4 And behold, there are many who are already lost from the knowledge of those who are at Jerusalem [*such as the ten lost tribes who were carried away about 721 B.C.*]. Yea, the more part [*the majority*] of all the tribes have been led away; and they are scattered to and fro upon the isles of the sea [*all over the world*]; and whither they are none of us knoweth, save that we know that they have been led away.

5 And since they have been led away, these things [*the words of Isaiah*] have been prophesied concerning them, and also concerning all those who shall hereafter be scattered and be confounded [*confused; stopped in their progression*], because of the Holy One of Israel; for against him [*Christ*] will they harden their hearts; wherefore, they [*Israel*]

First Nephi 22

shall be scattered among all nations and shall be hated of all men [*particularly the Jews; see 1 Nephi 19:13–14*].

6 Nevertheless, after they [*scattered Israel*] shall be nursed [*helped to gather*] by the Gentiles, and the Lord has lifted up his hand upon the Gentiles [*has blessed them with the restored gospel*] and set them up for a standard [*after the gospel has been restored among the Gentiles through the Prophet Joseph Smith*], and their [*Israel's*] children [*descendants*] have been carried in their [*the Gentiles*] arms, and their daughters [*descendants*] have been carried upon their [*the Gentiles*] shoulders, behold **these things of which are spoken are temporal** [*literal; they will actually happen, physically, to Israel*]; for thus are the covenants of the Lord with our fathers [*ancestors*]; and it meaneth us [*the Lamanites*] in the days to come, and also all our brethren who are of the house of Israel. [*In other words, all who are willing will be gathered in to God.*]

7 And it meaneth that the time cometh that after all the house of Israel have been scattered and confounded, that the Lord God will raise up a mighty nation [*the United States of America*] among the Gentiles, yea, even upon the face of this land [*America*]; and by them [*the Gentiles who came from Europe, etc. and settled America*] shall our seed [*the Lamanites*] be scattered.

> Next, Nephi will explain and apply Isaiah's prophecy specifically to the Lamanites.

8 And after our seed is scattered the Lord God will proceed to do a marvelous work among the Gentiles [*the restoration of the gospel through Joseph Smith*], which shall be of great worth unto our seed [*the Lamanites*]; wherefore, it is likened unto their being nourished by the Gentiles [*the members of the Church*] and being carried in their arms and upon their shoulders.

9 And it [*the restored gospel*] shall also be of worth unto the Gentiles; and not only unto the Gentiles but unto all the house of Israel, unto the making known of the covenants of the Father of heaven unto Abraham, saying: In thy seed shall all the kindreds of the earth be blessed.

> Remember, as noted previously, the word "Gentiles" has many different meanings, all of which are context sensitive. In verses 8 and 9, above, it means people who have the blood of Israel in them, but whose ancestors did not specifically come from the Holy Land in recent generations

(see Bible Dictionary, p. 679, under Gentiles).

10 And I would, my brethren, that ye should know that all the kindreds [*all peoples*] of the earth cannot be blessed unless he shall make bare his arm [*show forth His power*] in the eyes of the nations. [*In other words, it will take obvious intervention by God to cause the prophesied gathering to take place.*]

11 Wherefore [*therefore*], the Lord God will proceed to make bare his arm in the eyes of all the nations, in bringing about his covenants and his gospel unto those who are of the house of Israel.

> While the strict literal definition of Israel is anyone who has the blood of Abraham, Isaac, Jacob (Israel), and the twelve tribes of Israel in their veins, in our day virtually all people have the blood of Israel because of the widespread scattering of Israel to all the earth over thousands of years.
>
> Therefore, all who join the Church are considered to be covenant Israel with all the responsibilities and blessings of descendants of Abraham, Isaac, and Jacob.

12 Wherefore, he will bring them again out of captivity [*literal and spiritual bondage*], and they shall be gathered together to the lands [*not just one land, rather many lands*] of their inheritance; and they shall be brought out of obscurity and out of darkness; and they shall know that the Lord is their Savior and their Redeemer, the Mighty One of Israel.

13 And the blood of that great and abominable church, which is the whore of all the earth [*Satan's kingdom, including all the wicked who follow his evil ways; see verse 22*], shall turn upon their own heads; for they shall war among themselves, and the sword of their own hands shall fall upon their own heads, and they shall be drunken with their own blood. [*A description of conditions among the wicked, especially in the last days before the Second Coming.*]

14 And every nation which shall war against thee, O house of Israel, shall be turned one against another [*this is a very specific prophecy, which we are watching now as it proceeds into fulfillment*], and they shall fall into the pit which they digged to ensnare the people of the Lord. And all that fight against Zion shall be destroyed, and that great whore [*Satan's kingdom; the wicked*], who hath perverted [*polluted and twisted to satisfy their own lusts*] the right ways of the Lord, yea, that great and abominable church

First Nephi 22

[*the church of the devil; see 1 Nephi 14:10*], shall tumble to the dust and great shall be the fall of it.

> In verses 15–17, next, it appears that Nephi is quoting three verses from Isaiah's writings which are found nowhere else in scripture. We understand that these verses were on the brass plates, but were left out of the Bible somewhere along the way. They seem to fit at the end of 1 Nephi, chapter 21. They would fit between Isaiah, chapter 49 and Isaiah, chapter 50 in the Bible. (See *Old Testament Student Manual, 1 Kings through Malachi*, p. 194.)
>
> These three verses project ahead to the Second Coming of the Savior and scenes immediately preceding it.

15 For behold, saith the prophet [*Isaiah*], the time cometh speedily that Satan shall have no more power over the hearts of the children of men; for the day soon cometh that all the proud and they who do wickedly shall be as stubble; and the day cometh that they must be burned. [*They will be burned by the glory of the coming Christ; see D&C 5:19 plus 2 Nephi 12:10, 19, 21.*]

16 For the time soon cometh that the fulness of the wrath of God shall be poured out upon all the children of men [*all wicked people*]; for he will not suffer [*allow*] that the wicked shall destroy the righteous.

17 Wherefore, he will preserve the righteous by his power, even if it so be that the fulness of his wrath must come, and the righteous be preserved, even unto the destruction of their enemies by fire. Wherefore, the righteous need not fear [*a major message*]; for thus saith the prophet, they shall be saved, even if it so be as by fire.

> Next, Nephi will explain what he just quoted from Isaiah in verses 15–17, above. Remember, he is still answering the questions his brethren asked in verse 1 as to which prophecies of Isaiah are literal and which ones are symbolic or spiritual.

18 Behold, my brethren, I say unto you, that these things must shortly come [*will occur shortly after the restoration of the gospel*]; yea, even blood, and fire, and vapor of smoke must come [*these are signs of the times in the last days*]; and it must needs be upon the face of this earth [*it will literally happen upon the earth*]; and it cometh unto men according to the flesh [*it will literally happen to people*] if it so be that they will harden their hearts against the Holy One of Israel [*Christ*].

19 For behold, the righteous shall not perish; for the time surely must come that all they who fight against Zion shall be cut off.

20 And the Lord will surely prepare a way for his people, unto the fulfilling of the words of Moses, which he spake, saying: A prophet [*Christ*] shall the Lord your God raise up unto you, like unto me [*Moses*]; him shall ye hear in all things whatsoever he shall say unto you. And it shall come to pass that all those who will not hear that prophet [*Christ*] shall be cut off from among the people [*will be separated from the people of the Lord*].

21 And now I, Nephi, declare unto you, that this prophet of whom Moses spake was the Holy One of Israel [*the Savior*]; wherefore, he [*Christ*] shall execute [*carry out*] judgment in righteousness.

22 And the righteous need not fear, for they are those who shall not be confounded [*will not be stopped in their progress toward exaltation*]. But it is the kingdom of the devil [*the "church of the devil" in 1 Nephi 14:10*], which shall be built up among the children of men [*which will become powerful upon the earth*], which kingdom is established among them which are in the flesh. [*In other words, it is literal that Satan will gain tremendous power among the wicked in the last days upon the earth.*]

Nephi mentioned that the righteous do not need to fear, three times in the above verses (verses 17, 19, and 22). This indeed is a major message of Isaiah, Nephi, and the Savior.

Nephi will now describe motives of wicked people and organizations. We would do well to avoid such motives in our own thinking and behaviors. We will use **bold** for emphasis.

23 For the time speedily shall come that all churches [*organizations, whether they be religious, political, secret combinations, or whatever*] which are built up **to get gain**, and all those who are built up **to get power** over the flesh [*to exercise unrighteous dominion over people*], and those who are built up **to become popular in the eyes of the world**, and those who **seek the lusts of the flesh** and the **things of the world**, and to do all manner of iniquity; yea, in fine [*in summary*], all those who belong to the kingdom of the devil are they who need fear, and tremble, and quake; they are those who must [*because of the law of justice*] be brought low in the dust; they are those who must be consumed as stubble [*who will be burned like dry grain stalks*]; and this

First Nephi 22

is according to the words of the prophet [*Isaiah*].

Next, Nephi describes conditions of the world during the Millennium.

24 And the time cometh speedily that the righteous must be led up as calves of the stall [*will have peace and protection*], and the Holy One of Israel must reign in dominion, and might, and power, and great glory [*Christ will rule and reign on earth; Millennium*].

25 And he gathereth his children from the four quarters of the earth [*those who are willing to follow Christ will be gathered from throughout the earth*]; and he numbereth his sheep [*His faithful followers*], and they know him; and there shall be one fold and one shepherd; and he shall feed his sheep, and in him they shall find pasture.

26 And because of the righteousness of his people, Satan has no power; wherefore, he cannot be loosed for the space of many years [*a thousand years*]; for he hath no power over the hearts of the people, for they dwell in righteousness, and the Holy One of Israel reigneth.

Some people consider that the "righteousness of his people" (verse 26, above) during the Millennium will be the sole means of limiting Satan's power during the Millennium. This is not the case. D&C 101:28 teaches that Satan will not even have the power to tempt during the Millennium. While we can certainly limit his power over us by not yielding to his temptations, we know we cannot stop him from tempting. Christ is the only one who can stop him completely. And He will do so when He comes again. This doctrine is clearly taught in the 1981 Institute of Religion *Doctrine and Covenants Student Manual*, page 89, as follows:

"In speaking of the millennial era, Nephi said that 'because of the righteousness of his—the Lord's—people, Satan has no power; wherefore, he cannot be loosed for the space of many years; for he hath no power over the hearts of the people, for they dwell in righteousness, and the Holy One of Israel reigneth' (1 Nephi 22:26).

"President Joseph Fielding Smith taught concerning the binding of Satan: 'There are many among us who teach that the binding of Satan will be merely the binding which those dwelling on the earth will place upon him by their refusal to hear his enticings. This is not so. He will not have the privilege during that period of time to tempt any man (D&C 101:28)'" (Smith, *Church History and Modern Revelation*, 1:192).

"These two statements at first may seem to be at variance, but in reality they are not. It is true that the result of the righteousness of the Saints is that Satan cannot exert power over them. The restrictions that will come upon Satan will be a result of two important actions by the Lord: (1) he will destroy telestial wickedness from the earth at his second coming; and (2) as a reward for heeding his counsels, the Lord will pour out his Spirit upon the righteous who remain to the extent that Satan's power will be overwhelmed.

"Thus, Satan will not have the power to tempt or negatively influence the Lord's people. Both the righteousness of the Saints and the operation of the Lord's power are necessary to bind Satan: if the Saints do not give heed to God's word, he will not impart of his Spirit; and if the Lord's influence is not brought to bear to aid the Saints, they, on their own power, cannot withstand the force of the adversary" (*Doctrine and Covenants Student Manual*, p. 89).

27 And now behold, I, Nephi, say unto you that all these things must come according to the flesh [*all these things will be literally fulfilled*].

28 But, behold, all nations, kindreds, tongues, and people shall dwell safely in the Holy One of Israel if it so be that they will repent. [*The peace and safety brought by the Atonement of Christ and His gospel are available to all people, regardless of their lineage or any other factors.*]

Ultimately, whether in this life or in the spirit world that follows, all will receive a completely fair set of opportunities to use their agency to follow Christ (see D&C 138). Therefore, all

"shall dwell safely in the Holy One of Israel" if they so choose (see verse 28, above).

29 And now I, Nephi, make an end; for I durst not speak further as yet concerning these things [*this was all that I dared to say to my brethren at this time*].

30 Wherefore, my brethren, I would that ye should consider that the things [*particularly Isaiah*] which have been written upon the plates of brass are true; and they testify that a man must be obedient to the commandments of God.

31 Wherefore, ye need not suppose that I and my father are the only ones that have testified, and also taught them. [*Isaiah and others have taught them too.*] Wherefore, if ye shall be obedient to the commandments, and endure to the end, ye shall be saved at the last day. And thus it is. Amen.

THE SECOND BOOK OF NEPHI

SECOND NEPHI 1

In chapters 1–3, Lehi will give his final messages to his people. He will teach, review, prophesy, and bless his posterity.

1 AND now it came to pass that after I, Nephi, had made an end of teaching my brethren, our father, Lehi, also spake many things unto them, and rehearsed unto them, how great things the Lord had done for them in bringing them out of the land of Jerusalem.

2 And he spake unto them concerning their rebellions upon the waters, and the mercies of God in sparing their lives, that they were not swallowed up in the sea.

3 And he also spake unto them concerning the land of promise, which they had obtained—how merciful the Lord had been in warning us that we should flee out of the land of Jerusalem.

> In verses 1–3, above, Lehi tries again to strengthen the testimonies of his rebellious sons by reminding them of the mercies of the Lord. He encourages them to remember these things. Remembering past blessings from the Lord is a very powerful way to strengthen our testimonies and keep us faithful through trying times in our lives.

4 For, behold, said he, I have seen a vision, in which I know that Jerusalem is destroyed; and had we remained in Jerusalem we should [*would*] also have perished.

5 But, said he, notwithstanding [*in spite of*] our afflictions, we have obtained a land of promise, a land which is choice above all other lands [*literal; also symbolic of attaining heaven, despite hardships and trials during our lives on earth*]; a land which the Lord God hath covenanted with me should be a land for the inheritance of my seed [*descendants*]. Yea, the Lord hath covenanted this land unto me, and to my children forever, and also all those who should be led out of other countries by the hand of the Lord.

> Symbolism: We must be led by the Lord in order to enter celestial glory; covenants are required for entrance into the celestial kingdom—except for children who die before the age of accountability (see D&C 137:10), and the intellectually handicapped (see D&C 29:50).

6 Wherefore, I, Lehi, prophesy according to the workings of the Spirit which is in me, that there shall none come into this land save they shall be brought by the hand of the Lord.

> This (verse 6, above) is a fascinating prophecy. It is significant to realize that the New World remained undiscovered for all practical purposes, for many centuries until Columbus, and this despite the fact that numerous adventurers such as Vikings had come temporarily. It is a testimony that the Lord held others back from settling the Americas until the time was right for it to be discovered to the whole world (see verse 8, below).

> In verse 7, next, we find the formula for retaining freedom and liberty in this land. It is also a formula for retaining personal freedom from spiritual bondage. We will use **bold** for emphasis.

7 Wherefore, this land is consecrated unto [*set aside for*] him whom he [*the Lord*] shall bring. And **if** it so be that **they** [*the inhabitants of this land*] shall **serve him according to the commandments** which he hath given, **it shall be a land of liberty** unto them; wherefore, **they shall never be brought down into captivity**; if so, it shall be because of iniquity; for **if iniquity shall abound cursed shall be the land for their sakes**, but unto the righteous it shall be blessed forever.

> Next, Lehi explains the wisdom of the Lord in keeping others from discovering the Americas for the time being.

8 And behold, it is wisdom that this land should be kept as yet from the knowledge of other nations; for behold, many nations would overrun the land, that there would be no place for an inheritance.

9 Wherefore, I, Lehi, have obtained a promise, that inasmuch as those [*including the Mulekites (Mosiah 25:2) and Lehi's people*] whom the Lord God shall bring out of the land of Jerusalem shall keep his commandments, they shall prosper upon the face of this land; and they shall be kept from all other nations, that they may possess this land unto themselves. And if it so be that they shall keep his commandments they shall be blessed upon the face of this land, and there shall be none to molest them, nor to take away the land of their inheritance; and they shall dwell safely forever.

> Symbolism: This earth will become the celestial kingdom (D&C 130:9–11), and those who keep the commandments will live on it forever.

Second Nephi 1

10 But behold, when the time cometh that they [*the Lamanites*] shall dwindle in unbelief, after they have received so great blessings from the hand of the Lord—having a knowledge of the creation of the earth, and all men, knowing the great and marvelous works of the Lord from the creation of the world; having power given them to do all things by faith; having all the commandments from the beginning, and having been brought by his infinite goodness into this precious land of promise—behold, I say, if the day shall come that they will reject the Holy One of Israel, the true Messiah, their Redeemer and their God, behold, the judgments [*punishments*] of him [*God*] that is just shall rest upon them.

11 Yea, he will bring other nations unto them, and he will give unto them [*the other nations*] power, and he will take away from them [*the Lamanites*] the lands of their possessions, and he will cause them to be scattered and smitten.

12 Yea, as one generation passeth to another there shall be bloodsheds, and great visitations [*punishments*] among them; wherefore, my sons, I would that ye would remember; yea, I would that ye would hearken unto my words.

13 O that ye would awake; awake from a deep sleep [*spiritually asleep*], yea, even from the sleep of hell, and shake off the awful chains by which ye are bound, which are the chains which bind the children of men, that they are carried away captive down to the eternal gulf of misery and woe [*the "gulf" which separates the wicked from the righteous and God*].

> As Lehi continues to plead with Laman and Lemuel to repent and seek to keep the commandments, we learn an obvious and comforting truth, namely, that parents of rebellious children, who have tried to teach and guide them in the paths of righteousness, will themselves be saved. (**Bold** used for emphasis.)

14 Awake! and arise from the dust, and hear the words of a trembling parent, whose limbs ye must soon lay down in the cold and silent grave, from whence no traveler can return; a few more days and I go the way of all the earth [*I will die soon*].

15 But behold, **the Lord hath redeemed my soul from hell; I have beheld his glory, and I am encircled about eternally in the arms of his love.**

16 And I desire that ye should remember to observe the statutes [*laws and commandments*] and the judgments of the Lord; behold, this hath been the anxiety of my soul from the beginning.

17 My heart hath been weighed down with sorrow from time to time, for I have feared, lest for the hardness of your hearts the Lord your God should come out in the fulness of his wrath [*anger*] upon you, that ye be cut off and destroyed forever;

18 Or, that a cursing should come upon you for the space of many generations; and ye are visited by sword, and by famine, and are hated, and are led according to the will and captivity of the devil.

19 O my sons, that these things might not come upon you, but that ye might be a choice and a favored people of the Lord. But behold, his will be done; for his ways are righteousness forever.

20 And he hath said that: Inasmuch as ye [*if you*] shall keep my commandments ye shall prosper in the land; but inasmuch as ye will not keep my commandments ye shall be cut off from my presence [*a simple statement of eternal fact*].

21 And now that my soul might have joy in you, and that my heart might leave this world with gladness because of you, that I might not be brought down with grief and sorrow to the grave, arise from the dust, my sons, and be men, and be determined in one mind and in one heart, united in all things, that ye may not come down into captivity [*literal and spiritual*];

Next, Lehi defines the word "cursed" in the ultimate sense of the word. It means to be stopped in eternal progress and to be subject to Satan instead, eternally. (**Bold** used for emphasis.)

22 That ye may not be **cursed with a sore** [*very severe*] **cursing**; and also, that ye may not incur the displeasure of a just God upon you, unto the destruction, yea, **the eternal destruction of both soul** [*spirit*] **and body**.

We know that all will be resurrected, including even sons of perdition (see D&C 88:28–32 and 97–102). Thus, the spirit and body will continue inseparably forever after the resurrection and cannot be destroyed in the sense of ceasing to exist. Therefore, the "eternal destruction of both soul and body" has to refer to never again being privileged to dwell in the presence of God in celestial glory (see D&C 76:112).

23 Awake, my sons; put on the armor of righteousness. Shake off the chains with which ye are bound, and come forth out of obscurity, and arise from the dust.

24 Rebel no more against your brother, whose views have been glorious, and who hath kept the commandments from the time that we left Jerusalem; and who hath been an instrument in the hands of God, in bringing us forth into the land of promise; for were it not for him, we must have [*would have*] perished with hunger in the wilderness; nevertheless, ye sought to take away his life; yea, and he hath suffered much sorrow because of you.

25 And I exceedingly fear and tremble because of you, lest he shall suffer again; for behold, ye have accused him that he sought power and authority over you; but I know that he hath not sought for power nor authority over you, but he hath sought the glory of God, and your own eternal welfare.

> Next, we are given an excellent lesson in understanding that the perspectives held by the wicked differ sharply from the facts. It is difficult but important to realize that wicked people do not think like the righteous do.

26 And ye have murmured because he hath been plain unto you. Ye say that he hath used sharpness; ye say that he hath been angry with you; but behold, his sharpness was the sharpness of the power of the word of God, which was in him; and that which ye call anger was the truth, according to that which is in God, which he could not restrain, manifesting boldly concerning your iniquities.

27 And it must needs be [*it is necessary*] that the power of God must be with him, even unto his commanding you that ye must obey. But behold, it was not he, but it was the Spirit of the Lord which was in him, which opened his mouth to utterance that he could not shut it.

> Next, Lehi offers his "first" blessing to his sons and sons-in-law. The choice is up to them. This is a clear example of the fact that we each have moral agency and that we truly are free to choose our eternal destinies.

28 And now my son, Laman, and also Lemuel and Sam, and also my sons who are the sons of Ishmael, behold, if ye will hearken unto the voice of Nephi ye shall not perish. And if ye will hearken unto him I leave unto you a blessing, yea, even my first blessing [*the choicest blessing; perhaps, in this case, it*

could be called the "birthright" blessing].

> Each of us, regardless of birth order, is entitled to inherit all that the Father has, in other words, exaltation. This would be the first blessing or birthright blessing in the eternal gospel sense. It will come to each of us if we choose to keep the commandments.

29 But if ye will not hearken unto him I take away my first blessing [*you will lose your spiritual inheritance, including the right to lead our people*], yea, even my blessing, and it shall rest upon him.

30 And now, Zoram, I speak unto you: Behold, thou art the servant of Laban; nevertheless, thou hast been brought out of the land of Jerusalem, and I know that thou art a true friend unto my son, Nephi, forever.

31 Wherefore, because thou hast been faithful thy seed shall be blessed with his seed, that they dwell in prosperity long upon the face of this land; and nothing, save it shall be iniquity among them, shall harm or disturb their prosperity upon the face of this land forever.

> Zoram has been made a full family member in Lehi's family, just as promised by Nephi in 1 Nephi 4:31–37. This is certainly symbolic of the fact that anyone, regardless of lineage, can be made a full citizen in the household of God by making and keeping covenants.

32 Wherefore, if ye shall keep the commandments of the Lord, the Lord hath consecrated this land for the security of thy seed with the seed of my son.

SECOND NEPHI 2

This chapter contains one of the finest and most complete sermons anywhere in scripture on the Fall of Adam, justice, mercy, the Atonement, and agency. It describes the interrelationship of each of these elements with the others. It ties in very closely with 2 Nephi 9. In fact, you may wish to make a note in the heading of 2 Nephi 2 in your own scriptures, to the effect that chapters 2 and 9 go together.

Since the teachings in these two chapters are so vital to our understanding of the gospel of Christ, we will pause for a few moments here and depart from our usual format in order to invite you to check your knowledge about the fall, the Atonement and related topics. It is in the form of a true/false quiz. We will provide an answer key for you at the end of the quiz.

True or False Quiz for Second Nephi 2 and 9

Questions

1. True or False

Because of the Savior's Atonement, everyone but the very most wicked will be resurrected.

2. True or False

In a way, it is too bad Adam and Eve partook of the forbidden fruit, because our lives would have been much easier if they hadn't.

3. True or False

If Adam and Eve had not transgressed in the Garden of Eden, they and their children would never have become mortal and progressed.

4. True or False

Because of their transgression and the resulting Fall, Adam was cursed severely by God, but Eve got even a worse cursing.

5. True or False

Because of Christ's Atonement, people can be forgiven of all but two types of sin.

6. True or False

Bishops can forgive sins.

7. True or False

The only sins we have to confess to a bishop are sins listed in the temple recommend interview.

8. True or False

If you have a problem confessing your sins to your own bishop, it is sometimes permissible to confess to another bishop.

9. True or False

Part of the punishment for sinning is having to confess to the bishop.

10. True or False

It is not possible in this life to know for sure if you have been forgiven, but you can have a feeling of peace that gives you hope.

11. True or False

One way we can tell if we have been forgiven is that we won't remember the sin anymore.

12. True or False

If we repent of our sins, they will be taken off the records in heaven.

13. True or False

There is much, much more to repenting than the act of confessing.

14. True or False

It was a good thing that Adam and Eve ate the forbidden fruit.

15. True or False

Many people will have a very enjoyable judgment day.

16. True or False

Without the Savior's Atonement, we could not be resurrected and thus would have become like the devil.

17. True or False

It is okay to plan on making it to the highest part of heaven.

Answers

1. False.

Everyone will get resurrected (2 Nephi 9:22).

2. False.

The Fall was good plus essential
(2 Nephi 2:22–25).

3. False.

They would not have had children (2 Nephi 2:22–23).

4. False.

Neither of them was cursed. The Fall was a great blessing, and it gave Adam and Eve ownership of the consequences, which brought great joy along with hardships which promoted growth (see Moses 5:10–11). Satan was cursed. The ground was cursed for Adam's sake (Genesis 3:14–17).

5. True.

Denying the Holy Ghost (D&C 76:31–35) and first degree murder (D&C 42:18) are unforgivable. All other sins can be forgiven (Isaiah 1:18).

6. True or false, depending on how you are thinking.

Only God can forgive sins, but the bishop can forgive sins for the Church in terms of allowing people to go to the temple, etc.

7. Basically true.

This is because there is a question in the temple recommend interview which asks if there is any sin which should have been confessed to a bishop which hasn't been. However, you could answer "false" since not every possible sin is mentioned in the interview.

8. False.

Your bishop is the only one who has the keys of authority over you (except in the case of students who may have a campus ward plus a home ward). The issue here is the priesthood keys of authority and accompanying stewardship. If members have valid difficulty talking to their own bishops, they may confess to their stake president.

9. Absolutely false.

It is not punishment to be helped in overcoming sins.

10. False.

The Holy Ghost can give you a good feeling, which lets you know you are on the path to exaltation. We are counseled in 2 Nephi 31:20 to press forward with a "perfect brightness of hope."

11. False.

Alma could remember his sins but they pained him no more (Alma 36). Sometimes people seem to get D&C 58:42–43 mixed up where the Lord "remembers them no more," referring to Judgment Day, and they think that applies to us in terms of remembering them no more.

12. True.

D&C 58:42. However, if a student is being very observant, he or she might refer to D&C 82:7, where the Lord warns that "former sins return" if the sin is repeated again, and thus say correctly that, in this context, the answer is "false." The important result of the discussion for this question is that, upon deep and sincere repentance, our sins are forgiven and gone forever (Isaiah 1:18).

13. True.

D&C 58:42–43, and many more scriptures.

14. True.

See 2 Nephi 2:22–25 and Moses 5:10–11, among others.

15. True.

See 2 Nephi 9:14, second half of verse.

16. True.

See 2 Nephi 9:7–9.

17. True.

See 2 Nephi 31:20 and many other references. If we don't plan on it, we are less determined in our quest for exaltation.

Now that you have taken the above pretest, we will continue with Lehi's powerful teachings about agency, the Fall, the Atonement, justice and mercy. Lehi is speaking to his son, Jacob, who may be in his late teens to early twenties by now. Jacob was the first of two sons born in the wilderness to Lehi and Sariah. Joseph was born after Jacob. We will use **bold** for emphasis and teaching purposes throughout this chapter.

1 AND now, Jacob, I speak unto you: Thou art my first-born in the days of my tribulation in the wilderness. And behold, in thy childhood thou hast suffered afflictions and much sorrow, because of the rudeness of thy brethren.

"Rudeness" as used in verse 1, above, seems to be a much stronger word than the word "rudeness" today. It appears to include cruelty and wickedness.

2 Nevertheless, Jacob, my firstborn in the wilderness, thou knowest the greatness of God; and **he shall consecrate thine afflictions for thy gain.**

> Those who remain true and faithful to God through difficult trials and tribulations enable Him to bless them and strengthen them tremendously.

3 Wherefore, thy soul shall be blessed, and thou shalt dwell safely with thy brother, Nephi; and thy days shall be spent in the service of thy God. Wherefore, **I know that thou art redeemed, because of the righteousness** [*the Atonement*] **of thy Redeemer**; for thou hast beheld that in the fulness of time [*the time appointed by the Father*] he cometh to bring salvation unto men.

> Just a doctrinal comment, based on verse 3, above. The Atonement of Christ worked before it was actually performed by the Savior. Lehi says that it worked for Jacob, and Jacob and countless others lived before Christ. In fact, it even worked in premortality as we exercised our agency there. Elder Jeffrey R. Holland taught it as follows:
>
> "We could remember that even in the Grand Council of Heaven He loved us and was wonderfully strong, that we triumphed even there by the power of Christ and our faith in the blood of the Lamb" (Holland, " 'This Do in Remembrance of Me,' " p. 67).
>
> Referring to our premortal life, the Institute of Religion New Testament Student Manual, *The Life and Teachings of Jesus and His Apostles*, teaches: "We were given laws and agency, and commandments to have faith and repent from the wrongs that we could do there." "Man could and did in many instances, sin before he was born" (*The Life and Teachings of Jesus and His Disciples*, p. 336). The point is that the Atonement has been blessing our lives for countless eons of time already and will continue to do so if we strive to keep the commandments.

4 And thou hast beheld in thy youth his glory [*it appears that Jacob saw the Savior while still relatively young*]; wherefore, thou art blessed even as they unto whom he shall minister in the flesh; for the Spirit is the same, yesterday, today, and forever [*The same plan of salvation has been and always will be used to bring people to Christ.*] And the way is prepared from the fall of man [*the Fall of Adam*], and salvation is free [*available to all*].

Watch now, and note how skillfully Lehi builds one principle upon another as he teaches the basic plan of salvation. First, he teaches that in order to have and use agency, we must have sufficient knowledge of the gospel.

5 And **men are instructed sufficiently that they know good from evil**. And the law [*of Moses*] is given unto men. And by the law no flesh is justified [*no one can be saved by the law of Moses*]; or, by the law [*of Moses*] men are cut off [*cannot return to the presence of God*]. Yea, by the temporal law they were cut off; and also, by the spiritual law they perish from that which is good, and become miserable forever.

We understand the spiritual law in verse 5, above, to be the law governing spiritual death. In other words, wickedness leads to spiritual death, or the death of our spirituality. We are kept out of celestial glory.

Now that he has laid the doctrinal foundation, he shows us that we must have the Atonement of Christ.

6 Wherefore, redemption cometh in and through the Holy Messiah; for he is full of grace and truth [*fully capable of saving us*].

7 Behold, he [*Christ*] offereth himself a sacrifice for sin, to answer the ends of the law [*to satisfy the law of justice*], unto all those who have a broken [*humble; under proper control*] heart and a contrite spirit [*"contrite" means "desiring correction as needed"*]; and unto none else can the ends [*requirements*] of the law [*of justice*] be answered.

8 Wherefore, how great the importance to make these things known unto the inhabitants of the earth [*this is why the gospel must be taught to everyone*], that they may know that there is no flesh [*resurrected people*] that can dwell in the presence of God, save [*except*] it be through the merits, and mercy, and grace of the Holy Messiah [*the Atonement*], who layeth down his life according to the flesh [*as a mortal*], and taketh it again [*will be resurrected*] by the power of the Spirit, that he may bring to pass the resurrection of the dead, being the first that should rise. [*Christ will be the first one from this earth to be resurrected.*]

9 Wherefore, he is the firstfruits [*the first resurrected*] unto God [*the Father*], inasmuch as he shall make intercession for all the children of men [*His Atonement will be available to all people*]; and they that believe in him shall be saved [*exalted*].

Next, Lehi will teach about the laws of justice and mercy.

10 And because of the intercession [*the Atonement*] for all, all men come unto God [*all will ultimately be accountable*]; wherefore, they stand in the presence of him, to be judged of him according to the truth and holiness which is in him [*Christ's judgment will be completely fair*]. Wherefore, the ends of the law [*the purposes of the law of justice*] which the Holy One [*Christ*] hath given, unto the inflicting of the punishment which is affixed [*to violating laws of God*], which punishment that is affixed is in opposition to that of the happiness [*the law of mercy*] which is affixed, to answer the ends [*purposes, goals*] of the atonement—

> Lehi now explains that in order for our agency to be true agency, we must have choices. In order to have true choices, we must have opposites. In order to have opposites, we must be in an environment where opposition exists. We must have the laws of justice and mercy in order for the Atonement to work.

11 For it must needs be [*it is necessary*], that there is an opposition in all things. If not so, my firstborn in the wilderness [*Jacob*], righteousness [*the Atonement of Christ*] could not be brought to pass [*would not be able to work*], neither wickedness, neither holiness nor misery, neither good nor bad. Wherefore, all things must needs be a compound in one [*everything would be the same; nothing would work as far as personal progress is concerned*]; wherefore, if it should be one body [*if everything were the same, without opposing forces*] it must needs remain as dead [*nothing would happen*], having no life neither death, nor corruption nor incorruption, happiness nor misery, neither sense nor insensibility.

12 Wherefore, it must needs have been created for a thing of naught [*nothing would have purpose*]; wherefore there would have been no purpose in the end [*goal*] of its creation. Wherefore, this thing [*if there were no opposing forces, which require agency choices*] must needs destroy the wisdom of God and his eternal purposes, and also the power, and the mercy, and the justice of God.

> Next, you will see one of the greatest logical sequences ever!

13 And if ye shall say there is **no law**, ye shall also say there is **no sin**. [*This is the root philosophy of atheism.*] If ye shall say there is **no sin**, ye shall also say there

is **no righteousness**. And if there be **no righteousness** there be **no happiness**. And if there be **no righteousness nor happiness** there be **no punishment nor misery**. **And if these things are not there is no God. And if there is no God we are not** [*we don't exist*]**, neither the earth**; for there could have been no creation of things, neither to act nor to be acted upon [*there would be no opportunity for choice*]; wherefore, all things must have vanished away [*there would be no existence at all!*].

> Having taught the vital roles of justice and mercy, agency and opposition, Lehi will now bear testimony of God and the system He set up for us in order that we might have the option of using our agency to return to Him.

14 And now, my sons, I speak unto you these things for your profit and learning; for **there is a God**, and **he hath created all things**, both the heavens and the earth, and all things that in them are, **both things to act and things to be acted upon** [*so we can have true agency*].

> Next, Lehi will explain why Adam and Eve were faced with the opposing choices of the two trees in the Garden of Eden.

15 And to bring about his eternal purposes in the end [*His goals for His children*] of man, after he had created our first parents [*Adam and Eve*], and the beasts of the field and the fowls of the air, and in fine [*in summary*], all things which are created, it must needs be [*it is absolutely essential*] that there was an opposition; even **the forbidden fruit in opposition to the tree of life**; the **one** being **sweet** and **the other bitter**.

> Next, Lehi ties moral agency in with what he has taught above, and explains the absolute necessity for opposition in order to exercise agency.

16 Wherefore [*this is how*], **the Lord God gave unto man that he should act for himself**. Wherefore, man could not act for himself save it should be that he was enticed [*attracted*] by the one or the other.

> Next, Lehi explains how Lucifer opposes God and why he tries to get us to follow him.

17 And I, Lehi, according to the things which I have read, must needs suppose that an angel of God [*Lucifer*], according to that which is written, had fallen from heaven; wherefore, he became a devil, having sought that which was evil before God.

18 And because he had fallen

from heaven, and **had become miserable** forever, he **sought also the misery of all mankind.** Wherefore, he [*the fallen angel, verse 17, above; not a serpent*] said unto Eve, yea, even that old serpent [*one of Satan's nicknames*], who is the devil, who is the father of all lies, wherefore he said: Partake of the forbidden fruit, and ye shall not die, but ye shall be as God, knowing good and evil.

> Satan only told one lie in the Garden of Eden, namely, that they would not die. Otherwise, everything he said was true. This is a reminder that he is a master at mixing enough truth into his temptations that it makes them seem okay.

19 And after Adam and Eve had partaken of the forbidden fruit they were driven out of the garden of Eden, to till the earth.

20 And they have brought forth children; yea, even the family of all the earth. [*Adam and Eve are the origin of man.*]

> Now, Lehi will teach that we need sufficient time in this mortal state of being to exercise our agency amidst the many choices we have between good and evil. That way we have personal ownership of our final judgment. For those over age eight, whose lives are snuffed out before they have had sufficient time to be taught and exercise their agency, there is a great missionary work going on in the spirit world (see D&C 138).

21 And the **days of the children of men** [*mortal beings*] **were prolonged**, according to the will of God, **that they might repent while in the flesh** [*during mortality*]; wherefore, their state [*mortal lives*] became **a state of probation** [*testing and learning*], and their time was lengthened, according to the commandments which the Lord God gave unto the children of men. For **he gave commandment that all men must repent**; for he showed unto all men that they were lost, because of the transgression of their parents [*Adam and Eve*]. [*All people were—or will be—taught about the Fall of Adam and Eve, so they can exercise their moral agency under fair circumstances.*]

> Next, Lehi continues by teaching us what would have happened if Adam and Eve had not partaken of the forbidden fruit.

22 And now, behold, **if** Adam had **not transgressed** he would **not have fallen**, but he would have remained in the garden of Eden. And **all things** which were created **must have** [*would have*] **remained in the same state** in which they were after

Second Nephi 2

they were created; and they must have remained **forever**, and had no end.

> The word "end" in verse 22, above, can have two meanings in this context, both of which make sense. One meaning is "never ending" and the other is "no purpose."

23 And they would have had **no children**; wherefore they would have remained in a state of innocence, having **no joy**, for they knew **no misery**; doing **no good**, for they knew **no sin**.

> Next, Lehi answers a question which many members of the Church ask, namely, "Was God surprised when they ate the fruit? Was there a 'plan B' in case Adam and Eve did not partake of the forbidden fruit?" The answer is "No." because God knows all things as explained in verse 24, next.

24 But behold, **all things have been done in the wisdom of him who knoweth all things**.

> Both Brigham Young and Spencer W. Kimball likewise taught that there was no "plan B" as follows:
>
> "The Lord knew they would do this, and he had designed that they should" [*Young*, Discourses of Brigham Young, *p. 103*].
>
> "There were no guesses here, no trial and error" (Kimball, "The Blessings and Responsibilities of Womanhood," pp. 71–72).
>
> Furthermore, Joseph Smith said the following: "Adam did not commit sin in eating the fruits, for God had decreed that he should eat and fall" (*The Words of Joseph Smith*, p. 63).
>
> Next comes one of the most common and beautiful quotes from the Book of Mormon. It reminds us that mortal life is designed to be mostly enjoyable.

25 **Adam fell that men might be; and men are, that they might have joy.**

> Joseph Smith taught, "Happiness is the object and design of our existence" (Smith, *Teachings of the Prophet Joseph Smith*, pp. 255–56).
>
> Next, Lehi emphasized the role of the Atonement in overcoming the effects of the fall.

26 And **the Messiah cometh** in the fulness of time [*according to the timetable set by the Father*], **that he may redeem the children of men** [*mortals*] **from the fall**. And **because that they are redeemed from the fall** they **have become free forever, knowing good from evil; to act for themselves and not to be acted upon**, save [*except*] it be by the punishment of the law at the great and last day

[*Judgment Day*], according to the commandments which God hath given.

> We find a very interesting and significant teaching in verse 26, above. Many students of the gospel wonder why the wicked don't get "caught up with." In other words, why does the Lord let them get away with so much for so long? In verse 26, above, plus in previous verses, Lehi teaches that their days were prolonged in order to give them plenty of time to exercise their agency wisely. And here he teaches basically that (at least for most people) they won't get caught up with until the final day of judgment.

27 Wherefore, **men are free according to the flesh** [*people are free to choose during their entire mortal lives*]; and all things are given them which are expedient unto man [*ultimately, all people will get every chance to exercise their agency wisely, whether in mortality or in the spirit world; see D&C 138*]. And **they are free to choose liberty and eternal life,** through the great Mediator [*Christ*] of all men, **or to choose captivity and death,** according to the captivity and power of the devil; for he seeketh that all men might be miserable like unto himself.

28 And now, my sons, I would that ye should **look to the great Mediator**, and **hearken unto his great commandments**; and **be faithful unto his words**, and **choose eternal life** [*"eternal life" always means "exaltation" in the scriptures*] according to the will of his Holy Spirit;

29 And **not choose eternal death** [*"spiritual death"; being cut off forever from returning to live with God*], according to the will of the flesh [*by yielding to the lusts of the flesh*] and the evil which is therein, which giveth the spirit of the devil power to captivate, to bring you down to hell, that he may reign over you in his own kingdom.

30 I have spoken these few words unto you all, my sons, in the last days of my probation [*shortly before I die*]; and I have chosen the good part [*I have chosen eternal life*], according to the words of the prophet [*as taught by the prophets*]. And I have none other object save it be the everlasting welfare of your souls. Amen.

SECOND NEPHI 3

In this chapter, Lehi tells us of a great prophecy given by Joseph, who was sold into Egypt. This prophecy is not in the Bible. We learn from 2 Nephi 4:2 that it

Second Nephi 3

was on the brass plates. Lehi was thus able to study it and Nephi was able to transcribe it onto the small plates of Nephi, which we are reading now in the Book of Mormon. Joseph prophesies of one of his descendants, namely, the Prophet Joseph Smith.

Perhaps you will recall that the angel told Nephi during his vision that the brass plates contained more than the Old Testament (see 1 Nephi 13:23). It appears that this prophecy of Joseph in Egypt is one example of this fact.

1 AND now I [*Lehi*] speak unto you, Joseph, my last-born. Thou wast born in the wilderness of mine afflictions; yea, in the days of my greatest sorrow did thy mother bear thee.

> The word "sorrow," as used in verse 1, above, may help us understand the word "sorrow" as used in Genesis 3:16, where it says, "In sorrow thou shalt bring forth children." Some people believe the word "sorrow" implies punishment. Such thinking is out of harmony with 2 Nephi 2:25. President Spencer W. Kimball preferred the word "distress" (Kimball, "The Blessings and Responsibilities of Womanhood," p. 72).
>
> Rather than being a punishment to Eve for partaking of the forbidden fruit, "sorrow" means in distress, difficulty, toil, labor, etc., which is associated with mortal life. And, as Lehi taught his son, Joseph, in 2 Nephi 2:2, such difficult times are for our growth and good. The Lord taught Joseph Smith the same principle in Liberty Jail (see D&C 122:7). Certainly, Eve was being taught the same principle in Genesis, as the word "sorrow" was used in describing what was coming next.

2 And may the Lord consecrate also unto thee this land [*America*], which is a most precious land, for thine inheritance and the inheritance of thy seed with thy brethren, for thy security forever, **if it so be that ye shall keep the commandments of the Holy One of Israel**.

3 And now, Joseph, my last-born, whom I have brought out of the wilderness of mine afflictions, may the Lord bless thee forever, for thy seed [*descendants*] shall not utterly be destroyed.

4 For behold, thou art the fruit of my loins [*you are my offspring*]; and **I am a descendant of Joseph who was carried captive into Egypt**. And great were the covenants of the Lord which he made unto Joseph.

> It will be helpful for what comes next if we take a moment and point out the four "Josephs" who will be involved in Lehi's

teachings to his son, Joseph. We will number them:

1. Joseph who was sold into Egypt. Jacob's son, Isaac's grandson, Abraham's great-grandson.

2. Joseph, Lehi's son, addressed in this chapter.

3. Joseph Smith, Senior, the father of the Prophet Joseph Smith.

4. Joseph Smith, Junior, the prophet of the Restoration who reorganized Christ's church in the latter days.

5 Wherefore, **Joseph** [*who was sold into Egypt*] **truly saw our day**. And he obtained a promise of the Lord, that out of the fruit of his loins [*out of his posterity*] the Lord God would raise up a righteous branch [*a righteous people*] unto the house of Israel; not the Messiah, but a branch which was to be broken off [*scattered*], nevertheless, to be remembered in the covenants of the Lord that the Messiah should be made manifest unto them [*Israel?*] in the latter days, in the spirit of power, unto the bringing of them out of darkness unto light—yea, out of hidden darkness [*many who are in spiritual darkness think they are "enlightened" or living in the light, therefore, their spiritual darkness is "hidden" to them*] and out of captivity unto freedom [*the restoration of the gospel*].

6 For Joseph [*in Egypt*] truly testified, saying: A seer [*Joseph Smith, Junior*] shall the Lord my God raise up, who shall be a choice seer unto the fruit of my loins [*my posterity; both Ephraim and Manasseh*].

7 Yea, Joseph [*in Egypt*] truly said: Thus saith the Lord unto me: A choice seer [*Joseph Smith, Junior*] will I raise up out of the fruit of thy loins; and he shall be esteemed highly among the fruit of thy loins [*highly respected among your posterity*]. And unto him will I give commandment that he shall do a work [*restoration of the gospel in the last days*] for the fruit of thy loins, his brethren [*his fellow Israelites*], which shall be of great worth unto them, even to the bringing of them to the knowledge of the covenants which I have made with thy fathers [*Abraham, Isaac, and Jacob*].

8 And I will give unto him [*Joseph Smith, Junior*] a commandment that he shall do none other work, save the work which I shall command him [*Joseph Smith, Junior, will not prosper in things other than his work in the gospel; see D&C 24:9*]. And I will make him great in mine eyes; for he shall do my work.

Second Nephi 3

9 And he [*Joseph Smith, Junior*] shall be great like unto Moses, whom I have said I would raise up unto you [*the children of Israel in Egypt*], to deliver my people, O house of Israel.

10 And Moses will I raise up, to deliver thy people out of the land of Egypt.

11 But a seer [*Joseph Smith, Junior*] will I raise up out of the fruit of thy [*Joseph in Egypt*] loins; and unto him [*Joseph Smith, Junior*] will I give power to bring forth my word unto the seed of thy loins [*Ephraim and Manasseh*]—and not to the bringing forth my word only, saith the Lord, but to the convincing them of my word, which shall have already gone forth among them [*by way of the Bible*].

12 Wherefore, the fruit of thy [*Joseph in Egypt*] loins shall write [*the Book of Mormon*]; and the fruit of the loins of Judah shall write [*the Bible*]; and that which shall be written by the fruit of thy loins [*the Book of Mormon*], and also that which shall be written by the fruit of the loins of Judah [*the Bible*], shall grow together, unto the confounding [*stopping*] of false doctrines and laying down of contentions, and establishing peace among the fruit of thy loins, and bringing them to the knowledge of their fathers [*ancestors*] in the latter days, and also to the knowledge of my covenants, saith the Lord.

13 And out of weakness he [*Joseph Smith, Junior*] shall be made strong, in that day when my work shall commence among all my people, unto the restoring thee, O house of Israel, saith the Lord.

14 And thus prophesied Joseph [*in Egypt*], saying: Behold, that seer [*Joseph Smith, Junior*] will the Lord bless; and they that seek to destroy him shall be confounded [*unsuccessful*]; for this promise, which I have obtained of the Lord, of the fruit of my loins, shall be fulfilled. Behold, I [*Joseph in Egypt*] am sure of the fulfilling of this promise;

15 And his name shall be called after me [*Joseph Smith, Junior*]; and it shall be after the name of his father [*Joseph Smith, Senior*]. And he shall be like unto me [*a prophet and seer*]; for the thing, which the Lord shall bring forth by his hand, by the power of the Lord shall bring my people unto salvation.

16 Yea, thus prophesied Joseph [*in Egypt*]: I am sure of this thing, even as I am sure of the promise of Moses; for the Lord

hath said unto me, I will preserve thy seed forever.

17 And the Lord hath said: I will raise up a Moses; and I will give power unto him in a rod [*he will be a great leader with authority*]; and I will give judgment unto him in writing [*Moses will be a skilled writer—he wrote Genesis, Exodus, Leviticus, Numbers, and Deuteronomy*]. Yet I will not loose his tongue [*Moses won't be a great speaker; Exodus 4:10*], that he shall speak much, for I will not make him mighty in speaking. But I [*Jehovah, Jesus*] will write unto him my law, by the finger of mine own hand [*the stone tablets containing the commandments*]; and I will make a spokesman for him [*Aaron; Exodus 4:14–16*].

18 And the Lord said unto me [*Joseph in Egypt*] also: I will raise up unto the fruit of thy loins [*your posterity*]; and I will make for him [*Joseph Smith, Junior*] a spokesman [*perhaps Sidney Rigdon; see D&C 100:9*]. And I, behold, I [*the Lord*] will give unto him [*Joseph Smith, Junior*] that he shall write [*translate*] the writing of the fruit of thy loins [*the Book of Mormon plates*], unto the fruit of thy loins [*so that my gospel can come to your descendants*]; and the spokesman of thy loins shall declare it.

19 And the words [*from the golden plates*] which he [*Joseph Smith, Junior*] shall write [*translate*] shall be the words which are expedient [*essential*] in my wisdom should go forth unto the fruit of thy loins. And it shall be as if the fruit of thy loins [*the Book of Mormon prophets and people*] had cried unto them from the dust; for I know their faith.

20 And they [*the Book of Mormon prophets*] shall cry from the dust [*shall speak from the past*]; yea, even repentance unto their brethren, even after many generations have gone by them. And it shall come to pass that their cry shall go, even according to the simpleness of their words. [*The Book of Mormon will be instrumental in restoring the gospel's "plain and precious" truths.*]

21 Because of their [*prophets of the Book of Mormon*] faith their words shall proceed forth out of my [*the Lord's*] mouth unto their brethren who are the fruit of thy loins [*descendants of Joseph in Egypt*]; and the weakness of their words will I make strong in their faith, unto the remembering of my covenant [*keeping of my*

promise] which I made unto thy [*Joseph in Egypt*] fathers.

Lehi now briefly summarizes to his son, Joseph, the prophecies of Joseph in Egypt.

22 And now, behold, my son Joseph [*Lehi's son*], after this manner did my father [*my ancestor, Joseph in Egypt*] of old prophesy.

23 Wherefore, because of this covenant thou [*Joseph, Lehi's son*] art blessed; for thy seed [*your posterity*] shall not be destroyed, for they shall hearken unto the words of the book.

24 And there shall rise up one [*Joseph Smith, Junior; see 2 Nephi 3:24, footnote 24a*] mighty among them, who shall do much good, both in word and in deed, being an instrument in the hands of God, with exceeding faith, to work mighty wonders, and do that thing which is great in the sight of God, unto the bringing to pass much restoration [*the restoration of the gospel and true Church*] unto the house of Israel, and unto the seed of thy brethren.

25 And now, blessed art thou, Joseph [*Lehi's son*]. Behold, thou art little; wherefore hearken unto the words of thy brother, Nephi, and it shall be done unto thee even according to the words which I have spoken. Remember the words of thy dying father. Amen.

Before leaving this chapter, it is pleasant to note a wonderful little "miracle" which occurred in the naming of Joseph Smith, Junior. As recorded in verse 15, above, Joseph in Egypt prophesied that the prophet of the Restoration would be named after him as well as being named after his father.

Usually, when a husband and wife decide to name a son after the husband, it is the firstborn son who is so named. Therefore, we might imagine a little extra "urgent inspiration" from heaven when Joseph Smith, Senior, and his wife, Lucy Mack Smith, had their first child, a son. We can picture them looking at their newborn infant and thinking "Hi, Joseph." We then imagine inspiration whispering, "No, this is not Joseph." And so, they muse together that the name Joseph doesn't seem to fit. Therefore, they name him Alvin. Likewise, perhaps, with the second son. They name him Hyrum. The third child is a daughter. No problem. They name her Sophronia. Then the fourth child is born, a son who was chosen and foreordained in the premortal realms to be the prophet of the Restoration. They name him Joseph Smith, Junior, and the angels in heaven, who have charge of seeing that the prophecy of Joseph in Egypt is fulfilled, smile. (Actually, I am just letting my imagination go a bit in thinking that there might be angels assigned to help see that prophecy is fulfilled, but possibly. . . .)

We can read and study more of the prophecies of Joseph who was sold into Egypt in the Joseph Smith Translation of Genesis 50:24–38. It is contained in the Joseph Smith Translation section at the back of your LDS Bible. We will include it here for your convenience. If you read these verses in the JST section of your Bible, you will see that the words in *italics* are those added by the Prophet Joseph Smith.

JST, Genesis 50:24–38

24. And Joseph said unto his brethren, I die, *and go unto my fathers; and I go down to my grave with joy. The God of my father Jacob be with you, to deliver you out of affliction in the days of your bondage; for the Lord hath visited me, and I have obtained a promise of the Lord, that out of the fruit of my loins, the Lord God will raise up a righteous branch out of my loins; and unto thee, whom my father Jacob hath named Israel, a prophet; (not the Messiah who is called Shilo;) and this prophet shall deliver my people out of Egypt in the days of thy bondage.*

25. *And it shall come to pass that they shall be scattered again; and a branch shall be broken off, and shall be carried into a far country; nevertheless they shall be remembered in the covenants of the Lord, when the Messiah cometh; for he shall be made manifest unto them in the latter days, in the Spirit of power; and shall bring them out of darkness into light; out of hidden darkness, and out of captivity unto freedom.*

26. *A seer shall the Lord my God raise up, who shall be a choice seer unto the fruit of my loins.*

27. *Thus saith the Lord God of my fathers unto me, A choice seer will I raise up out of the fruit of thy loins, and he shall be esteemed highly among the fruit of thy loins; and unto him will I give commandment that he shall do a work for the fruit of thy loins, his brethren.*

28. *And he shall bring them to the knowledge of the covenants which I have made with thy fathers; and he shall do whatsoever work I shall command him.*

29. *And I will make him great in mine eyes, for he shall do my work; and he shall be great like unto him whom I have said I would raise up unto you, to deliver my people, O house of Israel, out of the land of Egypt; for a seer will I raise up to deliver my people out of the land of Egypt; and he shall be called Moses. And by this name*

he shall know that he is of thy house; for he shall be nursed by the king's daughter, and shall be called her son.

30. And again, a seer will I raise up out of the fruit of thy loins, and unto him will I give power to bring forth my word unto the seed of thy loins; and not to the bringing forth of my word only, saith the Lord, but to the convincing them of my word, which shall have already gone forth among them in the last days;

31. Wherefore the fruit of thy loins shall write, and the fruit of the loins of Judah shall write; and that which shall be written by the fruit of thy loins, and also that which shall be written by the fruit of the loins of Judah, shall grow together unto the confounding of false doctrines, and laying down of contentions, and establishing peace among the fruit of thy loins, and bringing them to a knowledge of their fathers in the latter days; and also to the knowledge of my covenants, saith the Lord.

32. And out of weakness shall he be made strong, in that day when my work shall go forth among all my people, which shall restore them, who are of the house of Israel, in the last days.

33. And that seer will I bless, and they that seek to destroy him shall be confounded; for this promise I give unto you; for I will remember you from generation to generation; and his name shall be called Joseph, and it shall be after the name of his father; and he shall be like unto you; for the thing which the Lord shall bring forth by his hand shall bring my people unto salvation.

34. And the Lord sware unto Joseph that he would preserve his seed forever, saying, I will raise up Moses, and a rod shall be in his hand, and he shall gather together my people, and he shall lead them as a flock, and he shall smite the waters of the Red Sea with his rod.

35. And he shall have judgment, and shall write the word of the Lord. And he shall not speak many words, for I will write unto him my law by the finger of mine own hand. And I will make a spokesman for him, and his name shall be called Aaron.

36. And it shall be done unto thee in the last days also, even as I have sworn. Therefore, Joseph said unto his brethren, God will surely visit you, and bring you out of this land, unto the land which he sware unto Abraham, and unto Isaac, and to Jacob.

37. And Joseph *confirmed many other things unto his brethren,* and took an oath of the children of Israel, saying unto them, God will surely visit you, and ye shall carry up my bones from hence.

38. So Joseph died *when he was* an hundred and ten years old; and they embalmed him,

and *they put him in a coffin in Egypt; and he was kept from burial by the children of Israel, that he might be carried up and laid in the sepulchre with his father. And thus they remembered the oath which they sware unto him.*

SECOND NEPHI 4

In this chapter, Lehi gives his final blessings to his posterity and then grows older and dies. As we listen in on Lehi's words, we will gain some very important doctrinal insights as to the fate of children whose parents are not faithful to the Lord. We will point these out when we get to them.

First, Nephi will review some of the words of his father and teach us, and then he will humbly express concern for his own shortcomings. We must pay close attention to all his conclusions about his inadequacies or we will miss a vital lesson for ourselves.

1 AND now, I, Nephi, speak concerning the prophecies of which my father hath spoken, concerning Joseph, who was carried into Egypt.

2 For behold, he [*Joseph in Egypt*] truly prophesied concerning all his seed [*posterity; Ephraim and Manasseh*]. And the prophecies which he wrote, there are not many greater. [*"Greater" can, of course, mean "more important." But it can also mean "which cover more territory about the subject."*] And he prophesied concerning us, and our future generations; and they are written upon the plates of brass.

Now, pay careful attention to what Lehi says by way of blessing to Laman's children, who will not have the same opportunities on earth to understand the gospel as Nephi's children will. You will see a major message about God's fairness.

3 Wherefore, after my father had made an end of speaking concerning the prophecies of Joseph, **he called the children of Laman, his sons, and his daughters, and said unto them**: Behold, my sons, and my daughters, who are the sons and the daughters of my first-born, I would that ye should give ear unto my words.

4 For the Lord God hath said that: **Inasmuch as ye shall keep my commandments ye shall prosper in the land; and inasmuch as ye will not keep my commandments ye shall be cut off from my presence.**

5 **But** behold, my sons and my daughters, I cannot go down to

my grave save I should leave a blessing upon you; for behold, **I know that if ye are brought up in the way ye should go ye will not depart from it.**

The last phrase in verse 5, above, is a most important doctrine concerning those who do not get a fair set of opportunities to learn about and accept the gospel while on earth, because of poor parental example or whatever. Lehi says that he knows that if they had been given a proper gospel upbringing, they would have remained faithful to it.

A similar doctrine is taught in **D&C 137:7–8** as follows:

7 Thus came the voice of the Lord unto me, saying: All who have died without a knowledge of this gospel, **who would have received it** if they had been permitted to tarry, shall be heirs of the celestial kingdom of God;

8 Also **all that shall die henceforth without a knowledge of it, who would have received it with all their hearts, shall be heirs of that kingdom**;

Thus we see that God is completely fair, and that all His children will get a completely fair set of opportunities to accept and live the gospel before final judgment, even if it means getting that opportunity in the spirit world (see D&C 138) and during the Millennium. Now, we will continue with Lehi's blessing to Laman's children.

6 Wherefore, if ye are cursed [*stopped in gospel progression because you haven't been taught properly*], behold, I leave my blessing upon you, that the cursing may be taken from you and be answered upon the heads of your parents [*your parents will be held accountable*].

What about parents who repent, but it is too late for them to reclaim their wayward children? Answer: That is what the Atonement is all about, namely, to lift sins and burdens off our shoulders which we cannot fix ourselves. In other words, parents can be forgiven too, and God will make sure that their children do get a fair chance before Judgment Day, as stated in the above quotes.

7 Wherefore, because of my blessing the Lord God will not suffer [*allow*] that ye shall perish [*spiritually*]; wherefore, he will be merciful unto you and unto your seed forever.

8 And it came to pass that after my father had made an end of speaking to the sons and daughters of Laman, **he caused the sons and daughters of Lemuel to be brought before him.**

9 And he spake unto them, saying: Behold, my sons and my daughters, who are the sons and

the daughters of my second son; behold **I leave unto you the same blessing which I left unto the sons and daughters of Laman**; wherefore, thou shalt not utterly be destroyed; but **in the end** [*ultimately*] **thy seed shall be blessed**. [*Ultimately, you will have the opportunity to receive the full blessings of the gospel. Another clear statement that God is completely fair to all His children.*]

10 And it came to pass that when my father had made an end of speaking unto them, behold, he spake unto the sons of Ishmael, yea, and even all his household [*all of Ishmael's descendants*].

11 And after he had made an end of speaking unto them, he spake unto Sam, saying: Blessed art thou, and thy seed; for thou shalt inherit the land like unto thy brother Nephi. And thy seed shall be numbered with his seed; and thou shalt be even like unto thy brother, and thy seed like unto his seed; and thou shalt be blessed in all thy days.

> Now, we will say "Goodbye" to Lehi, at least for a while until we meet him in the next life. Hopefully, you have a strong feeling of appreciation for this great prophet and father.

12 And it came to pass after my father, **Lehi,** had spoken unto all his household, according to the feelings of his heart and the Spirit of the Lord which was in him, he waxed [*grew*] old. And it came to pass that he **died**, and was buried.

13 And it came to pass that not many days after his death, Laman and Lemuel and the sons of Ishmael were angry with me because of the admonitions [*warnings and counsels*] of the Lord.

14 For I, Nephi, was constrained [*required by the Spirit*] to speak unto them, according to his word; for I had spoken many things unto them, and also my father, before his death; many of which sayings are written upon mine other plates [*the large plates of Nephi*]; for a more history part are written upon mine other plates.

15 And upon these [*the small plates of Nephi*] I write the things of my soul, and many of the scriptures which are engraven upon the plates of brass. For **my soul delighteth in the scriptures, and my heart pondereth them, and writeth them for the learning and the profit of my children.**

> Verses 15–35 are known as "The Psalm of Nephi." In these verses, he both rejoices in the scriptures and the things of the

Lord, while at the same time expressing concern for his mortal frailties and shortcomings. Certainly, we can relate to him. You may wish to underline or highlight some of the things we **bold,** in your own Book of Mormon by way of emphasis and learning.

16 Behold, **my soul delighteth in the things of the Lord; and my heart pondereth continually upon the things which I have seen and heard**.

17 **Nevertheless,** notwithstanding [*in spite of*] the great goodness of the Lord, in showing me his great and marvelous works, my heart exclaimeth: **O wretched man that I am!** Yea, my heart sorroweth because of my flesh [*my mortal weaknesses*]; my soul grieveth because of mine iniquities [*my sins and shortcomings*].

18 I am encompassed about [*surrounded*], because of the temptations and the sins which do so easily beset me.

There is certainly comfort for us in the fact that even the great and righteous, such as Nephi, have feelings of being overwhelmed by their weaknesses. Isaiah expresses similar feelings in Isaiah 6:5.

We might ask a question here, namely, why would such a righteous man as Nephi be so concerned, when we know that he is solidly on the strait and narrow path leading to exaltation? Perhaps the answer is found in the fact that the more righteous people become, the more little imperfections glare at them in the light of truth. Things bother them now that formerly hardly registered in their minds. Actually, **such people can rejoice** that they are noticing such things in their lives now. It is a witness that they are well along on the path back to God. You will see Nephi teaching us this principle of rejoicing in verses 28 and 30. This rejoicing is possible because of the Atonement of Christ.

Now back to Nephi's teaching. Pay careful attention to the "progression" from being weighed down with feelings of falling short to the rejoicing which comes from relying completely upon the "Rock of our salvation" who is Christ the Lord.

19 And when I desire to rejoice, **my heart groaneth** because of my sins; **nevertheless, I know in whom I have trusted.**

20 **My God hath been my support**; he hath led me through mine afflictions in the wilderness; and he hath preserved me upon the waters of the great deep.

21 **He hath filled me with his love,** even unto the consuming of my flesh.

22 He hath confounded [*stopped*] **mine enemies**, unto the causing of them to quake before me.

23 Behold, **he hath heard my cry** by day, and **he hath given me knowledge** by visions in the night-time.

24 And by day have I waxed [*grown*] bold in **mighty prayer** before him; yea, my voice have I sent up on high; and angels came down and ministered unto me.

25 And upon the wings of his Spirit hath **my body been carried away upon exceedingly high mountains** [*I have been given mighty perspectives, in order to see things as God sees them*]. And mine eyes have beheld great things, yea, even too great for man; therefore I was bidden that I should not write them.

26 O then, if I have seen so great things, if the Lord in his condescension unto the children of men hath visited men in so much mercy, **why should my heart weep and my soul linger in the valley of sorrow** [*why should I keep holding on to the past*], and my flesh waste away, and my strength slacken, because of mine afflictions?

27 And **why should I yield to sin, because of my flesh?** Yea, why should I give way to **temptations**, that the evil one have place in my heart to destroy my peace and afflict my soul? **Why am I angry because of mine enemy?** [*Why am I so human?*]

> Pay close attention now to where this goes. If we fail to see and feel and accept this next teaching of Nephi, we will likely fall into the carefully laid trap of low self esteem, discouragement, and depression.

28 **Awake**, my soul! No longer droop in sin. **Rejoice, O my heart** [*the center of feelings; allow you to feel good about yourself*], and give place no more for the enemy of my soul.

29 Do not anger again because of mine enemies. Do not slacken my strength because of mine afflictions.

30 **Rejoice, O my heart**, and cry unto the Lord, and say: O Lord, I will **praise thee forever**; yea, **my soul will rejoice in thee**, my God, and **the rock of my salvation**. [*Rejoice because you know you can make it because of the Savior!*]

31 O Lord, wilt thou redeem my soul? Wilt thou deliver me out of the hands of mine enemies? Wilt thou make me that I may shake at the appearance of sin? [*The answer is "Yes!"*]

32 May the gates of hell be shut continually before me, **because that my heart is broken and my spirit is contrite!** [*"Contrite" means "I want to be corrected."*] O Lord, wilt thou not shut the gates of thy righteousness before me, that I may walk in the path of the low valley, that I may be strict in the plain road!

> The final phrase in verse 32, above, is a pure Bedouin term still used in the Near East. It is another internal evidence that the Book of Mormon has its origins in the Holy Land.

33 O Lord, wilt thou encircle me around in the robe of thy righteousness! O Lord, wilt thou make a way for mine escape before mine enemies! Wilt thou make my path straight before me! Wilt thou not place a stumbling block in my way—but that thou wouldst **clear my way before me**, and hedge not up my way, but the ways of mine enemy.

34 O Lord, **I have trusted in thee, and I will trust in thee forever** [*one hundred percent commitment*]. I will not put my trust in the arm of flesh [*I will not place my trust in man*]; for I know that cursed is he that putteth his trust in the arm of flesh. Yea, cursed [*stopped*] is he that putteth his trust in man or maketh flesh his arm [*those who rely on the philosophies and counsels of men, rather than using God as their standard*].

35 Yea, I know that **God will give liberally to him that asketh**. Yea, my God will give me, if I ask not amiss [*if I do not ask for inappropriate things; compare with D&C 46:30 and 50:30*]; therefore **I will lift up my voice unto thee**; yea, I will cry unto thee, my God, **the rock of my righteousness**. Behold, **my voice shall forever ascend up unto thee, my rock and mine everlasting God. Amen**.

> You watched as Nephi moved from potential overwhelming discouragement to solid and firm confidence in his future with God. This Psalm of Nephi is one of the most beautiful and powerful in all scripture. It applies to every one of us, and has power to lift each of us from discouragement. It is unfortunately a badly underused segment of the Book of Mormon.

SECOND NEPHI 5

Chapter 5 is a pivotal chapter. In it we will see the separation of Nephi and his righteous followers from Laman and Lemuel and their wicked associates. We will be taught many principles of spiritual survival, including the fact that you sometimes have to get away from those you have tried so hard to save, for fear of being destroyed spiritually or literally yourself.

1 BEHOLD, it came to pass that I, Nephi, did cry much unto the Lord my God, because of the anger of my brethren.

> What do you think Nephi asked for in his prayers to God on behalf of his wicked brothers? What do you think he hoped for? No doubt he asked that their hearts be softened, as had happened many times before. But—and here is an important lesson—God respects agency and their "chances" seem to be running out.

2 But behold, their anger did increase against me, insomuch that they did seek to take away my life.

3 Yea, they did murmur against me, saying: Our younger brother thinks to rule over us; and **we have had much trial because of him**; wherefore, now let us slay him, that we may not be afflicted more because of his words. For behold, we will not have him to be our ruler; for it belongs unto us, who are the elder brethren, to rule over this people.

> The bolded phrase in verse 3, above, points out one of Satan's much-used tools, namely, blame others for your current inappropriate behavior. Many people spend years trying to find out whom to blame for their present sinful behavior. They would be best served by forgiving, fleeing if necessary, and repenting and changing their own behavior.

4 Now I do not write upon these plates [*the small plates*] all the words which they murmured against me. But it sufficeth me to say, that they did seek to take away my life.

5 And it came to pass that the Lord did warn me, that **I, Nephi, should depart from them and flee** into the wilderness, and all those who would go with me.

> A young lady once came to me in tears because her friends were getting deeper and deeper involved in sinful behaviors and associations, and her efforts to save them were not working. She now feared that she was on the verge of being corrupted herself. In fact, she was now hanging her clothing, which smelled of tobacco and some drugs, out on the deck of her home so they would not transfer the smells to her Sunday clothes which she wore to church.
>
> She had associated with these friends for years and had initially felt that she was strong enough in the gospel to weather the storms of evil influence, and still be available to them to drive

SECOND NEPHI 5

if they were drunk. She wanted to be around to try to talk them out of viewing the videos they chose, or at least to chat about gospel values and standards if and when they might be receptive. But now her own mind and spirit were being tainted, and it scared her. Her biggest fear was that if she no longer associated with them, they would have no one to rescue them. As she contemplated leaving the group, she felt like a deserter.

When we talked, I asked her if she had read the Book of Mormon. She said, "Yes, several times." Then I said, "Do you remember what Nephi had to do when it got too dangerous for him?" And with visible relief, she said, "Yes. He had to flee from Laman and Lemuel." And then, with even more relief, she said, "Then, it would be okay with God if I left the group? I wouldn't be responsible for their souls? I wouldn't be a deserter?" Verse 5 answered her concerns and solved her dilemma.

She left the group, though they tried to get her to come back. She went on to serve a mission and is happily married and is a Primary president at the time of the writing of this book.

Nephi obeys the Lord and flees the environment and people who could destroy him and his people.

6 Wherefore, it came to pass that I, Nephi, did take my family, and also Zoram and his family, and Sam, mine elder brother and his family, and Jacob and Joseph, my younger brethren, and also my sisters [*he apparently had sisters who were not yet married; see note, next*], and all those who would go with me. And **all those who would go with me were those who believed in the warnings and the revelations of God**; wherefore, they did hearken unto my words.

Verse 6, above, mentions Nephi's sisters. We will use a quote from the 1996 *Book of Mormon Student Manual*, used at BYU and in Institutes of Religion, on this topic.

"This is the only specific reference in the Book of Mormon that Nephi had sisters as well as brothers. How many sisters there were, whether they were older or younger than Nephi, or what their names may have been are questions not answered in our present Book of Mormon. However, the following statement by Erastus Snow may provide information on some of the sisters of Nephi:

" 'The Prophet Joseph informed us that the record of Lehi was contained on the 116 pages that were first translated and subsequently stolen, and of which an abridgment is given us in the first book of Nephi, which is the record of Nephi individually, he himself being of the lineage of Manasseh; but that Ishmael was of the lineage of Ephraim, and that his sons married into Lehi's family, and Lehi's sons married Ishmael's daughters' (Snow, *Journal of Discourses,* 23:184).

"The words that Ishmael's sons 'married into Lehi's family' would seem to indicate that the two sons of Ishmael (see 1 Nephi 7:6) were married to Lehi's daughters (and thus to two of the sisters of Nephi). However, the sisters referred to in 2 Nephi 5:6 are evidently still other sisters, because the sisters mentioned here follow Nephi when the schism with Laman occurs, whereas the sisters of Nephi who were married to the sons of Ishmael evidently stayed with their husbands and joined with Laman (see Alma 3:7 and 47:35)" (Ludlow, *Companion to Your Study of the Book of Mormon,* pp. 131–32).

7 And we did take our tents and whatsoever things were possible for us, and did journey in the wilderness for the space of many days. And after we had journeyed for the space of many days we did pitch our tents.

8 And my people would that we should call the name of the place Nephi; wherefore, we did call it Nephi.

9 And all those who were with me did take upon them to call themselves the people of Nephi.

Next, Nephi tells us that he and his people were still living according to the law of Moses. They knew of Christ and that He would be born six hundred years from the time Lehi left Jerusalem. The law of Moses was designed to point toward Christ and to prepare people for the full gospel of Christ. Following it properly allowed Nephi and his people to live "after the manner of happiness" (see verse 27). This is a reminder that the law of Moses was actually a rather high law, compared to the ways of the world. (You may wish to take time to read Exodus, chapters 20, 22:1–9; 23:1–9, and others, for a quick reminder that the laws which Moses gave his people, under the direction of the Lord, were much higher than most in our society today live.

10 And we did observe to keep the judgments, and the statutes, and the commandments of the Lord in all things, according to the law of Moses.

11 And the Lord was with us; and we did prosper exceedingly; for we did sow seed, and we did reap again in abundance. And we began to raise flocks, and herds, and animals of every kind.

12 And I, Nephi, had also brought the records which were engraven upon the plates of brass [*their scriptures*]; and also the ball

Second Nephi 5

[*Liahona*], or compass, which was prepared for my father by the hand of the Lord, according to that which is written.

13 And it came to pass that we began to **prosper exceedingly, and to multiply in the land** [*the result of living the gospel as a society*].

> Some people wonder whether or not it is proper and righteous to make military preparations for self-defense. In fact, protesters often make much of their opposition to this practice. Here again we see that the Book of Mormon is written to help us in our day. Verse 14, next, reminds us that there is wisdom in making such preparations.

14 And I, Nephi, did take the sword of Laban, and after the manner of it [*using it for a pattern*] did make many swords, lest by any means the people who were now called Lamanites should come upon us and destroy us; for I knew their hatred towards me and my children and those who were called my people.

15 And I did teach my people to build buildings, and to work in all manner of wood, and of iron, and of copper, and of brass, and of steel, and of gold, and of silver, and of precious ores, which were in great abundance.

[*Industriousness and education go hand in hand with living the gospel.*]

16 And I, Nephi, did build a temple; and I did construct it after the manner of the temple of Solomon [*ninety feet long by thirty feet wide by thirty feet high; see 1 Kings 6:2*] save [*except*] it were not built of so many precious things; for they were not to be found upon the land, wherefore, it could not be built like unto Solomon's temple. But the manner of the construction was like unto the temple of Solomon; and the workmanship thereof was exceedingly fine.

> Some people criticize us and the Church for spending so much money on temples and making them so beautiful, as opposed to giving to the poor. We do both. There is simple symbolism in putting our finest materials into the building of our temples, as did Nephi and his people. The putting of our finest work and efforts into temple building is symbolic of putting our best efforts and resources into living worthy of exaltation.

17 And it came to pass that I, Nephi, did cause my people to be industrious, and to labor with their hands.

18 And it came to pass that they would that I should be their king.

But I, Nephi, was desirous that they should have no king; nevertheless, I did for them according to that which was in my power.

19 And behold, the words of the Lord had been fulfilled unto my brethren, which he spake concerning them [*see 1 Nephi 2:21–22*], that I should be their ruler and their teacher. Wherefore, I had been their ruler and their teacher, according to the commandments of the Lord, until the time they sought to take away my life.

20 Wherefore, the word of the Lord was fulfilled which he spake unto me, saying that: Inasmuch as they will not hearken unto thy words they shall be cut off from the presence of the Lord. And behold, they were cut off from his presence. [*The prophecy had been fulfilled. Symbolism: The day will come that the wicked are cut off from ever returning to the presence of God, if they continually ignore His invitations to repent and be happy eternally.*]

Next, the topic of people's being cursed comes up. It is important to understand that the "curse" spoken of is when the Spirit of the Lord withdraws. Thus, we can "curse" ourselves as far as present and eternal blessings are concerned. People have agency, and when they continually ignore the light of Christ and the invitations which the Lord sends out to come unto Him, they are "cursed" or stopped in spiritual progression by their own choices.

21 And he had caused the cursing to come upon them [*He had withdrawn His Spirit*], yea, even a sore [*very severe*] cursing, because of their iniquity [*wickedness*]. For behold, they had hardened their hearts against him, that they had become like unto a flint [*unyielding in their evil ways*]; wherefore, as they were white, and exceedingly fair and delightsome, that they might not be enticing unto my people the Lord God did cause a skin of blackness to come upon them.

The skin of blackness in verse 21, above, is a sensitive subject and must be kept absolutely within the context here. The curse is the withdrawal of the Lord's Spirit. Joseph Fielding Smith explained it as follows:

"The dark skin was placed upon the Lamanites so that they could be distinguished from the Nephites and to keep the two peoples from mixing. The dark skin was the sign of the curse. **The curse was the withdrawal of the Spirit of the Lord** and the (withdrawal of the Spirit was the cause of the) Lamanites becoming a 'loathsome and filthy people, full of idleness and all manner of abominations' (I Nephi 12:23). The Lord commanded the Nephites not to intermarry with them, for if they did they would partake of the curse (they would also become spiritually dead). The dark skin of those who have come into the Church is no longer to be considered a sign of the curse" (Smith, *Answers to Gospel Questions,* 3:123–24).

22 And thus saith the Lord God: I will cause that they shall be loathsome [*not attractive*] unto thy people, save [*unless*] they shall repent of their iniquities.

23 And cursed shall be the seed of him that mixeth with their seed; for they shall be cursed even with the same cursing [*because of their choices, the Spirit of the Lord will have to withdraw from them too*]. And the Lord spake it, and it was done.

24 And because of their cursing [*because the Spirit of the Lord had withdrawn*] which was upon them they did become an idle people, full of mischief and subtlety, and did seek in the wilderness for beasts of prey.

25 And the Lord God said unto me: They shall be a scourge [*trouble, problem*] unto thy seed, to stir them up in remembrance of me; and inasmuch as they will not remember me, and hearken unto my words, they [*the Lamanites*] shall scourge them even unto destruction.

26 And it came to pass that I, Nephi, did consecrate Jacob and Joseph, that they should be priests and teachers over the land of my people.

Students of the scriptures often ask whether the priesthood spoken of here was Aaronic or Melchizedek. It was Melchizedek. Joseph Fielding Smith explains this as follows (**bold** added for emphasis):

"The Nephites were descendants of Joseph. Lehi discovered this when reading the brass plates. He was a descendant of Manasseh. And Ishmael, who had accompanied Lehi with his family, was of the tribe of Ephraim (Alma 10:3; *Improvement Era,* 8:781; *Journal of Discourses,* 23:184).

"Therefore there were no Levites who accompanied Lehi to the Western Hemisphere. Under these conditions **the Nephites officiated by virtue of the Melchizedek Priesthood from the days of Lehi to the days of the appearance of our Savior among them**. It is true that Nephi 'consecrated Jacob and Joseph' that they should be priests and teachers over the land of the Nephites, but the fact that plural terms *priests and teachers* were used indicates that this was not a reference to the definite office in the priesthood in either case, but it was a general assignment to teach, direct, and admonish the people. Otherwise the terms *priest and teacher* would have been given, in the singular. Additional light is thrown on this appointment showing that these two brothers of Nephi held the Melchizedek Priesthood, in the sixth chapter, second verse of 2 Nephi, where Jacob makes this explanation regarding the priesthood which he and Joseph held: 'Behold, my beloved brethren, I, Jacob, having been called of God, and ordained *after the manner of his holy order*, and having been consecrated by my brother Nephi, unto whom ye look as a king or a protector, and on whom ye depend for safety, behold ye know that I have spoken unto you exceeding many things.'

"This seems to be a confirmation of the ordinations that he and his brother Joseph received in the Melchizedek Priesthood. All through the Book of Mormon we find references to the Nephites officiating by virtue of the Higher Priesthood after the holy order" (Melchizedek Priesthood) (Smith, *Answers to Gospel Questions*, 1:124).

27 And it came to pass that **we lived after the manner of happiness.**

28 And thirty years had passed away from the time we left Jerusalem.

29 And I, Nephi, had kept the records upon my plates [*the large plates of Nephi*], which I had made, of my people thus far.

30 And it came to pass that the Lord God said unto me: Make other plates [*the small plates of Nephi, the translation of which we are reading now*]; and thou shalt engraven many things upon them [*the small plates*] which are good in my sight, for the profit of thy people.

31 Wherefore, I, Nephi, to be obedient to the commandments of the Lord, went and made these plates [*the small plates*] upon which I have engraven these things.

32 And I engraved that which is pleasing unto God. And if my people are pleased with the things of God they will be pleased with mine engravings which are upon these plates.

33 And if my people desire to know the more particular part of the history of my people they must search mine other plates [*the large plates of Nephi*].

34 And it sufficeth me to say that forty years had passed away,

SECOND NEPHI 6

Nephi now records some teachings of his brother, Jacob, as Jacob teaches Nephi's people. Jacob is probably thirty-five to forty-five years old by now. He will review Jewish history and in so doing will remind all of us that we, Israel, have much to do and that we must come unto Christ and remain faithful in order to return to God.

1 THE words of Jacob, the brother of Nephi, which he spake unto the people of Nephi:

2 Behold, my beloved brethren, I, Jacob, having been called of God, and ordained after the manner of his holy order [*I hold the Melchizedek Priesthood*], and having been consecrated [*set apart*] by my brother Nephi, unto whom ye look as a king or a protector, and on whom ye depend for safety, behold ye know that I have spoken unto you exceedingly many things [*I have already taught you many things*].

3 Nevertheless, I speak unto you again; for I am desirous for the welfare of your souls. Yea, mine anxiety is great for you; and ye yourselves know that it ever has been. For I have exhorted you with all diligence; and I have taught you the words of my father [*Lehi*]; and I have spoken unto you concerning all things which are written, from the creation of the world.

> Just as Nephi turned to the words of Isaiah to teach his people (see 1 Nephi 20–21), so also will Jacob use Isaiah. The last sentence of verse 4, next, summarizes what studying Isaiah will do for us. It will help us glorify God by living worthy of returning to Him and becoming gods ourselves (compare with Moses 1:39).

4 And now, behold, I would speak unto you concerning things which are, and which are to come [*the future*]; wherefore [*in order to do this*], I will read you the words of Isaiah. And they are the words which my brother has desired that I should speak unto you. And I speak unto you for your sakes, **that ye may learn and glorify the name of your God**.

5 And now, the words which I shall read are they which Isaiah spake concerning all [*this includes us*] the house of Israel; wherefore, they may be likened unto you, for ye are of the house of Israel. And there are many things which have been spoken

by Isaiah which may be likened unto you [*which apply to you*], because ye are of the house of Israel.

> Jacob basically quotes the same portions of Isaiah that Nephi used in 1 Nephi 20–21. First, he quotes Isaiah in verses 6 and 7; then he explains how these verses apply to the Jews.

6 And now, these are the words: Thus saith the Lord God: Behold, I will lift up mine hand to the Gentiles, and set up my standard [*the gospel; the true Church*] to the people; and they shall bring thy sons in their arms, and thy daughters shall be carried upon their shoulders [*leaders of nations will aid in the last days gathering of Israel*].

7 And kings [*leaders of nations*] shall be thy nursing fathers [*will help you gather*], and their queens thy nursing mothers; they shall bow down to thee with their faces towards the earth [*they will be humbled in your presence*], and lick up the dust of thy feet [*and serve you and be awed by you*]; and thou shalt know that I am the Lord [*and then you will see that My promises are fulfilled*]; for they shall not be ashamed [*disappointed*] that wait for me [*who trust in Me*].

8 And now I, Jacob, would speak somewhat concerning these words [*I will now explain these words*]. For behold, the Lord has shown me that those who were at Jerusalem [*the Jews*], from whence we came, have been slain and carried away captive [*the Babylonian captivity; see Bible Dictionary, p. 639*].

9 Nevertheless, the Lord has shown unto me that they [*the Jews*] should [*will*] return again. [*They did, in about 538 B.C. when Cyrus the Persian easily conquered Babylon and allowed the Jewish captives to return to Jerusalem.*] And he also has shown unto me that the Lord God, the Holy One of Israel [*Christ*], should manifest himself unto them in the flesh [*Jesus will show Himself to the Jews and live among them as a mortal*]; and after he should manifest himself they [*the Jews*] should [*will*] scourge him and crucify him, according to the words of the angel who spake it unto me.

10 And after they [*the Jews*] have hardened their hearts and stiffened their necks against the Holy One of Israel [*against the Savior*], behold, the judgments [*punishments*] of the Holy One of Israel shall come upon them. And the day cometh that **they** [*the Jews*]

SECOND NEPHI 6

shall be smitten and afflicted.

11 Wherefore, after they are **driven to and fro**, for thus saith the angel [*this is what the angel explained to me*], many shall be afflicted in the flesh [*they shall suffer much physical suffering*], and shall not be suffered to perish [*the Jews will not be destroyed completely*], because of the prayers of the faithful; they shall be **scattered**, and **smitten**, and **hated; nevertheless**, the Lord will be merciful unto them, that **when they shall come to the knowledge of their Redeemer, they shall be gathered together again to the lands of their inheritance.**

12 And blessed are the Gentiles [*in this context, the non-Jews*], they of whom the prophet has written; for behold, if it so be that they shall repent and fight not against Zion, and do not unite themselves to that great and abominable church [*the church of the devil, meaning Satan's kingdom, evil, wickedness, etc.; see 1 Nephi 22:23*], they shall be saved; for the Lord God will fulfill his covenants which he has made unto his children; and for this cause the prophet has written these things.

13 Wherefore, they that fight against Zion and the covenant people of the Lord shall lick up the dust of their feet [*the righteous will ultimately triumph over the wicked*]; and the people of the Lord shall not be ashamed [*will not be disappointed*]. For the people of the Lord are they who wait for him [*who trust and rely on Him*]; for they still wait for the coming of the Messiah [*at this point, about 550 B.C.*].

In verse 14, next, Jacob explains that Isaiah referred to two major times when the Jews will return. The first was when they returned from Babylonian captivity in two major waves, 538 B.C. and 520 B.C. (see 2 Kings 24). The second major return of the Jews will occur in the last days. We are watching the fulfillment of this prophecy now. However, we note that part of the gathering, to their homelands, is under way, but that the most important "gathering" prophesied, namely, being gathered to Christ, has not really made much headway. Joseph Fielding Smith speaks of this as follows:

"Not many of the Jews, I take it from my reading of the scriptures, will believe in Christ before he comes. The Book of Mormon tells us that they shall begin to believe in him (see 2 Nephi 30:7). They are now beginning to believe in him. The Jews today look upon Christ as a great Rabbi. They have accepted him as one of their great teachers; they have said that, 'He is Jew of Jew, the greatest Rabbi of them all,' as one has stated it. When the gospel was restored in 1830, if a Jew had mentioned the name of Christ in one of the synagogues, he would have been rebuked. Had a rabbi referred to him, the congregation would have arisen and left the building. And so, we see the sentiment has changed. Now I state this on Jewish authority that they are beginning to believe in Christ, and some of them are accepting the gospel.

"But in the main they will gather to Jerusalem in their unbelief; the gospel will be preached to them; some of them will believe. Not all of the Gentiles have believed when the gospel has been proclaimed to them, but the great body of the Jews who are there assembled will not receive Christ as their Redeemer until he comes himself and makes himself manifest unto them" (Smith, *Doctrines of Salvation*, 3:9; *Book of Mormon Student Manual*, p. 27).

14 And behold, according to the words of the prophet [*Isaiah*], the Messiah will set himself again the second time to recover them [*the return of the Jews in the last days*]; wherefore, he will manifest himself unto them in power and great glory [*perhaps referring, among other things, to the appearance of the Savior on the Mount of Olives*], unto the destruction of their enemies, when that day cometh when they shall believe in him; and none will he destroy that believe in him.

Some of the signs of the times are mentioned next.

15 And they that believe not in him shall be destroyed, both by fire, and by tempest, and by earthquakes, and by bloodsheds, and by pestilence, and by famine. And they shall know that the Lord is God, the Holy One of Israel.

Next, Jacob quotes Isaiah as he asks a most significant question. In this context, since Jacob is prophesying about the Jews, we will add notes which reference the Jews.

16 For shall the prey [*the Jews, who have been victims over the centuries*] be taken from the mighty [*be set free from their mighty enemies*], or the lawful captive [*the covenant people*] delivered [*be set free from their enemies*]? [*The answer is "Yes!" as emphasized in verse 17, next.*]

17 But thus saith the Lord: Even the captives of the mighty [*the Jews who have been so terribly persecuted by powerful enemies*] shall be taken away [*liberated*], and the prey [*victims*] of the terrible [*tyrants*] shall be delivered

[*set free*]; [*And this is how.*] for the Mighty God shall deliver his covenant people. For thus saith the Lord: I will contend with them that contendeth with thee [*I, the Lord, will fight your battles*]—

18 And I will feed them that oppress thee, with their own flesh [*I will turn your enemies against each other*]; and they shall be drunken with their own blood as with sweet wine [*they will revel at fighting against each other*]; and all flesh shall know that I the Lord am thy Savior and thy Redeemer, the Mighty One of Jacob [*because the prophecies about the gathering of the Jews will be so obviously fulfilled*].

SECOND NEPHI 7

Since Isaiah uses much symbolism, and since the Lord uses symbolism in many settings, including the temple, to teach us, we will include here a list of several items of symbolism commonly used in the scriptures.

Symbolism Often Used in the Scriptures

Colors

white	purity; righteousness; exaltation (Example: Rev. 3:4–5)
black	evil; famine; darkness (Example: Rev. 6:5–6)
red	sins; bloodshed (Example: Rev. 6:4; D&C 133:51)
blue	heaven; godliness; remembering and keeping God's commandments (Example: Num. 15:37–40)
green	life; nature (Example: Rev. 8:7)
amber	sun; light; divine glory (Example: D&C 110:2; Rev. 1:15; Ezek. 1:4, 27; 8:2)
scarlet	royalty (Example: Dan. 5:29; Matt. 27:28–29)
silver	worth, but less than gold (Example: Ridges, *Isaiah Made Easier*, Isa. 48:10 notes)
gold	the best; exaltation (Example: Rev. 4:4)

Body parts

eye	perception; light and knowledge
head	governing
ears	obedience; hearing
mouth	speaking
hair	modesty; covering
members	offices and callings
heart	inner man; courage
hands	action, acting
right hand	covenant hand; making covenants
bowels	center of emotion; whole being
loins	posterity; preparing for action (gird up your loins)
liver	center of feeling
reins	kidneys; center of desires, thoughts
arm	power
foot	mobility; foundation
toe	associated with cleansing rites (Example: Lev. 14:17)
nose	anger (Example: 2 Sam. 22:16; Job 4:9)
tongue	speaking
blood	life of the body
knee	humility; submission

Second Nephi 7

shoulder	strength; effort
forehead	total dedication, loyalty (Example: Rev. 14:1—loyalty to God; Rev. 13:16—loyalty to wickedness, Satan)

Numbers

1	unity; God
3	God; Godhead; A word repeated three times means superlative, "the most" or "the best" (see Isaiah 6:3)
4	mankind; earth (see *Smith's Bible Dictionary*, p. 456) (Example: Rev. 7:1. Four angels over four parts of the earth)
7	completeness; perfection. When man lets God help, it leads to perfection. (man + God = perfection) 4 + 3 = 7
10	numerical perfection; well-organized (Example: Ten Commandments, tithing) (Example: Satan is well-organized, Rev. 13:1)
12	divine government; God's organization (Example: JST Rev. 5:6)
40 days	literal; sometimes means "a long time" as in 1 Samuel 17:16
forever endless	can sometimes be a specific period or age, not endless (see *BYU Religious Studies Center Newsletter*, Vol. 8, No. 3, May 1994)

Other

horse	victory; power to conquer (Example: Rev. 19:11; Jer. 8:16)
donkey	peace (Example: Christ came in peace at the Triumphal Entry)
palms	joy; triumph, victory (Example: John 12:13; Rev. 7:9)
wings	power to move, act, etc. (Example: Rev. 4:8; D&C 77:4)
crown	power; dominion; exaltation (Example: Rev. 2:10; 4:4)
robes	royalty; kings, queens; exaltation (Example: Rev. 6:11; 7:14; 2 Ne. 9:14; D&C 109:76; 3 Ne. 11:8)

As we continue with 2 Nephi 7, Jacob now quotes what is basically known as Isaiah, chapter 50, in the Bible. A major question here is who has left whom when people find themselves far away from God spiritually? Another question that Isaiah asks is essentially "Why don't you come unto Christ? Has He lost His power to save you?"

In this chapter we learn that one of the terrible tortures inflicted upon the Savior during His trial and crucifixion was the pulling out of His whiskers. In this chapter, Isaiah speaks of the future as if it had already happened.

1 [*The Lord asks the question, "Did I divorce you or did you divorce me?" "Did I leave you or did you leave me? Did I break My covenants with you or did you break your covenants with Me?"*] Yea, for thus saith the Lord: Have I put thee away [*divorced you*], or have I cast thee off forever? For thus saith the Lord: Where is the bill of your mother's divorcement? To whom have I put thee away, or to which of my creditors have I sold you [*Was it I who sold you*]? Yea, to whom have I sold you? Behold, for your iniquities have ye sold yourselves [*you brought it upon yourselves!*], and for your transgressions is your mother [*your apostate nation; Hosea 2:2*] put away [*scattered and smitten*].

2 Wherefore [*this is why*], when I [*Jesus*] came, there was no man [*who received me as the Messiah*]; when I called, yea, there was none to answer [*nobody responded*]. O house of Israel, is my hand shortened at all that it cannot redeem, or have I no power to deliver [*have I lost my power*]? Behold, at my rebuke [*command*] I dry up the sea, I make their rivers a wilderness and their fish to stink because the waters are dried up, and they die because of thirst [*I haven't lost my power*].

3 I clothe the heavens with blackness, and I make sackcloth their covering [*I can cause the sky to be dark during the day as if it were mourning the dead. In fact it will at Jesus' crucifixion; see Matt 27:45*].

4 The Lord God [*the Father*] hath given me [*Jesus; see verse 6*] the tongue of the learned [*Father taught Me well*], that I should know how to speak a word [*a strengthening and comforting word*] in season unto thee, O house of Israel. When ye are weary he waketh morning by morning. He waketh

mine ear to hear as the learned [*German Bible, Luther edition: "He, the Father, is constantly communicating with me and I hear as his disciple"*].

5 The Lord God [*the Father*] hath opened mine ear, and I was not rebellious [*hint, hint, Israel*], neither turned away back [*I accomplished my calling, the Atonement; you should do yours as given in 1 Nephi 21:6*].

Isaiah now prophesies some very specific details surrounding Christ's crucifixion.

6 I gave my back to the smiter [*scourging; see Matthew 27:26*], and my cheeks to them that plucked off the hair [*pulled out whiskers of my beard*]. I hid not my face from shame and spitting [*as My time for crucifixion came*].

7 For the Lord God [*Father*] will help me, therefore shall I not be confounded [*I'll not be stopped*]. Therefore have I set my face like a flint [*I have braced Myself for the ordeal*], and I know that I shall not be ashamed [*will not fail*].

8 And the Lord [*the Father; see verse 9*] is near, and he justifieth me [*approves of everything I do; could refer to Isaiah too*].

Who will contend with me [*who is willing to go against such odds*]? Let us stand together [*go to court as in a court of law*]. Who is mine adversary? Let him come near me [*face me*], and I will smite him with the strength of my mouth [*the truth from My mouth will ultimately win*].

The phrase "and I will smite him with the strength of my mouth," in verse 8, above, is not in our Bible, thus showing us that the brass plates contained a more accurate record of Isaiah's teachings.

9 For the Lord God [*the Father*] will help me. And all they who shall condemn me, behold, all they shall wax old as a garment, and the moth shall eat them up [*the wicked will have their day, then reap the punishment*].

10 Who is among you that feareth [*respects*] the Lord, that obeyeth the voice of his servant [*prophets*], that walketh in darkness and hath no light? [*Answer. No one because the Lord blesses his followers with light.*]

11 Behold all ye [*the wicked*] that kindle fire, that compass [*surround*] yourselves about with sparks, walk in the light of your fire and in the sparks which ye

have kindled [*trying to live without God, according to your own "light" and philosophies*]. This shall ye have of mine hand—ye shall lie down in sorrow [*misery awaits those who try to live without God*].

SECOND NEPHI 8

Next, Isaiah first speaks to the righteous and teaches a course in perspective. He reminds all of us not to sell ourselves short. Rather, remember who we are and live to fulfill our potential.

1 Hearken unto me, ye that follow after righteousness [*the Lord is now speaking to the righteous*]. Look unto the rock [*the good, solid rock—Abraham and Sarah*] from whence ye are hewn, and to the hole of the pit [*the rock quarry*] from whence ye are digged [*consider your origins; you are really somebody!*].

2 Look unto Abraham, your father, and unto Sarah, she that bare you [*Sarah is side by side with Abraham in importance*]; for I called him alone [*when he was childless*], and blessed him [*see Abraham 2:9–11*].

3 For the Lord shall comfort Zion, he will comfort all her waste places; and he will make her wilderness like Eden, and her desert like the garden of the Lord [*the Garden of Eden*]. Joy and gladness shall be found therein, thanksgiving and the voice of melody [*wonderful reward for the righteous*].

4 Hearken unto me [*Christ*], my people; and give ear unto me, O my nation; for a law shall proceed from me [*teachings, doctrines; see Isaiah 51:4, footnote a*], and I will make my judgment to rest for a light for the people [*my laws will bring light to the nations*].

> The Lord reminds the righteous that His Atonement and His gospel are always closely available to them.

5 My righteousness [*My ability to save you; triumph*] is near [*is close to you; is available to you*]; my salvation is gone forth, and mine arm shall judge the people. The isles [*nations of the world*] shall wait [*trust, rely*] upon me, and on mine arm [*My power*] shall they trust.

> Next, Isaiah reminds us that the salvation that comes through the Lord is completely and totally reliable. No matter what else happens, it will always come through.

6 Lift up your eyes to the heavens, and look upon the earth

SECOND NEPHI 8

beneath; for the heavens shall vanish away like smoke [*D&C 29:23–24*], and the earth shall wax [*grow*] old like a garment; and they that dwell therein shall die in like manner. But my salvation [*the salvation I bring*] shall be forever, and my righteousness [*triumph, victory*] shall not be abolished [*glad message of hope; see D&C 1:38*].

7 Hearken unto me, ye that know righteousness [*you who are righteous*], the people in whose heart I have written my law [*you who have taken My gospel to heart*], fear ye not the reproach [*insults*] of men, neither be ye afraid of their revilings [*stinging criticisms*].

8 For the moth shall eat them [*the wicked who revile against the righteous*] up like a garment [*they will vanish like moth-eaten clothing*], and the worm shall eat them like wool. But my righteousness [*salvation and deliverance*] shall be [*last*] forever, and my salvation from generation to generation [*throughout eternity*].

> Isaiah now depicts Israel as replying to the Lord's assurances in the previous verses. Righteous Israel now invites the Lord to exercise His power in their behalf like he did in ancient times.

9 Awake, awake! Put on strength, O arm [*symbolic of power*] of the Lord; awake as in the ancient days [*help us like You did in days gone by*]. Art thou not he that hath cut Rahab [*trimmed Egypt down to size. Rahab is a mythical sea monster and symbolically represents Satan and nations who serve him*], and wounded the dragon [*Satan; see Revelation 12:7–9*]?

10 Art thou not he who hath dried the sea [*Red Sea*], the waters of the great deep; that hath made the depths of the sea a way [*pathway*] for the ransomed [*redeemed, You redeemed the children of Israel from Egypt; symbolic of the Atonement's redeeming us from our sins*] to pass over [*parting of the Red Sea*]?

11 Therefore [*because of your power*], the redeemed of the Lord shall return [*the gathering*], and come with singing unto Zion; and everlasting joy and holiness shall be upon their heads; and they shall obtain gladness and joy; sorrow and mourning shall flee away [*ultimate results of righteousness*].

> The Lord now replies to righteous Israel's request in verse 9, above.

12 I am he; yea, I am he that comforteth you. Behold, who art thou, that thou shouldst be afraid of man [*mortal man*], who shall die [*trust in God, not man*], and of the son of man [*mortal men*], who shall be made like unto grass [*short-lived glory*]?

13 And forgettest the Lord thy maker, that hath stretched forth the heavens, and laid the foundations of the earth [*how could you forget Me, your Creator, after all I've done for you?*], and hast feared continually every day, because of the fury of the oppressor [*Israel's captors who have oppressed them; see 2 Nephi 8, footnote 13c*], as if he were ready to destroy [*German Bible: whose intent is to destroy, why should you live in fear of mortal men*]? And where is the fury of the oppressor? [*If you live righteously, the day will come when enemies won't be able to hurt you anymore.*]

14 The captive exile hasteneth, that he may be loosed [*the day will come when Israel will be set free; see Isaiah 52:1–2*], and that he should not die in the pit [*not die in captivity*], nor that his bread should fail [*run out; famine, etc.*]

15 But I am the Lord thy God, whose waves roared [*as they drowned Pharaoh's armies in the Red Sea; see 1 Nephi 4:2*]; the Lord of Hosts is my name.

16 And I have put my words in thy mouth [*have given you My gospel*], and have covered [*protected*] thee in the shadow of mine hand, that I may plant the heavens and lay the foundations of the earth [*I created the heavens and the earth*], and say unto Zion: Behold, thou art my people [*I haven't deserted you*].

17 Awake, awake, stand up, O Jerusalem, which hast drunk at the hand of the Lord the cup of his fury—thou hast drunken the dregs [*bitter residue at the bottom of a cup*] of the cup of trembling wrung out [*you have paid a terrible price for your wickedness*]—

18 And none to guide her [*Israel*] among all the sons she hath brought forth [*you have spent many years without prophets*]; neither that taketh her by the hand, of all the sons she hath brought up.

19 These two sons [*two prophets in the last days who will help keep enemies of the Jews from totally destroying them; see Revelation 11*] are come unto thee, who shall be sorry for thee

[*who will care about you*]—thy desolation and destruction, and the famine and the sword—and by whom shall I comfort thee?

20 Thy sons [*your people*] have fainted [*German Bible: are on their last leg*], save these two [*the two prophets in Revelation 11*]; they [*your people*] lie at the head of all the streets [*German Bible: are being destroyed right and left*]; as a wild bull in a net [*implies that they are trapped in a net woven by their own wickedness*], they are full of the fury of the Lord [*they are catching the full fury of the Lord*], the rebuke of thy God [*the punishments of God*].

21 Therefore hear now this, thou [*Israel*] afflicted, and drunken [*out of control*], and not with wine [*rather, with wickedness*]:

22 Thus saith thy Lord, the Lord and thy God pleadeth the cause of his people [*I have not deserted you*]; behold, I have taken out of thine hand the cup of trembling, the dregs of the cup of my fury; thou shalt no more drink it again [*Christ will save the Jews in the last days; see 2 Nephi 9:1–2*].

23 But I will put it [*the cup in verse 22*] into the hand of them that afflict thee [*your enemies will get what they gave you*]; who have said to thy soul: Bow down, that we may go over [*lie down while we walk all over you!*]—and thou hast laid thy body as the ground and as the street to them that went over [*you have been walked on by your enemies*].

24 Awake, awake, put on thy strength, O Zion [*return to the proper use of the priesthood; see D&C 113:7, 8*]; put on thy beautiful garments [*dress in your finest and prepare to be with the Savior; see Revelation 21:2–3*], O Jerusalem, the holy city; for henceforth there shall no more come into thee the uncircumcised and the unclean [*the wicked*].

25 Shake thyself from the dust [*from being walked on, verse 23; see also 2 Nephi 13:26*]; arise [*from being walked on, verse 23*], sit down [*in dignity, redeemed at last*], O Jerusalem; loose thyself [*free yourself*] from the bands of thy neck [*from captivity, bondage, wickedness*], O captive daughter of Zion.

SECOND NEPHI 9

Jacob has quoted Isaiah. He has used this great prophet to emphasize that the Atonement of Christ can truly set us free from sin. He has, in effect, pleaded with his people to accept the gift of the Atonement which the Savior offers all. He will now explain these teachings of Isaiah to his people.

Again, the fact that Book of Mormon prophets explain Isaiah's writings gives us an advantage over all others, and also a responsibility to share our understanding of the gospel with all others.

1 AND now, my beloved brethren, I [*Jacob*] have read these things [*Isaiah's writings*] that ye might know concerning the covenants of the Lord that he has covenanted with all the house of Israel [*in other words, with all of us*]—

2 That he has spoken unto the Jews, by the mouth of his holy prophets, even from the beginning down, from generation to generation, until the time comes that they shall be restored to the true church and fold of God [*this hasn't happened yet, to any significant degree as far as numbers are concerned*]; when they shall be gathered home to the lands of their inheritance, and shall be established in all their lands of promise.

3 Behold, my beloved brethren, I speak unto you these things that ye may rejoice, and lift up your heads forever, because of the blessings which the Lord God shall bestow upon your children.

4 For I know that ye have searched much, many of you, to know of things to come; wherefore I know that ye know that our flesh must waste away and die; nevertheless, in our bodies we shall see God [*we will all be resurrected; see verse 22*].

5 Yea, I know that ye know that in the body [*in a physical, mortal body*] he [*Christ*] shall show himself unto those at Jerusalem, from whence we came; for it is expedient [*necessary*] that it should be among them [*it has to be that Christ is born and lives among the Jews*]; for it behooveth [*is required of*] the great Creator [*Christ*] that he suffereth [*allows*] himself to become subject unto man in the flesh, and die for all men, that all men might become subject unto him. [*In other words, Christ had to "buy" us with His life so that we would be in complete debt to Him, in order to be able to offer us the law of mercy and have a chance that we would accept it.*]

Jacob will now build a case

for his people as to why they need the Atonement.

6 For as **death** hath passed upon all men [*everyone will eventually die*], to fulfil the merciful plan of the great Creator [*death is a blessing; without it, we couldn't be resurrected*], there must needs be [*there has to be*] a power of **resurrection**, and the resurrection must needs come unto man by reason of **the fall**; and the fall came by reason of **transgression**; and because man became fallen they were **cut off from the presence of the Lord.**

7 Wherefore, it must needs be [*there has to be*] an infinite **atonement**—save it should be an infinite atonement this corruption [*mortal body*] could not put on incorruption [*we could not be resurrected*]. Wherefore, the first judgment [*the fall*] which came upon man must needs have remained to an endless duration [*without the Atonement, the effects of the fall would have lasted forever*]. And if so, this flesh [*our mortal bodies*] must have laid down to rot and to crumble to its mother earth, to rise no more [*we would have died and never resurrected*].

As you know, the Atonement made it possible for us to overcome two types of death, physical death and spiritual death. At this point, Jacob is emphasizing what would have happened to us if Christ had not overcome physical death for us. This is very sobering doctrine.

8 O the wisdom of God, his mercy and grace! For behold, if the flesh should rise no more [*if we were not to resurrect*] our spirits must become subject to that angel [*the devil*] who fell from before the presence of the Eternal God, and became the devil, to rise no more [*Satan will never get a physical body; therefore, he will never gain a resurrected body*].

9 And our spirits must have [*would have*] become like unto him, and we become devils, angels to a devil, to be shut out from the presence of our God, and to remain with the father of lies [*Satan*], in misery, like unto himself; yea, to that being who beguiled our first parents [*Adam and Eve*], who transformeth himself nigh unto an angel of light [*who tries to appear as an angel of God in order to deceive people; see D&C 129 for keys to prevent being so deceived by him*], and stirreth up the children of men unto secret combinations of murder and all manner of secret works of darkness.

10 O how great the goodness of

our God, who prepareth a way [*the Atonement*] for our escape from the grasp of this awful monster; yea, that monster, death and hell, which I call the death of the body, and also the death of the spirit [*spiritual death; a spirit can't be killed in the sense of ceasing to exist*]. [*Through the Atonement, we can overcome both types of death.*]

11 And because of the way of deliverance of our God, the Holy One of Israel, this death [*physical death*], of which I have spoken, which is the temporal [*physical*], shall deliver up its dead; which death is the grave.

12 And this death of which I have spoken, which is the **spiritual death** [*being cut off from the presence of God forever*], shall deliver up its dead [*through repentance and being forgiven because of Christ's Atonement for sins*]; which **spiritual death is hell**; wherefore, death and hell must deliver up their dead, and hell [*spiritual death*] must deliver up its captive spirits, and the grave must deliver up its captive bodies [*physical death*], and the bodies and the spirits of men will be restored one to the other [*through the resurrection*]; and it is by the power of the resurrection of the Holy One of Israel.

13 O how great the plan of our God! For on the other hand [*now we will talk about the righteous*], the paradise of God must deliver up the spirits of the righteous, and the grave deliver up the body of the righteous; and the spirit and the body is restored to itself again, and all men become incorruptible [*receive permanent, resurrected bodies*], and immortal, and they are living souls, having a perfect knowledge like unto us in the flesh, save it be that our knowledge shall be perfect [*except we don't have perfect knowledge yet*].

> Verse 14, next, is a great doctrinal verse. It clearly teaches that it is possible to have an enjoyable Judgment Day! The first half of the verse shows the misery of the wicked on the day of final judgment, but the last half teaches the joy and enjoyment of the righteous on that day.

14 Wherefore, we [*Jacob graciously and humbly includes himself in this category, even though we know he belongs with the righteous*] shall have a perfect knowledge of all our guilt, and our uncleanness, and our nakedness [*i.e., the wicked have no "cover up" or no excuses left*]; and the **righteous** shall have a perfect knowledge of their **enjoyment**, and their righteousness, being **clothed with purity**, yea,

even **with the robe of righteousness.**

> Jacob emphasizes differences between the wicked and the righteous, like Isaiah does, to encourage us to be righteous and to gain eternal happiness and joy. Next, he emphasizes accountability. No one fully capable of accountability escapes accountability to God.

15 And it shall come to pass that when all men shall have passed from this first death [*the death of the mortal body*] unto life [*and are resurrected*], insomuch as they have become immortal, **they must appear before the judgment-seat of the Holy One of Israel**; and then cometh the judgment, and then must they be judged according to the holy judgment of God.

> With respect to verse 15, above, John 5:22 informs us that Christ is the final judge, that the Father has turned this responsibility over to Him.

16 And assuredly, as the Lord liveth, for the Lord God hath spoken it, and it is his eternal word, which cannot pass away, that **they who are righteous shall be righteous still**, and **they who are filthy shall be filthy still**; wherefore, they who are filthy are the devil and his angels [*and that's how the wicked will end up if they don't repent*]; and they shall go away into everlasting fire [*remorse and punishment*], prepared for them; and their torment is as [*is like*] a lake of fire and brimstone, whose flame ascendeth up forever and ever and has no end.

17 O the greatness and the justice of our God! For he executeth all his words, and they have gone forth out of his mouth, and his law must be fulfilled. [*Both the laws of justice and mercy will have their own.*]

> Now Jacob emphasizes again the joy and pleasant status the righteous will have eternally and reviews what it takes to become a "saint" or a "holy one," "free from blemish" (see Bible Dictionary, pp. 767–68).

18 But, behold, **the righteous, the saints** of the Holy One of Israel, they who have believed in the Holy One of Israel, they **who have endured the crosses** [*the tests and tribulations of remaining righteous*] **of the world**, and despised the shame of it, **they shall inherit the kingdom of God**, which was prepared for them from the foundation of the world [*which was planned in the premortal councils*], and **their joy shall be full forever.**

19 O the greatness of the mercy

of our God, the Holy One of Israel! For he delivereth his saints from that awful monster the devil, and death, and hell, and that lake of fire and brimstone [*symbolic of being engulfed in severe anguish for evil deeds etc.*], which is endless torment [*see D&C 19:4–12 for more about endless torment*].

20 O how great the holiness of our God! For he knoweth all things, and there is not anything save he knows it.

> Sometimes, members of the Church wonder whether or not Christ paid for the sins of all people or just for those which are ultimately repented of. Jacob answers this question in the next verse.

21 And he [*Christ*] cometh into the world that he may save all men **if** they will hearken unto his voice; for behold, he suffereth the pains of all men, yea, the pains of every living creature, both men, women, and children, who belong to the family of Adam [*Christ paid for all sins, whether repented of or not*].

> Christ paid for all sins, whether repented of or not. However, those who refuse to accept His payment by repenting and becoming righteous, will, in effect, be given back the "receipt" for payment of their sins, and will have to be punished for them themselves (see D&C 19:15–19).

22 And he suffereth this [*Christ went through His atoning sacrifice*] that the resurrection might pass upon all men [*Christ overcame physical death for everyone*], that all might stand before him at the great and judgment day [*so that it is completely fair for everyone to ultimately be accountable*].

> Next, Jacob reviews again what we must do to overcome spiritual death, which is dying as far as spirituality is concerned and being refused the privilege of returning to live with God eternally.

23 And he commandeth all men that they must **repent**, and **be baptized** in his name, **having perfect faith in the Holy One of Israel** [*having complete faith that Christ can make them clean and fit to be in the presence of God*], or they cannot be saved in the kingdom of God.

24 And **if they will not repent and believe in his name, and be baptized in his name, and endure to the end, they must be damned** [*they will be stopped from eternal progression*]; for the Lord God, the Holy One of Israel, has spoken it.

Eternal progression only applies to those who attain exaltation in the celestial kingdom. In other words, only those who live in the family unit eternally will have eternal progression. Those who go to any other category in the three degrees of glory or into outer darkness will be limited eternally.

25 Wherefore, he has given a law; and where there is no law given there is no punishment; and where there is no punishment there is no condemnation; and where there is no condemnation the mercies of the Holy One of Israel have claim upon them, because of the atonement; for they are delivered by the power of him.

Verse 25, above, is context sensitive, meaning that it must be studied in the context of all the scriptures. Verse 25 teaches that God is completely fair and that a person who has not been properly taught is not yet accountable for those laws. Taken alone, it sounds like some lucky people (who have passed the age of accountability) will make it simply because they were never taught the gospel. However, we know from D&C 131:6 that we cannot be saved in ignorance of the gospel. And we know from D&C 138 that all who did not get a fair opportunity to learn and accept the gospel in this life will get those opportunities in the spirit world. Therefore, there is no "free" salvation. Verse 26, next, must be studied in the same context.

26 For the atonement satisfieth the demands of his justice upon all those who have not the law given to them, that they are delivered from that awful monster, death and hell, and the devil, and the lake of fire and brimstone [*molten sulphur; a figurative expression to remind us that suffering for one's own sins is not a small thing; see D&C 19:15–19*], which is endless torment; and they are restored [*by way of merciful opportunities provided in the spirit world mission field*] to that God who gave them breath, which is the Holy One of Israel.

27 But wo unto him that has the law given, yea, that has all the commandments of God, like unto us [*in other words, those who have a full set of opportunities here on earth*], and that transgresseth them, and that wasteth the days of his probation, for awful is his state!

Jacob now gives his famous sermon on the fate of those who waste their mortal lives in wicked living. He begins with a warning to those who gain much education without having faith in Christ. (Compare with D&C 88:118.)

28 O that cunning plan of the

evil one! O the vainness, and the frailties, and the foolishness of men! **When they are learned they think they are wise, and they hearken not unto the counsel of God, for they set it aside, supposing they know of themselves**, wherefore, **their wisdom is foolishness** and it profiteth them not. And they shall perish.

29 But **to be learned is good if they hearken unto the counsels of God**.

30 But **wo unto the rich**, who are rich as to the things of the world. For because they are rich **they despise the poor**, and they persecute the meek, and **their hearts are upon their treasures**; wherefore, **their treasure is their god**. And behold, their treasure shall perish with them also.

31 And **wo unto the deaf** [*spiritually deaf*] **that will not hear** [*refuse to listen to the gospel*]; for they shall perish.

32 **Wo unto the blind** [*spiritually blind*] **that will not see** [*do not want to see spiritual truths*]; for they shall perish also.

33 **Wo unto the uncircumcised of heart** [*those who are not loyal to God in their innermost feelings*], for a knowledge of their iniquities shall smite them at the last day [*see verse 14*].

34 **Wo unto the liar**, for he shall be thrust down to hell.

35 **Wo unto the murderer** who deliberately killeth [*in other words, first degree murder*], for he shall die.

36 **Wo unto them who commit whoredoms** [*those who delight in sexual immorality of any form*], for they shall be thrust down to hell.

37 Yea, **wo unto those that worship idols**, for the devil of all devils delighteth in them.

38 And, in fine [*in summary*], **wo unto all those who die in their sins; for they shall return to God, and behold his face, and remain in their sins**.

39 O, my beloved brethren, **remember the awfulness in transgressing against that Holy God**, and also the awfulness of yielding [*as an agency choice*] to the enticings of that cunning one [*the devil*]. Remember, **to be carnally-minded is death** [*brings spiritual death*], and **to be spiritually-minded is life eternal** [*brings exaltation in celestial glory*].

40 O, my beloved brethren, give ear to my words. Remember the greatness of the Holy One of

Israel. Do not say that I have spoken hard things against you [*do not have a bad attitude about what I have taught you*]; for if ye do, ye will revile [*rebel*] against the truth; for I have spoken the words of your Maker. I know that the words of truth are hard against all uncleanness; but **the righteous fear them not, for they love the truth and are not shaken**.

> Now, having spoken in clear, unmistakable terms, Jacob tenderly invites his people to be loyal to Christ and to remember that the ways of righteousness are simple. By the way, perhaps you've noticed that righteousness is simple and wickedness is complex.

41 O then, my beloved brethren, come unto the Lord, the Holy One. Remember that his paths are righteous. Behold, the way for man is narrow, but it lieth in a straight course before him [*there is nothing complicated about righteousness*], and the keeper of the gate is the Holy One of Israel; and he employeth no servant there [*you can trust the Savior completely*]; and there is none other way save it be by the gate [*there is only one path which leads to salvation*]; for he cannot be deceived, for the Lord God is his name.

42 And whoso knocketh [*an agency choice for each of us*], to him will he open; and the wise [*in their own minds*], and the learned [*who don't have faith in Christ*], and they that are rich [*whose hearts are set on their wealth*], who are puffed up [*prideful*] because of their learning, and their wisdom, and their riches—yea, they are they whom he despiseth [*whom He will reject*]; and save [*unless*] they shall cast these things away, and consider themselves fools [*not wise in their own eyes; humble*] before God, and come down in the depths of humility, he will not open [*the "door" of heaven*] unto them.

43 But the things of the wise and the prudent [*the truly wise and careful*] shall be hid from them forever—yea, that happiness which is prepared for the saints.

44 O, my beloved brethren, remember my words. Behold, I take off my garments, and I shake them before you [*a token in Jacob's Jewish culture that he has delivered the message God asked him to and that the responsibility for it now lies with them*]; I pray the God of my salvation that he view me with his all-searching eye; wherefore, ye

shall know at the last day, when all men shall be judged of their works, that the God of Israel did witness that I shook your iniquities from my soul, and that I stand with brightness before him, and am rid of your blood [*not responsible in any way for your sins*].

45 O, my beloved brethren, **turn away from your sins; shake off the chains of him that would bind you fast; come unto that God who is the rock of your salvation.**

> Next, Jacob reminds his listeners that they will play a role in their final judgment. The wicked will have a perfect recollection of all their sins. As far as the righteous are concerned, they can take comfort in the statement of the Lord in D&C 58:42 concerning sins which have been repented of. He said, "Behold, he who has repented of his sins, the same is forgiven, and I, the Lord, remember them no more." Thus, the sins which have been properly repented of will not even be brought up or mentioned on Judgment Day.

46 Prepare your souls for that **glorious day** [*Judgment Day*] when **justice shall be administered unto the righteous**, even the day of judgment, that ye may not shrink with awful fear; that ye may not remember your awful guilt in perfectness, and be constrained to exclaim: Holy, holy are thy judgments, O Lord God Almighty—but I know my guilt; I transgressed thy law, and my transgressions are mine; and the devil hath obtained me, that I am a prey to his awful misery.

47 But behold, my brethren, is it expedient [*necessary*] that I should awake you to an awful reality of these things? Would I harrow up [*tear up*] your souls if your minds were pure? Would I be plain unto you according to the plainness of the truth if ye were freed from sin?

48 Behold, if ye were holy I would speak unto you of holiness; but as ye are not holy, and ye look upon me as a teacher, it must needs be expedient [*it is necessary*] that I teach you the consequences of sin.

49 Behold, my soul abhorreth sin [*is completely repulsed by sin*], and my heart delighteth in righteousness; and I will praise the holy name of my God.

50 Come, my brethren, every one that thirsteth, come ye to the waters [*the "living water" of Christ; see John 4:10*]; and he that hath no money [*you don't have to be wealthy to make it to heaven*], come buy and eat;

yea, come buy wine and milk [*the very best, in other words, exaltation*] without money and without price. [*In other words, the gospel of Christ is available to all, without regard to social status, personal wealth, etc.*]

51 Wherefore, do not spend money for that which is of no worth, nor your labor for that which cannot satisfy [*eternally*]. Hearken diligently unto me, and remember the words which I have spoken; and come unto the Holy One of Israel [*Christ*], and feast upon that which perisheth not, neither can be corrupted, and let your soul delight in fatness. [*"Fatness" is a word which means the very best, the finest. Thus, in verse 51, above, it would be symbolic of exaltation.*]

52 Behold, my beloved brethren, **remember the words of your God; pray unto him continually by day**, and **give thanks unto his holy name by night. Let your hearts rejoice.**

The phrase "Let your hearts rejoice" in verse 52, above, can be very important for personal joy and satisfaction. In one sense, it can simply mean, "Rejoice." However, in another sense, it can mean, "Allow yourself to be happy and confident that, with the Savior's help, you will make it."

King Benjamin was apparently concerned about his standing with the Lord as he considered his responsibilities for his people. When the angel appeared to him and helped him prepare for his address to his people, one of the first things he told Benjamin was that the Lord had heard his prayers and that "thou mayest rejoice" (Mosiah 3:4).

53 And behold how great the covenants of the Lord, and how great his condescensions unto the children of men [*His willingness to work with us who are so far beneath Him*]; and because of his greatness, and his grace [*ability to help us*] and mercy, he has promised unto us that our seed shall not utterly be destroyed, according to the flesh [*here in mortality*], but that he would preserve them; and in future generations they shall become a righteous branch unto the house of Israel [*a prophecy of the Restoration through Joseph Smith and the conversion of the Lamanites in the last days; see D&C 49:24*].

54 And now, my brethren, I would speak unto you more; but on the morrow [*tomorrow*] I will declare unto you the remainder of my words. Amen.

SECOND NEPHI 10

It is now "tomorrow" and Jacob continues his address to his people. He will first teach more about the Lamanites, then about the Jews and their scattering and last days gathering. He will then teach about the bringing of the gospel to the Lamanites. Finally, he will teach his people about Zion in the last days.

1 AND now I, Jacob, speak unto you again, my beloved brethren, concerning this righteous branch [*the Lamanites, referred to in 2 Nephi 9:53*] of which I have spoken.

2 For behold, the promises [*that the gospel will someday be brought back to the Lamanites*] which we have obtained are promises unto us according to the flesh [*that is to say, these promises will be literally fulfilled*]; wherefore, as it has been shown unto me that many of our children [*descendants*] shall perish in the flesh because of unbelief, nevertheless, God will be merciful unto many; and our children [*descendants*] shall be restored [*compare with D&C 49:24*], that they may come to that which will give them the true knowledge of their Redeemer.

3 Wherefore, as I said unto you, it must needs be expedient [*it is necessary*] that **Christ**—for in the last night the angel spake unto me that this should be his name—should **come among the Jews**, among those who are the more wicked part of the world; **and they shall crucify him**—for thus it behooveth our God [*Christ has to do this*], and there is none other nation on earth that would crucify their God.

Often when members read the last phrase of verse 3, above, they ask, "Is it true that this is the wickedest world?" The answer is "Yes"; see Moses 7:36.

The next question is usually, "What did we do wrong in the premortal life to deserve to be sent to this earth?" The answer is, "You should consider it a great honor to come to this world, where the Atonement for this and all other worlds belonging to Heavenly Father, ever, was performed. Your being here is a reminder to you of the trust and confidence the Father has in you."

4 For should the mighty miracles be wrought [*if such mighty miracles were done*] among other nations they would repent, and know that he be their God.

5 But because of priestcrafts [*the Jewish religious leaders exercising religious power and authority*

Second Nephi 10

for personal prestige and gain; see Alma 1:16] and iniquities, they at Jerusalem will stiffen their necks against him [*Jesus Christ*], that he be crucified.

6 Wherefore, because of their iniquities, destructions, famines, pestilences, and bloodshed shall come upon them [*the Jews*]; and they who shall not be destroyed shall be scattered among all nations.

> The gathering of the Jews spoken of next is one of the very visible signs of the times in the last days before the Second Coming of the Savior. We are privileged to live in the time when this great prophecy is being fulfilled.

7 But behold, thus saith the Lord God: When the day cometh that they [*the Jews*] shall believe in me, that I am Christ, then have I covenanted with their fathers [*ancestors*] that they shall be restored in the flesh [*in other words, the restoration of the Jews spoken of is not just symbolic; rather, it is a literal gathering*], upon the earth, unto the lands of their inheritance.

8 And it shall come to pass that they shall be gathered in from their long dispersion [*they will remain scattered for a long time*], from the isles of the sea [*from all nations of the earth*], and from the four parts of the earth; and the nations of the Gentiles shall be great in the eyes of me, saith God, in carrying them forth to the lands of their inheritance. [*In other words, non-Jewish nations will assist in bringing the Jews back to their homelands.*]

> As mentioned previously, Great Britain and other nations voted in the United Nations to restore the Jews to the land of Palestine and to create the nation of Israel in 1948. We understand these to be the "nations of the Gentiles" spoken of in verse 8, above.

9 Yea, the kings [*political leaders*] of the Gentiles shall be nursing fathers [*provide assistance*] unto them [*the Jews*], and their queens shall become nursing mothers; wherefore, the promises of the Lord are great unto the Gentiles [*it is a great privilege to help the Lord fulfill prophecies*], for he hath spoken it, and who can dispute?

10 But behold, this land [*America*], said God, shall be a land of thine inheritance [*Lehi's posterity; the Lamanites*], and the Gentiles [*immigrants from Europe, etc.*] shall be blessed upon the land.

> It is a tremendous promise with a miraculous fulfillment that this land will never have a king in

our day (see verse 11, next). In that, alone, we can see the hand of the Lord, especially when we look at the nearly universal trend over the centuries to have kings as political leaders.

11 And this land [*America; see heading to chapter 10*] shall be a land of liberty unto the Gentiles, and **there shall be no kings upon the land, who shall raise up unto the Gentiles.**

12 And I will fortify this land against all other nations.

13 And he that fighteth against Zion shall perish, saith God.

14 For he that raiseth up a king against me shall perish, for I, the Lord, the king of heaven, will be their king, and I will be a light unto them forever, that hear my words.

15 Wherefore, for this cause, that my covenants may be fulfilled which I have made unto the children of men, that I will do unto them while they are in the flesh [*during their mortal lives*], I must needs destroy the secret works of darkness, and of murders, and of abominations.

The next verse is fair warning to all people that no one will ultimately, successfully, fight against Zion (the Lord's work; the restoration of the gospel in the last days).

16 Wherefore, **he that fighteth against Zion, both Jew and Gentile, both bond and free, both male and female, shall perish;** for **they are they who are the whore of all the earth;** for they who are not for me are against me, saith our God.

The phrase "they are they who are the whore of all the earth" in verse 16, above, is unmistakably strong. You may recall that the "whore of all the earth" is the "church of the devil" (see 1 Nephi 14:10). The message is clear; if we are not helping the Lord build up His kingdom here on earth, we are helping the devil. There is no neutral ground.

17 For **I will fulfil my promises** which I have made unto the children of men, that I will do unto them while they are in the flesh—

18 Wherefore, my beloved brethren, thus saith our God: I will afflict thy seed [*the Lamanites*] by the hand of the Gentiles [*the Lamanites will be badly treated by those who settle America*]; nevertheless, I will soften the hearts of the Gentiles, that they shall be like unto a father to them; wherefore, the Gentiles shall be blessed and numbered among the house of Israel.

19 Wherefore, I will consecrate

this land [*America; North and South America*] unto thy seed, and them who shall be numbered among thy seed, forever, for the land of their inheritance; for **it is a choice land**, saith God unto me, **above all other lands**, wherefore I will have all men that dwell thereon that they shall worship me, saith God.

> The last phrase of verse 19, above, is sobering. It reminds us that to have the Lord's promises fulfilled concerning America, the inhabitants of America must live the gospel.

20 And now, my beloved brethren, seeing that our merciful God has given us so great knowledge concerning these things, let us remember him, and lay aside our sins, and not hang down our heads, for we are not cast off; nevertheless, we have been driven out of the land of our inheritance; but we have been led to a better land, for the Lord has made the sea our path, and we are upon an isle of the sea.

> As mentioned in previous notes, the phrase "we are upon an isle of the sea" in verse 20, above, means the Americas. In Jewish culture and language at the time of Lehi, the phrase "isles of the sea" means all lands and continents other than Asia and Africa.

21 But great are the promises of the Lord unto them who are upon the isles of the sea; wherefore as it says isles [*plural*], there must needs be more than this [*there must be other continents besides this one on which we live*], and they are inhabited also by our brethren. [*In other words, all people are our brothers and sisters.*]

> Next, Jacob teaches us that there are many peoples who have been led away by the Lord. In other words, there have been many "scatterings" throughout history. It will be fascinating someday to meet them and learn of their history.

22 For behold, the Lord God has led away from time to time from the house of Israel, according to his will and pleasure. And now behold, the Lord remembereth all them who have been broken off [*all people will eventually be "gathered in" as part of the gathering of Israel*], wherefore he remembereth us also [*keeps his covenants to restore us and our people also*].

> Next, in verse 23, we find one of Jacob's most famous teachings. We will emphasize this in **bold**.

23 Therefore, cheer up your hearts, and remember that **ye are free to act for yourselves—to choose the way of everlasting**

death or the way of eternal life.

Just a reminder, with respect to verse 23, above. There is no such thing as the actual destruction of a person's spirit. Therefore, the term "everlasting death" means "spiritual death" or what is often referred to as the "second death." In other words, being cut off from being in the presence of God forever. Another way to put it might be to say "never having the personal spirituality needed to be comfortable in the presence of God and other celestial beings forever."

"Eternal life" is also used in verse 23. The celestial glory has three degrees in it (see D&C 131:1–3) and "eternal life" always means "exaltation" in the highest degree of the celestial kingdom. D&C 14:7 teaches this by telling us that "eternal life . . . is the greatest of all the gifts of God." Exaltation means living in the family unit forever, becoming gods, having spirit children, creating worlds for them to live on, and using the same plan of salvation for them as our Heavenly Father used for us. The First Presidency made this clear in 1916 in the following statement (**bold** added for emphasis):

"Only resurrected and glorified beings can become parents of spirit offspring. Only such **exalted souls** have reached maturity in the appointed course of eternal life; and **the spirits born to them in the eternal worlds will pass in due sequence through the several stages or estates by which the glorified parents have attained exaltation**" (Smith, Lund, and Smith, 1916 First Presidency Statement, p. 942).

24 Wherefore, my beloved brethren, reconcile yourselves to the will of God, and not to the will of the devil and the flesh; and remember, after ye are reconciled unto God, that it is only in and through the grace of God that ye are saved.

The word "reconcile" as used in verse 24, above, comes from Latin and means "to sit with again." The word breakdown is:

"re" means "again"

"con" means "with"

"cile" means "sit"

Therefore, in this context, "reconcile" basically means to make agency choices which will allow you to return to God and sit down with Him again in His kingdom.

Revelation 3:20–21 teaches this concept of sitting down with Christ and the Father as follows (**bold** added for emphasis):

20 Behold, I stand at the door, and knock: if any man hear my voice, and open the door, I will come in to him, and will sup

with him, and he with me.

21 To him that overcometh will I grant to **sit with me in my throne, even as I also overcame, and am set down with my Father in his throne**.

25 Wherefore, may God raise you from death [*physical death*] by the power of the resurrection, and also from everlasting death [*spiritual death; dying as to things which are spiritual*] by the power of the atonement, that ye may be received into the eternal kingdom of God [*celestial glory*], that ye may praise him through grace divine. Amen.

SECOND NEPHI 11

2 Nephi, chapters 12–24 and 27, are the writings of Isaiah. In this chapter, Nephi will explain why he "delighteth" (2 Nephi 11:2) in the words of Isaiah. He will explain why he is going to quote Isaiah at such length.

Many members of the Church find these chapters of Isaiah very difficult to understand. Some skip them in their reading of the Book of Mormon, while others read every word without getting much out of them. Yet others see some beautiful concepts and gain some understanding but miss much.

Pay close attention to what Nephi says about why the writings and teachings of Isaiah are so valuable. It will help as we study the chapters of Isaiah which lie ahead. When we get to them, we will include many helps within the verses.

We will use **bold** to highlight the reasons Nephi says he delights in Isaiah's words.

1 AND now, Jacob spake many more things to my people at that time; nevertheless only these things have I caused to be written, for the things which I have written sufficeth me [*are sufficient as far as my purposes are concerned*].

2 And now I, Nephi, write more of the words of Isaiah, for my soul delighteth in his words. For **I will liken his words unto my people** [*the words of Isaiah apply to my people*], and I will send them forth unto all my children, for he verily saw my Redeemer [*see 2 Nephi 16:1–5*], even as I have seen him [*Nephi has seen the Savior*].

3 And my brother, Jacob, also has seen him as I have seen him; wherefore, I will send their words forth unto my children to prove unto them that my words are true. Wherefore, by the words of

three [*the law of witnesses*], God hath said, I will establish my word. Nevertheless, God sendeth more witnesses, and he proveth all his words.

> Now, some reasons Nephi wants his people to study Isaiah.

4 Behold, **my soul delighteth in proving unto my people the truth of the coming of Christ**; for, for this end [*purpose*] hath the law of Moses been given [*this is the purpose of the law of Moses*]; and **all things which have been given of God from the beginning of the world, unto man, are the typifying of him** [*"typifying of" means "symbolic of."*]

5 And also **my soul delighteth in the covenants of the Lord which he hath made to our fathers** [*ancestors*]; yea, **my soul delighteth in his grace, and in his justice, and power, and mercy in the great and eternal plan of deliverance from death.**

6 And **my soul delighteth in proving unto my people that save Christ should come all men must perish** [*if it were not for Christ, we would all be destroyed*].

> Sometimes we shy away from logic in gospel discussions and gospel teaching because shallow logic, based on falsehoods or half truths, has been used so pervasively to try to prove that there is no God, etc. However, when logic is based on truth, it has tremendous power. Watch Nephi's powerful "true logic" in verse 7, next.

7 For if there be no Christ there be no God; and if there be no God we are not [*we do not exist*], for there could have been no creation. But there is a God, and he is Christ, and he cometh in the fulness of his own time [*He will come to live on earth when the time is right*].

8 And now **I write some of the words of Isaiah, that whoso of my people shall see these words may lift up their hearts and rejoice for all men.** Now these are the words, and **ye may liken them unto you and unto all men** [*they apply to you and to everyone*].

> Many who observe the widespread wickedness among people on earth feel that there is little hope for the majority of people who now live or who ever have lived on earth or ever will. Nephi's statement in verse 8, above, provides an inspired contradiction to such philosophy and thinking. He in effect invites us to see the "big picture" of how far the Atonement will ultimately reach, and to

"rejoice for all men." This is a wonderful and serious reminder that God is completely fair to all people. We can be optimists about them rather than pessimists.

We have seen Lehi bless Laman and Lemuel's children who would not get a fair chance because of their wayward parents. He blessed them that they would get a fair chance, before Judgment Day. In his blessing he stated that "if (they had been) brought up in the way ye should go (they would) not depart from it" (see 2 Nephi 4:5 and 9). God is completely fair!

We read Doctrine and Covenants, section 138, and see that all who did not get a fair set of opportunities to accept the gospel here during mortality, regardless of why, will get that opportunity before Judgment Day. And D&C 137:7 and 8 reinforce this truth. No wonder Nephi invites us to "lift up [our] hearts and rejoice for all men." And no wonder he wants us to read and understand Isaiah's great message, because it shows how effective and far-reaching Christ's Atonement is.

One last thing, before we go to the Isaiah chapters Nephi presents to us. In order to get a feel for the teaching of Isaiah with respect to the power of the Atonement to cleanse and heal, we will take time here to read Isaiah, chapter one, from the Bible. Notes are added within the verses to help with understanding. (**Bold** added for emphasis.)

Isaiah 1

1 The vision of Isaiah the son of Amoz, which he saw concerning Judah and Jerusalem in the days of Uzziah, Jotham, Ahaz, and Hezekiah, kings of Judah [*an introduction to the whole book—a superscription similar to "An account of Lehi . . ." at the beginning of First Nephi. The kings mentioned above reigned from about 740 BC to 701 BC*].

2 Hear, O heavens, and give ear, O earth: for the Lord hath spoken, I have nourished and brought up children, and they have rebelled against me [*the main problem*].

3 The ox knoweth his owner, and the ass his master's crib [*manger*]: but Israel doth not know [*know God*], my people doth not consider [*think seriously, i.e., Israel, you are acting dumber than animals!*].

4 Ah **sinful nation, a people laden with iniquity** [*loaded with wickedness*], **a seed of evildoers, children that are corrupters:** they have **forsaken the Lord**, they have provoked the Holy One of Israel unto anger, **they are gone away backward** [*retrogressing; they are "in the world" and "of the world"*].

5 Why should ye be stricken any more [*why do you keep asking for more punishment*]? ye will revolt more and more: the **whole head** [*leadership*] **is sick**, and **the whole heart** [*the people*] **faint** [*is diseased*].

6 **From the sole of the foot even unto the head there is no soundness in it** [*you are completely sick*]; but wounds [*you have spiritual wounds*], and bruises [*spiritual bruises*], and putrifying sores [*you have oozing spiritual sores all over you*]: they have not been closed, neither bound up, neither mollified with ointment [*you are sick, and you don't even care; you won't try the simplest first aid*].

7 Your country is desolate [*prophecy of coming destruction*], your cities are burned with fire: your land, strangers devour it in your presence, and it is desolate as overthrown by strangers [*foreigners, specifically the Assyrians*].

8 And the daughter of Zion [*Israel*] is left as a cottage [*temporary shade structure built of straw and leaves*] in a vineyard, as a lodge [*same as cottage*] in a garden of cucumbers, as a besieged city [*you are about as secure as a flimsy shade shack in a garden*].

9 Except the Lord of hosts had left unto us a very small remnant [*if God hadn't intervened and saved a few of Israel*], we should have been as Sodom, and we should have been like unto Gomorrah [*totally destroyed*].

10 Hear the word of the Lord, ye rulers of Sodom [*"Listen up, you wicked leaders!"*]; give ear unto the law of our God, ye people of Gomorrah [*Sodom and Gomorrah symbolize total wickedness*].

11 To what purpose is the multitude of your sacrifices unto me [*what good are your insincere, empty rituals*]? saith the Lord: I am full [*"I've had it to here!"*] of the burnt offerings of rams, and the fat of fed beasts; and I delight not in the blood of bullocks, or of lambs, or of he goats.

12 When ye come to appear before me, who hath required this at your hand, to tread my courts [*who authorized you to be such hypocrites*]?

13 Bring no more vain [*useless*] oblations [*offerings*]; incense is an abomination unto me; the new moons [*special Sabbath ritual at beginning of month—Bible Dictionary, p. 738, under "New Moon"*] and sabbaths, the calling of assemblies, I cannot [*"I can't stand it!"*] away with; it is iniquity, even the solemn meeting [*solemn assembly*].

14 Your new moons and your appointed feasts my soul hateth: they are a trouble unto me; I am weary to bear them.

15 And when ye spread forth

your hands [*pray*], I will hide mine eyes from you: yea, when ye make many prayers, I will not hear: your hands are full of blood [*bloodshed; murder, see verse 21*].

You probably can't imagine anyone more spiritually sick than the people Isaiah has described in the foregoing verses. Watch, now, as he invites even people who are so far gone into wickedness to repent and become completely clean through the Atonement of the Savior.

16 **Wash you** [*be baptized*], **make you clean; put away the evil of your doings from before mine eyes** [*repent*]; **cease to do evil**;

17 **Learn to do well** [*don't just cease to do evil, but replace evil with good*]; seek judgement [*be fair*], relieve the oppressed, judge the fatherless [*be kind and fair to them*], plead for the widow.

18 **Come now, and let us reason together, saith the Lord: though your sins be as scarlet** [*cloth dyed with scarlet, a colorfast dye*], **they shall be as white as snow** [*even though you think your sins are colorfast, the Atonement can cleanse you*]; **though they be red like crimson, they shall be as wool** [*a long process is required to get wool white, but it can be done*].

19 **If ye be willing and obedient, ye** [*even people who have been as wicked as you*] **shall eat the good of the land** [*you will prosper with the blessings of the Lord upon you*]:

20 But if ye refuse and rebel, ye shall be devoured with the sword: for the mouth of the Lord hath spoken it.

21 How is the faithful city [*Jerusalem*] become an harlot [*unfaithful to the Lord; a willful sin*]! it was full of judgement [*justice*]; righteousness lodged in it; but now murderers.

22 Thy silver is become dross [*surface scum on molten metal*] thy wine mixed with water [*you are polluted!*].

23 Thy princes [*rulers*] are rebellious, and companions of thieves: every one loveth gifts [*bribes*], and followeth after rewards: they judge not [*do not justice to*] the fatherless, neither doth the cause of the widow come unto them [*never penetrates their hearts*].

24 Therefore saith the Lord, the Lord of hosts, the mighty One of Israel, Ah, I will ease me of [*be rid of*] mine adversaries, and avenge me of mine enemies:

25 And I will turn [*return; i.e., repeatedly chastise*] my hand upon thee, and purely purge away thy dross, and take away all thy tin [*slag; i.e., I will refine thee*]:

26 And I will restore thy judges as at the first, and thy counsellors as at the beginning:

afterward thou shalt be called, The city of righteousness, the faithful city [*gathering*].

27 Zion shall be redeemed [*a fact!*] with judgment, and her converts with righteousness [*message of hope*].

28 And the destruction of the transgressors and of the sinners shall be together [*at the same time; Second Coming*], and they that forsake the Lord shall be consumed.

29 For they shall be ashamed of [*shamed because of*] the oaks [*trees and gardens used in idol worship*] which ye have desired, and ye shall be confounded for the [*because of the*] gardens [*used in idol worship*] that ye have chosen.

30 For ye shall be as an oak whose leaf fadeth, and as a garden that hath no water [*drought; destruction*].

31 And the strong shall be as tow [*as a tuft of inflammable fibers*], and the maker of it as a spark, and they shall both burn together, and none shall quench them [*destruction of the wicked is sure to happen*].

Now we will go ahead and study the next chapters of Isaiah in Second Nephi. We will continue using **bold** occasionally for emphasis.

SECOND NEPHI 12

Chapters 12, 13, and 14 go together. Also note that of the 433 verses of Isaiah quoted in the Book of Mormon, over half of them are given differently than in the King James Bible, while about two hundred of them are the same; see 2 Nephi 12, footnote 2a. Thus, the Book of Mormon is a major source of clarification and help for understanding Isaiah. This chapter, 2 Nephi 12, is similar to Isaiah 2 in the Bible. It deals with the gathering of Israel to the true Church in the last days, the Millennium, and the destruction of the proud and the wicked at the Second Coming.

1 The word that Isaiah, the son of Amoz, saw concerning Judah [*the Jews as a political kingdom as well as the Jews as Israelites*] and Jerusalem:

> As you know, because Isaiah uses so much symbolism, his writings can have many different meanings and applications. Next, in verse 2 for instance, the phrase "mountain of the Lord's house" can mean the headquarters of the Church in Salt Lake City in the Rocky Mountains in the last days. Also, since "mountains" are often symbolic of temples ("high places" where we can draw closer to God), "mountain of the Lord's house"

can have a dual meaning referring to temples.

2 And it shall come to pass in the last days, when the mountain of the Lord's house [*"high place," or Church headquarters in the last days; also temples will be established*] shall be established in the top of the mountains, and shall be exalted above the hills [*you can get "higher," or closer to God in the temples through covenant-making than on the highest mountains*], and all nations [*the gathering involves people from every nation*] shall flow unto it [*the true Church in the last days*].

LeGrand Richards, an Apostle and scholar, explained how "mountain" can refer to temples as follows:

"The word mountain is used in the scriptures in different allegorical or figurative senses. In 2 Nephi 12:1–4 the word mountain refers to a high place of God, a place of revelation, even the temple of the Lord.

"This temple (Salt Lake Temple) on this temple block is that house of the God of Jacob that our pioneer fathers started to build when they were a thousand miles from transportation, and it took them forty years to build it" (Richards, "Prophets and Prophecy," in Conference Report, p. 77; or *Ensign*, p. 51).

3 And many people shall go and say, Come ye, and let us go up to the mountain [*to the true Church; temple*] of the Lord, to the house [*temples*] of the God of Jacob [*Israel*]; and he will teach us of his ways, and we will walk in his paths [*we will be obedient*]; for out of Zion shall go forth the law, and the word of the Lord from Jerusalem [*"law" and "word" are synonyms*].

There will be two headquarters of the Church during the Millennium, one in Zion (Jackson County, Missouri) and one in Old Jerusalem.

4 And he [*Christ*] shall judge among the nations, and shall rebuke many people: and they shall beat their swords into plow-shares [*the promised millennial peace will come*], and their spears into pruning-hooks [*there will be peace*]—nation shall not lift up sword against nation, neither shall they learn war any more [*the Millennium*].

Isaiah now switches from the future back to his own time and people who have become very wicked, inviting them to repent and return to the Lord.

5 O house of Jacob [*Israel*], come ye and let us walk in the light of the Lord; yea, come, for ye have all gone astray,

every one to his wicked ways.

> Next, Isaiah explains why the blessings of the Lord are not coming upon the Israelites of his day. Remember that the phrase "house of Jacob" means "family of Jacob" or in other words, "descendants of Abraham, Isaac, and Jacob," who are the covenant people of the Lord. Remember also that all people are invited by the gospel of Jesus Christ to join with the "covenant people of the Lord" through baptism, whether or not they are bloodline descendants of Jacob. Thus all can become covenant people and ultimately enter into celestial exaltation.

6 Therefore [*this is the reason why*], O Lord, thou hast forsaken thy people, the house of Jacob [*the Israelites*], because they be replenished from the east [*they are adopting false eastern religions*], and hearken unto soothsayers like the Philistines [*are into witchcraft, sorcery etc.; see 3 Nephi 21:16*], and they please themselves in the children of strangers [*they are mixing and marrying with foreigners, people not of covenant Israel; they are "marrying" themselves right out of the Church, so to speak*].

> The word "strangers," as used in Isaiah's writings (see verse 6, above), almost always means "foreigners" or in other words, non-Israelites.

7 Their land also is full of silver and gold, neither is there any end of their treasures [*they have become materialistic*]; their land is also full of horses, neither is there any end of their chariots.

> Horses and chariots are symbolic of military equipment and preparations for war in Isaiah's writings. They can also represent military might and ability to conquer.

8 Their land is also full of idols [*they are in a condition of deep apostasy; they have left God*]; they worship the work of their own hands, that which their own fingers have made [*an absurd thing to do; emphasizing that wickedness does not promote rational thought, a theme Isaiah pursues throughout his writings*].

9 And the mean man [*poor, low in social status*] boweth not down [*is not humble*], and the great [*wealthy, powerful, high in social status*] man humbleth himself not, therefore, forgive him not [*nobody is humble, therefore, no forgiveness!*].

> Verse 9, above, is a great example of the value of the Book of Mormon Isaiah verses. In the Bible, the equivalent of verse 9 reads as follows:

Isaiah 2:9

9 And the mean man boweth down, and the great man humbleth himself: therefore forgive them not.

When you compare 2 Nephi 12:9 with Isaiah 2:9, you see that the word "not" is left out twice in the Bible version and makes all the difference! If you were reading Isaiah in the Bible and trying to understand God's mercy and His dealings with people based on Isaiah 2:9, you would be in trouble. This is an example of the meaning of the eighth article of faith which says: "We believe the Bible to be the word of God as far as it is translated correctly; we also believe the Book of Mormon to be the word of God" (Pearl of Great Price, Article of Faith 1:8).

10 O ye wicked ones, enter into the rock [*caves; see verse 19*], and hide thee in the dust, for the fear of the Lord and **the glory of his majesty shall smite thee** [*you will not be able to stand the brightness of his glory at the Second Coming and will thus be consumed; see D&C 5:19*].

Many people wonder how the wicked will be burned at the time of the actual Second Coming. We learned the answer in verse 10, above. As stated, they will be burned by His glory. This is stated again in verses 19 and 21.

Some years ago, a student asked me how the temples would survive the burning at the Second Coming. Verses 10, 19, 21, plus D&C 5:19 provide a simple answer. Temples can stand the glory of the Lord. Therefore, they will not be burned.

11 And it shall come to pass that the lofty looks [*pride*] of man shall be humbled, and the haughtiness [*pride*] of men shall be bowed down [*put down*], and the Lord alone shall be exalted in that day [*the Lord will demonstrate that He has power over all things at the Second Coming*].

Verse 11, above, is a good example of the fact that Isaiah repeats important concepts as he writes and teaches. The phrases "lofty looks" and "haughtiness of men" both mean pride. If people do not understand that Isaiah uses repetition as a technique for emphasizing important points, they could spend a lot of time and fruitless effort in trying to figure out the difference in message between these two phrases. In fact, in verse 12, next, Isaiah says "pride" three different ways. They are in **bold**. This emphasis against pride continues in succeeding verses. We will **bold** some of them too.

12 For the day of the Lord of Hosts [*the Second Coming*]

soon cometh upon [*Hebrew: "against"*] all nations, yea, upon every one [*who is wicked*]; yea, upon the **proud** and **lofty**, and upon every one who is **lifted up** [*prideful*], and he shall be brought low [*humbled*].

13 Yea, and the day of the Lord shall come upon all the **cedars** [*symbolic of high and mighty people; can also mean groves of trees which idol worshipers often used for seclusion when they participated in sexual immorality with temple prostitutes as a part of their idol worship*] **of Lebanon**, for they are **high and lifted up** [*full of pride*]; and upon all the **oaks** [*people*] **of Bashan**;

> As mentioned in verse 13, above, sexual immorality was often a part of idol worship among apostate Israelites as they joined in the false religions of their pagan neighbors. The Bible Dictionary confirms this abominable practice on page 706, under the topic "Idol." It describes various aspects of idol worship in practice in ancient times and, among other things, says, "Such idolatry being some form of nature worship, **which encouraged** as a rule **immoral practices**."
>
> Perhaps you have wondered why conquering Israelite armies were often commanded to cut down groves of trees as part of their conquering of their enemies. Most of us are environmentally conscientious and would prefer that they leave these trees standing. But, when we understand that the groves represented sexual immorality associated with apostasy, we understand. An example of such a command to destroy the groves is found in **Exodus 34:13** as follows:
>
> "But ye shall destroy their altars, break their images, and cut down their groves."

14 And upon all the high mountains [*where people worship idols*], and upon all the hills [*where they worship idols*], and upon all the nations which are **lifted up** [*in pride, etc.*], and upon every people;

15 And upon every high tower, and upon every fenced wall [*symbolic of the pride and "trusting in the arm of flesh" which can go along with man-made defenses*];

16 And upon all the ships of the sea, and upon all the ships of Tarshish [*noted for ability to travel long distances, carry large cargos, and have the strength of a warship; apparently symbolic of pride and materialism*], and upon all pleasant pictures [*pleasure ships upon which the wealthy traveled*].

17 And the **loftiness** [*pride*] of man shall be bowed down [*shall be brought down*], and the **haughtiness** of men shall be made low [*brought* down]; and the Lord alone shall be exalted in that day.

18 And the idols he [*Christ*] shall utterly abolish [*at the Second Coming*].

In verse 19, next, Isaiah paints a picture with words of the terror of the wicked as the Savior actually comes at the time of His Second Coming.

19 And they [*the wicked*] shall go into the holes of the rocks [*caves*], and into the caves of the earth, for the fear of the Lord shall come upon them and **the glory of his majesty shall smite them** [*D&C 5:19*], when he ariseth [*becomes active*] to shake terribly the earth.

20 In that day [*the Second Coming*] a man shall cast his idols of silver, and his idols of gold, which he hath made for himself to worship [*an absurd thing to do*], to the moles and to the bats [*creatures who live in darkness; symbolic of wicked people who live in spiritual darkness*];

21 To go into the clefts of the rocks, and into the tops of the ragged rocks [*to try to hide from God*], for the fear of the Lord shall come upon them and **the majesty of his glory shall smite them** [*D&C 5:19*], when he ariseth to shake terribly the earth.

22 Cease ye from man, whose breath is in his nostrils; for wherein is he to be accounted of [*why trust in man, why trust in the arm of flesh when God is truly powerful and can save you*]?

SECOND NEPHI 13

This chapter is to be compared with Isaiah 3 in the Bible. In this chapter as well as others, Isaiah uses a literary technique known as "chiasmus," a writing form in which the author says certain things and then repeats them in reverse order for emphasis. Usually, the middle element or elements of the chiasmus are the main point being emphasized. An example of a simple chiasmus is found in Isaiah 6:10 as follows. We will use **bold** to point it out.

Chiastic structure in Isaiah 6:10:

"Make the **heart** of this people fat, and make their **ears** heavy, and shut their **eyes**; lest they see with their **eyes**, and hear with their **ears**, and understand with their **heart**, and convert, and be healed."

A way of showing the flow of the above chiasmus would be:

A, B, C, C', B', A'

The ancient use of chiasmus as a literary technique was not discovered until after the coming forth of the Book of Mormon. Therefore, the fact that chiasmus is found in other places in the Book of Mormon is a very strong internal evidence of its authenticity as an ancient document. Two examples of chiasmus in the Book of Mormon, other than in the Isaiah passages, follow. We will again use **bold** to point out the ancient chiastic writing form.

Example 1: Mosiah 3:18–19

18 For behold he judgeth, and his judgment is just; and the infant perisheth not that dieth in his infancy; but men drink damnation to their own souls except they **humble (A)** themselves and become as **little children (B)**, and believe that salvation was, and is, and is to come, in and through the **atoning blood of Christ (C)**, the Lord Omnipotent.

19 **For the natural man (D)** is an enemy to God, and has been from the fall of Adam, and will be, forever and ever, unless he yields to the enticings of the Holy Spirit, and putteth off **the natural man (D')** and becometh a saint through the **atonement of Christ (C')** the Lord, and becometh as a **child (B')**, submissive, meek, **humble (A')**, patient, full of love, willing to submit to all things which the Lord seeth fit to inflict upon him, even as a child doth submit to his father.

In the case of the above chiasmus, we could show the flow of concepts as follows:

A, B, C, D, D', C', B', A'

Example 2: Alma 36

1 My son, give ear to my **words (A)**; for I swear unto you, that inasmuch as ye shall **keep the commandments (B)** of God ye shall prosper in the land.

2 I would that ye should do as I have done, in remembering the captivity of our fathers; for they were **in bondage (C)**, and none could deliver them except it was the God of Abraham, and the God of Isaac, and the God of Jacob; and he surely did deliver them in their afflictions.

3 And now, O my son Helaman, behold, thou art in thy youth, and therefore, I beseech of thee that thou wilt hear my words and learn of me; for I do know that whosoever shall put their trust in God shall be **supported in their trials (D)**, and their troubles, and their afflictions, and shall be lifted up at the last day.

Second Nephi 13

4 And I would not that ye think that I know of myself—not of the temporal but of the spiritual, not of the carnal mind but of God.

5 Now, behold, I say unto you, if I had not been **born of God (E)** I should not have known these things; but God has, by the mouth of his holy angel, made these things known unto me, not of any worthiness of myself;

6 For I went about with the sons of Mosiah, seeking to destroy the church of God; but behold, God sent his holy angel to stop us by the way.

7 And behold, he spake unto us, as it were the voice of thunder, and the whole earth did tremble beneath our feet; and we all fell to the earth, for the fear of the Lord came upon us.

8 But behold, the voice said unto me: Arise. And I arose and stood up, and beheld the angel.

9 And he said unto me: If thou wilt of thyself be destroyed, seek no more to destroy the church of God.

10 And it came to pass that I fell to the earth; and it was for the space of three days and three nights that I could not open my mouth, neither had I the use of my limbs.

11 And the angel spake more things unto me, which were heard by my brethren, but I did not hear them; for when I heard the words—If thou wilt be destroyed of thyself, seek no more to destroy the church of God—I was struck with such great fear and amazement lest perhaps I should be destroyed, that I fell to the earth and I did hear no more.

12 But I was racked with eternal torment, for my soul was harrowed up to the greatest degree and racked with all my sins.

13 Yea, I did remember all my sins and iniquities, for which I was tormented with the pains of hell; yea, I saw that I had rebelled against my God, and that I had not kept his holy commandments.

14 Yea, and I had murdered many of his children, or rather led them away unto destruction; yea, and in fine so great had been my iniquities, that the very thought of coming into the presence of my God did rack my soul with inexpressible horror.

15 Oh, thought I, that I could be banished and become extinct both soul and body, that I might not be brought to stand in the presence of my God, to be judged of my deeds.

16 And now, for three days and for three nights was I racked, even with the pains of a damned soul.

17 And it came to pass that as I was thus racked with torment, while I was harrowed up by **the memory of my many sins (F)**, behold, I remembered also to have heard my father prophesy unto the people concerning the coming of one Jesus Christ, a Son of God, to atone for the sins of the world.

18 Now, as my mind caught hold upon this thought, I cried within my heart: O Jesus, thou Son of God, have mercy on me, who am in the gall of bitterness, and am encircled about by the everlasting chains of death.

19 And now, behold, when I thought this, I could remember my pains no more; yea, I was harrowed up by **the memory of my sins (F')** no more.

20 And oh, what joy, and what marvelous light I did behold; yea, my soul was filled with joy as exceeding as was my pain!

21 Yea, I say unto you, my son, that there could be nothing so exquisite and so bitter as were my pains. Yea, and again I say unto you, my son, that on the other hand, there can be nothing so exquisite and sweet as was my joy.

22 Yea, methought I saw, even as our father Lehi saw, God sitting upon his throne, surrounded with numberless concourses of angels, in the attitude of singing and praising their God; yea, and my soul did long to be there.

23 But behold, my limbs did receive their strength again, and I stood upon my feet, and did manifest unto the people that I had been born of God.

24 Yea, and from that time even until now, I have labored without ceasing, that I might bring souls unto repentance; that I might bring them to taste of the exceeding joy of which I did taste; that they might also be born of God, and be filled with the Holy Ghost.

25 Yea, and now behold, O my son, the Lord doth give me exceedingly great joy in the fruit of my labors;

26 For because of the word which he has imparted unto me, behold, many have been **born of God (E')**, and have tasted as I have tasted, and have seen eye to eye as I have seen; therefore they do know of these things of which I have spoken, as I do know; and the knowledge which I have is of God.

27 And I have been **supported under trials (D')** and troubles of every kind, yea, and in all manner of afflictions; yea, God has delivered me from prison, and from bonds, and from death; yea, and I do put my trust in him, and he will still deliver me.

28 And I know that he will raise me up at the last day, to dwell

SECOND NEPHI 13

with him in glory; yea, and I will praise him forever, for he has brought our fathers out of Egypt, and he has swallowed up the Egyptians in the Red Sea; and he led them by his power into the promised land; yea, and he has delivered them out of bondage and captivity from time to time.

29 Yea, and he has also brought our fathers out of the land of Jerusalem; and he has also, by his everlasting power, delivered them **out of bondage (C')** and captivity, from time to time even down to the present day; and I have always retained in remembrance their captivity; yea, and ye also ought to retain in remembrance, as I have done, their captivity.

30 But behold, my son, this is not all; for ye ought to know as I do know, that inasmuch as ye shall **keep the commandments (B')** of God ye shall prosper in the land; and ye ought to know also, that inasmuch as ye will not keep the commandments of God ye shall be cut off from his presence. Now this is according to his **word (A')**.

By the way, did you notice the center of the "chiasmus"? It deals with "memory of sins" and teaches very strongly that memory of sins need not devastate members for the rest of their lives if they repent and are cleansed by the Atonement. Also, if you look closely, there is much more of chiasmus in Alma 36. In fact, there is a chiasmus containing thirty-four elements, seventeen going forward and seventeen going backward.

We will now go ahead with 2 Nephi 13, which contains a chiastic structure also. Isaiah uses chiasmus to show the destruction of stability within a society which smiles upon gross sin and wickedness.

1 For behold, the Lord, **the Lord of Hosts, doth take away from Jerusalem (A)**, and from Judah, the stay [*supply*] and the staff [*support*], **the whole staff of bread (B)**, and the whole stay of water [*the Lord is going to pull the props out and the whole kingdom of the Jews will collapse*]—

2 **The mighty man (C), and the man of war**, the judge, and the prophet, and the prudent, and the ancient [*all the stable, capable leaders will be gone*];

3 **The captain of fifty, and the honorable man, and the counselor (D), and the cunning artificer** [*skilled craftsman*], **and the eloquent orator** [*all capable leaders and craftsman will be gone*].

4 And I will **give children unto them to be their princes** [*leaders*], **and babes (E) shall rule**

over them [*immature, irresponsible leaders will take over*].

5 And **the people shall be oppressed (F), every one by another** [*anarchy, gangs, citizens against citizens, etc.*], and every one by his neighbor; the **child shall behave himself proudly against the ancient (E')**, and the base [*crude, rude*] against the honorable [*no respect for authority*].

> Next, Isaiah describes how bad things will get when stable society crumbles.

6 When a man shall take hold of his brother of the house of his father, and shall say: Thou hast clothing, **be thou our ruler (D'), and let not this ruin come under thy hand** [*don't let this happen to us, you've got half decent clothing, you be our leader*]—

7 In that day shall he swear [*protest*], saying: **(C') I will not be a healer** [*I can't lead you nor defend and protect you!*]; for in my house there is neither **bread (B')** nor clothing [*I've got my own problems*]; make me not a ruler of the people.

> Next, Isaiah describes the end result of a society that allows open evil and wickedness.

8 **For Jerusalem is ruined, (A') and Judah is fallen**, because their tongues and their doings have been against the Lord, to provoke the eyes of his glory [*in word and actions, the people are completely against the Lord*].

9 The show of their countenance doth witness against them [*they even look wicked*], and doth declare their sin to be even as Sodom [*wicked through and through, including homosexuality; see Gen. 19, footnote 5a*], and they cannot hide it [*blatant sin, can't be rationalized away or hidden from God*]. Wo unto their souls, for they have rewarded evil unto themselves [*they are getting what they deserve*]!

> So far, this chapter is pretty dismal. In order to make sure that the righteous do not despair, who are trying to survive spiritually and otherwise in such a society, the Lord assures them that they will ultimately be rewarded for their righteousness.

10 Say unto the righteous that it is well with them; for they shall eat the fruit of their doings.

11 Wo unto the wicked, for they shall perish; for the reward of their hands shall be upon them! [*As ye sow, so shall ye reap.*]

Isaiah continues to describe the end results of such uncontrolled wickedness among the Jews. This of course applies to any nation, any time in history, anywhere.

12 And my people, children [*immature leaders*] are their oppressors, and women rule over them [*breakdown of traditional family; men are weak leaders*]. O my people, they who lead thee cause thee to err and destroy the way of thy paths [*leadership without basic gospel values causes terrible damage*].

Next, Isaiah will take the wicked leaders of the Jews to task for selfishly taking all they possibly can from the very people they are supposed to protect as leaders.

13 The Lord standeth up to plead [*Hebrew: contend, or, you are in big trouble*], and standeth to judge the people.

14 The Lord will enter into judgment with the ancients [*the wicked elders and leaders*] of his people and the princes [*leaders*] thereof; for ye have eaten up the vineyard [*you have ruined, destroyed the country*] and the spoil of the poor in your houses [*you have all kinds of loot in your houses which you have taken from the poor; you were*] *supposed to protect them, but, instead, you ruin them*].

15 What mean ye [*what have you got to say for yourselves*]? Ye beat my people to pieces, and grind the faces of the poor [*push the poor farther into poverty*], saith the Lord God of Hosts.

Isaiah now shows what happens when women get as wicked as men, and points out that when this happens, society is doomed as pointed out in verses 25 and 26.

16 Moreover, the Lord saith: Because the daughters of Zion are haughty [*full of wicked pride*], and walk with stretched-forth necks [*pride*] and wanton [*lustful*] eyes, walking and mincing [*short, rapid steps; see Isaiah 3, footnote 16e*] as they go, and making a tinkling with their feet [*German Bible: wearing expensive shoes so people will notice them*]—

17 Therefore [*for these reasons*] the Lord will smite with a scab the crown of the head [*German Bible: make them bald; perhaps the "scab" is a result of being shaved as slaves*] of the daughters of Zion, and the Lord will discover their secret parts [*expose their evil deeds*].

In verse 17, above, Isaiah prophesied that the Lord's covenant people would go into captivity because of their wickedness. Below, he describes the taking away of all that has been precious in the hearts and minds of the women who have become wicked in Isaiah's day. This same scene is typical of any society whose morals and values decay.

18 In that day the Lord will take away the bravery [*German Bible: decoration, beauty*] of their tinkling ornaments [*German Bible: expensive shoes*], and cauls, and round tires like the moon [*female ornamentations representing high status in materialistic society*];

19 The chains [*necklaces*] and the bracelets, and the mufflers [*veils*];

20 The bonnets, and the ornaments of the legs, and the headbands, and the tablets [*German Bible: musk boxes, perfume boxes*], and the ear-rings;

21 The rings, and nose jewels;

22 The changeable suits of apparel [*German Bible: party clothes*], and the mantles [*German Bible: gowns, robes*], and the wimples [*medieval women's head coverings*], and the crisping-pins [*German Bible: money purses*];

23 The glasses [*German Bible: mirrors; Hebrew: see-through clothing; see Isaiah 3, footnote 23a*], and the fine linen, and hoods [*turbans*], and the veils.

As indicated above, Isaiah has described female high-society fashions, arrogance, sexual immorality, and materialism in terms of such things in his day. Next, he prophetically describes the end results of such wickedness for these women, and literally and symbolically for Jerusalem and the kingdom of Judah.

24 And it shall come to pass, instead of sweet smell [*perfume*] there shall be stink [*from corpses of people killed by invading armies; also the stench associated with miserable slavery conditions*]; and instead of a girdle [*German Bible: nice waistband*], a rent [*rags*]; and instead of well set hair, baldness [*slaves had shaved heads*]; and instead of a stomacher [*a nice robe*], a girding of sackcloth; burning [*branding, a mark of slavery; see Isaiah 3, footnote 24d*] instead of beauty.

In the above verses, Isaiah spoke of "shaved" heads. Symbolically, this represents slavery or bondage. Literally, conquering armies often kept the best captives who would bring a good price in the slave markets back home. They shaved the hair off of these slaves for three basic reasons:

1. Humiliation

2. Identification (makes it easier to spot a runaway slave)

3. Sanitation

25 Thy men shall fall by the sword and thy mighty in the war [*wars will deplete your male population*].

26 And her [*Jerusalem's; see verse 8*] gates shall lament and mourn; and she shall be desolate [*empty, cleaned out; see Isaiah 3, footnote 26d*], and shall sit upon the ground [*Jerusalem, symbolic of the wicked, will be brought down completely and conquered—one fulfillment of this prophecy was the Babylonian captivity which ended about 587 B.C.*].

SECOND NEPHI 14

The Joseph Smith Translation, the Hebrew Bible, and the German Bible put this next verse at the end of Isaiah, chapter 3 in the Bible. Thus, 2 Nephi 14:1 fits in the context of Jerusalem's destruction and the scarcity of men resulting from that invasion (see Isaiah 4, footnote 1a). Verses 2–6 refer to the Millennium.

1 And in that day [*referred to in chapter 13:25–26*], seven women shall take hold of one man, saying: We will eat our own bread, and wear our own apparel [*we will pay our own way*]; only let us be called by thy name [*please marry us*] to take away our reproach [*the stigma of being unmarried and childless*].

Verse 2, below, starts a new topic, namely conditions during the Millennium.

2 In that day shall the branch of the Lord [*The "branch" can have dual meaning. In Jer. 23:5 and footnote 5b, this "branch" refers to Christ. In Isaiah 60:21; 61:3, it refers to righteous people during the Millennium*] be beautiful and glorious; the fruit of the earth excellent and comely [*pleasant to look at*] to them that are escaped of Israel [*the righteous who have escaped the destruction of the wicked*].

3 And it shall come to pass, they [*the righteous remnant of Israel*] that are left in Zion and remain in Jerusalem shall be called holy [*will be righteous*], every one that is written among the living [*those saved by approval of the Messiah*] in Jerusalem—

4 When the Lord shall have washed away the filth of the daughters of Zion [*when the Lord has cleansed the earth*], and shall have purged the blood of Jerusalem from the midst

thereof by the spirit of judgment [*Hebrew: carrying out a sentence; punishment*] and by the spirit of burning [*the earth will be cleansed by fire*].

The Angel Moroni quoted verses 5 and 6 to Joseph Smith in reference to the last days (see *Messenger and Advocate*, Apr., 1835, p. 110). Next, Isaiah depicts the peace and security that will prevail for the righteous during the Millennium as a result of having the presence of the Savior here on earth.

5 And the Lord will create upon every dwelling-place of mount Zion [*Jerusalem; the earth during the Millennium*], and upon her assemblies, a cloud and smoke by day [*represents the presence of the Lord as in Exodus 19:16–19 when He spoke from Mount Sinai and the children of Israel heard Him*] and the shining of a flaming fire by night [*presence of God*]; for upon all [*everyone*] the glory of Zion shall be a defence.

6 And there shall be a tabernacle [*shelter; can symbolize Hebrew marriage canopy, thus representing the remarriage of Christ and his people who were worthy to meet Him when He came at the time of the Second Coming; see Jeremiah 3:1*] for a shadow [*protection*] in the daytime from the heat, and for a place of refuge, and a covert [*protection*] from storm and from rain [*millennial peace and protection; verses 5 and 6 could be dual, referring also to the stakes of Zion as protection, defense, refuge in the last days—see D&C 115:6*].

SECOND NEPHI 15

Isaiah is a master at creating intrigue and interest among his students such that they become motivated to find out the end of the story. Here, he will compose a "song" or poetic parable of a vineyard, showing God's mercy and Israel's unresponsiveness to His invitations to come unto Him and have peace and security. It causes the reader to become quite exasperated with the people of Judah. But we would do well to look into the mirror and make sure the person we see does not fall into similar foolishness and wickedness.

1 And then will I sing to my well-beloved a song of my beloved [*Christ*], touching his vineyard [*Israel*]. My well-beloved [*the Lord of Hosts; see verse 7*] hath a vineyard [*Israel; see verse 7*] in a very fruitful hill [*in Israel*].

2 And he fenced it [*protected it*], and gathered out the stones thereof [*removed stumbling blocks or gave it every chance to succeed*], and planted it with the choicest vine [*the men of Judah; see verse 7*], and built a tower [*put prophets*] in the midst of it, and also made a wine-press therein [*indicates potential for a good harvest*]; and he looked that it should bring forth grapes [*the desired product, such as faithful people*], and it brought forth wild grapes [*apostasy, wickedness*].

3 And now, O inhabitants of Jerusalem, and men of Judah, judge, I pray you, betwixt me [*Christ*] and my vineyard [*apostate Israel; I'll give you the facts and you be the judge*].

4 What could have been done more to my vineyard that I have not done in it [*the main question: have I not done my job? Is that why you are wicked*]? Wherefore [*Why*], when I looked [*planned*] that it should bring forth grapes [*righteous people*] it brought forth wild grapes [*apostasy*].

5 And now go to [*German Bible: All right. That's settled*]; I will tell you what I will do to my vineyard [*Israel*]—I will take away the hedge thereof [*I will take away divine protection*], and it [*Israel*] shall be eaten up [*destroyed*]; and I will break down the wall [*withdraw my protection*] thereof, and it shall be trodden down;

6 And I will lay it waste; it shall not be pruned nor digged [*the Spirit will withdraw; no prophets to "prune" out false doctrines and warn against evil*]; but there shall come up briers and thorns [*apostate doctrines and behaviors*]; I will also command the clouds that they rain no rain upon it [*drought, famine*].

Isaiah now explains what the elements in his parable represent.

7 For the vineyard of the Lord of Hosts [*Christ*] is the house of Israel, and the men of Judah his pleasant plant; and he looked for judgment [*expected justice, fairness, kindness etc. from them*], and behold, oppression [*instead, He found them oppressing one another*]; for righteousness, but behold, a cry [*in place of righteousness, He found riotous living*].

On occasions, people have been known to use the phrase "join house to house" verse 8, next, to condemn builders and contractors who construct and sell apartment buildings and condominiums. While this is perhaps amusing, it also shows how badly Isaiah can be misinterpreted.

8 Wo unto them [*the powerful, wealthy*] that join house to house [*who grab up house after house*], till there can be no place, that they [*the poor*] may be placed alone in the midst of the earth [*those in power cheat and push the poor farmers off their land, taking their houses from them in the process*]!

9 In mine ears [*German Bible: Isaiah's ears*], said the Lord of Hosts, of a truth many houses shall be desolate, and great and fair cities without inhabitant [*great troubles are coming because of your wickedness; many of you will be captured and taken far away and your cities will be deserted*].

> As we have said many times, Isaiah is a master at painting mental images with words. Watch now as he describes the abject poverty that awaits rebellious Israel when He withdraws His help and protection from them.

10 Yea, ten acres of vineyard [*fields where grapes are grown*] shall yield [*produce*] one bath [*about 8¼ U.S. gallons*], and the seed of a homer [*6½ bushel of seed*] shall yield an ephah [*½ bushel of harvest, a terrible famine is coming!*].

> Next, Isaiah condemns the riotous lifestyle of the wicked, which includes drunkenness.

11 Wo unto them that rise up early in the morning, that they may follow strong drink, that continue until night, and wine inflame them!

> Isaiah now describes the hypocritical religious worship services among the apostate Israelites. They go through the motions of true religious worship, having all the elements of that proper worship as prescribed by past prophets, but their lives make a mockery of it. As he "paints" this picture with words, he will describe musical instruments that were properly a part of their religious services in his day. It would be like describing the proper components of our worship services today by saying "You have your music, your prayers, your meetings, and your sacrament. You pay your tithing and fast offering, hold temple recommends, attend the temple, etc., but then you cheat, lie, steal at work, take unfair advantage of your neighbors, view pornography, break the Sabbath, get involved in sexual immorality, gossip, etc." In other words, your worship and ritual are hollow and empty. You are hypocrites.

12 And the harp, and the viol [*Hebrew: lyre; a small stringed instrument of the harp family*], the tabret [*drums or tambourines*],

and pipe [*Hebrew: flute, or musical instruments associated with worship of the Lord*], and wine are in their feasts; but they regard not [*don't pay attention to*] the work of the Lord, neither consider the operation of his hands [*their worship is empty, hypocritical; they do not actually acknowledge God nor do they hardly even think about Him*].

13 Therefore [*this is why*], my people are gone into captivity [*prophecy about Israel's future captivity*], because they have no knowledge [*they have become ignorant of the true gospel; see D&C 131:6*]; and their honorable men are famished [*they have lost their righteous leaders*], and their multitude dried up with thirst [*dual: fits with Amos 8:11–12 about a famine of hearing the words of the Lord; also, literal results of famine*].

Next, Isaiah uses very interesting language and imagery to describe where Israel is going because of her wickedness.

14 Therefore [*this is why*], hell hath enlarged herself [*they've had to add on to hell to make room for you!*], and opened her mouth without measure [*seemingly without limit because there are so many of you heading for it*]; and their [*the wicked*] glory, and their multitude, and their pomp, and he that rejoiceth [*in wicked, riotous living*], shall descend into it [*hell*].

Next, Isaiah explains that the whole society is riddled with pride. In other words, no one is humble. Isaiah's writing here demonstrates his use of repetition for emphasis.

15 And the mean [*poor*] man shall be brought down [*humbled*], and the mighty [*wealthy, powerful*] man shall be humbled, and the eyes of the lofty [*proud*] shall be humbled [*everyone needs humbling*].

16 But the Lord of Hosts shall be exalted [*will be victorious*] in judgment, and God that is holy shall be sanctified in righteousness [*the Lord will triumph*]. [*This verse is another example of how Isaiah says the same thing two different ways.*]

Next, Isaiah describes the completeness of the devastation that will come upon wicked Israel unless they repent.

17 Then shall the lambs feed [*graze where the Lord's vineyard, Israel, once stood; the destruction will be so complete that animals will graze where wicked Israelites once lived*] after their manner [*German: where the city once stood*], and

the waste places of the fat ones [*the former wealthy, wicked*] shall strangers [*foreigners*] eat.

18 Wo unto them that draw [*pull*] iniquity with cords of vanity [*pride*], and sin as it were with a cart rope [*you are tethered to your sins; they follow you around like a cart follows the animal pulling it!*];

> In verse 19, next, we see the arrogance which wickedness can bring upon individuals and societies. We see the wicked challenging God to be more obvious about His existence if He actually expects people to pay any attention to Him. This reminds us of some of the antichrists in the Book of Mormon, such as Sherem, Nehor, and Korihor, who demanded a sign from God to prove His existence.

19 That say: Let him [*the Lord*] make speed, hasten his work, that we may see it [*it is up to God to prove to us that he exists*]; and let the counsel [*plans*] of the Holy One of Israel draw nigh and come, that we may know it [*we are "calling his bluff"; tell him to follow through with his threats so we can know he really exists!*].

> Next comes one of the most famous of all the writings and teachings of Isaiah. We are witnessing this problem on every side today in our world. It seems that one of Satan's most effective tools is getting people to think and act just the opposite of what God says.

20 Wo unto them that call evil good, and good evil, that put darkness for light, and light for darkness, that put bitter for sweet, and sweet for bitter!

21 Wo unto the wise in their own eyes [*full of evil pride*] and prudent in their own sight [*the wicked, who make their own rules*]!

22 Wo unto the mighty to drink wine, and men of strength to mingle strong drink [*drunkenness and riotous living*];

> Next, Isaiah reminds us that corrupt judicial systems and processes go along with the downfall of a society.

23 Who justify the wicked for reward [*take bribes, corrupt judicial system, etc.*], and take away the righteousness of the righteous from him [*deprive the innocent of his rights*]!

> Next, Isaiah describes the downfall and destruction of the wicked. Watch as he masterfully says the same thing in many different ways.

24 Therefore [*because of such wickedness*], as the fire devo-

ureth the stubble [*just as fire burns dry grain stocks*], and the flame consumeth the chaff [*highly flammable byproduct of harvesting grain*], their root shall be rottenness [*the wicked lose their roots, anchor, stability; family ties*], and their blossoms [*potential to bear fruit; families*] shall go up as dust [*in summary: the wicked will not bear fruit; no posterity in the next life and destruction of many in this life*]; because they have cast away the law of the Lord of Hosts, and despised the word of the Holy One of Israel.

You've noticed by now that Isaiah always explains the "why" of what is going to happen. This reminds us that the Lord wants us to have understanding, so we can make wise and advantageous agency choices.

25 Therefore [*for these reasons*], is the anger of the Lord kindled against his people, and he hath stretched forth his hand against them, and hath smitten them; and the hills did tremble, and their carcasses were torn in the midst of the streets [*terrible destruction resulting from Israel's wickedness*]. For [*because of*] all this his anger is not turned away, but his hand is stretched out still [*inviting you to repent; in other words, despite all this, you can still repent; compare with 2 Nephi 28:32 and Jacob 6:4 and 5*].

The end of verse 25, above, is a strong and very comforting reminder that the Lord is very desirous that we use His Atonement and be freed from the burden of sin, even if we have a long history of not living the gospel. Elder Neal A. Maxwell of the Quorum of the Twelve Apostles taught the following:

"Our merciful and long-suffering Lord is ever ready to help. His 'arm is lengthened out all the day long' " (Maxwell, "According to the Desire of [Our] Hearts," p. 21; October 1996 General Conference of the Church; 2 Nephi 28:32).

It appears that Isaiah was shown our day in vision and that he saw modern forms of transportation involved in the gathering process. It is interesting to consider his dilemma as far as how to describe trains, airplanes, etc. when such things did not exist in his day. Watch as he uses terminology and objects of his time and day to describe objects of our time and day.

26 And he will lift up an ensign [*flag, rallying point; the true gospel*] to the nations from far, and will hiss [*whistle; a signal to gather*] unto them from the end of the earth; and behold, they [*the righteous*] shall come

with speed swiftly [*because of modern transportation?*]; none shall be weary nor stumble among them. [*They will travel so fast and arrive so soon that they won't even hardly get tired.*]

27 None shall slumber nor sleep; neither shall the girdle of their loins be loosed, nor the latchet of their shoes be broken [*perhaps meaning that they will travel so fast via modern transportation that they won't need to change clothes; get pajamas on, or even take their shoes off*];

28 Whose arrows shall be sharp [*airplane fuselages perhaps looked to Isaiah like arrows poised in a bow?*], and all their bows bent [*like airplane wings?*], and their horses' hoofs shall be counted like flint [*making sparks like train wheels do?*], and their wheels like a whirlwind [*going around extremely fast?*], their roaring like a lion [*the deafening roar of trains, airplanes?*].

29 They shall roar [*airplanes, etc.?*] like young lions; yea, they shall roar, and lay hold of the prey [*passengers, converts will board them?*], and shall carry away safe [*will transport them safely, securely*], and none shall deliver [*no enemies can stop them or prevent the gathering*].

Elder LeGrand Richards of the Quorum of Twelve Apostles commented on verses 26–29, above, as follows:

"In fixing the time of the great gathering, Isaiah seemed to indicate that it would take place in the day of the railroad train and the airplane (Isaiah 5:26–29):

"Since there were neither trains nor airplanes in that day, Isaiah could hardly have mentioned them by name. However, he seems to have described them in unmistakable words. How better could 'their horses' hoofs be counted like flint, and their wheels like 'a whirlwind' than in the modern train? How better could 'their roaring? be like a lion' than in the roar of the airplane? Trains and airplanes do not stop for night. Therefore, was not Isaiah justified in saying: 'none shall slumber nor sleep; neither shall the girdle of their loins be loosed, nor the latchet of their shoes be broken'? With this manner of transportation the Lord can really 'hiss unto them from the end of the earth,' that 'they shall come with speed swiftly.' Indicating that Isaiah must have foreseen the airplane, he stated: 'Who are these that fly as a cloud, and as the doves to their windows?' (Isaiah 60:8)" (Richards, *Israel! Do You Know?*, p. 182).

30 And in that day [*the last days*] they shall roar against them like the roaring of the sea; and if they look unto the land, behold, darkness and sorrow, and the light is darkened in the heavens thereof [*perhaps referring to conditions in the last days, war, smoke, pollutions, etc., while the righteous are gathering to Zion and the gospel in various locations throughout the world*].

SECOND NEPHI 16

Since this chapter is relatively short and has beautiful Atonement symbolism, it is perhaps one of the very best chapters of Isaiah to study to get a feel for the power and majesty of Isaiah's inspired writings. This chapter deals with Isaiah's call, either his initial call or a subsequent call to major responsibility.

1 In the year that king Uzziah [*king of Judah*] died [*about 750–740 B.C.*], I [*Isaiah*] saw also the Lord [*Jesus; see verse 5*] sitting upon a throne, high and lifted up [*exalted*], and his train [*skirts of his robe; Hebrew: wake, light; can also mean His power and authority*] filled the temple.

2 Above it [*the Savior's throne*] stood the seraphim [*angelic beings*]; each one had six wings [*wings are symbolic of power to move, act etc. in God's work; see D&C 77:4*]; with twain [*two*] he covered his face, and with twain he covered his feet, and with twain he did fly.

To cover one's face (verse 2, above) is a way of showing respect and humility before God in many cultures.

3 And one cried unto another, and said: Holy, holy, holy [*repeated three times means the very best in Hebrew, or, superlative*], is the Lord of Hosts; the whole earth is full of his glory.

4 And the posts of the door moved [*shook*] at the voice of him that cried, and the house was filled with smoke [*symbolic of God's presence, as with the shaking of the mountain at Sinai, Exodus 19:18, when the Lord was there*].

Next, Isaiah expresses profound feelings of inadequacy and unworthiness to be in the presence of the Lord. Watch as the Atonement takes away his shortcomings and feelings of falling short and gives him confidence to do the work to which the Lord is calling him. The same principle applies to each of us as we realize our dependence on the Lord as we strive to do His work.

5 Then said I [*Isaiah*]: Wo is unto

me! for I am undone [*feel completely overwhelmed*]; because I am a man of unclean lips [*I am so imperfect, inadequate!*]; and I dwell in the midst of a people of unclean lips [*none of us mortals is worthy to be in the presence of God*]; for mine eyes have seen the King, the Lord of Hosts [*I am feeling completely overwhelmed because I have just seen the Savior*].

Watch the beautiful symbolism now, in verses 6 and 7, as the Atonement is represented and its power to cleanse and heal is taught.

6 Then flew one of the seraphim [*symbolic of a being with authority*] unto me, having a live coal [*symbolic of the Holy Ghost's power to cleanse "by fire"*] in his hand, which he had taken with the tongs from off the altar [*symbolic of the Atonement; Christ was sacrificed for us on the "altar" cross*];

7 And he laid it upon my mouth [*applied the Atonement to me*], and said: Lo, this [*the Atonement*] has touched thy lips [*symbolic of his shortcomings, imperfections, and feelings of inadequacy*]; and thine iniquity is taken away, and thy sin purged [*cleansed; the results of the Atonement; compare with Isaiah 1:18*].

Next, watch what the application of the Atonement did to Isaiah's confidence to embark in the service of the Lord. We will use **bold** for emphasis.

8 Also I heard the voice of the Lord, saying: Whom shall I send, and who will go for us [*plural deity*]? Then I [*Isaiah*] said: **Here am I; send me** [*the cleansing power of the Atonement gave Isaiah the needed confidence to accept the call*].

Now, the Lord will give Isaiah a brief description of the people to whom he will be preaching as a prophet. You will note that the people are going to be extremely difficult to reach. Perhaps this is a bit of an "MTC" experience for Isaiah to help him brace for the difficulties ahead.

9 And he [*the Lord*] said: Go and tell this people—Hear ye indeed, but they understood not; and see ye indeed, but they perceived not [*Isaiah's task is not going to be easy with these kinds of people*].

As discussed in notes at the beginning of 2 Nephi, chapter 13, Isaiah often uses a literary technique known as chiasmus as he teaches. It involves an intentional listing of key elements of the teaching in reverse order for emphasis, after having given them in regular order.

10 Make [*picture in your mind*] the **heart** [A] of this people fat [*insulated against truth*], and make their **ears** [B] heavy [*picture them as being spiritually deaf*], and shut their **eyes** [C] [*picture them as being spiritually blind*]—lest they see with their **eyes** [C'], and hear with their **ears** [B'], and understand with their **heart** [A'], and be converted and be healed.

> It may be that verse 11, next, can be viewed as a reminder that the Lord has a sense of humor.

11 Then said I [*Isaiah*]: Lord, how long [*will people be like this*]? And he said: Until the cities be wasted without inhabitant, and the houses without man, and the land be utterly desolate [*empty; in other words, when you go to preach some morning and no one is left in the city, you will not be confronted with such people; as long as people are around, you will run into such people*];

12 And the Lord have removed men far away, for there shall be a great forsaking [*many deserted cities*] in the midst of the land.

> Verse 13, next, is a great example of Isaiah's use of symbolism understood by people in his time and culture. It is also an example of a verse that is virtually impossible for us in our time and culture to understand without help.

13 But yet there shall be a tenth [*remnant of Israel*], and they [*Israel*] shall return, and shall be eaten [*pruned, as by animals eating the limbs, leaves, and branches; the Lord "prunes" his vineyard, cuts out old false doctrines and apostates, etc., destroys old unrighteous generations so new may have a chance*], as a teil-tree [*like pruning a lime tree? See Bible Dictionary, page 780*], and as an oak whose substance [*sap*] is in them when they cast their leaves [*shed the old, non-functioning leaves and look dead in winter*]; so the holy seed shall be the substance thereof [*Israel may look dead, but there is still life in it*].

> In summary, verse 13, above, explains that although various Israelites will be carried away into captivity and thus be scattered and seemingly die out as a people, yet the Lord will eventually "prune" them, shape them and guide them to become a righteous covenant people again. They will look dead, as a people, like a fruit tree does in winter, but Israel will be gathered again and become powerful in the last days. We are

watching the fulfillment of this prophecy as we see the great gathering now taking place.

SECOND NEPHI 17

This next chapter compares with Isaiah chapter 7 in the Bible. It deals with literal historical events, including the virgin birth of the Savior.

King Ahaz is a wicked, idol-worshiping king of Judah (the nation of the Jews and part of the tribe of Benjamin, who are in the southern part of the Holy Land at this time). His nation is being threatened from the north by both Israel (the ten tribes who have their own nation called Israel) and by Syria. Israel and Syria are plotting to take over Judah and Jerusalem and to set up a puppet regime in Jerusalem, controlled by themselves. Watch Ahaz's reaction as the Lord tells Isaiah to bring him the news that if he will trust in the Lord, he has no need to fear these two enemy nations. It is a reminder, among other things, that the wicked live in fear, despite the availability of help and safety with the Lord.

1 And it came to pass in the days of Ahaz [*a wicked, idol-worshipping king of Judah about 734 B.C.*] the son of Jotham, the son of Uzziah, king of Judah [*the Jews*], that Rezin, king of Syria, and Pekah the son of Remaliah, king of Israel [*the ten tribes or northern Israel*], went up toward Jerusalem to war against it, but could not prevail against it [*didn't win, but they did kill 120,000 men of Judah and take 200,000 captives in one day; see 2 Chr. 28:6–15*].

2 And it was told the house of David [*Jerusalem*], saying: Syria is confederate [*has joined*] with Ephraim [*the ten tribes; northern Israel*]. And his [*Ahaz's*] heart was moved [*shaken*], and the heart of his people, as the trees of the wood are moved with the wind [*the people of Judah were trembling with fear, "shaking in their boots"*].

3 Then said the Lord unto Isaiah: Go forth now to meet Ahaz [*king of Judah living in Jerusalem*], thou and Shear-jashub [*Hebrew, meaning "the remnant shall return"*] thy son, at the end of the conduit of the upper pool in the highway of the fuller's field [*Ahaz is hiding where the women do their laundry, or, he is hiding behind the women's skirts; a coward*];

4 And say unto him [*King Ahaz*]: Take heed, and be quiet [*Relax!*]; fear not, neither be faint-hearted for [*because of*]

Second Nephi 17

the two tails of these smoking firebrands [*don't worry because of the threats from Syria and Israel*], for the fierce anger of Rezin with Syria, and of the son of Remaliah [*don't worry about continued threats from Syria and Israel; they think they are "hot stuff" but are nothing but smoldering stubs of firewood; they are "have beens"*].

5 Because Syria, Ephraim [*Syria and northern Israel*], and the son of Remaliah [*northern Israel's king*], have taken evil counsel [*are plotting*] against thee, saying:

6 Let us go up against Judah and vex it [*cause trouble for Judah*], and let us make a breach [*an opening*] therein for us, and set a king in the midst of it [*let's set up our own king in Jerusalem*], yea, the son of Tabeal.

7 Thus saith the Lord God: It shall not stand, neither shall it come to pass [*the plot will fail, so don't worry about it, Ahaz*].

8 For the head [*capital city*] of Syria is Damascus, and the head [*leader*] of Damascus, Rezin; and within three score and five years [*sixty-five years*] shall Ephraim [*the ten tribes*] be broken that it be not a people [*within sixty-five years the ten tribes will be lost*].

9 And the head [*capital city*] of Ephraim is Samaria [*about 35 miles north of Jerusalem*], and the head [*leader*] of Samaria is Remaliah's son. If ye [*Ahaz and his people, the tribe of Judah, plus some of Benjamin*] will not believe surely ye shall not be established [*not be saved by the Lord's power; see Isaiah 7, footnote 9b*].

10 Moreover, the Lord spake again unto Ahaz, saying:

11 Ask thee a sign [*to assure you that the Lord is speaking to you*] of the Lord thy God; ask it either in the depths, or in the heights above [*ask anything you want*].

12 But Ahaz said: I will not ask, neither will I tempt [*test*] the Lord [*refuses to follow prophet's counsel; is deliberately evasive because he is already secretly depending on Assyria for help*].

13 And he [*Isaiah*] said: Hear ye now, O house of David [*Ahaz and his people, Judah*]; is it a small thing for you to weary men, but will ye weary my God also [*try the patience of God*]?

14 Therefore [*because of your disobedience*], the Lord himself shall give you a sign—Behold, a virgin shall conceive, and shall bear a son, and shall call his

name Immanuel [*the day will come when the Savior will be born*].

15 Butter and honey [*curd and honey, the only foods available to the poor at times; see Isaiah 7, footnote 15a*] shall he eat [*Jesus will eat what the poor people eat; in other words, He will not be considered high in social status*], that he may know to refuse the evil and to choose the good.

16 For before the child shall know to refuse the evil and choose the good [*in as many years as it takes for the child to be old enough to know good from evil, or in just a few years*], the land [*northern Israel*] that thou [*Judah*] abhorrest [*are afraid of*] shall be forsaken of both her kings [*both Syria and the northern ten tribes will be taken by Assyria; see Isaiah 8:4, 2 Nephi 17:17*].

17 The Lord shall bring upon thee [*Ahaz*], and upon thy people [*Judah*], and upon thy father's house, days that have not come from the day that Ephraim departed [*northern ten tribes split*] from Judah, the king of Assyria [*the king of Assyria will bring troubles like you have not seen since the twelve tribes of Israel split apart, about 975 B.C., into the northern kingdom under Jeroboam I, and the tribe of Judah under Rehoboam*].

18 And it shall come to pass in that day that the Lord shall hiss [*signal, call for*] for the fly [*associated with plagues, troubles; this will remind you of the plagues in Egypt*] that is in the uttermost part of Egypt, and for the bee [*sting*] that is in the land of Assyria [*the Assyrians will come like flies and bees*].

19 And they shall come, and shall rest all of them in the desolate valleys, and in the holes of the rocks, and upon all thorns, and upon all bushes [*your enemies will be everywhere, will overrun your land*].

20 In the same day [*when this terrible day comes upon you because you refuse to turn to the Lord*] shall the Lord shave with a razor [*fate of captives, slaves—for humiliation, sanitation, identification*] that is hired [*Assyria will be "hired" to do this to Judah*], by them beyond the river, by the king of Assyria, the head, and the hair of the feet; and it shall also consume the beard [*they will shave you completely; will conquer you completely*].

21 And it shall come to pass

in that day [*after the above-mentioned devastation*], a man shall nourish a young cow and two sheep;

22 And it shall come to pass, for the abundance of milk they [*the few remaining domestic animals*] shall give he shall eat butter; for butter and honey shall every one eat that is left in the land [*not many people left, so a few animals can supply them well*].

23 And it shall come to pass in that day, every place shall be, where there were [*used to be*] a thousand vines at a thousand silverlings [*worth a thousand pieces of silver*], which shall be for briers and thorns [*formerly valuable, cultivated land will become overgrown with weeds; this can be symbolic of apostasy*].

> Isaiah continues emphasizing that Judah will be conquered and her inhabitants scattered to the point that relatively few of them will remain. The Babylonian captivity in about 587 B.C. was one fulfillment of this prophecy. Other devastations and scatterings of the Jews have also occurred.

24 With arrows and with bows shall men come thither, because all the land shall become briers and thorns [*previously cultivated land will become wild and overgrown such that hunters will hunt wild beasts there where you used to live*].

25 And all hills that shall be digged with the mattock [*that were once cultivated with the hoe*], there [*you*] shall not come thither [*because of*] the fear of briers and thorns; but it shall be for the sending forth [*pasturing*] of oxen, and the treading of lesser cattle [*sheep or goats; your once cultivated lands will revert to wilds; symbolic of apostasy*].

SECOND NEPHI 18

The Lord has Isaiah continue spreading the unpopular word that an attack by the Assyrians (a large, wicked, powerful nation in approximately the region occupied by Iraq today) is coming unless the people and their political leaders repent and return to their God. He will be asked by the Lord to use a large scroll on which he can write a warning in large letters for all to see. He is also asked to give his son a name, the meaning of which is that the Assyrians will be quick to ruin the country.

In contrast to the cruel devastation coming at the hands of the Assyrians, Isaiah invites the people to enjoy the gentle "waters of Shiloah" (verse 6), symbolic of the mercy and kindness of the Savior. If they turn to Christ, He will protect them. The choice is theirs. There is much symbolism in this for us.

1 Moreover, the word of the Lord said unto me [*Isaiah*]: Take thee a great [*large*] roll [*scroll*], and write in it with a man's pen, concerning Maher-shalal-hash-baz [*a Hebrew saying, meaning "destruction is imminent" or "to speed to the spoil, he hasteneth the prey"; in other words, Assyria will be here soon and destruction will overtake you soon*].

2 And I [*Isaiah*] took unto me faithful witnesses to record, Uriah the priest, and Zechariah the son of Jeberechiah [*these were required witnesses and legal authorities for a proper Hebrew wedding*].

3 And I went unto the prophetess [*Isaiah's wife*]; and she conceived and bare a son. Then said the Lord to me: Call his name, Maher-shalal-hash-baz [*meaning "destruction" is imminent"*].

Next, Isaiah indicates that the Assyrians will be upon Syria and the northern ten tribes in about as much time as it takes his baby boy to learn to say "Daddy" or "Mommy."

4 For behold, the child shall not have knowledge to cry, My father, and my mother, before the riches of Damascus [*Syria*] and the spoil [*wealth*] of Samaria [*northern Israel*] shall be taken away before [*by*] the king of Assyria [*before my son is old enough to say "Daddy" or "Mommy," Assyria will attack northern Israel and Syria*].

5 The Lord spake also unto me [*Isaiah*] again, saying:

6 Forasmuch as this people [*Judah, Jerusalem*] refuseth the waters of Shiloah [*the gentle help of Christ, John 4:14*] that go softly [*mercifully*], and rejoice in [*place more trust in*] Rezin and Remaliah's son [*Syria and northern Israel instead of the Lord*];

7 Now therefore, behold, the Lord bringeth up upon them [*Judah*] the waters of the river [*you'll be flooded with Assyrians*], strong and many, even the king of Assyria and all his glory [*his pomp and armies*]; and he shall come up over all his channels, and go over all his banks [*you will have a flood of Assyrians*].

8 And he [*Assyria*] shall pass through Judah; he shall overflow and go over, he shall reach even to the neck [*you will be up*

*to your neck in Assyrians; can also mean "will reach clear to Jerusalem, the head or capital city," which Assyria did before being stopped via the death by plague of 185,000 soldiers; see 2 Kings 19:32–36]; and the stretching out of his wings [*Assyria*] shall fill the breadth of thy land [*Judah*], O Immanuel [*the land of the future birth and ministry of Christ*].

9 Associate yourselves [*if you form political alliances with other nations for protection rather than turning to God*], O ye people [*of Judah*], and ye shall be broken in pieces; and give ear all ye of far countries [*foreign nations who might rise against Judah*]; gird yourselves [*prepare for war*], and ye [*foreign nations who attack Judah*] shall be broken in pieces; gird yourselves, and ye shall be broken in pieces [*note that "broken in pieces" is repeated three times for emphasis; three times in Hebrew is a form of superlative*].

10 Take counsel together [*go ahead, plot against Judah, you foreign nations*], and it shall come to naught [*won't succeed*]; speak the word, and it shall not stand [*and it will still not happen*]; for God is with us [*Judah won't be destroyed completely*].

The Lord has asked Isaiah, His prophet, to give some very unpopular messages to the citizens and political leaders of wicked Judah. This must have been extremely hard on Brother and Sister Isaiah and their little family. Next, the Lord gives Isaiah strong instructions not to give in to peer pressure and tell the Jews what they want to hear concerning making treaties with other nations for protection from their enemies, rather than turning to righteousness for God's protection. He then counsels Isaiah to stick with the Lord no matter what.

11 For the Lord spake thus to me [*Isaiah*] with a strong hand [*firmly*], and instructed me that I should not walk in the way of this people [*Judah*], saying:

12 Say ye not, A confederacy [*a treaty*], to all to whom this people shall say, A confederacy; neither fear ye their fear, nor be afraid [*"Isaiah, don't endorse Judah's plan for confederacy with Assyria. Don't tell them what they want to hear."*].

13 Sanctify the Lord of Hosts himself, and let him be your fear, and let him be your dread [*"Isaiah, you rely on the Lord, not public approval."*].

14 And he [*the Lord*] shall be for a sanctuary [*for you, Isaiah*]; but for a stone of stumbling, and for a rock of

offense [*a rock that makes them fall rather than the Rock of their salvation*] to both the houses of [*wicked*] Israel [*Judah and Ephraim—the ten tribes*], for a gin [*a trap*] and a snare to the inhabitants of Jerusalem.

> Notice how simple but powerful Isaiah's wording is in the next verse.

15 And many among them shall **stumble** and **fall**, and be **broken**, and be **snared**, and be **taken**.

16 Bind up the testimony [*record your testimony, Isaiah*], seal the law among my disciples [*righteous followers*].

> We discover from verse 16, above, that there were other faithful Saints among the people of Judah, in addition to Isaiah and his family.
>
> Next, Isaiah responds to the Lord's admonition to him to remain faithful at all costs.

17 And I [*Isaiah*] will wait upon [*trust*] the Lord, that hideth his face [*is holding His blessings back*] from the house of Jacob [*Israel*], and I will look for him.

18 Behold, I and the children whom the Lord hath given me are for signs and for wonders in Israel from the Lord of Hosts, which dwelleth in Mount Zion. [*My family and I are a reminder to Israel that the Lord lives.*]

> It seems that too often, the wicked just can't get the obvious! They are so blind that they can't see that the only way to preserve their freedom is to follow the commandments and guidelines of the gospel of Christ. In this case, rather than repenting and returning to the God of Israel, which would restore civil peace and security to them, they turn to witchcraft and sorcery which are controlled by forces other than and alien to God. Wickedness certainly does not promote rational thought!

19 And when they [*the wicked*] shall say unto you: Seek unto them [*spiritualists, mediums, fortune tellers, and so forth*] that have familiar spirits [*who contact dead relatives and friends*], and unto wizards that peep and mutter [*into their "crystal balls"*]—should not a people seek unto their God for the living to hear from the dead? [*In other words, wouldn't it be wise for them to turn to God for help?*]

> Next, Isaiah wisely counsels his people to compare any advice, counsel, etc. they receive from any source, to the scriptures. We often refer to our scriptures as the "standard works," which means "the

standard by which all things should be measured."

20 To the law and to the testimony [*to the scriptures*]; and if they [*the spiritualists and their media*] speak not according to this word [*the scriptures*], it is because there is no light in them [*the fortunetellers, mediums, and so forth*].

21 And they [*the wicked of Judah*] shall pass through it [*the land; the trouble described in verses 7 and 8*] hardly bestead [*severely distressed*] and hungry; and it shall come to pass that when they shall be hungry, they shall fret themselves [*become enraged*], and curse their king and their God, and look upward [*proud, defiant*].

22 And they shall look unto the earth [*will look around them*] and behold [*see only*] trouble, and darkness, dimness of anguish [*gloom; Hebrew: dark affliction*], and shall be driven to darkness [*thrust into utter despair; results of wickedness*].

SECOND NEPHI 19

This is a continuation of the topic in chapter 18. King Ahaz of Judah ignored the Lord's counsel and made an alliance with Assyria anyway. Symbolism here can include that Assyria would represent the devil and his evil, prideful ways. King Ahaz could symbolize foolish and wicked people who make alliances with the devil or his evil ways and naively think that they are thus protected from destruction spiritually and often physically.

In this next chapter, which can be compared to Isaiah 9, Isaiah gives one of the most famous and beautiful of all his messianic prophecies. He prophesies that Christ will come. Handel's *Messiah* puts some of this chapter to magnificent music.

1 [*This verse is the last verse of chapter 8 in the Hebrew Bible and in the German Bible. It serves as a natural transition from chapter 18 to verse 2.*] Nevertheless, the dimness [*affliction referred to in 18:22*] shall not be such as was in her vexation, when at first [*the first Assyrian attacks in Isaiah's day*] he lightly [*German: strictly*] afflicted the land of Zebulun [*the Nazareth area, part of northern Israel; see maps 5 & 14 in the first editions of the new LDS Bible*], and the land of Naphtali [*in northern Israel*], and afterwards did more grievously afflict [*Hebrew: gloriously bless, German: brought honor to*] by the way of the Red Sea beyond Jordan in Galilee of

the nations [*Jesus grew up in Galilee and righteous Israel has been gloriously blessed through him, whereas wicked Israel has been grievously afflicted as a result of rejecting him*].

2 The people that walked in darkness [*spiritual darkness; apostasy and captivity*] have seen a great light [*the Savior and his teachings*]; they that dwell in the land of the shadow of death, upon them hath the light shined [*the gospel of Christ is made available to them*].

3 Thou [*the Savior*] hast multiplied the nation, and increased the joy—they joy before thee according to the joy in harvest, and as men rejoice when they divide the spoil [*Christ and his faithful followers will ultimately triumph and divide the spoils; reap the rewards of righteous living as they enjoy celestial exaltation*].

> Next, Isaiah continues prophesying about the future and the redemption made available by the Savior.

4 For thou [*Christ*] hast broken the yoke of his burden [*Israel's captivity, bondage*], and the staff of his shoulder, the rod [*power*] of his [*Israel's*] oppressor.

5 For every battle of the warrior is with confused noise, and garments rolled in blood; but this shall be with burning [*the burning at the Second Coming, according to Joseph Smith; see Isaiah 9, footnote 5b*] and fuel of fire.

6 For unto us a child [*Christ*] is born, unto us a son is given; and the government shall be upon his shoulder; and his name shall be called, Wonderful, Counselor, The Mighty God, The Everlasting Father, The Prince of Peace.

7 Of the increase of government and peace there is no end [*for the righteous*], upon the throne of David, and upon his kingdom to order it, and to establish it with judgment [*fairness*] and with justice from henceforth, even forever. The zeal of the Lord of Hosts will perform this [*God will do this*].

> The Lord now continues his message of warning to the northern ten tribes (known at this point in history as Israel). He addresses their arrogance and prideful claims that they can get along well without Him or His help.

8 The Lord sent his word unto Jacob [*Israel*] and it [*the message from the Lord*] hath lighted upon Israel.

9 And all the people shall know,

even Ephraim [*the northern ten tribes, Israel*] and the inhabitants of Samaria [*the northern ten tribes, Israel*], that say [*boast*] in the pride and stoutness of heart:

10 The bricks are fallen down, but we will build with hewn stones [*boastful Israel claims they can't be destroyed successfully, but would simply rebuild with better materials than before*]; the sycamores [*trees*] are cut down, but we will change them into cedars [*more valuable trees*].

11 Therefore [*this is why, or, because of wicked pride*] the Lord shall set up the adversaries of Rezin [*Syria*] against him [*Israel*], and join his enemies together;

> A very important theme is repeated over and over in Isaiah's writings. It is, "but his hand is stretched out still." We will see it in verse 12 and again in verses 17 and 21. The message is that no matter what mistakes you have made in the past, the mercy of the Atonement is still being offered to you by the outstretched hand of the Savior. We will **bold** this in these three verses for teaching emphasis.
>
> Remember too that when something is repeated three times in Hebrew culture, it means it is the very best, the very most important, etc. The message, "but his hand is stretched out still" is repeated three times in this chapter!

12 The Syrians before [*on the East*] and the Philistines behind [*on the West*]; and they shall devour Israel with open mouth. For all this his anger is not turned away, **but his hand is stretched out still** [*the Lord will still let you repent if you will turn to him; see Jacob 6:4 and 5; see also Isaiah 9, footnote 12d. Laman and Lemuel need to hear this message of mercy, as do we in our day*].

13 For the [*wicked*] people turneth not unto him [*the Lord*] that smiteth [*punishes*] them, neither do they seek the Lord of Hosts [*the people won't repent; they are going through the pain without learning the lesson*].

14 Therefore [*for this reason*] will the Lord cut off from Israel head [*leaders*] and tail [*false prophets*], branch [*Hebrew: palm branch, triumph and victory; see John 12:13*] and rush [*reed; people low in social status*] in one day.

> Isaiah now explains some of the imagery above.

15 The ancient [*elders, leaders*], he is the head; and the prophet that teacheth lies, he is the tail.

16 For the leaders of this people cause them to err; and they that are led of them are destroyed.

17 Therefore the Lord shall have no joy in their young men, neither shall have mercy on their fatherless and widows [*all levels of society have gone bad; no one qualifies for mercy*]; for every one of them is a hypocrite and an evildoer, and every mouth speaketh folly [*foolishness*]. For all this his anger is not turned away, **but his hand is stretched out still** [*you can still repent; please do*].

18 For wickedness burneth as the fire [*wickedness destroys like wildfire*]; it shall devour the briers and thorns [*symbolic of wicked people and apostate philosophies and doctrines*], and shall kindle in the thickets of the forests, and they shall mount up like the lifting up of smoke [*when destruction comes it will come rapidly like wildfire*].

19 Through the wrath of the Lord of Hosts is the land darkened [*bad conditions prevail*], and the [*wicked*] people shall be as the fuel of the fire; no man shall spare his brother [*when people turn so wicked, they are no longer loyal, even to family members*].

20 And he shall snatch on the right hand and be hungry; and he shall eat on the left hand and they shall not be satisfied; they shall eat every man the flesh of his own arm [*the wicked will turn on each other*]—

21 Manasseh, Ephraim; and Ephraim, Manasseh; they together shall be against Judah. For all this his anger is not turned away, **but his hand is stretched out still** [*you can still repent; please do!*].

SECOND NEPHI 20

In the heading to chapter 20 in your Book of Mormon, you will find the phrase, "Destruction of Assyria is a type of destruction of wicked at the Second Coming." The word "type" means something that is symbolic of something else. For example, both Joseph who was sold into Egypt and Isaac were "types" of Christ, that is to say, many of the things that happened to them were symbolic of the Savior. The following charts show some of the ways in which these great prophets were types of Christ.

"TYPES" OF CHRIST

JOSEPH IN EGYPT

Was sold for the price of a common slave

Was thirty years old when he began his mission as prime minister to save his people

Gathered food for seven years to save his people

Forgave his persecutors

CHRIST

Was sold for the price of a common slave

Was thirty years old when He began His formal mission to save His people

Used seven "days" to create the earth in which to offer salvation to us

Forgave His persecutors

ISAAC

Was the only begotten of Abraham and Sarah

Was to be sacrificed by his father

Carried the wood for his sacrifice

Volunteered to give his life (Abraham was too old to restrain him.)

CHRIST

Is the Only Begotten of the Father

Was allowed to be sacrificed by His Father

Carried the cross for His sacrifice

Gave His life voluntarily

Even in Leviticus 14, the priest is a "type" of Christ as he presents the privilege of being cleansed to the leper (who is a "type" of all sinners—that is to say, the leper can be symbolic of the need we all have to be cleansed from sin). We will include Leviticus 14:1–9 here as a brief lesson on the power of understanding the use of "types" in the scriptures.

Leviticus 14:1–9

1 And the LORD spake unto Moses, saying,

2 This shall be the law of the leper [*a "type" for all sinners; symbolic of serious sin and great need for help and cleansing*] in the day of his cleansing: He shall be brought unto the priest [*authorized servant of God; bishop, stake president, etc.; can also be a "type" of Christ—symbolic of Christ*]:

3 And the priest shall go forth out of the camp [*the person with leprosy did not have fellowship with the Lord's people and was required to live outside the main camp of the children of Israel; the bishop, symbolically, goes out of the way to help sinners who want to repent*]; and the priest shall look, and, behold, if the plague of leprosy be healed in the leper [*the bishop serves as a judge to see if the repentant sinner is ready to return to full membership privileges*];

4 Then shall the priest command to take for him that is to be cleansed [*the person who has repented*] two birds [*one represents the Savior, the other represents the person who has repented*] alive and clean, and cedar wood [*symbolic of the cross*], and scarlet [*associated with mocking Christ before His crucifixion, Mark 15:17*], and hyssop [*associated with Christ on the cross, John 19:29*]:

5 And the priest shall command that one of the birds [*a "type" for the Savior; symbolic of the Savior*] be killed in an earthen vessel [*Christ was sent to earth to die for us*] over running water [*Christ offers "living water," John 7:37–38, which cleanses us*]:

6 As for the living bird [*a "type," representing the person who has repented*], he [*the priest; symbolic of the bishop, stake president*] shall take it [*the living bird*], and the cedar wood, and the scarlet, and the hyssop [*all associated with the Atonement*], and shall dip them and the living bird in the blood of the bird that was killed over the running water [*representing the Savior's blood which was shed for us*]:

7 And he shall sprinkle upon him that is to be cleansed from the leprosy [*cleansed from sin, symbolically*] seven times [*seven is the number which, in numeric symbolism, represents perfection*], and shall pronounce him clean, and shall

Second Nephi 20

let the living bird [*the person who has repented*] loose into the open field [*representing the wide open opportunities again available in the kingdom of God for the person who truly repents*].

8 And he that is to be cleansed shall wash his clothes, and shave off all his hair [*symbolic of becoming like a newborn baby; fresh start*], and wash himself in water [*symbolic of baptism*], that he may be clean: and after that he shall come into the camp [*rejoin the Lord's people*], and shall tarry abroad out of his tent seven days.

9 But it shall be on the seventh day, that he shall shave all his hair off his head and his beard and his eyebrows, even all his hair he shall shave off [*symbolic of being "born again"*]: and he shall wash his clothes, also he shall wash his flesh in water [*symbolic of baptism*], and **he shall be clean** [*a simple fact, namely that we can truly be cleansed and healed by the Savior's Atonement*].

Having considered the use of "types" [*sometimes called "types and shadows"*] in the scriptures, we will now continue with Isaiah's teachings and watch as Assyria is used as a "type" of the destruction of the wicked at the Second Coming.

1 Wo unto them [*political leaders; kings*] that decree unrighteous decrees [*unrighteous laws*], and that write grievousness [*laws designed to oppress their people*] which they have prescribed;

2 To turn away the needy from judgment [*designed to keep the needy from fair treatment*], and to take away the right from the poor of my people, that widows may be their prey [*victims*], and that they may rob the fatherless [*they are greedy and brutal*]!

3 And what will ye [*the wicked*] do in the day of visitation [*punishment*], and in the desolation which shall come from far [*from Assyria; in other words, what will you wicked, greedy leaders do when the Assyrians attack you*]? to whom will ye flee for help? and where will ye leave your glory [*wealth, etc.*]?

4 Without me [*the Lord; without the help of the Lord*] they shall bow down under the prisoners [*huddle among the prisoners*], and they shall fall under the slain [*be killed*]. For all this his anger is not turned away, **but his hand is stretched out still** [*you can still repent*].

> Now Isaiah gives a message from the Lord to the Assyrian king, Sargon. Sargon thinks that he is terrific in and of himself. He isn't.

5 O Assyrian, the rod [*tool of destruction used by the Lord to punish Israel*] of mine anger, and the staff in their hand is their indignation.

6 I will send him [*Assyria*] against a hypocritical nation [*Israel*], and against the people of my wrath [*Israel*] will I give him [*Assyria*] a charge [*an assignment*] to take the spoil [*Israel's wealth*], and to take the prey [*Israel*], and to tread them [*Israel*] down like the mire [*mud*] of the streets [*see 2 Nephi 8:23*].

7 Howbeit he meaneth not so [*doesn't think so*], neither doth his heart think so [*the king of Assyria doesn't realize he is a tool in God's hand; thinks he doing it on his own*]; but in his heart it is to destroy and cut off nations not a few [*he is a wicked man, takes pleasure in destroying others*].

8 For he [*the Assyrian king*] saith [*boasts*]: Are not my princes [*military commanders*] altogether kings [*just like kings in other countries*]?

Isaiah portrays the Assyrian king, who is a "type" of Satan, naming off the cities he has easily conquered en route toward Jerusalem.

9 Is not Calno as Carchemish? Is not Hamath as Arpad? Is not Samaria as Damascus [*cities conquered by Assyria; see Map 10 in LDS Bible, first editions; see also 2 Kings 19:8–13 for Sennacherib's boastful letter to Hezekiah, King of Judah*]?

10 As my hand [*Assyria's*] hath founded [*Hebrew: acquired*] the kingdoms of the idols, and whose graven images did excel them of Jerusalem and of Samaria [*I've taken many cities whose idols are more powerful than those of Jerusalem and Samaria*];

11 Shall I not, as I have done unto Samaria and her idols, so do to Jerusalem and to her idols [*Assyria's king boasts that other nations' idols, gods, did not stop him and neither will Jerusalem's*]?

12 Wherefore it shall come to pass that when the Lord hath performed his whole work upon Mount Zion and upon Jerusalem [*when the Lord is through using Assyria to punish Israel*], I [*the Lord*] will punish the fruit of the stout heart of the king of Assyria, and the glory [*German Bible: pompousness*] of his high looks [*when I'm through using Assyria against Israel, then proud, haughty Assyria will get its deserved punishment*].

13 For he [*the Assyrian king*] saith: By the strength of my hand and by my wisdom I have done these things; for I am prudent; and I have moved the borders of the people, and have robbed their treasures, and I have put down the inhabitants like a valiant [*mighty*] man [*bragging*];

14 And my hand hath found as a nest the riches of the people; and as one gathereth eggs that are left have I gathered all the earth [*I'm mighty powerful!*]; and there was none that moved the wing, or opened the mouth, or peeped [*everybody is afraid of me!*].

Isaiah next uses some very fascinating imagery in describing the absurdity of the king of Assyria's taking credit to himself for his "amazing" accomplishments. There is an important message in this for all of us who might at times take or accept credit for accomplishments in the work of the Lord.

As you read verse 15, you might even find it a bit humorous.

15 Shall the ax [*king of Assyria*] boast itself against him [*the Lord*] that heweth [*chops*] therewith [*shall the ax brag that it is doing all the work by itself*]? Shall the saw magnify itself against [*German Bible: defy*] him that shaketh it [*uses it*]? As if the rod [*wooden club*] should shake itself against them that lift it up [*as if a wooden club should suddenly turn to the man who is swinging it and say, "Let go of me. I can do it myself!"*], or as if the staff should lift up itself as if it were no wood [*as if the staff were not simply a piece of wood*]!

16 Therefore [*because of the King of Assyria's wicked deeds and cocky attitude*] shall the Lord, the Lord of Hosts, send among his fat [*powerful*] ones, leanness [*Hebrew: disease, or trouble is coming to Assyria*]; and under his [*Assyria's*] glory he shall kindle a burning like the burning of a fire [*the Lord will trim Assyria down to size*].

17 And the light of Israel [*Christ*] shall be for a fire, and his [*Israel's*] Holy One [*Christ*] for a flame, and shall burn and shall devour his [*Assyria's*] thorns and his briers **in one day**;

The prophecy of destruction upon Assyria, given in verse 17, above, happened suddenly. 185,000 Assyrians died of devastating sickness in one night as they prepared to attack Jerusalem; see 2 Kings 19:35–37. The prophecy is continued with additional repetition in verses 18 and 19. We will use **bold** to point these out.

18 And **shall consume** the glory of **his forest** [*Assyria's armies*], and of **his fruitful field** [*his very productive military*], both **soul and body**; and they shall be **as when a standard-bearer fainteth** [*as when the last flag bearer falls, and the flag with him; your armies will be destroyed*].

19 And **the rest of the trees of his forest** [*the remnants of Assyria's army*] **shall be few**, that a child may write them [*so few Assyrians will remain that a small child could count them with his limited counting ability*].

20 And it shall come to pass in that day [*the last days*], that the remnant of Israel, and such as are escaped [*survive*] of the house of Jacob [*Israel*], shall no more again stay [*be dependent*] upon him [*Israel's enemies*] that smote them [*Israel*], but shall stay [*depend*] upon the Lord, the Holy One of Israel, in truth. [*In other words, the day will come in which Israel will become a righteous people who depend on and trust in the Lord.*]

> Next, Isaiah again emphasizes the future return of Israel to their God.

21 The remnant shall return, yea, even the remnant of Jacob, unto the mighty God [*Dual: 1. A remnant remains in the land after Assyrian destruction. 2. In the future, a righteous remnant of Israel will be gathered in; see 2 Nephi 21:11–12*].

22 For though [*although*] thy people Israel be as the sand of the sea, yet a remnant of them shall return [*German Bible: only a remnant will be converted; gathering*]; the consumption decreed [*destruction at the end of the world*] shall overflow [*will overcome the wicked*] with righteousness [*because of God's power or under God's direction; see the following verse*].

23 For the Lord God of Hosts shall make a consumption, even determined [*the decreed or prophesied destruction; see Isaiah 10, footnote 23a*] in all the land.

> Next, Isaiah emphasizes and repeats again the prophecy that the Lord will stop the Assyrians in their tracks. He adds that they will be stopped at the very last moment, just as they position themselves to enter Jerusalem.

24 Therefore, thus saith the Lord God of Hosts: O my people that dwellest in Zion, be not afraid of the Assyrian; he [*the Assyrian armies*] shall smite thee with a

rod, and shall lift up his staff against thee, after the manner of Egypt [*like Egypt did in earlier times*].

25 For yet a very little while, and the indignation [*the anger of the Lord against Israel*] shall cease, and mine anger in their destruction [*my anger will be directed toward the destruction of the Assyrians*].

26 And the Lord of Hosts shall stir up a scourge for him [*the Assyrians*] according to [*like*] the slaughter of Midian at the rock of Oreb [*Judges 7:23–25 where Gideon and his three hundred miraculously defeated the overwhelming armies of the Midianites*]; and as his rod was upon the sea [*His power came upon the Red Sea to drown the Egyptian armies*] so shall he lift it up after the manner of Egypt [*God will stop Assyria like he did the Egyptians when they pursued the children of Israel*].

27 And it shall come to pass in that day that his [*Israel's enemies, such as Assyria and others*] burden shall be taken away from off thy [*Israel's*] shoulder, and his yoke [*bondage*] from off thy neck, and the yoke shall be destroyed because of the anointing [*because of Christ, the "Anointed One"*].

As previously stated, Isaiah is a master of drama. Next, he will create a high degree of tension as he prophesies the advance of the Assyrian armies upon Jerusalem. It will look like Assyria will not be stopped; Assyrians will easily take several cities leading right up to the outskirts of Jerusalem and it will look like Jerusalem is doomed despite Isaiah's prophecies to the contrary in verse 26. We will **bold** the names of the cities that the Assyrian king conquers as he heads toward Jerusalem.

28 He [*the Assyrian king with his powerful armies*] is come to **Aiath**, he is passed to **Migron**; at **Michmash** he hath laid up his carriages [*horses and carriages are symbolic of military might*].

29 They [*Assyria*] are gone over the passage [*they have come over the pass*]; they have taken up their lodging at **Geba**; **Ramath** is afraid; **Gibeah** of Saul is fled.

30 Lift up the voice [*weep!*], O daughter of **Gallim**; cause it to be heard unto **Laish**, O poor **Anathoth**.

31 **Madmenah** is removed; the inhabitants of **Gebim** gather themselves to flee.

32 As yet shall he [*Assyria*] remain at **Nob** [*just outside of Jerusalem*] that day; he shall shake his hand against the mount of the daughter of Zion [*Jerusalem*], the hill of Jerusalem.

33 Behold, the Lord, the Lord of Hosts shall lop the bough with terror [*when Assyrian armies get right to Jerusalem, the Lord will "trim them down to size," "clip their wings," stop them in their tracks*]; and the high ones [*leaders of Assyrian armies*] of stature shall be hewn down; and the haughty shall be humbled.

34 And he shall cut down the thickets of the forests [*the Assyrian armies*] with iron [*an axe*], and Lebanon shall fall by a mighty one [*the Lord did stop Assyria by sending a sudden plague which killed 185,000 of them in one night as they camped outside Jerusalem; see 2 Kings 19:32–35*].

> The Assyrian armies came up to Jerusalem, as prophesied, and were stopped suddenly by the Lord, as promised. This was one fulfillment of this prophecy.
>
> However, this may be a dual prophecy, that is, one with more than one fulfillment. It also could refer to the attacks on Jerusalem and Israel in the last days, as powerful nations gather together to attempt to destroy them. In this case also, the Jews and Jerusalem will be spared also because of the Savior. He will appear on the Mount of Olives, which will split in two. The Jews will flee into the valley caused by the split and will see their Savior there. They will ask questions and He will answer. We will use prophecies recorded in Zechariah to review these future events and will use **bold** for teaching purposes.

Zechariah 12:8–9

8 **In that day shall the LORD defend the inhabitants of Jerusalem**; and he that is feeble among them at that day shall be as David; and the house of David shall be as God, as the angel of the LORD before them.

9 And it shall come to pass **in that day**, that **I will seek to destroy all the nations that come against Jerusalem**.

Zechariah 14:4–5

4 **And his** [*Christ's*] **feet shall stand in that day upon the mount of Olives**, which is before [*across the valley from*] Jerusalem on the east, **and the mount of Olives shall cleave** in the midst thereof **toward the east and toward the west**, and there shall be **a very great valley**; and half of the mountain shall remove toward the north, and

half of it toward the south.

5 And **ye** [*the Jews*] **shall flee to the valley** of the mountains; for the valley of the mountains shall reach unto Azal: yea, ye shall flee, like as ye fled from before the earthquake in the days of Uzziah king of Judah: and the LORD my God shall come, and all the saints with thee.

Zechariah 13:6

6 And **one shall say unto him, What** *are* **these wounds in thine hands?** Then he shall answer, *Those* **with which I was wounded** *in* **the house of my friends**.

SECOND NEPHI 21

This chapter compares to Isaiah 11 in the Bible. Joseph Smith said that Moroni quoted this chapter and said that it was about to be fulfilled. We find this statement in Joseph Smith—History, in the Pearl of Great Price, as follows (**bold** added for emphasis):

Joseph Smith—History 1:40

40 In addition to these, **he quoted the eleventh chapter of Isaiah, saying that it was about to be fulfilled**. He quoted also the third chapter of Acts, twenty-second and twenty-third verses, precisely as they stand in our New Testament. He said that that prophet was Christ; but the day had not yet come when "they who would not hear his voice should be cut off from among the people," but soon would come.

In this chapter, we are taught that powerful leaders will come forth in the last days to lead the gathering of Israel. We are instructed in Christlike qualities of leadership. We will be shown the peace that will abound during the Millennium and Isaiah will also teach about the last days gathering of Israel.

1 And there shall come forth a rod [*Hebrew: "twig"; D&C 113:3–4 defines this "rod" as "a servant in the hands of Christ, who is partly a descendant of Jesse as well as of Ephraim . . . on whom there is laid much power."*] out of the stem of Jesse [*Christ; see D&C 113:1–2*], and a branch shall grow out of his roots.

Perhaps the imagery here in verse one grows out of the last two verses of chapter 20, where the wicked leaders end up as "stumps" and have been destroyed. In the last days, new, righteous, powerful leaders will be brought forth to replace the "stumps" of the past and will have their origins from the "roots" of Christ. "Roots" can symbolically represent being solid and firmly rooted in God.

2 [*Christlike qualities of leadership described next.*] And the Spirit of the Lord shall rest upon him, the spirit of wisdom and understanding, the spirit of counsel and might, the spirit of knowledge and of the fear of the Lord;

3 And shall make him of quick understanding in the fear of the Lord; and he shall not judge after the sight of his eyes, neither reprove after the hearing of his ears.

4 But with righteousness shall he judge the poor, and reprove with equity for the meek of the earth; and he shall smite the earth with the rod of his mouth, and with the breath of his lips shall he slay the wicked.

5 And righteousness shall be the girdle of his loins, and faithfulness the girdle of his reins [*desires, thoughts*].

Isaiah now makes the transition directly into the Millennium.

6 The wolf also shall dwell with the lamb, and the leopard shall lie down with the kid [*young goat*], and the calf and the young lion and fatling together; and a little child shall lead [*herd*] them [*Millennial conditions*].

7 And the cow and the bear shall feed [*graze*]; their young ones shall lie down together; and the lion shall eat straw like the ox.

8 And the suckling child [*nursing child*] shall play on the hole of the asp [*viper*], and the weaned child [*toddler*] shall put his hand on the cockatrice's [*venomous serpent's*] den.

9 They shall not hurt nor destroy in all my holy mountain, for the earth shall be full of the knowledge [*Hebrew: devotion*] of the Lord, as the waters cover the sea. [*There will be great and wonderful peace on earth during the Millennium.*]

10 And in that day there shall be a root of Jesse [*probably Joseph Smith, but we don't know for sure*], which shall stand for an ensign of the people [*will signal that the gathering of Israel in the last days is about to begin*]; to it [*the "ensign" or flag signaling the beginning of an event*] shall the Gentiles seek; and his rest shall be glorious.

11 And it shall come to pass in that day that the Lord shall set his hand again the second time [*dual: a remnant returned after the Babylonian captivity/ last days gathering of Israel*] to recover the remnant of his

people which shall be left, from Assyria, and from Egypt, and from Pathros, and from Cush, and from Elam, and from Shinar, and from Hamath, and from the islands of the sea. [*In other words, in the last days, Israel will be gathered from every nation in the world.*]

12 And he shall set up an ensign [*the Church in the last days*] for the nations, and shall assemble the outcasts of Israel, and gather together the dispersed of Judah [*the Jews*] from the four corners of the earth.

> As you will recall from your study of Isaiah so far, and from the history of the Holy Land, the twelve tribes split into two nations in a bitter dispute over high taxes, etc. after the death of Solomon. Over the years, Ephraim (the ten tribes whose nation was in the northern portion of the Holy Land) and Judah (the southern kingdom with Jerusalem as their capital city) became bitter enemies. Therefore, the prophecy that follows is marvelous! It is a prophecy that the day will come when the Jews and the descendants of Ephraim will get along well. We are seeing this today (**bold** added for emphasis).

13 The envy of Ephraim also shall depart, and the adversaries of Judah shall be cut off; **Ephraim shall not envy Judah, and Judah shall not vex Ephraim** [*the United States and others will be on good terms with the Jews*].

> Next, Isaiah addresses conditions in the Middle East in the last days before the Second Coming of the Savior.

14 But they [*the Jews, with Ephraim's help*] shall fly upon the shoulders of the Philistines towards the west [*attack the western slopes that were once Philistine territory*]; they shall spoil them of the east together; they shall lay their hand upon Edom and Moab; and the children of Ammon shall obey them [*the Jews will be powerful against the enemy nations which surround them in the last days rather than being easy prey for their enemies as they have been throughout history*].

15 And the Lord shall utterly destroy the tongue of the Egyptian sea [*productivity of Nile River ruined?—see Isaiah 19:5–10*]; and with his mighty wind he shall shake his hand over the river, and shall smite it in the seven streams, and make men go over dry shod.

16 And there shall be a highway

for the remnant of his people which shall be left, from Assyria, like as it was to Israel in the day that he came up out of the land of Egypt [*the Lord will establish His gospel which will serve as a "highway" for Israel to return to Him*].

SECOND NEPHI 22

This chapter compares to Isaiah, chapter 12. It is a short but beautiful chapter referring to the Millennium. It describes the faithful who survive the destruction at the Second Coming of Christ as praising the Lord and rejoicing at the salvation that has come to them.

1 And in that day [*the Millennium*] thou [*Israel*] shalt say: O Lord, I will praise thee; though thou wast angry with me thine anger is turned away, and thou comfortedst me.

2 Behold, God is my salvation; I will trust, and not be afraid; for the Lord JEHOVAH [*Jesus*] is my strength and my song; he also has become my salvation.

3 Therefore, with joy shall ye draw water [*"living water," John 4:10; 7:38–39*] out of the wells of salvation.

4 And in that day shall ye say: Praise the Lord, call upon his name, declare his doings among the people, make mention that his name is exalted.

5 Sing unto the Lord; for he hath done excellent things; this is known in all the earth [*knowledge of the Lord will cover the earth*].

6 Cry out and shout, thou inhabitant of Zion; for great is the Holy One of Israel [*Christ*] in the midst of thee.

SECOND NEPHI 23

In chapter 20, the destruction of Assyria was a "type" of (or symbolic of) the destruction of the wicked at the Second Coming of Christ. We discussed the definition of "type" in the notes at the beginning of that chapter. In this chapter, the destruction of Babylon is likewise a "type" of the destruction of Satan's kingdom at the time of the Second Coming.

It will be helpful to understand that the ancient city of Babylon was a huge city full of wickedness. Over time, Babylon has come to symbolize the wickedness of the world. A brief description of Babylon is given in your Bible Dictionary

Second Nephi 23

under "Babylon" as follows:

"**Babylon.** The capital of Babylonia. According to Gen. 10:8–10 it was founded by Nimrod and was one of the oldest cities of the land of Shinar; in 11:1–9 we have the record of the Tower of Babel and the 'Confusion of Tongues' (see Ether 1:3–5, 34–35). During the Assyrian supremacy (see Assyria) it became part of that empire, and was destroyed by Sennacherib. After the downfall of Assyria, Babylon became Nebuchadnezzar's capital. He built an enormous city of which the ruins still remain. The city was square, and the Euphrates ran through the middle of it. According to Herodotus the walls were 56 miles in circumference, 335 ft. high, and 85 ft. wide. A large part of the city consisted of beautiful parks and gardens. The chief building was the famous temple of Bel. Inscriptions that have been recently deciphered show Babylonian accounts of the Creation and the Deluge in many ways similar to those given in Genesis. Other inscriptions recount events referred to in the Bible histories of the kingdoms of Israel and Judaea, and also give valuable information as to the chronology of these periods."

A sketch of the history of the Babylonian empire will be found under Assyria.

1 The burden of [*message of doom to*] Babylon, which Isaiah the son of Amoz did see.

> Verses 2–5, next, describe how the Lord will gather his righteous forces together.

2 Lift ye up a banner upon the high mountain, exalt [*raise*] the voice unto them [*the righteous*], shake the hand [*wave the hand, signal*], that they may go into the gates of the nobles [*gather with the righteous*].

3 I have commanded my sanctified ones [*my Saints*], I have also called my mighty ones, for mine anger is not upon them that rejoice in my highness.

4 The noise of the multitude in the mountains like as of a great people [*the gathering*], a tumultuous noise of the kingdoms of nations gathered together, the Lord of Hosts mustereth the hosts of the battle.

5 They come from a far country, from the end of heaven, yea, the Lord, and the weapons of his indignation, to destroy the whole land [*the wicked*].

> Next, Isaiah switches topics from the gathering of the righteous to fight together against

wickedness to a strong warning to the wicked who will soon be facing the consequences of their evil ways.

6 Howl ye [*the wicked*], for the day of the Lord [*Second Coming*] is at hand; it shall come as a destruction from the Almighty.

7 Therefore shall all hands be faint [*hang limp*], every man's [*wicked men*] heart [*courage*] shall melt;

8 And they shall be afraid; pangs and sorrows shall take hold of them; they shall be amazed [*will look in fear*] one at another; their faces shall be as flames [*burn with shame*].

9 Behold, the day of the Lord [*Second Coming*] cometh, cruel [*it will appear cruel to the wicked*] both with wrath and fierce anger, to lay the land desolate; and he [*the Lord*] shall destroy the sinners thereof out of it [*a purpose of the Second Coming*].

10 For the stars of heaven and the constellations thereof shall not give their light; the sun shall be darkened in his going forth, and the moon shall not cause her light to shine [*signs of the times preceding the Second Coming of Christ*].

11 And I will punish the world for evil, and the wicked for their iniquity; I will cause the arrogancy of the proud to cease, and will lay down the haughtiness [*pride*] of the terrible [*tyrants; typical Isaiah repetition to drive home a point*].

12 I will make a man more precious [*scarce*] than fine gold; even a man than the golden wedge of Ophir [*a land rich in gold, possibly in southern Arabia; there will be relatively few survivors of the Second Coming*].

13 Therefore [*because of the wickedness on earth prior to the Second Coming*], I will shake the heavens, and the earth shall remove out of her place, in the wrath of the Lord of Hosts, and in the day of his fierce anger.

14 And it [*dual: Babylon literally as a city; also the wicked in general*] shall be as the chased roe [*hunted deer*], and as a sheep that no man taketh up [*no shepherd, no one to defend it*]; and they shall every man turn to his own people, and flee every one into his own land [*foreigners who have had safety in Babylon, because of Babylon's great power, will return to their homelands because Babylon is no longer powerful and safe*].

15 Every one that is proud shall be thrust through [*stabbed*]; yea, and every one that is joined to the wicked shall fall by the sword.

16 Their children, also shall be dashed to pieces before their eyes; their houses shall be spoiled and their wives ravished [*fate of Babylon; innocent people suffer because of the wicked*].

Next, Isaiah gives a very specific prophecy regarding how the ancient city of Babylon was to be conquered.

17 Behold, I will stir up the Medes against them [*the Medes, from Persia, conquered Babylon easily in 538 B.C.*], which shall not regard silver and gold, nor shall they delight in it [*you Babylonians will not be able to bribe the Medes not to destroy you*].

18 Their bows shall also dash the young men to pieces, and they shall have no pity on the fruit of the womb [*babies*]; their eyes shall not spare children.

19 And Babylon, the glory of kingdoms, the beauty of the Chaldees' excellency, shall be as when God overthrew Sodom and Gomorrah.

Isaiah prophesied that Babylon would be completely destroyed and never inhabited again. And that is exactly what happened. It remains in ruins even today. The symbolism is clear. Satan's kingdom will be destroyed by the Savior at the time of His Second Coming, and again after the "little season" at the end of the Millennium, never again to be rebuilt. (See D&C 88:111–14.)

20 It shall never be inhabited, neither shall it be dwelt in from generation to generation: neither shall the Arabian pitch tent there; neither shall the shepherds make their fold there.

21 But wild beasts of the desert shall lie there; and their houses [*the ruins*] shall be full of doleful creatures [*such as owls*]; and owls shall dwell there, and satyrs [*male goats*] shall dance there.

22 And the wild beasts of the islands shall cry in their desolate houses, and dragons [*hyenas, wild dogs, jackals*] in their pleasant palaces; and her time is near to come, and her day shall not be prolonged [*Babylon's time is up, her days are almost over*]. For I will destroy her speedily; yea, for I will be merciful unto my people [*the righteous*], but the wicked shall perish.

SECOND NEPHI 24

Isaiah uses very colorful style and imagery as he now prophesies concerning the future downfall of the King of Babylon and, symbolically, the downfall of Satan's kingdom. Compare with Isaiah 14 in the Bible.

1 For the Lord will have mercy on Jacob [*Israel*], and will yet choose Israel, and set them in their own land [*One historical fulfillment of this was when Cyrus the Great of Persia allowed Jewish captives in Babylon to return, 538 B.C.; another group returned in 520 B.C. This is also being fulfilled in our day.*]; and the strangers shall be joined with them [*foreigners will live with them*], and they shall cleave to the house of Jacob.

2 And the people [*many nations who will help Israel return*] shall take them [*Israel*] and bring them to their place; yea, from far unto the ends of the earth; and they [*Israel*] shall return to their lands of promise. And the house of Israel shall possess them and the land of the Lord shall be for servants and handmaids; and they [*Israel*] shall take them [*nations who used to dominate Israel*] captives unto whom they [*Israel*] were captives; and they [*Israel*] shall rule over their oppressors [*the tables will be turned in the last days*].

Notice that "lands" in verse 2, above, is plural. Among other things, this reminds us that in the last days there are to be several gathering places for Israel. In our day, members are being gathered into stakes of Zion throughout the world.

3 And it shall come to pass in that day [*Millennium*] that the Lord shall give thee [*Israel; the Lord's covenant people; the members of the Church*] rest, from thy sorrow, and from thy fear, and from the hard bondage wherein thou wast made to serve [*Israel will finally be free from subjection by foreigners*].

Next, Isaiah paints a future scene with words in which he depicts two things, namely, the literal fall of Babylon and her wicked king, and also, symbolically, the future fall of Satan and his wicked kingdom. Such prophecies of Isaiah are known as "dual meaning" prophecies.

As he sets things up for his students, Isaiah creates interest and intrigue by telling them that downtrodden Israel will someday come to the point when they will see the king of Babylon (symbolic of wicked earthly leaders) as well as Satan himself trimmed down to size, with no more power to afflict and distress them. Isaiah then creates fascinating imagery to drive home his point that the faithful righteous will eventually triumph over all evil by staying close to God.

4 And it shall come to pass in that day, that thou [*Israel*] shalt take up this proverb [*taunting, saying*] against the king of

SECOND NEPHI 24

Babylon [*dual: literally King of Babylon. Refers also to Satan plus any wicked leader*], and say: How hath the oppressor ceased [*what happened to you!*], the golden city ceased [*your unconquerable city, kingdom, is gone*]!

> In verse 5, below, Isaiah confirms that it is the power of the Lord that will ultimately break the power of the wicked to afflict the righteous.

5 The Lord hath broken the staff of the wicked, the scepters [*power*] of the [*wicked*] rulers.

6 He [*dual: King of Babylon; Satan*] who smote the people in wrath with a continual stroke [*never ceasing*], he that ruled the nations in anger, is persecuted [*is now being punished*], and none hindereth [*nobody can stop it*].

7 The whole earth is at rest, and is quiet [*Millennium*]; they break forth into singing [*during the Millennium*].

8 Yea, the fir-trees [*people*] rejoice at thee [*at what has happened to Satan*], and also the cedars [*people*] of Lebanon, saying: Since thou art laid down [*since you got chopped down*] no feller [*tree cutter, lumberjack*] is come up against us.

9 Hell [*spirit prison*] from beneath is moved for thee [*is getting ready to receive you*] to meet thee at thy coming; it stirreth up the dead for thee, even all the chief ones [*dead wicked leaders*] of the earth; it hath raised up from their thrones all the [*wicked*] kings of the nations.

10 All they shall speak and say unto thee [*dual: Satan; King of Babylon*]: Art thou also become weak as we [*what happened to your power*]? Art thou become like unto us [*did you get your power taken away too, like us*]?

11 Thy pomp is brought down to the grave [*was destroyed with you*]; the noise of thy viols [*royal harp music*] is not heard; the worm is spread under thee, and the worms cover thee. [*Maggots are destroying your dead body just like they destroyed ours. You're no better off here in hell than we are, so hah, hah, hah! Refers to the King of Babylon since Satan has no mortal body.*]

> Next comes one of the most famous quotes from Isaiah regarding Lucifer. It deals with his fall from heaven, after his rebellion in the premortal life.

12 How art thou fallen from heaven [*What happened to you?*], O Lucifer, son of the morning! Art thou cut down to the ground, which did weaken the nations [*you used to destroy*

nations; now your power is destroyed]!

13 For thou hast said in thy heart [*these were your motives*]: I will ascend into heaven, I will exalt my throne above the stars of God [*I will be the highest*]; I will sit also upon the mount of the congregation, in the sides of the north [*mythical mountain in the north where gods assemble*];

14 I will ascend above the heights of the clouds; I will be like the Most High [*Moses 4:1 indicates he wanted to be the Most High!*].

15 Yet thou [*Lucifer*] shalt be brought down to hell, to the sides of the pit [*to the lowest part of the world of the dead, outer darkness*].

16 They [*the residents of hell*] that see thee [*Lucifer; King of Babylon*] shall narrowly look upon thee [*scorn you, mock you*], and shall consider [*look at*] thee, and shall say: Is this the man that made the earth to tremble, that did shake kingdoms?

17 And made the world as a wilderness, and destroyed the cities thereof, and opened not the house of his prisoners [*refused to free his prisoners*]?

18 All the kings of the nations, yea, all of them, lie in glory, every one of them in his own house [*all other kings have magnificent tombs*].

19 But thou [*dual: King of Babylon literally; Satan figuratively because he doesn't even have a physical body*] art cast out of thy grave like an abominable branch [*pruned off and thus worthless*], and the remnant of those that are slain [*you are just like any other dead wicked person*], thrust through with a sword, that go down to the stones of the pit [*to the very bottom*]; as a carcass trodden under feet.

20 Thou [*King of Babylon; Satan*] shalt not be joined with them in burial, because thou hast destroyed thy land and slain thy people; the seed of evil-doers shall never be renowned [*none of your evil family will survive, King of Babylon*].

21 Prepare slaughter for his [*King of Babylon*] children for the iniquities of their fathers, that they do not rise, nor possess the land, nor fill the face of the world with cities [*none of your children will rule the earth like you have*].

Next, Isaiah reiterates that it is ultimately the Lord who will stop Lucifer and all powerful wicked leaders and rulers. Note how thoroughly Isaiah defines the destruction. We will use **bold** to point it out.

SECOND NEPHI 24

22 For I will rise up against them [*the Lord will stop Lucifer; King of Babylon*], saith the Lord of Hosts, and **cut off** from Babylon the **name**, and **remnant**, and **son**, and **nephew** [*I will destroy Babylon completely*], saith the Lord.

One of Isaiah's favorite methods of driving home the point that a wicked kingdom will be destroyed completely is to picture it desolate, deserted—where only birds and animals live, avoiding humans. We see this technique in the next verse.

23 I will also make it [*Babylon*] a possession for the bittern [*owls*], and pools of water; and I will sweep it with the besom [*broom*] of destruction [*a "clean sweep"*], saith the Lord of Hosts.

Isaiah has finished with Babylon, and starts a new topic now, namely, the fate of Assyria.

24 The Lord of Hosts hath sworn [*covenanted*], saying: Surely as I have thought [*planned*], so shall it come to pass [*here is something else I will do*]; and as I have purposed [*planned*], so shall it stand [*it will happen*]—

25 That I will bring the Assyrian in my land [*Judah*], and upon my mountains [*the mountains of Judah*] tread him [*Assyria*] under foot; then shall his yoke [*Assyrian bondage*] depart from off them [*my people*], and his burden depart from off their shoulders [*dual: the Assyrian downfall in Judah, 701 B.C.; also, the forces of the wicked will be destroyed at the Second Coming and again at the end of the earth*].

26 This is the purpose [*the plan*] that is purposed upon the whole earth; and this is the hand [*the power of the Lord*] that is stretched out upon all nations [*the eventual fate of all wicked*].

27 For the Lord of Hosts hath purposed [*planned*], and who shall disannul [*prevent it*]? And his [*the Lord's*] hand is stretched out, and who shall turn it back [*who can stop the Lord*]?

Isaiah has finished with the Assyrians and now switches to the Philistines.

28 In the year that king Ahaz died [*about 720 B.C.*] was this burden [*message of doom to the Philistines*].

29 Rejoice not [*don't get happy and start celebrating*] thou, whole Palestina [*Philistia*], because the rod [*power*] of him [*Shalmaneser, King of Assyria from 727–22 B.C.*] that smote thee is broken; for out of the

serpent's root [*"snakes lay eggs," or, from the same source, Assyria*] shall come forth a cockatrice [*One "snake" is dead—Shalmaneser—and a worse one will yet come—Sennacherib, King of Assyria, 705–687 B.C. The Philistines rejoiced when Sargon, King of Assyria from 722–705 B.C. took over at Shalmaneser's death. Sargon was not as hard on them as his predecessor was.*], and his fruit [*his son, Senacherib*] shall be a fiery flying serpent.

30 And the first-born of the poor shall feed, and the needy shall lie down in safety [*if you Philistines will join with the Lord, repent etc., you too can enjoy peace and safety, otherwise . . .*]; and I will kill thy [*Philistines*] root with famine, and he shall slay thy remnant [*you will be utterly destroyed*].

31 Howl, O gate; cry, O city; thou, whole Palestina [*Philistia*], art dissolved [*reduced to nothing*]; for there shall come from the north a smoke [*cloud of dust made by an approaching enemy army*], and none shall be alone in his appointed times [*the enemy army will have no cowards in it*].

32 What shall then answer the messengers of the nations [*what will one say when people ask, "What happened to the Philistines?"*]? [*Answer:*] That the Lord hath founded Zion, and the poor of his people shall trust in it [*that the Lord is the one who caused the destruction of the wicked and established Zion*].

SECOND NEPHI 25

One of the great advantages that we enjoy as far as understanding Isaiah is concerned, is that Nephi explains what we have just read in the previous Isaiah chapters. As of verse 9, he will begin giving specific explanations. In verses 1–8, he will explain that his own people had difficulty understanding Isaiah also. We will use **bold** for emphasis.

1 NOW I, Nephi, do speak somewhat concerning the words which I have written, which have been spoken by the mouth of Isaiah. For behold, **Isaiah spake many things which were hard for many of my people to understand; for they know not concerning the manner of prophesying among the Jews**.

2 For I, Nephi, have not taught them many things concerning the manner of the Jews; for their works were works of darkness,

Second Nephi 25

and their doings were doings of abominations.

3 Wherefore, I write unto my people, unto all those that shall receive hereafter these things which I write, that they may know the judgments of God, that they come upon all nations, according to the word which he hath spoken.

4 Wherefore, hearken, O my people, which are of the house of Israel, and give ear unto my words; for because the words of Isaiah are not plain unto you, nevertheless they are plain unto all those that are filled with the spirit of prophecy [*the Holy Ghost*]. But I give unto you a prophecy, according to the spirit which is in me; wherefore I shall prophesy according to the plainness which hath been with me from the time that I came out from Jerusalem with my father; for behold, **my soul delighteth in plainness unto my people, that they may learn**.

> Often, people ask whether or not the Jews themselves understood the words of Isaiah. Next, in verse 5, Nephi answers this question. The answer is "Yes."

5 Yea, and my soul delighteth in the words of Isaiah, for I came out from Jerusalem, and mine eyes hath beheld the things of the Jews, and **I know that the Jews do understand the things of the prophets**, and there is **none other people** that **understand the things which were spoken unto the Jews like unto them**, save it be that they are taught after the manner of the things of the Jews.

> As stated in verse 2, above, Nephi has avoided teaching his people many things about life among the Jews in the Jerusalem area because of the wicked lifestyle of that culture. Therefore, his people are a lot like us in the sense that they don't understand the background, setting and symbolism used by Isaiah. In the next verses, Nephi tells us that he will remedy this by teaching us in plain words what Isaiah was teaching.

6 But behold, **I, Nephi, have not taught my children after the manner of the Jews**; but behold, I, of myself, have dwelt at Jerusalem, wherefore **I know concerning the regions round about**; and I have made mention unto my children concerning the judgments of God, which hath come to pass among the Jews, unto my children, according to all that which Isaiah hath spoken, **and I do not write them**.

7 But behold, I proceed with mine own prophecy [*I will teach*

Isaiah in my own words], according to my plainness; in the which I know that no man can err; nevertheless, in the days that the prophecies of Isaiah shall be fulfilled men shall know of a surety, at the times when they shall come to pass.

> In verse 8, below, Nephi prophesies that in the last days, people will understand the writings of Isaiah. You are part of the fulfillment of this prophecy as you grow in ability to understand them because of the Book of Mormon and Nephi's explanations.

8 Wherefore, they [*the words of Isaiah*] are of worth unto the children of men, and he that supposeth that they are not, unto them will I speak particularly, and confine the words unto mine own people; for I know that they shall be of great worth unto them **in the last days**; for in that day **shall they understand them**; wherefore, for their good have I written them.

> Now, Nephi begins his explanation of the Isaiah chapters which he included in his small plates which we are reading now at this point in the Book of Mormon. We will continue to use **bold** for teaching purposes.

9 And **as one generation hath been destroyed among the Jews because of iniquity, even so have they been destroyed from generation to generation** [*the scattering of Israel*] **according to their iniquities** [*see 2 Nephi 13:11*]; and never hath any of them been destroyed save it were foretold them by the prophets of the Lord.

> In verse 9, above, near the end, we find an important doctrine, namely, that the Lord always gives fair warning of impending destruction or scattering because of wickedness. This way, people have a chance to use their moral agency wisely and are accountable for what happens.

10 Wherefore, it hath been told them [*the Jews*] concerning the destruction [*the Babylonian captivity*] which should come upon them, immediately after my father left Jerusalem; nevertheless, they hardened their hearts [*refused to repent*]; and according to my prophecy they have been destroyed [*Jerusalem has been destroyed*], save [*except*] it be those which are carried away captive into Babylon.

> Next, Nephi explains that one of Isaiah's most dominant teachings is the "gathering" of Israel. On a personal note, each of us is invited constantly by the Lord to be "gathered" to Him.

11 And now this I speak because

of the spirit which is in me. And notwithstanding [*even though*] they [*the Jews*] have been carried away they shall return again [*the gathering*], and possess the land of Jerusalem [*this became a fact when the Nation of Israel was formed by the United Nations in 1948*]; wherefore, they shall be restored again to the land of their inheritance [*the Holy Land*].

Next, Nephi explains that Isaiah prophesied that the Son of God would actually come to earth and live among the Jews.

12 But, behold, they [*the Jews*] shall have wars, and rumors of wars; and when the day cometh that the Only Begotten of the Father [*Jesus*], yea, even the Father of heaven and of earth [*yes, I mean Heavenly Father*], shall manifest himself unto them in the flesh, behold, they [*the Jews*] will reject him, because of their iniquities [*because of their wickedness*], and the hardness of their hearts, and the stiffness of their necks [*their pride and lack of humility*].

13 Behold, they will crucify him; and after he is laid in a sepulchre [*a tomb*] for the space of three days he shall rise from the dead [*he will be resurrected*], with healing in his wings [*with full power to heal all of us from our sins*]; and all those who shall believe on his name shall be saved in the kingdom of God. Wherefore, my soul delighteth to prophesy concerning him [*this is why I love to teach about Christ*], for I have seen his day, and my heart doth magnify his holy name [*I have indescribable feelings of appreciation for Him in my heart*].

The phrase "healing in his wings" in verse 13, above, has beautiful symbolism. "Healing" is, of course, the Savior's ability and power to heal all of us of the effects of sins and inadequacies. "Wings" symbolize the power to be wherever He is needed instantly, in order to minister to us. See D&C 77:4 for a brief explanation of "wings" given by the Prophet Joseph Smith.

14 And behold it shall come to pass that after the Messiah hath risen from the dead, and hath manifested himself unto his people, unto as many as will believe on his name, behold, Jerusalem shall be destroyed again [*by the Romans, about A.D. 70–73*]; for wo unto them that fight against God and the people of his church.

Nephi now continues teaching what Isaiah taught, namely, that the Jews would be scattered and smitten for centuries after they crucify Christ. And then, a wonderful thing begins to happen as the Jews begin to believe in Christ and His Atonement. A great gathering begins among them.

15 Wherefore, **the Jews shall be scattered among all nations**; yea, and also Babylon shall be destroyed [*it was, in 538 B.C. by the Persians*]; wherefore, the Jews shall be scattered by other nations [*this would include Rome as well as Hitler and other tyrants*].

16 And after they have been scattered, and the Lord God hath scourged [*punished*] them by other nations for the space of many generations, yea, even down from generation to generation until they shall be persuaded to believe in Christ, the Son of God, and the atonement, which is infinite for all mankind—and **when that day shall come that they shall believe in Christ, and worship the Father in his name, with pure hearts and clean hands, and look not forward any more for another Messiah** [*this time is just beginning to happen among the Jews*], then, at that time, the day will come [*is still future*] that it must needs be expedient that they should believe these things.

For several verses, Nephi has been speaking very specifically about the Jews. You will notice that his prophecy now begins to broaden in scope to include the gathering of all of Israel in the last days. This is typical of Isaiah and other Bible prophets. They will be talking about one thing and even in the middle of a verse, they will make the transition to other related topics.

17 And the Lord will set his hand again the second time [*in the last days; see Jacob 6:2 and the heading to Jacob 6*] to restore his people from their lost and fallen state. Wherefore, he will proceed to do **a marvelous work and a wonder** [*the restoration of the gospel through Joseph Smith*] among the children of men [*in all the earth*].

18 Wherefore [*in this whole process of restoring the gospel*], he shall bring forth his words unto them [*the Jews*], which words shall judge them at the last day, for they shall be given them for the purpose of convincing them of the true Messiah, who was rejected by them; and unto the convincing of them that they need not look forward any more for a Messiah to come, for there should not any come, save it should be a false Messiah which should deceive the people; for **there is save** [*only*] **one Messiah spoken of by the prophets, and**

that Messiah is he who should be rejected of the Jews.

19 For according to the words of the prophets, the Messiah cometh in six hundred years from the time that my father left Jerusalem [*600 B.C.*]; and according to the words of the prophets, and also the word of the angel of God, **his name shall be Jesus Christ, the Son of God.**

Nephi certainly does teach clearly! He emphasizes the simplicity of the gospel next by calling to his readers' minds the brass serpent set up by Moses, so his people could be healed if they would simply look at it. But it was too simple for many of them! He reminds us that Isaiah's message, too, is beautifully simple. Turn to Christ and live.

20 And now, my brethren, **I have spoken plainly** that ye cannot err [*you can not misunderstand what I have taught*]. And as the Lord God liveth that brought Israel up out of the land of Egypt, and gave unto Moses power that he should heal the nations [*the twelve tribes of Israel*] after they had been bitten by the poisonous serpents, **if they would cast their eyes unto the serpent** which he did raise up before them, and also gave him power that he should smite the rock and the water should come forth [*symbolic of the "living waters" from Christ; see John 10:4*]; yea, behold I say unto you, that **as these things are true**, and as the Lord God liveth, **there is none other name given under heaven save it be this Jesus Christ, of which I have spoken, whereby man can be saved.** [*In other words, it is just that simple. You can be saved by Christ. No one else can save you.*]

21 Wherefore, for this cause hath the Lord God promised unto me that these things [*the Book of Mormon*] which I write shall be kept and preserved, and handed down unto my seed [*posterity; the Lamanites*], from generation to generation, that the promise may be fulfilled unto Joseph, that his seed should never perish as long as the earth should stand.

22 Wherefore, these things [*Nephi's writings on the small plates, which have become part of our Book of Mormon*] shall go from generation to generation as long as the earth shall stand; and they shall go according to the will and pleasure of God [*according to His timetable*]; and the nations who shall possess them shall be judged of them [*will be held accountable for their knowledge of them*] according to the words which are written.

23 For we labor diligently to write [*it is very difficult to make metal plates and engrave them*], to persuade our children, and also our brethren, to believe in Christ, and to be reconciled to God [*to be at peace with God*]; for we know that **it is by grace that we are saved, after all we can do.**

> The last phrase of verse 23, above, is a very important doctrinal statement. Many Christians today are taught that it is by grace that they are saved, and that works are not a part of the requirements for salvation. They misquote Paul and ignore James, chapter 2:17–24. Nephi leaves no doubt as to the need for both faith and works in order to have the grace of Christ save us. "Grace" in the simplest terms means "help of Christ."

24 And, notwithstanding [*even though*] we believe in Christ, we keep the law of Moses, and look forward with steadfastness unto Christ, until the law shall be fulfilled.

> The law of Moses was designed to point the people's minds toward Christ and the great sacrifice for their sins which He would offer through the Atonement.

25 For, for this end [*purpose*] was the law [*the law of Moses*] given; wherefore [*this is why*] the law hath become dead unto us [*is no longer uppermost in our minds, even though we keep it*], and we are made alive in Christ [*we are being saved through the Atonement of Christ*] because of our faith; yet we keep the law because of the commandments [*because we are told to do so by God for the time being until Christ comes to begin His mortal ministry*].

> The next verse is an excellent one to quote to anyone who claims that we do not believe in Christ.

26 And **we talk of Christ, we rejoice in Christ, we preach of Christ, we prophesy of Christ**, and we write according to our prophecies, that our children may know to what source they may look for a remission of their sins.

> Verse 27, next, is perhaps one of the best and simplest summaries anywhere in scripture of the purpose of the law of Moses in relationship to the gospel of Christ. If the Jews at the time of Christ had allowed themselves to understand this, which was clearly taught by Old Testament prophets according to Nephi, they would have welcomed Jesus.

27 Wherefore, we speak concerning the law [*the law of Moses*] that our children may know the deadness of the law [*that it does not have the power*

to save us]; and they, by knowing the deadness of the law, may look forward unto that life [*eternal life; exaltation*] which is in Christ, and know for what end [*purpose*] the law was given [*so that our children will understand why the law of Moses was given*]. And after the law [*of Moses*] is fulfilled in Christ, that they need not harden their hearts against him [*like the Jews will when He comes among them*] when the law ought to be done away [*it was intended that the law of Moses be done away with by Christ*].

> It appears that Nephi's people are becoming less committed to God and hardened, and that some apostasy is settling in among them. We conclude this because of what Nephi says next.

28 And now behold, my people, ye are a stiffnecked people; wherefore, **I have spoken plainly unto you, that ye cannot misunderstand**. And the words which I have spoken shall stand as a testimony against you; for they are sufficient to teach any man the right way; for **the right way is to believe in Christ and deny him not**; for by denying him ye also deny the prophets and the law [*the Old Testament teachings about Christ*].

> The "prophets" are the Old Testament prophets such as Abraham, Enoch, Isaiah, Jeremiah, and so forth. The "law" consists of the writings of Moses, namely, Genesis, Exodus, Leviticus, Numbers, and Deuteronomy.

29 And now behold, I say unto you that **the right way is to believe in Christ**, and deny him not; and **Christ is the Holy One of Israel**; wherefore **ye must bow down before him, and worship him with all your might, mind, and strength, and your whole soul**; and if ye do this ye shall in nowise be cast out.

> Nephi is speaking to his own people next as he tells them that they are obligated to keep the law of Moses until Christ comes to earth to fulfill it.

30 And, inasmuch as it shall be expedient [*necessary*], ye must keep the performances and ordinances of God [*the sacrifices and detailed rules of the law of Moses*] until the law shall be fulfilled which was given unto Moses.

SECOND NEPHI 26

Having explained the simple, basic messages of Isaiah to his people, in chapter 25, Nephi now continues, prophesying about the ministry of the Savior to the people in America, after He has been crucified by the Jews.

1 AND after Christ shall have risen from the dead he shall show himself unto you, my children, and my beloved brethren [*my righteous descendants, the Nephites, who are around when Christ comes to America*]; and the words which he shall speak unto you shall be the law which ye shall do. [*In other words, you will no longer be required to live the law of Moses. Rather, you will live according to the gospel as taught by Christ.*]

2 For behold, I say unto you that I have beheld [*I have seen in vision*] that many generations shall pass away, and there shall be great wars and contentions among my people [*including those recorded in Alma and Helaman*].

Next, after prophesying about the signs which will be given among the Nephites and Lamanites in America concerning the Savior's mortal mission, Nephi will explain why some people will be killed in the destructions which precede the coming of Christ to America.

Many gospel students ask, "How good do you have to be to not be destroyed at the Second Coming?" We deduce from verse 3, below, that those who live telestial lifestyles or below will be destroyed by fire at the Second Coming. Therefore, anyone who is living a terrestrial (D&C 76:71–79) lifestyle or a celestial (D&C 76:50–53) lifestyle will be spared.

3 And after the Messiah shall come [*is born in Bethlehem*] there shall be signs given unto my people of his birth [*see Helaman 14:3–6*], and also of his death and resurrection [*see Helaman 14:20–28*]; and **great and terrible shall that day** [*when Christ comes to visit the Nephites*] **be unto the wicked**, for they shall perish; and **they perish because they cast out the prophets, and the saints, and stone them, and slay them**; wherefore the cry of the blood of the saints shall ascend up to God from the ground against them.

Nephi's prophecy of burning in verse 4, next, can apply to those of his descendants who were destroyed by fire (3 Nephi 9:9) as well as to the burning of the wicked at the time of the Second Coming.

4 Wherefore, all those who are proud, and that do wickedly, the day that cometh shall burn them up, saith the Lord of Hosts, for they shall be as stubble [*dry grain stalks, straw*].

5 And they that kill the prophets, and the saints, the depths of the earth shall swallow them up, saith

the Lord of Hosts; and mountains shall cover them, and whirlwinds shall carry them away, and buildings shall fall upon them and crush them to pieces and grind them to powder.

6 And they shall be visited with thunderings, and lightnings, and earthquakes, and all manner of destructions, for the fire of the anger of the Lord shall be kindled against them, and they shall be as stubble [*they will be like dry straw in a wildfire*], and the day that cometh [*the coming of the Lord*] shall consume them, saith the Lord of Hosts.

As we read the previous verses about the destruction of the wicked at the coming of Christ to the Nephites, we see many parallels between that and the Second Coming.

This vision was very hard on Nephi because of his kindness and tenderness, as we see in verse 7, next. While he wishes that such destructions might not take place, he realizes that the law of justice must not be robbed (see Alma 42:25).

7 O the pain, and the anguish of my soul for the loss of the slain of my people! For I, Nephi, have seen it, and it well nigh consumeth me before the presence of the Lord; but I must cry unto my God: Thy ways are just.

Next, Nephi reminds us of the attitudes and behaviors of the righteous who will not be destroyed.

8 But behold, **the righteous** that **hearken unto the words of the prophets**, and destroy them not [*literally, don't destroy the prophets; symbolically, don't destroy the words of the prophets by ignoring them*], but **look forward unto Christ with steadfastness** for the signs which are given, notwithstanding [*in spite of*] all persecution—behold, **they are they which shall not perish.**

9 But the Son of righteousness [*Christ*] shall appear unto them; and he shall heal them, and they shall have peace with him, until three generations shall have passed away, and many of the fourth generation shall have passed away in righteousness [*200 years of peace among the Nephites, after the Savior's visit to them; see 4 Nephi 1:1–22*].

10 And when these things [*the two hundred years of peace*] have passed away a speedy destruction cometh unto my people; for, notwithstanding the pains of my soul, I have seen it; wherefore, I know that it shall come to pass; and **they sell themselves for naught** [*things of no value*]; for,

for the reward of their **pride** and their **foolishness** they shall reap destruction; for because **they yield unto the devil and choose works of darkness rather than light**, therefore they must go down to hell.

> A very sobering warning is given to all of us in verse 11, next. There are eternal laws by which the Lord is bound, such that He will never violate our agency. Therefore, if we so choose and demonstrate by our actions, His Spirit must withdraw from us.

11 For the Spirit of the Lord will not always strive with man. And when the Spirit ceaseth to strive with man then cometh speedy destruction, and this grieveth my soul.

> As we have previously noted, the word "Gentile" has many different meanings and is always context sensitive. Verse 12, next, is an example of this. In this case it means everyone who is not a Jew.

12 And as I spake concerning the convincing of the Jews, that Jesus is the very Christ, it must needs be [*it is necessary that*] that the Gentiles be convinced also that Jesus is the Christ, the Eternal God;

> The term "Eternal God" is context sensitive. In this case, it means Christ. In other contexts it can mean the Father.

> Next, Nephi teaches the vital role of the Holy Ghost in bearing witness of Christ and teaching us about the Savior.

13 And that he manifesteth himself unto all those who believe in him, by the power of the Holy Ghost; yea, unto every nation, kindred, tongue, and people, working mighty miracles, signs, and wonders, among the children of men according to their faith.

> Next, Nephi teaches things of extra interest to us, since we live in the last days and are watching first hand the fulfillment of many of these prophecies. We will use **bold** for teaching purposes.

14 But behold, **I prophesy unto you concerning the last days**; concerning the days when the Lord God shall bring these things [*the Book of Mormon*] forth unto the children of men.

> Nephi uses military imagery next as he describes the Lord's efforts to humble his people sufficiently that they will return to Him.

15 After my seed [*the Nephites*] and the seed of my brethren [*the Lamanites*] shall have dwindled in unbelief, and shall have been smitten by the Gentiles [*the early immigrants and settlers who came to America*]; yea, after the Lord

God shall have camped **against them** round about [*surrounded them with punishments because of their wickedness*], and shall have laid siege against them with a mount [*a "mountain" of dirt thrown up for protection during a military attack*], and raised forts against them; and after they shall have been brought down low in the dust [*after they have been humbled*], even that they are not [*even to the point that they are virtually destroyed as a people*], yet the words of the righteous [*the Book of Mormon prophets*] shall be written, and the prayers of the faithful shall be heard, and all those who have dwindled in unbelief shall not be forgotten [*the gospel restored to them*].

16 For those who shall be destroyed [*the Book of Mormon peoples*] shall speak unto them [*all people in the last days*] out of the ground [*out of the Hill Cumorah*], and their speech shall be low out of the dust, and their voice shall be as one that hath a familiar spirit; for the Lord God will give unto him power, that he may whisper concerning them, even as it were out of the ground; and their speech shall whisper out of the dust.

The people speaking "out of the dust" and the term "familiar spirit" as used in verse 16, above, would be familiar phrases to those in Isaiah's and Nephi's day. We will quote a quote from Daniel H. Ludlow in the 1996 Book of Mormon Student Manual used in the Institutes of Religion of the Church for explanation of these terms. It is as follows (**bold** added for emphasis):

"Nephi is evidently quoting from a statement found in **Isaiah 29:4** when he refers to a destroyed people whose record shall come '**out of the ground, and their speech shall be low out of the dust, and their voice shall be as one that hath a familiar spirit**' (2 Nephi 26:16)

"A careful reading of this scripture, particularly when read together with Nephi's explanation, would indicate that the term it '**hath a familiar spirit**' means that this record (the Book of Mormon) would **speak with a 'familiar voice' to those who already have the Bible**. In other words, Nephi is evidently saying here that **the doctrinal teachings of the Book of Mormon would seem familiar to people who had already read and accepted the Bible**" (Ludlow, A Companion to Your Study of the Book of Mormon, pp. 37 and 146; Book of Mormon Student Manual, p. 36).

17 For thus saith the Lord God: They [*Book of Mormon prophets*] shall write the things which shall be done among them, and

they shall be written and sealed up in a book [*the gold plates*], and those who have dwindled in unbelief shall not have them, for they seek to destroy the things of God. [*In other words, the gold plates will be protected from those wicked who would destroy them, perhaps by melting them down for profit.*]

18 Wherefore, as those who have been destroyed have been destroyed speedily; and the multitude of their terrible ones [*tyrants, powerful wicked leaders*] shall be as chaff that passeth away [*that blows away in the wind*]—yea, thus saith the Lord God: It [*the prophesied destruction*] shall be at an instant, suddenly—

19 And it shall come to pass, that those [*Lamanites*] who have dwindled in unbelief shall be smitten by the hand of the Gentiles [*such as Cortez, etc.*].

Nephi is reviewing many of the prophecies he saw in vision in 1 Nephi 13. Next, he reviews the building up of many churches during the dark ages and beyond, which led up to the time of Joseph Smith and the Restoration. He points out the motives adopted by many of these churches. As usual, we will use **bold** for emphasis.

20 And the Gentiles are lifted up in the **pride** of their eyes, and have stumbled, because of the greatness of their stumbling block, that they have built up **many churches**; nevertheless, **they put down the power and miracles of God**, and preach up unto themselves **their own wisdom and their own learning, that they may get gain** and grind upon the face of the poor [*they don't really care about the poor*].

21 And there are many churches built up which cause **envyings**, and **strifes**, and **malice** [*hatred; evil feelings toward one another*].

As Nephi continues, we see our day and age in his prophetic description of the future.

22 And there are also **secret combinations** [*secret groups organized to tear down that which is righteous and to get power and to rob and murder; compare with Helaman 6:17–39*], even as in times of old, according to the combinations of the devil, for he is the founder of all these things; yea, the founder of **murder**, and **works of darkness**; yea, and he leadeth them by the neck with a flaxen cord [*a light, thin string; symbolic of temptations and sins which could be relatively easily overcome; compare with 2 Nephi 28:8*], until he bindeth them with

his strong cords [*the chains of hell*] forever.

> Nephi is a powerful teacher and has a great desire to alert us and warn us about Satan's methods for pulling people down. We would do well to listen carefully to what he is teaching us here.

23 For behold, my beloved brethren, I say unto you that the Lord God worketh not in darkness.

24 He doeth not anything save it be for the benefit of the world; for he loveth the world, even that **he layeth down his own life that he may draw all men unto him** [*giving His own life gave Christ the power to give eternal life to all of us*]. Wherefore, he commandeth none that they shall not partake of his salvation [*salvation is available to all people*].

25 Behold, doth he cry unto any, saying: Depart from me? Behold, I say unto you, Nay; but he saith: **Come unto me all ye ends of the earth**, buy milk and honey, without money and without price. [*In other words, it makes no difference how rich or poor you are. The gospel of Jesus Christ is available to all.*]

26 Behold, hath he commanded any that they should depart out of the synagogues, or out of the houses of worship? Behold, I say unto you, Nay.

> Be careful how you interpret the word "free" in the next verse. Misinterpreted, it could lead to the false beliefs associated with predestination, being saved by grace alone, etc. In the context of Nephi's teachings, it means that Christ's gospel—His Atonement and exaltation—is available to all people, regardless of status or circumstance. By the final judgment, everyone, whether here on earth or later in the spirit world [*see D&C 138*] will have been given an absolutely fair and just opportunity to exercise agency to accept or reject the Savior's gift of exaltation.

27 Hath he commanded any that they should not partake of his salvation? Behold I say unto you, Nay; but he hath given it **free** for all men; and he hath commanded his people that they should persuade all men to repentance.

28 Behold, hath the Lord commanded any that they should not partake of his goodness? Behold I say unto you, Nay; but **all men are privileged the one like unto the other, and none are forbidden** [*God is completely fair*].

> Next, Nephi defines priestcraft. There is much of priestcraft in our world today.

29 He commandeth that there shall be no priestcrafts; for, behold, **priestcrafts are that**

men preach and set themselves up for a light unto the world, that they may get gain and praise of the world; but they seek not the welfare of Zion.

Next, Nephi reviews things which lead to exaltation.

30 Behold, the Lord hath forbidden this thing; wherefore, the Lord God hath given a commandment that **all men should have charity**, which charity is love. And except they should have charity they were nothing. Wherefore, **if they should have charity they would not suffer the laborer in Zion to perish.**

31 But the laborer in Zion shall labor for Zion; for **if they labor for money** [*if material possessions become their main goal*] **they shall perish.**

32 And again, the Lord God hath commanded that men should **not murder**; that they should not lie; that they should **not steal**; that they should **not take the name of the Lord their God in vain**; that they should **not envy**; that they should **not have malice** [*hatred*]; that they should **not contend one with another**; that they should **not commit whoredoms** [*sexual immorality*]; and that they should do none of these things; for whoso doeth them shall perish [*die spiritually, and sometimes physically*].

Nephi summarizes his powerful sermon here by emphasizing again that the gospel of Christ is available to all.

33 For none of these iniquities come of the Lord; for he doeth that which is good among the children of men; and he doeth nothing save it be plain unto the children of men; and **he inviteth them all to come unto him and partake of his goodness; and he denieth none that come unto him, black and white, bond and free, male and female; and he remembereth the heathen; and all are alike unto God, both Jew and Gentile.**

SECOND NEPHI 27

This chapter compares with Isaiah 29 in the Bible. It was given by Isaiah about 700 B.C., near the end of his ministry. It deals with the last days, including the restoration of the gospel through the Prophet Joseph Smith and many specific details about the coming forth of the Book of Mormon. It is one of those chapters of scripture which bear extra strong witness of the truth of prophecies given by the Lord's prophets.

Isaiah begins by prophesying

about the out-of-control wickedness which will prevail among all peoples upon the earth in the last days. **Bold** is used for teaching purposes.

1 But, behold, in the last days, or in the days of the Gentiles [*when the times of the Gentiles are being fulfilled; see Luke 21:24*]—yea, behold all the nations of the Gentiles and also the Jews, both those who shall come upon this land [*the land of the Book of Mormon*] and those who shall be upon other lands, yea, even **upon all the lands of the earth**, behold, **they will be drunken** [*out of control*] **with iniquity and all manner of abominations**—[*they will be hooked on wickedness; wickedness will be very widespread*]

2 And when that day shall come they shall be visited of the Lord of Hosts, with thunder and with earthquake, and with a great noise, and with storm, and with tempest, and with the flame of devouring fire [*the burning at the Second Coming; see D&C 5:19*].

Next, Isaiah prophesies that once the gospel is restored in the last days, none will be successful in stopping its progress.

3 And all the nations that fight against Zion [*the Lord's work and his people*], and that distress her, shall be as a dream of a night vision [*will be gone suddenly*]; yea, it shall be unto them [*wicked nations*], even as unto a hungry man which dreameth, and behold he eateth [*in his dream*] but he awaketh and his soul is empty [*he is still hungry*]; or like unto a thirsty man which dreameth, and behold he drinketh but he awaketh and behold he is faint [*still hungry and thirsty*], and his soul hath appetite; yea, even so shall the multitude of all the nations be that fight against Mount Zion [*the Lord's work; they, the wicked, will never be satisfied and will ultimately come up empty. Persecutors of the Saints never feel satisfied and can't seem to leave them alone*].

4 For behold, all ye that doeth iniquity, stay yourselves and wonder [*stop and think*], for ye shall cry out, and cry; yea, ye shall be drunken [*out of control*] but not with wine, ye shall stagger but not with strong drink [*you will stagger about in wickedness because you reject the prophets; see verse 5*].

5 For behold, the Lord hath poured out upon you the spirit of deep sleep [*has had to withdraw His spirit; spiritual darkness; compare with Alma 12:11*]. For behold, **ye have closed your eyes**, and **ye have rejected the**

prophets; and your rulers [*righteous leaders*], and the seers [*prophets*] hath he [*the Lord*] covered [*taken away*] because of your iniquity.

Next begins an incredibly detailed prophecy of the coming forth of the Book of Mormon.

6 And it shall come to pass [*in the last days; see verse 1*] that the Lord God shall bring forth unto you the words of a book [*the Book of Mormon*], and they shall be the words of them which have slumbered [*people who have already passed away such as Nephi, Mormon, Moroni, etc.*].

7 And behold the book shall be sealed [*referring to the sealed portion of the plates; see verses 10, 21; also Ether 5:1*]; and in the book shall be a revelation from God, from the beginning of the world to the ending thereof.

8 Wherefore, because of the things which are sealed up, **the things which are sealed** [*the sealed portion of the plates*] **shall not be delivered** [*translated, etc.*] **in the day of the wickedness and abominations of the people.** Wherefore, the book [*sealed portion*] shall be kept from them.

The fact that the sealed portion of the plates will not be translated and given to the people while "wickedness and abominations" exist makes us wonder if it might not be until the Millennium before we get the rest of the Book of Mormon.

9 But the book [*the gold plates*] shall be delivered unto a man [*Joseph Smith*], and he shall deliver [*translate, etc.*] the words of the book, which are the words of those who have slumbered in the dust [*Book of Mormon prophets*], and he [*Joseph Smith*] shall deliver these words unto another [*refers prophetically to the incident in which Martin Harris gave a copy of characters taken from the plates to Professor Charles Anthon; see JS—H 1:63–65*];

10 But the words which are sealed [*sealed portion of the plates*] he shall not deliver [*translate, etc.*], neither shall he deliver the book. For the book shall be sealed by the power of God, and the revelation which was sealed [*the sealed portion*] shall be kept in the book [*kept with the plates*] until the own due time of the Lord [*until the Lord says it is time to translate it; see verse 22*], that they [*the contents of the sealed portion*] may come forth; for behold, they reveal all things from the foundation of the world unto the end thereof.

People often wonder what is in

the sealed portion of the Book of Mormon plates. Verse 10, above, at least gives us a hint, namely, that they contain "all things from the foundation of the world unto the end thereof." What a treasure that will be!

11 And the day cometh that the words of the book which were sealed [*the sealed portion, see verses 8 and 10*] shall be read upon the house tops [*shall be made available to everyone*]; and they shall be read by the power of Christ; and all things [*compare with D&C 101:32–34*] shall be revealed unto the children of men which ever have been among the children of men, and which ever will be even unto the end of the earth.

Having spoken some about the sealed portion of the plates which Joseph Smith received from Hill Cumorah, next, Isaiah gives specific details about the coming forth of the Book of Mormon as we have it. He will begin by telling about the Three Witnesses to the Book of Mormon.

12 Wherefore, at that day when the book [*gold plates*] shall be delivered [*by Angel Moroni*] unto the man [*Joseph Smith*] of whom I have spoken, the book shall be hid from the eyes of the world [*no one will be allowed to see the gold plates*], that the eyes of none shall behold it save [*except*] it be that three witnesses [*Oliver Cowdery, David Whitmer and Martin Harris; see D&C 17, heading and verse 1*] shall behold it, by the power of God, besides him [*Joseph Smith*] to whom the book shall be delivered; **and they shall testify to the truth of the book and the things therein.**

We will take a moment here and read the testimony of these three witnesses. Note how they adhered carefully to the guidelines given in Isaiah's prophecy, above. In fact, the Lord gave additional instructions to Martin Harris, Oliver Cowdery, and David Whitmer as to what they should say in their testimony, as follows (**bold** added):

D&C 17:3–6

3 And after that you have obtained faith, and have seen them with your eyes, **you shall testify of them, by the power of God**;

4 And this you shall do that my servant Joseph Smith, Jun., may not be destroyed, that I may bring about my righteous purposes unto the children of men in this work.

5 And **ye shall testify that you have seen them**, even as my servant Joseph Smith, Jun., has seen them; for it is by my power that he has seen them, and it is because he had faith.

6 And he has translated the book, even that part which I have commanded him, **and** as your Lord and your God liveth **it is true**.

Now, let us read the Testimony of Three Witnesses (**bold** used for emphasis):

THE TESTIMONY OF THREE WITNESSES

BE IT KNOWN unto all nations, kindreds, tongues, and people, unto whom this work shall come: That **we**, through the grace of God the Father, and our Lord Jesus Christ, **have seen the plates** which contain this record, which is a record of the people of Nephi, and also of the Lamanites, their brethren, and also of the people of Jared, who came from the tower of which hath been spoken. And **we** also **know** that they have been **translated by the gift and power of God**, for his voice hath declared it unto us; wherefore **we know of a surety that the work is true**. And we also testify that we have seen the engravings which are upon the plates; and **they have been shown unto us by the power of God**, and not of man. And we declare with words of soberness, that an angel of God came down from heaven, and he brought and laid before our eyes, that **we beheld and saw the plates, and the engravings thereon; and we know that it is by the grace of God the Father, and our Lord Jesus Christ, that we beheld and bear record that these things are true**. And it is marvelous in our eyes. Nevertheless, the voice of the Lord commanded us that we should bear record of it; wherefore, to be obedient unto the commandments of God, **we bear testimony of these things**. And we know that if we are faithful in Christ, we shall rid our garments of the blood of all men, and be found spotless before the judgment-seat of Christ, and shall dwell with him eternally in the heavens. And the honor be to the Father, and to the Son, and to the Holy Ghost, which is one God. Amen.

OLIVER COWDERY

DAVID WHITMER

MARTIN HARRIS

13 And there is **none other which shall view it** [*the gold plates*], **save it be a few** [*the Eight Witnesses; see their witness at the beginning of your Book of Mormon*] **according to the will of God**, to bear testimony of his word unto the children of men; for the Lord God hath said that the words of the faithful [*Book of Mormon prophets*] should speak as if it were from the dead.

There is one other recorded witness of the gold plates who

SECOND NEPHI 27

was not called upon to bear witness to the world, as directed in verse 13, but who, nevertheless, saw the gold plates. Her name was Mary Whitmer. She is the mother of David Whitmer. Her husband, Peter Whitmer, Senior, invited Joseph Smith and Oliver Cowdery to come to the family farm in Fayette, New York, and continue the work of translating the gold plates there, after persecution became too dangerous for them to remain in Harmony, Pennsylvania.

David Whitmer came with his horse and buggy to Harmony and transported Joseph and Oliver to Fayette. Emma Smith stayed behind to finish some details and soon joined Joseph at the Whitmer home in Fayette. Having extra people to feed and take care of was an extra burden for Mother Whitmer, which overwhelmed her at times, but she never complained. One evening, as she went to the barn to milk the cows, Moroni appeared to her and expressed appreciation for her kindness in hosting the Prophet and Oliver and offered to show her the plates so she would know for sure that she was helping with the work of the Lord. He did so. Mary Whitmer's son, David, reported this incident as follows:

"She was met out near the yard by the same old man (the Angel Moroni seen earlier by David, judging by her description of him) who said to her: 'You have been very faithful and diligent in your labors, but you are tired because of the increase of your toil; it is proper therefore that you should receive a witness that your faith may be strengthened.' Thereupon he showed her the plates" (Report of Elders Orson Pratt and Joseph F. Smith, pp. 772–73; spelling standardized). This quote is used in the Institute of Religion student manual for Church history, *Church History in the Fulness of Times*, pp. 57–58).

14 Wherefore, the Lord God will proceed to bring forth the words of the book; and in the mouth of as many witnesses [*missionaries, you, me, etc.*] as seemeth him good will he establish his word; and wo be unto him that rejecteth the word of God!

15 But behold, it shall come to pass that the Lord God shall say unto him [*Joseph Smith*] to whom he shall deliver the book: Take these words which are not sealed and deliver them to another [*Martin Harris*], that he may show them unto the learned [*Professor Charles Anthon and Dr. Mitchell; see JS—H 1:64–65*], saying: Read this, I pray thee. And the learned [*Charles Anthon*] shall say: Bring hither the book, and I will read them.

Isaiah even gives details as

to the motives of Mitchell and Anthon.

16 And now, **because of the glory of the world and to get gain** will they [*Anthon and Mitchell*] say this, and not for the glory of God.

17 And the man [*Martin Harris*] shall say: I cannot bring the book, for it is sealed.

18 Then shall the learned say: I cannot read it.

19 Wherefore it shall come to pass, that the Lord God will deliver again the book and the words thereof to him [*Joseph Smith*] that is not learned; and the man that is not learned shall say: I am not learned.

20 Then shall the Lord God say unto him [*Joseph Smith*]: The learned shall not read [*translate*] them, for they have rejected them, and I am able to do mine own work; wherefore thou shalt read [*translate*] the words which I shall give unto thee [*with the help of the Urim and Thummim*].

21 Touch not the things which are sealed [*don't even peek at the sealed portion*], for I will bring them forth in mine own due time; for I will show unto the children of men that I am able to do mine own work.

22 Wherefore, when thou [*Joseph Smith*] hast read the words which I have commanded thee [*finished the translation of the Book of Mormon plates*], and obtained the witnesses which I have promised unto thee, then shalt thou seal up the book again, and **hide it up unto me**, that I may preserve the words which thou hast not read [*the sealed portion*], until I shall see fit in mine own wisdom to reveal all things unto the children of men.

With respect to the instruction to "hide it up unto me" in verse 22, above, it is interesting to note that as Joseph Smith finished the translation of the plates, he and Oliver Cowdery did just that. Brigham Young relates that they took the plates back to the Hill Cumorah where the hill opened up for them and they entered a large room filled with other plates and records. This incident is related by Brigham Young in the *Journal of Discourses*, 19:38 as follows.

"I will take the liberty to tell you of another circumstance that will be as marvelous as anything can be. This is an incident in the life of Oliver Cowdery, but he did not take the liberty of telling such things in meeting as I take. I tell these things to you, and I have a motive for doing so. I want to carry them to the ears of my brethren

Second Nephi 27

and sisters, and to the children also, that they may grow to an understanding of some things that seem to be entirely hidden from the human family. Oliver Cowdery went with the Prophet Joseph when he deposited these plates. Joseph did not translate all of the plates; there was a portion of them sealed, which you can learn from the Doctrine and Covenants. When Joseph got the plates, the angel instructed him to carry them back to the hill Cumorah, which he did. Oliver says that when Joseph and Oliver went there, the hill opened, and they walked into a cave, in which there was a large and spacious room. He says he did not think, at the time, whether they had the light of the sun or artificial light; but that it was just as light as day.

"They laid the plates on a table; it was a large table that stood in the room. Under this table there was a pile of plates as much as two feet high, and there were altogether in this room more plates than probably many wagon loads; they were piled up in the corners and along the walls. The first time they went there the sword of Laban hung upon the wall; but when they went again it had been taken down and laid upon the table across the gold plates; it was unsheathed, and on it was written these words: 'This sword will never be sheathed again until the kingdoms of this world become the kingdom of our God and his Christ.' I tell you this as coming not only from Oliver Cowdery, but others who were familiar with it, and who understood it just as well as we understand coming to this meeting, enjoying the day, and by and by we separate and go away, forgetting most of what is said, but remembering some things. So is it with other circumstances in life. I relate this to you, and I want you to understand it. I take this liberty of referring to those things so that they will not be forgotten and lost." (Young, *Journal of Discourses,* 19:38–39)

23 For behold, I am God; and I am a God of miracles; and I will show unto the world that I am the same yesterday, today, and forever [*I use the same gospel to save people; I am totally reliable, dependable*]; and **I work not among the children of men save it be according to their faith**.

> Isaiah teaches an important lesson to us at the end of verse 23, above. It is basically that we determine how much the Lord is involved in our lives by our agency as we exercise faith in Him or as we chose not to exercise faith in Him.

24 And again it shall come to pass that the Lord shall say unto him [*Joseph Smith; see JS—H. 1:19*] that shall read [*translate*] the words that shall be delivered him:

Jesus quoted Isaiah, next, as He answered Joseph Smith's question as to which church to join, during the First Vision.

25 Forasmuch as this people draw near unto me with their mouth, and with their lips do honor me, but have removed their hearts far from me, and their fear towards me [*their concept of God*] is taught by the precepts of men—

26 Therefore, I will proceed to do a marvelous [*Hebrew: "astonishing"*] work among this people, yea, a marvelous work and a wonder [*the Restoration of the gospel through Joseph Smith*], for the wisdom [*the false wisdom*] of their wise and learned shall perish, and the understanding of their prudent shall be hid [*pushed aside by revealed truth*].

27 And wo unto them [*the wicked*] that seek deep to hide their counsel [*evil plots*] from the Lord! And their works are in the dark; and they say: Who seeth us, and who knoweth us? And they also say: Surely, your turning of things upside down [*perversion of truth*] shall be esteemed as the potter's clay [*claiming they can get along without God, like the situation described in Isaiah 45:9 where the potter's clay tries to tell the potter what to do*]. But behold, I will show unto them [*the wicked*], saith the Lord of Hosts, that I know all their works. For shall the work [*the pot*] say of him [*the potter*] that made it, he made me not? Or shall the thing framed [*the building or whatever*] say of him [*the carpenter, craftsman*] that framed it [*built it*], he had no understanding [*he doesn't know me; "God doesn't know us. We can be wicked and successfully hide from God"; or, "You wicked are just as foolish as potters clay that claims it made itself into a pot and has no accountability to its maker."*]?

Next, Isaiah will prophesy that Israel will blossom with literal forests and with truth, spiritual growth, etc., after the Restoration. This is being very dramatically fulfilled, literally, today, as millions upon millions of trees are being planted in the southern portions of the Holy Land. It appears that significant spiritual growth is yet future.

28 But behold, saith the Lord of Hosts: I will show unto the children of men [*all people*] that it is yet a very little while [*after the Book of Mormon comes forth*] and Lebanon [*the Holy Land*] shall be turned into a fruitful field; and the fruitful field shall be esteemed as a forest.

Next, we are shown what the

results of the coming forth of the Book of Mormon and the restoration of the true Church will be. (**Bold** added for emphasis.)

29 And in that day shall **the deaf hear** the words of the book, and the eyes of **the blind shall see** out of obscurity and out of darkness [*the spiritually deaf and blind will be healed as a result of the Restoration, Book of Mormon, etc.*].

30 And **the meek also shall increase** [*shall gain strength and power with God*], and **their joy shall be in the Lord**, and **the poor among men shall rejoice in the Holy One of Israel** [*the righteous will know the Savior again*].

31 For assuredly as the Lord liveth they shall see that the terrible one [*tyrant*] is brought to naught [*is reduced to nothing*], and the scorner [*one who ridicules the work of the Lord*] is consumed, and all that watch for iniquity [*in Church leaders and members; see D&C 45:50*] are cut off;

32 And they that make a man an offender for a word [*via corrupt lawyers and corrupt judicial system*], and lay a snare for him that reproveth in the gate [*try to destroy the honest person who attempts to straighten out corrupt governments, etc.; the "gate" was an alcove in Jerusalem's wall where officials and citizens met to discuss matters*], and turn aside the just for a thing of naught [*destroy good people for unimportant matters*].

In a fascinating and ingenious way, Isaiah next portrays Jacob, the father of the twelve tribes of Israel, as having been embarrassed over the centuries to admit that the Israelites are related to him. However, in the last days, when Israelites (including us) are strong, faithful Saints, Jacob is no longer embarrassed to claim us as his posterity. Rather, he is proud to be our ancestor.

33 Therefore, thus saith the Lord, who redeemed Abraham, concerning the house of Jacob [*Israel*]: **Jacob shall not now be ashamed**, neither shall his face now wax pale [*Father Jacob will no longer have to be embarrassed about the behavior of his posterity*].

34 But **when he seeth his children** [*his posterity being faithful to God in the last days*], **the work of my** [*the Lord's*] **hands** [*now righteous*], in the midst of him, **they** [*righteous Israel*] **shall sanctify my [*God's*] name**, and sanctify the Holy One of Jacob, and **shall fear** [*respect*] **the God of Israel** [*Christ*].

Isaiah now summarizes the results of the Restoration and the coming forth of the Book of Mormon in one final sentence.

35 They also that erred in spirit shall come to understanding, and they that murmured shall learn doctrine [*via truths of the Restoration*].

SECOND NEPHI 28

Nephi has just quoted Isaiah regarding the last days and the coming forth of the Book of Mormon. Now he will explain what Isaiah said and teach us many lessons from it.

1 AND now, behold, my brethren, I have spoken unto you, according as the Spirit hath constrained [*instructed*] me; wherefore, I know that they [*the prophecies of Isaiah*] must surely come to pass.

2 And the things which shall be written out of the book [*the Book of Mormon*] shall be of great worth unto the children of men, and especially unto our seed [*the Lamanites*], which is a remnant of [*a part of*] the house of Israel [*the descendants of Abraham, Isaac, and Jacob*].

Nephi now explains that there will be much contention between churches in the last days and warns that such churches will claim to be the Lord's church.

3 For it shall come to pass in that day [*in the last days especially*] that the churches which are built up, and not unto the Lord [*are not the Lord's true church*], when the one shall say unto the other: Behold, I, I am the Lord's; and the others shall say: I, I am the Lord's; and thus shall every one say that hath built up churches, and not unto the Lord—

4 And they shall contend one with another; and their priests shall contend one with another, and they shall teach with their learning, and deny the Holy Ghost, which giveth utterance.

> The phrase "deny the Holy Ghost" in verse 4, above, is not the same as denying the Holy Ghost as in becoming a son of perdition. In this context, it means to refuse to be inspired by the Holy Ghost or to live unworthily of inspiration.

5 And they deny the power of God, the Holy One of Israel; and they say unto the people: Hearken unto us, and hear ye our precept; for behold there is no God today, for the Lord

and the Redeemer hath done his work, and he hath given his power unto men; [*In other words, among other things, they will teach that there is no such thing as more scripture, continuing revelation, prophets, Apostles, etc. The Bible is it and there is nothing beyond that.*]

Nephi continues to describe what false priests and teachers will teach their followers in the last days.

6 Behold, hearken ye unto my precept; if they shall say there is a miracle wrought by the hand of the Lord, believe it not; for this day he is not a God of miracles; he hath done his work. [*In other words, there are no such things as miracles today. They ceased with the Bible.*]

Next, Nephi prophesies that there will be many in the last days who believe in the philosophy that sin is not that big of a deal. Therefore, don't worry about it.

7 Yea, and there shall be many which shall say: Eat, drink, and be merry, for tomorrow we die; and it shall be well with us.

Next, Nephi warns against those who believe in God and believe in accountability but do not believe that the standards of the gospel are all that strict, nor that God's punishments will be all that bad. We see this all around us today, even among some members of the Church. Satan is quite successful with this philosophy.

8 And there shall also be many which shall say: Eat, drink, and be merry; nevertheless, fear God—he will justify in committing a little sin; yea, lie a little, take the advantage of one because of his words, dig a pit for thy neighbor; there is no harm in this; and do all these things, for tomorrow we die; and if it so be that we are guilty, God will beat us with a few stripes [*punish us with a few gentle lashes*], and at last we shall be saved in the kingdom of God.

9 Yea, and there shall be many which shall teach after this manner, false and vain and foolish doctrines, and shall be puffed up in their hearts [*full of pride, thinking that they can change or water down God's commandments*], and shall seek deep to hide their counsels from the Lord; and their works shall be in the dark [*as Isaiah said in 2 Nephi 27:27*].

10 And the blood of the saints [*who gave their lives to keep the standards of the gospel*] shall cry from the ground [*shall witness*] against them.

11 Yea, they have all gone out of the way [*they have all gone astray*]; they have become corrupted.

> Nephi warns us against some of the things which can lead people into such foolish thinking and rebellious behaviors. We will **bold** these to point them out.

12 Because of **pride**, and because of **false teachers**, and **false doctrine**, their churches have become corrupted, and their churches are lifted up; because of pride they are puffed up.

13 They rob the poor because of their fine sanctuaries; they rob the poor because of their fine clothing; and they persecute the meek and the poor in heart, because in their **pride** they are puffed up.

14 They wear stiff necks and high heads [*they are full of pride*]; yea, and because of **pride**, and **wickedness**, and **abominations** [*very evil and wicked deeds*], and **whoredoms** [*sexual immorality*], they have all gone astray save it be a few, who are the humble followers of Christ; nevertheless, they are led, that in many instances they do err because they are taught by the precepts of men. [*All the more reason to stick very strictly to the words of our modern prophets.*]

15 O the wise [*in their own minds*], and the learned [*the highly educated who do not have faith in God*], and the rich, that are **puffed up in the pride of their hearts**, and all those who preach **false doctrines**, and all those who **commit whoredoms**, and **pervert** [*twist and misrepresent*] **the right way of the Lord**, wo, wo, wo be unto them, saith the Lord God Almighty, for they shall be thrust down to hell!

> Nephi is giving us one of the most powerful sermons ever on the attitudes, philosophies, and behaviors which will lead to the downfall of stable and safe society in the last days.

16 Wo unto them that turn aside the just [*the righteous; this can include corrupt judicial systems*] for a thing of naught [*worth nothing*] and revile against that which is good [*tear down that which is good*], and say that it is of no worth! For the day shall come that the Lord God will speedily visit [*punish*] the inhabitants of the earth; and in that day that they are fully ripe in iniquity they shall perish [*when they get to the point that they are completely wicked, they will be destroyed*].

> After describing such gross wickedness and disregard for God and His commandments,

Nephi reminds us that it is still not too late for such a society to repent. This is a wonderful reminder of the kindness and mercy of the Lord. He paid for all sins and is very desirous that people accept His gift of the Atonement.

17 But behold, if the inhabitants of the earth shall repent of their wickedness and abominations they shall not be destroyed, saith the Lord of Hosts.

18 But behold, that great and abominable church [*the kingdom of the devil; see 1 Nephi 14:10, 22:22–23*], the whore of all the earth, must tumble to the earth, and great must be the fall thereof. [*In other words, when the time is right, Satan's kingdom with all his evil followers will fall.*]

Next, Nephi shows that the Lord will use strong means to try to wake the wicked up so that they can still repent and return to Him.

19 For the kingdom of the devil must shake, and they [*the wicked*] which belong to it must needs be [*have to be*] stirred up unto repentance, or the devil will grasp them with his everlasting chains, and they be stirred up to anger, and perish;

In verse 20, below, Nephi reminds us that one of the devil's most powerful tools is anger against righteousness.

20 For behold, at that day shall he rage in the hearts of the children of men, and **stir them up to anger against that which is good**.

Perhaps you've noticed that Satan is very cunning. If he can't get people involved in gross wickedness, which often leads to anger against the righteous, he gently convinces them that things aren't as bad as the prophets say, so that they relax in their worldly lifestyles and become sloppy in living the gospel, while still "active in the Church" in their own minds. Nephi describes this next in verse 21.

21 And others will he pacify, and **lull them away into carnal security**, that they will say: All is well in Zion; yea, Zion prospereth, all is well—and thus the devil cheateth their souls, and leadeth them away **carefully** down to hell.

Apostle George Albert Smith, who later became the President of the Church, described how Satan leads people "carefully down to hell" as follows:

"Now, I want you to note that: 'And thus the devil cheateth their souls and leadeth them away carefully down to hell.' And that is the way he does it, that's exactly the way he does it. He does not grab you bodily and take you into his territory, but he whispers, 'Do this little evil,' and when he succeeds in that, another little evil and another, and, to use the expression, 'He cheateth their souls.' That's what he does. He makes you believe you are gaining something when you are losing. So it is every time we fail to observe a law of God or keep a commandment; we are being cheated, because there is no gain in this world or in the world to come but by obedience to the law of our heavenly Father. Then again, that peculiar suggestion, 'And he leadeth them carefully away down to hell' is significant, that is his method. Men and women in the world today are subject to that influence, and they are being drawn here and there, and that whispering is going on and they do not understand what the Lord desires them to do, but they continue in the territory of the evil one, subject to his power where the Spirit of the Lord will not go" (Smith, in Conference Report, Apr. 1918, p. 40).

Next, Nephi describes yet another tool of the devil.

22 And behold, others he **flattereth** away, and telleth them there is no hell; and he saith unto them: I am no devil, for there is none—and thus he **whispereth** in their ears, **until he grasps them with his awful chains**, from whence there is no deliverance.

23 Yea, they are grasped with death [*spiritual death; the death of their spirituality*], and hell; and death, and hell, and the devil, and all that have been seized therewith must stand before the throne of God, and be judged according to their works, from whence they must go into the place prepared for them, even a lake of fire and brimstone, which is endless torment.

Nephi now summarizes what he has taught so eloquently in the previous verses.

24 Therefore, wo be unto him that is at ease in Zion!

25 Wo be unto him that crieth: All is well!

26 Yea, wo be unto him that hearkeneth unto the precepts [*teachings and philosophies*] of men, and denieth the power of God, and the gift of the Holy Ghost!

27 Yea, wo be unto him that saith: We have received, and we need no more!

28 And in fine [*in summary*], wo unto all those who tremble, and are angry because of the truth of God! For behold, he that is built upon the rock [*Christ*

and His gospel] receiveth it with gladness; and he is built upon a sandy foundation *[the devil's ways]* trembleth lest he shall fall.

Next, Nephi prophesies that there will be many who will oppose the doctrine of continuing revelation through modern prophets.

29 Wo be unto him that shall say: We have received the word of God, and we need no more of the word of God, for we have enough!

Verse 30, next, is a great lesson in how we can qualify to receive continuing revelation ourselves, both through our prophets and through the Holy Ghost for our personal stewardships and growth toward God.

30 For behold, thus saith the Lord God: I will give unto the children of men **line upon line, precept upon precept** *[commandment upon commandment; rule upon rule; instruction upon instruction, etc.]*, here a little and there a little; and **blessed are those who hearken unto my precepts, and lend an ear unto my counsel**, for they shall learn wisdom; for **unto him that receiveth I will give more**; and **from them that shall say, We have enough, from them shall be taken away even that which they have.**

Perhaps you've noticed someone whom you know who once had a strong testimony but who now does not have it anymore. The last phrase of verse 30, above, explains what has happened.

31 Cursed is he that putteth his trust in man, or maketh flesh his arm, or shall hearken unto the precepts *[the philosophies and teachings]* of men, save *[unless]* their precepts shall be given by the power of the Holy Ghost.

32 Wo be unto the Gentiles, saith the Lord God of Hosts! For notwithstanding *[even though]* I shall lengthen out mine arm unto them from day to day *[even though I keep reaching out to them, inviting them to repent and come unto Me]*, they will deny me *[they refuse]*; nevertheless, I will be merciful unto them, saith the Lord God, if they will repent and come unto me; for **mine arm is lengthened out all the day long** *[I will keep trying to save them]*, saith the Lord God of Hosts.

SECOND NEPHI 29

Nephi continues in this chapter to speak the words of the Lord to us. Among other things, he prophesies that there will be much opposition to the Book of Mormon because Satan will have entrenched in the minds of people so thoroughly that revelation came to an end with the end of the Bible. In fact, you may have encountered that thinking yourself, on the part of someone to whom you spoke about the Book of Mormon.

Such people often quote from the last chapter of Revelation in the Bible, suggesting that verse 18 teaches that there can be no more scripture. We will take a moment here and quote Revelation 22:18, and then show what is incorrect about their interpretation. We will use **bold** to highlight what they quote to oppose the Book of Mormon and other LDS scriptures.

Revelation 22:18

> 18 For I testify unto every man that heareth the words of the prophecy of this book, **If any man shall add unto these things, God shall add unto him the plagues that are written in this book:**

One of the academic problems with their interpretation is that the book of Revelation is not the last book of the New Testament. Bible scholars agree that the Gospel of John was written after John wrote Revelation. Therefore, much in the Bible was written after the book of Revelation. Not only that, but Ezekiel specifically prophesies that there will be a book of scripture that will be added to the Bible (see Ezekiel 37:16–20).

We will now continue with Nephi's prophecy.

1 BUT behold, there shall be many—at that day [*in the last days*] when I [*the Lord*] shall proceed to do a marvelous work among them [*when I restore the gospel among them, including bringing forth the Book of Mormon*], that I may remember [*keep*] my covenants which I have made unto the children of men, that I may set my hand again the second time to recover my people, which are of the house of Israel;

2 And also, that I may remember [*keep*] the promises which I have made unto thee, Nephi, and also unto thy father, that I would remember your seed [*posterity*]; and that the words of your seed should proceed forth out of my mouth unto your seed [*through the Book of Mormon*]; and my words shall hiss [*signal*] forth unto the ends of the earth, for a standard unto my people, which are of the house of Israel;

> Next, the specific prophecy that people will oppose the Book of

Mormon because they already have the Bible.

3 And because my words shall hiss forth—many of the Gentiles shall say: A Bible! A Bible! We have got a Bible, and there cannot be any more Bible.

> The Lord answers this reasoning for opposing additional scripture in no uncertain terms! Also, He will give a wonderful compliment to the Jews for giving us what we have in the Bible.

4 But thus saith the Lord God: O fools, they shall have a Bible; and it shall proceed forth from the Jews, mine ancient covenant people. And what thank they the Jews for the Bible which they receive from them? Yea, what do the Gentiles mean? **Do they remember the travails, and the labors, and the pains of the Jews, and their diligence unto me, in bringing forth salvation unto the Gentiles?**

5 O ye Gentiles, have ye remembered the Jews, mine ancient covenant people? Nay; but ye have cursed them, and have hated them, and have not sought to recover them. But behold, I will return all these things upon your own heads; for I the Lord have not forgotten my people [*the Jews*].

> Next comes one of the favorite quotes of many returned missionaries.

6 Thou fool, that shall say: A Bible, we have got a Bible, and we need no more Bible. Have ye obtained a Bible save it were by the Jews?

> We are taught next that we are not the only ones who have received scriptures from the Lord. This reminds us that there are many records yet to come forth in the due time of the Lord.

7 Know ye not that there are more nations than one? Know ye not that I, the Lord your God, have created all men, and that I remember those who are upon the isles of the sea [*upon all the continents and in all nations*]; and that I rule in the heavens above and in the earth beneath; and I bring forth my word unto the children of men, yea, even upon all the nations of the earth?

8 Wherefore murmur ye [*why do you complain*], because that ye shall receive more of my word? Know ye not that the testimony of two nations is a witness unto you that I am God, that I remember one nation like unto another? Wherefore, I speak the same words unto one nation like unto another. And when the two nations shall run together the

testimony of the two nations shall run together also.

9 And I do this that I may prove unto many that I am the same yesterday, today, and forever [*I am completely fair to all people*]; and that I speak forth my words according to mine own pleasure. And **because that I have spoken one word ye need not suppose that I cannot speak another; for my work is not yet finished; neither shall it be until the end of man, neither from that time henceforth and forever.** [*In other words, there will be no end to continuous revelation.*]

10 Wherefore, **because that ye have a Bible ye need not suppose that it contains all my words**; neither need ye suppose that I have not caused more to be written.

11 For I command all men, both in the east and in the west, and in the north, and in the south, and in the islands of the sea, that they shall write the words which I speak unto them; for out of the books which shall be written I will judge the world, every man according to their works, according to that which is written.

12 For behold, I shall speak unto the Jews and they shall write it [*the Bible*]; and I shall also speak unto the Nephites and they shall write it [*the Book of Mormon*]; and I shall also speak unto the other tribes of the house of Israel, which I have led away, and they shall write it [*they have written scriptures too*]; and I shall also speak unto all nations of the earth and they shall write it [*still more written scriptures*].

13 And it shall come to pass that the Jews shall have the words of the Nephites [*the Book of Mormon*], and the Nephites shall have the words of the Jews [*the Bible*]; and the Nephites and the Jews shall have the words of the lost tribes of Israel; and the lost tribes of Israel shall have the words of the Nephites and the Jews. [*What a "triple combination" this will be!*]

It is important to note in verse 14, next, that there are many lands to which the house of Israel will be gathered. In a significant sense, members today are being "gathered" to stakes of Zion wherever they live.

14 And it shall come to pass that my people, which are of the house of Israel, shall be gathered home unto the lands of their possessions; and my word also shall be gathered in one [*all of the written scriptures will support and strengthen each other, as is the case with the Bible and*

the Book of Mormon]. And I will show unto them that fight against my word and against my people, who are of the house of Israel, that I am God, and that I covenanted with Abraham that I would remember [*keep My promises to*] his seed [*posterity*] forever.

SECOND NEPHI 30

As Nephi finishes his message to his people (and to us) in this chapter, he teaches a course in perspective. He reminds all of us that God is completely fair and that no one is favored over another as the big picture unfolds.

This may create a dilemma in the minds of some as they think, "Wait. The Lord does have His chosen people, His covenant people of Israel, the descendants of Abraham, Isaac, and Jacob. So all people are not treated the same in His eyes." While it is true that He has a chosen or covenant people, we must remember that the responsibility of these people, of whom we are a part, is to make sure that the gospel and its priesthood covenants are made available to all within our sphere of influence. This is made clear in our patriarchal blessings, when our lineage is declared and we are reminded of the blessings and responsibilities of the lineage of Abraham, Isaac, and Jacob. These are summarized in Abraham 2:9–11 as follows (**bold** added for emphasis):

Abraham 2:9–11

9 And I will make of thee [*Abraham*] a great nation, and I will bless thee above measure, and make thy name great among all nations, and **thou shalt be a blessing unto thy seed** [*posterity*] after thee, that in their hands **they shall bear this ministry and Priesthood unto all nations**;

10 And I will bless them through thy name; for **as many as receive this Gospel shall be called after thy name** [*shall receive the same blessings as you, namely, exaltation, the highest degree in the celestial kingdom (Abraham has already become a god; see D&C 132:37)*], and shall be accounted thy seed, and shall rise up and bless thee, as their father [*ancestor*];

11 And I will bless them that bless thee, and curse them that curse thee; and in thee [*that is, in thy priesthood*] and **in thy seed** [*through your posterity*] [*that is, thy priesthood*], for I give unto thee a promise that this right shall continue in thee, and in thy seed after thee [*that is to say, the literal seed, or the seed of the body*] **shall all**

the families of the earth be blessed, even with the blessings of the Gospel, which are the blessings of salvation, even of life eternal.

Much of this work of equalizing things out will be done in the spirit world. By the time of final judgment, all will have been given a completely fair set of opportunities to use their agency to accept or reject the gospel of Christ.

We will continue now with Nephi's teachings as he defines a covenant people and teaches us about the success of the gospel as it brings others into the fold. We will continue our use of **bold** for teaching purposes.

1 AND now behold, my beloved brethren, I would speak unto you; for **I, Nephi, would not suffer** [*allow*] **that ye should suppose that ye are more righteous than the Gentiles shall be.** For behold, except ye shall keep the commandments of God ye shall all likewise perish; and because of the words which have been spoken **ye need not suppose that the Gentiles are utterly destroyed.**

Next, Nephi emphasizes that whether or not to become part of the covenant people is a matter of individual agency.

2 For behold, I say unto you that as many of the Gentiles as will repent are the covenant people of the Lord [*all people who are baptized and remain faithful are part of the Lord's covenant people*]; and as many of the Jews as will not repent shall be cast off; for the Lord covenanteth with none save it be with them that repent and believe in his Son, who is the Holy One of Israel.

We have seen the terms "Jew" and "Judah" many times in the Book of Mormon so far. We will take a brief moment to quote the Institute of Religion *Book of Mormon Student Manual* as it explains these terms.

"Jew and Judah are national names as well as tribal names. From about 1800 B.C. to about 750 B.C. the terms Jew and Judah applied specifically to only one of the thirteen tribes (counting Joseph as two tribes, Ephraim and Manasseh, as in Numbers 2). After that time, the terms increasingly began to be used to name any citizen of the kingdom of Judah, which consisted primarily of the tribes of Judah and Benjamin, but included many people from other tribes, especially Levi.

"The term Jew first appears in the Old Testament in 2 Kings 16:6, at the time just before the northern kingdom of Israel fell to Assyria. Thereafter, the Jews, or the southern kingdom of Judah, became the

SECOND NEPHI 30

only known surviving remnant of Israel. Nephi referred to the Jews as "them from whence I came" (2 Nephi 33:8).

Mulek, and possibly all of the Mulekites, were Jews of the tribe of Judah. They were "exceedingly numerous" (Omni 1:17) when discovered by the people of King Mosiah. In addition to being descendants of the Jews in the national sense, there is also a blood relationship to the tribe of Judah among the modern Lamanites" (*Book of Mormon Student Manual*, p. 41).

As Nephi continues, he teaches about the coming forth of the Book of Mormon and shows that it is a pivotal event in ushering in the last days. In other words, when the Book of Mormon comes on the scene, we know that the last days are beginning.

3 And now, I would prophesy somewhat more concerning the Jews and the Gentiles. For after the book [*the Book of Mormon*] of which I have spoken shall come forth, and be written unto the Gentiles [*translated and be taken out to the Gentiles by missionaries from the Church*], and sealed up again unto the Lord [*and the gold plates are returned to the Hill Cumorah for safe keeping; see Journal of Discourses, volume 19, page 38*], there shall be many which shall believe the words which are written [*many will be converted to the Church*]; and they [*the converts*] shall carry them [*the words of the Book of Mormon*] forth unto the remnant of our seed [*the Lamanites*].

4 And then shall the remnant of our seed know concerning us [*the Book of Mormon peoples*], how that we came out from Jerusalem, and that they are descendants of the Jews [*see note after verse 2, above*].

5 And the gospel of Jesus Christ shall be declared among them [*the Lamanites*]; wherefore, they shall be restored unto the knowledge of their fathers [*ancestors*], and also to the knowledge of Jesus Christ, which was had among their fathers.

6 And then shall they rejoice; for they shall know that it is a blessing unto them from the hand of God; and their scales of darkness [*spiritual darkness*] shall begin to fall from their eyes; and many generations shall not pass away among them, save they shall be a pure and a delightsome people.

> You and I are witnesses of the tremendous work now taking place among the Lamanites, especially in places such as Mexico, Central America, and

South America. The fulfillment of Nephi's prophecy about the Book of Mormon being taken to his descendants is under way on a grand scale!

Next, the Lord turns our attention to the future gathering and conversion of the Jews.

7 And it shall come to pass that the Jews which are scattered also shall begin to believe in Christ; and they shall begin to gather in upon the face of the land; and as many as shall believe in Christ shall also become a delightsome people. [*In other words, they too will be set free from spiritual darkness and unbelief in Christ.*]

Again, a reminder that the coming forth of the Book of Mormon is a tremendously significant pivotal point in the history of the earth. Its coming forth signals the final restoration of the gospel before the Second Coming of the Lord. It heralds the final great gathering of Israel to the true gospel, out of all the earth, in preparation for the final prophesied scenes before the Savior comes. In order for this gathering to be accomplished, we must take the gospel to all nations. This work is certainly under way. In fact, President Gordon B. Hinckley seems to be leading the Church in bringing it "out of obscurity" as spoken of in D&C 1:30. There, we read:

"And also those to whom these commandments were given, might have power to lay the foundation of this church, **and to bring it forth out of obscurity** and out of darkness, the only true and living church upon the face of the whole earth, with which I, the Lord, am well pleased, speaking unto the church collectively and not individually."

8 And it shall come to pass that the Lord God shall commence his work among all nations, kindreds, tongues, and people, to bring about the restoration of his people upon the earth [*the gathering of Israel*].

As the gathering continues, Nephi tells us that we will see more and more of the hand of the Lord in the affairs of the world.

9 And with righteousness shall the Lord God judge the poor, and reprove with equity for the meek of the earth. And he shall smite the earth with the rod of his mouth; and with the breath of his lips shall he slay the wicked.

Next, you will see that it is prophesied that in the last days, as the Second Coming gets closer, there will be a more and more obvious division between those who stay loyal to the gospel of Christ and those who do not. It appears that there will be less and less "gray area." You are either with the Lord or far away from Him.

These divisions between the righteous and the wicked will become wider and wider until the actual Second Coming at which time the wicked will be burned and thus the "division" will be complete.

10 For the time speedily cometh that the Lord God shall cause a great division among the people, and the wicked will he destroy; and he will spare his people, yea, even if it so be that he must destroy the wicked by fire [*which He will at the Second Coming*].

11 And righteousness shall be the girdle of his loins [*Christ will be clothed in righteousness*], and faithfulness the girdle of his reins [*reins or kidneys symbolized the deepest feelings and desires of the heart; Nephi is quoting Isaiah's prophecy in 2 Nephi 21:5*].

The great, final division between the righteous and the wicked, spoken of above, will usher in the Millennium, as depicted in the remaining verses of this chapter.

12 And then shall the wolf dwell with the lamb; and the leopard shall lie down with the kid, and the calf, and the young lion, and the fatling, together; and a little child shall lead them. [*There will be peace during the Millennium.*]

13 And the cow and the bear shall feed [*graze*]; their young ones shall lie down together; and the lion shall eat straw like the ox.

14 And the sucking [*nursing*] child shall play on the hole of the asp [*will play with formerly poisonous serpents*], and the weaned child [*toddler*] shall put his hand on the cockatrice's [*poisonous serpent's*] den.

15 They shall not hurt nor destroy in all my holy mountain [*the entire world will be at peace during the Millennium*]; for the earth shall be full of the knowledge of the Lord as the waters cover the sea [*the gospel of Christ will eventually cover the whole earth*].

16 Wherefore, the things of all nations shall be made known; yea, all things shall be made known unto the children of men. [*If it hasn't already happened by this time, this sounds like the time when all the records or scriptures of other nations will come forth.*]

17 There is nothing which is secret save it shall be revealed; there is no work of darkness save it shall be made manifest in the light; and there is nothing which is sealed upon the earth save it shall be loosed.

18 Wherefore, all things which have been revealed unto the children of men shall at that day be revealed; and Satan shall have power over the hearts of the children of men no more, for a long time [*for a thousand years; see D&C 29:11*]. And now, my beloved brethren, I [*Nephi*] make an end of my sayings.

SECOND NEPHI 31

In the next three chapters, Nephi will, in effect, say "Goodbye" to us. Knowing that he has very little time remaining as our teacher, we will want to pay close attention to what he says by way of counsel in these last few pages. We will use **bold** to point out some of these things.

1 AND now I, Nephi, make an end of my prophesying unto you, my beloved brethren. And I cannot write but a few things, which I know must surely come to pass; neither can I write but a few of the words of my brother Jacob.

> First, Nephi will teach us about what is known as "the doctrine of Christ."

2 Wherefore, the things which I have written sufficeth me [*will have to do*], save it be [*except for*] a few words which I must speak concerning **the doctrine of Christ**; wherefore, I shall speak unto you plainly, according to the plainness of my prophesying.

> The word "prophesying" as used here, in context, can mean two things. First: Literally prophesying of future events. Second: It can also mean "teaching."

3 For my soul delighteth in plainness; for after this manner doth the Lord God work among the children of men. [*In other words, the true gospel, properly taught, is very plain and simple.*] For the Lord God giveth light unto the understanding [*to our minds*]; for he speaketh unto men according to their language, unto their understanding.

4 Wherefore, I would that ye should remember that I have spoken unto you concerning that prophet [*John the Baptist*] which the Lord showed unto me, that should baptize the Lamb of God [*Jesus*], which should take away the sins of the world.

> Members often wonder why Christ had to be baptized, or if He actually had to be baptized, or if perhaps He did it only to serve as an example for all of us. Nephi will give us the correct answer in the next verses.

5 And now, **if the Lamb of God**, he being holy [*perfectly free*

from sin], **should have need to [*had to be*] be baptized by water**, to fulfil all righteousness [*to be obedient to the will of the Father*], **O then, how much more need have we, being unholy, to be baptized, yea, even by water!**

6 And now, I would ask of you, my beloved brethren, wherein [*in what way*] the Lamb of God did fulfil all righteousness in being baptized by water?

7 Know ye not that he was holy? But notwithstanding [*even though*] he being holy, he showeth [*set an example*] unto the children of men that, according to the flesh [*as a mortal*] **he humbleth himself before the Father, and witnesseth unto the Father that he would be obedient unto him in keeping his commandments.**

8 Wherefore, after he was baptized with water the Holy Ghost descended upon him in the form of a dove.

> Occasionally, in gospel discussions centered in the Savior's baptism, students wonder if the Holy Ghost really turns Himself into a dove on occasions, as He bears witness of Christ. The Prophet Joseph Smith taught about the mission of John the Baptist and his greatness as a prophet. And in the course of that teaching, answered this question as follows (**bold** added for emphasis):
>
> "How is it that John was considered one of the greatest prophets? His miracles could not have constituted his greatness.
>
> "First. He was entrusted with a divine mission of preparing the way before the face of the Lord. Whoever had such a trust committed to him before or since? No man.
>
> "Second. He was entrusted with the important mission, and it was required at his hands, to baptize the Son of Man. Whoever had the honor of doing that? Whoever had so great a privilege and glory? Whoever led the Son of God into the waters of baptism, and had the privilege of beholding the Holy Ghost descend in the form of a dove, or rather in the *sign* of the dove, in witness of that administration? **The sign of the dove was instituted before the creation of the world, a witness for the Holy Ghost**, and the devil cannot come in the sign of a dove. **The Holy Ghost is a personage, and is in the form of a personage. It does not confine itself to the *form* of the dove, but in *sign* of the dove. The Holy Ghost cannot be transformed into a dove**; but the sign of a dove was given to John to signify the truth of the deed, as the dove is an

emblem or token of truth and innocence (Smith, *Teachings of the Prophet Joseph Smith*, p. 275).

9 And again, it showeth unto the children of men the straitness [*narrowness*] of the path, and the narrowness of the gate [*baptism*], by which they should enter, **he having set the example before them.**

10 And he said unto the children of men: **Follow thou me.** Wherefore, my beloved brethren, can we follow Jesus save we shall be willing to keep the commandments of the Father?

11 And the Father said: Repent ye, repent ye, and be baptized in the name of my Beloved Son.

12 And also, the voice of the Son came unto me, saying: **He that is baptized in my name, to him will the Father give the Holy Ghost**, like unto me [*Christ*]; wherefore, follow me, and do the things which ye have seen me do.

Another question which often comes up in gospel classes is, "Did Jesus have the Holy Ghost?" or, "Was the Holy Ghost functioning upon the earth at the time of the Savior's mortal ministry?" That question is clearly answered in verse 12, above. The answer is "Yes." Additional scriptural proof of this fact is found in Luke 4:1 as follows (**bold** added for emphasis):

Luke 4:1

1 And **Jesus being full of the Holy Ghost** returned from Jordan, and was led by the Spirit into the wilderness,

Additional questions arise when class members wonder if the gift of the Holy Ghost was functional during the time of the Savior's ministry. Our Bible Dictionary, page 704, under "Holy Ghost," helps clarify this matter as follows (**bold** added for emphasis):

Holy Ghost. The third member of the Godhead and, as the name implies, a personage of Spirit, not possessing a body of flesh and bones (D&C 130:21–22). **The Holy Ghost has been manifest in every dispensation of the gospel since the beginning**, being first made known to Adam (1 Ne. 10:17–22; Moses 6:51–68). **The Holy Ghost is manifested to men on the earth both as the *power* of the Holy Ghost and as the *gift* of the Holy Ghost**. The **power** can come upon one before baptism, and is the convincing witness that the gospel is true. It gives one a testimony of Jesus Christ and of his work and the work of his servants upon the earth. The **gift** can come only after proper and authorized baptism, and is conferred by the laying on of hands, as in Acts 8:12–25 and Moroni 2:1–3. The gift of the Holy Ghost is the right to have, whenever one is worthy, the companionship of the Holy Ghost. More powerful than that which is available before baptism, it acts as a cleansing agent to purify a person and sanctify him from all sin. Thus it is often spoken of as "fire" (Matt. 3:11; 2 Ne. 31:17; D&C 19:31). **The manifestation on the day of Pentecost (Acts 2) was the gift of the Holy Ghost** that came upon the Twelve, without which they were not ready for their ministries to the world.

"For some reason not fully explained in the scriptures, **the Holy Ghost did not operate in the fulness among the Jews during the years of Jesus' mortal sojourn** (John 7:39; 16:7). **Statements to the effect that the Holy Ghost did not come until after Jesus was resurrected must of necessity refer to that particular dispensation only**, for it is abundantly clear that the Holy Ghost was operative in earlier dispensations. Furthermore, **it has reference only to the *gift* of the Holy Ghost not being present, since the *power* of the Holy Ghost was operative during the ministries of John the Baptist and Jesus**; otherwise no one would have received a testimony of the truths that these men taught (cf. Matt. 16:16–17; 1 Cor. 12:3). When a person speaks by the power of the Holy Ghost that same power carries a conviction of the truth into the heart of the hearer (2 Ne. 33:1). The Holy Ghost knows all things (D&C 35:19) and can lead one to know of future events (2 Pet. 1:21).

"Other names for the Holy Ghost are Holy Spirit, Spirit of God, Spirit of the Lord, Comforter, and Spirit."

Now we will continue with Nephi's teachings of the doctrine of Christ.

13 Wherefore, my beloved brethren, I know that if ye shall **follow the Son**, with full purpose of heart, acting **no hypocrisy** and no deception before God, but with real intent, **repenting of your sins**, witnessing unto the Father that ye are willing to take upon you the name of Christ, by **baptism** —yea, by following your Lord and your Savior down into the water, according to his word, behold, then shall ye **receive the Holy Ghost**; yea, then cometh the baptism of fire and of the Holy Ghost; and then can ye speak with the tongue of angels [*you can speak with the same testimony and understanding which angels have about Christ*], and shout praises unto the Holy One of Israel [*Christ*].

14 But, behold, my beloved brethren, thus came the voice of the Son unto me, saying: **After ye have repented** of your sins, and witnessed unto the Father that ye are willing to keep my commandments, by the **baptism of water**, and have received the **baptism of fire and of the Holy Ghost**, and can speak with a new tongue [*you can speak as one who has a true testimony of Christ and His gospel*], yea, even with the tongue of angels, and after this should deny me, it would have been better for you that ye had not known me. [*This is a serious warning about the accountability of one who has gained a testimony from the Holy Ghost.*]

> The imagery of being "baptized by fire" by the Holy Ghost is a reminder that the Holy Ghost works with us after we receive the Gift of the Holy Ghost, to purge and cleanse us from sin and inappropriate behaviors. The symbolism of burning imperfections out of us through the help of the Holy Ghost comes from what is known as the refiner's fire.
>
> A refiner of gold, for instance, heats ore until both the rock (imperfections) and the gold (the person being refined or prepared for exaltation) melts. The gold is heavier than the rock; therefore, it settles to the bottom of the crucible, and the rock floats to the top where it can be scraped off. As the "refiner's fire" continues, more ore is added, and the level of gold rises, and more "imperfections" are taken away by the Refiner (Christ and His Atonement). Eventually, the crucible is filled with pure gold (a person ready for exaltation).
>
> Next, Nephi bears testimony to us that he has heard the voice of Heavenly Father.

15 And I heard a voice from the Father, saying: Yea, the words of my Beloved are true and faithful. He that **endureth to the end**, the same shall be saved.

> Enduring to the end is more than merely "surviving white knuckled." It is living the gospel and having the most satisfying and rewarding journey through mortal life possible. The perspective of the righteous is much different than that of the wicked. The wicked live in fear and turmoil interspersed by temporary times of deceiving satisfactions brought by gratification of lusts. The righteous, on the other hand, have the help of the Holy Ghost to bear them up, even during times of severe trial, such that they can "bear up their burdens with ease, and . . . submit cheerfully and with patience to all the will of the Lord" (see Mosiah 24:15).

16 And now, my beloved brethren, I know by this that unless

a man shall **endure to the end**, in following the example of the Son of the living God, he cannot be saved.

> There is another way to look at the phrase "endure to the end." The word "end" often means "goal" or "purpose" as used in the scriptures. Therefore, "endure to the end" could also mean "endure until you have reached the goal of exaltation," or "endure until you have satisfied the purpose of your having been sent to earth," which would obviously be that you live the gospel as best you can right up until you die.

17 Wherefore, **do the things** which I have told you I have seen that **your Lord and your Redeemer should** [*will*] **do** [*be baptized and keep your commitments like Christ will*]; for, for this cause have they been shown unto me, that ye might know the gate by which ye should enter. For **the gate by which ye should enter is repentance and baptism by water**; and then cometh a remission of your sins by fire and by the Holy Ghost.

18 And then are ye in this strait [*narrow*] and narrow path [*the "narrow and narrowing path"; in other words, the more righteous you become, the narrower the path you allow yourself to walk because of the "light" which the Holy Ghost is shining for you*] which leads to eternal life [*exaltation*]; yea, **ye have entered in by the gate; ye have done according to the commandments** of the Father and the Son; and **ye have received the Holy Ghost**, which witnesses of the Father and the Son, unto the fulfilling of the promise which he hath made, that if ye entered in by the way ye should receive.

19 And now, my beloved brethren, **after ye have gotten into this strait and narrow path, I would ask if all is done?** Behold, I say unto you, **Nay**; for ye have not come thus far save it were by the word of Christ with unshaken faith in him, relying wholly upon the merits of him who is mighty to save.

> Verse 20, next, is a strong reminder that it is all right to humbly plan on exaltation. Many members might think that planning on being exalted is a bit arrogant and smacks of pride. Not so, according to Nephi in verse 20. The word "hope" as used in the Book of Mormon is a much more positive and a much stronger word than hope as used in modern English. An explanation of this is found by association with other words in Alma 58:11 as follows (**bold** added for emphasis):

Alma 58:11

11 Yea, and it came to pass that the Lord our God did visit us with **assurances** that he would deliver us; yea, insomuch that he did speak **peace to our souls**, and did grant unto us **great faith**, and did cause us that we should **hope** for our deliverance in him.

We will now study Nephi's teachings about hope. **Bold** will be used to make the point.

20 Wherefore, ye must **press forward** with a steadfastness in Christ, **having a perfect brightness of hope**, and a love of God and of all men. Wherefore, if ye shall **press forward, feasting upon the word of Christ**, and **endure to the end**, behold, thus saith the Father: **Ye shall have eternal life** [*exaltation in the highest degree in the celestial kingdom; see D&C 131:1–4*].

> Another way to say "endure to the end" in verse 20, above, might be "continue improving to the end." Elder Marvin J. Ashton gave a marvelous talk on the role of "improving" in the April 1989 General Conference of the Church. He said, "the speed with which we head along the straight and narrow path isn't as important as the direction in which we are traveling." This gives the honest in heart great confidence that they will make it.

Nephi now concludes his sermon on the doctrine of Christ.

21 And now, behold, my beloved brethren, **this is the way**; and there is **none other way nor name given under heaven whereby man can be saved in the kingdom of God**. And now, behold, **this is the doctrine of Christ**, and **the only and true doctrine of the Father, and of the Son, and of the Holy Ghost**, which is one God [*three members of the Godhead, working together in perfect unity*], without end. Amen.

SECOND NEPHI 32

As Nephi continues his final teachings to us, he will see by the power of prophecy and the Holy Ghost that many of us still do not understand what he meant in 2 Nephi 31:13 when he said, "Then can ye speak with the tongue of angels." Therefore, he will proceed to explain this vital concept again as he begins this chapter. We will continue to use **bold** for teaching purposes.

1 AND now, behold, my beloved brethren, I suppose that ye ponder somewhat in your hearts concerning that which ye should do after ye have entered in by the way. But, behold, why do ye

ponder these things in your hearts?

2 Do ye not **remember that I said unto you that after ye had received the Holy Ghost ye could speak with the tongue of angels?** And now, how could ye speak with the tongue of angels save it were by the Holy Ghost?

> As mentioned in 2 Nephi 31:13, in the note in brackets, a major part of "speaking with the tongue of angels" is that of having the same testimony and understanding of the Savior and His gospel that angels have. The logic in this is that since angels speak by the power of the Holy Ghost (verse 3, next) and since we can also speak or bear testimony by that same power, we can have the same understanding as they do about Christ. This is a very powerful and wonderful truth!

3 **Angels speak by the power of the Holy Ghost**; wherefore [*therefore*], they speak the words of Christ. Wherefore [*this is the reason*], I said unto you, feast upon the words of Christ; for behold, the words of Christ will tell you all things what ye should do.

4 Wherefore, now after I have spoken these words, **if ye cannot understand them it will be because ye ask not, neither do ye knock; wherefore, ye are not brought into the light, but must perish in the dark.** [*In other words, now it is up to us to use our moral agency to choose to ask the Father for additional inspiration from the Holy Ghost if needed, to understand Nephi's inspired words.*]

> Nephi repeats again to help us understand his teaching. He is very anxious that we understand what he has taught us about the doctrine of Christ in chapter 31. It appears from Nephi's emphasis, that the doctrine of Christ is the gospel of Christ in its most basic form. Therefore, understanding the doctrine of Christ is essential for any other thorough understanding of any doctrines of the plan of salvation.

5 For behold, again I say unto you that **if ye will enter in by the way** [*repentance and baptism*]**, and receive the Holy Ghost, it will show unto you all things what ye should do.**

6 Behold, **this is the doctrine of Christ**, and there will be no more doctrine given until after he shall manifest himself unto you in the flesh [*until after He comes to perform His mortal ministry*]. And when he shall manifest himself unto you in the flesh, the things which he shall say unto you shall ye observe to do.

Nephi is a tender-hearted teacher and prophet, and he wishes he could do even more to help save every soul. But there are limits, set by individual agency. And although this has to be, it still causes pain in the hearts of righteous teachers.

7 And now I, Nephi, cannot say more; the Spirit stoppeth mine utterance, and I am left to mourn because of the unbelief, and the wickedness, and the ignorance, and the stiffneckedness [*pride and lack of humility*] of men; for **they will not search** knowledge [*this requires effort; it is an agency choice that many people will not make*], nor understand great knowledge, when it is given unto them in plainness, even as plain as word can be.

Next, Nephi emphasizes the role of fervent prayer in gaining knowledge through the Holy Ghost. He also warns us to pray even if we do not feel like praying. As people yield to Satan's temptations, they generally stop praying to God. Thus, they cut off communication with the very Being who could help them keep from being pulled down by the devil.

8 And now, my beloved brethren, I perceive that ye ponder still in your hearts; and it grieveth me that I must speak concerning this thing. **For if ye would hearken unto the Spirit which teacheth a man to pray ye would know that ye must pray; for the evil spirit** [*Satan*] **teacheth not a man to pray, but teacheth him that he must not pray.**

9 But behold, I say unto you that **ye must pray always, and not faint** [*not give up*]; that ye must not perform any thing unto the Lord save in the first place ye shall pray unto the Father in the name of Christ, that he will consecrate thy performance unto thee [*He will see that it benefits you*], that thy performance may be for the welfare of thy soul.

SECOND NEPHI 33

This is the last chapter of Nephi, and we will feel his great love for his people and for us as he carefully chooses his final words to us. In verse 1, below, he humbly claims that he is not "mighty in writing," but we would humbly disagree. He is a mighty prophet and teacher, and we will look forward to meeting him in the next life.

Next, in **bold** for emphasis, is another famous quote from the Book of Mormon dealing with the role of the Holy Ghost in teaching.

SECOND NEPHI 33

1 AND now I, Nephi, cannot write all the things which were taught among my people; neither am I mighty in writing, like unto speaking; **for when a man speaketh by the power of the Holy Ghost the power of the Holy Ghost carrieth it unto the hearts of the children of men.**

> There is a subtle misquote which is often used in place of the last part of verse 1, above. The misquote is "carrieth it **into** the hearts" instead of "carrieth it **unto** the hearts" as it is written in the verse. While this may not be that big of a concern, yet there could be an important lesson taught with the correct wording. The word "unto" implies that the Holy Ghost will carry the message right up to your heart, but you must let it in.

2 But behold, there are many that harden their hearts against the Holy Spirit, that it hath no place in them; wherefore, they cast many things away which are written and esteem them as things of naught [*they consider them to be of no worth*].

3 But I, Nephi, have written what I have written, and I esteem [*consider*] it as of great worth, and especially unto my people. For I pray continually for them by day, and mine eyes water my pillow by night, because of them; and I cry unto my God in faith, and I know that he will hear my cry [*prayer*].

4 And I know that the Lord God will consecrate my prayers for the gain of my people [*I know my prayers will be effective*]. And the words which I have written in weakness will be made strong unto them; for it persuadeth them to do good; it maketh known unto them of their fathers; and it speaketh of Jesus, and persuadeth them to believe in him, and to endure to the end, which is life eternal.

5 And it speaketh harshly against sin, according to the plainness of the truth; wherefore, no man will be angry at the words which I have written save [*unless*] he shall be of the spirit of the devil.

6 I glory in plainness; I glory in truth; I glory in my Jesus, for he hath redeemed my soul from hell.

> Above, Nephi expresses his love of "plainness." You may have noticed that Christ is the author of plainness and that Satan is the author of complexity. In fact, many false doctrines, which compete with the simple "plain and precious" truths of the gospel, become so complex that they are unfathomable.

7 I have charity for my people, and **great faith in Christ that I**

shall meet many souls spotless at his judgment-seat.

There is a major message which is very encouraging, taught by Nephi in verse 7, above. It is that he has confidence that many of us will make it to exaltation. We should pay close attention to his choice in using the word "spotless." Many members of the Church have the mistaken idea that we have to be perfect as we get to the final judgment. This is not true. Christ was the only completely perfect individual to ever live on earth. If we get confused and use the word "perfect" in place of the word "spotless," we will get very discouraged.

If we understand and follow the doctrine of Christ as taught by Nephi in the previous chapter, we will qualify for the Savior's Atonement to cleanse us completely from sins. Thus, we will be spotless or, in other words, perfectly clean and pure and we will be fit to be in the presence of God. This is the definition of the word "sanctified."

The Prophet Joseph Smith taught very clearly that we will still have much work to do beyond the veil as we go on to gain exaltation. He said (**bold** added for emphasis):

*"When you climb up a ladder, you must begin at the bottom, and ascend step by step, until you arrive at the top; and so it is with the principles of the gospel—you must begin with the first, and go on until you learn all the principles of exaltation. But **it will be a great while after you have passed through the veil before you will have learned them. It is not all to be comprehended in this world; it will be a great work to learn our salvation and exaltation even beyond the grave**"* (Smith, *Teachings of the Prophet Joseph Smith*, 348).

8 I have charity for the Jew—I say Jew, because I mean them from whence I came [*in other words, geographically speaking; there were people from all of the tribes of Israel living in the Jerusalem area*].

9 I also have charity for the Gentiles. But behold, for none of these can I hope except they shall be reconciled unto Christ [*put their lives in harmony with Christ*], and enter into the narrow gate [*repentance and baptism; see 2 Nephi 31:17*], and walk in the strait [*note that the word is "strait," not "straight." The word "strait" means "narrow"*] path which leads to life [*eternal life; exaltation*], and continue in the path until the end of the day of probation [*until the time of your testing is over*].

10 And now, my beloved brethren, and also Jew, and all ye ends of the earth, hearken unto these

words and believe in Christ; and if ye believe not in these words believe in Christ. And if ye shall believe in Christ ye will believe in these words, for they are the words of Christ, and he hath given them unto me; and **they teach all men that they should do good**.

11 And if they are not the words of Christ, judge ye—for Christ will show unto you, with power and great glory, that they are his words, at the last day [*on Judgment Day*]; and you and I shall stand face to face before his bar; and ye shall know that I have been commanded of him to write these things, notwithstanding [*in spite of*] my weakness.

12 And I pray the Father in the name of Christ that many of us, if not all, may be saved in his kingdom at that great and last day.

Nephi now bids us all a powerful and emotional farewell. Feel his deep and sincere concern for our eternal welfare.

13 And now, my beloved brethren, all those who are of the house of Israel, and all ye ends of the earth, I speak unto you as the voice of one crying from the dust: Farewell until that great day shall come.

14 And you that will not partake of the goodness of God, and respect the words of the Jews [*the Bible*], and also my words [*Nephi's portion of the Book of Mormon*], and the words which shall proceed forth out of the mouth of the Lamb of God, behold, I bid you an everlasting farewell, for these words shall condemn you [*will stop your eternal progression*] at the last day [*on final Judgment Day*].

15 For what I seal on earth, shall be brought against you at the judgment bar; for thus hath the Lord commanded me, and I must obey. Amen.

THE BOOK OF JACOB

Jacob is the older of Lehi's two sons born during the eight years of journeying in the wilderness (see 1 Nephi 18:7). He is Nephi's younger brother and would be in the neighborhood of forty-five to fifty years old at this point. In chapter one, Jacob will talk to us about the commandment Nephi gave him to take over the small plates of Nephi and to engrave a few of his own things on them. Nephi's death is recorded by Jacob, also in chapter one.

Jacob will give some powerful messages, not the least of which will concern the growing practice of plural marriage among his people (chapter 2).

Perhaps the most famous chapter of Jacob is chapter 5 which is the allegory of the tame olive tree and the wild olive trees. We will spend considerable time on this chapter.

Jacob has seen the Savior (2 Nephi 11:3) and has been well schooled in the gospel by Nephi. He is kind and gentle and it bothers him to have to speak bluntly and boldly to his people in order to wake them up to the reality that they are going into apostasy (see chapter two). We are greatly blessed to have these inspired teachings of Jacob and we can see that Mormon selected them for us (Words of Mormon 1:3–8) as he was inspired to include the small plates of Nephi in the plates which Moroni would later bury in the stone box in the Hill Cumorah.

JACOB 1

In this chapter, Jacob will introduce himself to us and will explain some differences between the large plates and the small plates. He will redefine the terms "Lamanites" and "Nephites" and then give a little background to the sermon he delivered to his people in the temple.

1 FOR behold, it came to pass that fifty and five years had passed away from the time that Lehi left Jerusalem [*so it is now a little over 540 years before Christ*]; wherefore, Nephi gave me, Jacob, a commandment concerning the small plates [*the small plates of Nephi*], upon which these things are engraven.

For more information about the various sets of plates referred to in the Book of Mormon, see "A Brief Explanation About The Book Of Mormon" in the introductory pages to your Book of Mormon.

2 And he gave me, Jacob, a commandment that I should write upon these plates [*the small plates*] a few of the things which I considered to be most precious; that I should not touch, save it were lightly, concerning the history of this people which are called the people of Nephi.

3 For he said that the history of his people should be engraven upon his other plates [*the large plates of Nephi*], and that I should preserve these plates and hand them down unto my seed, from generation to generation.

4 And if there were preaching which was sacred, or revelation which was great, or prophesying, that I should engraven the heads [*main points*] of them upon these plates [*the small plates*], and touch upon them as much as it were possible, for Christ's sake, and for the sake of our people.

5 For because of faith and great anxiety, it truly had been made manifest unto us concerning our people, what things should happen unto them.

6 And we also had many revelations, and the spirit of much prophecy; wherefore, we knew of Christ and his kingdom, which should come.

7 Wherefore we labored diligently among our people, that we might persuade them to come unto Christ, and partake of the goodness of God, that they might enter into his rest [*exaltation in the celestial kingdom; see D&C 84:24*], lest by any means he should swear in his wrath they should not enter in, as in the provocation [*the "provoking of God," in other words, the forty years the children of Israel spent in the wilderness because they provoked God to anger*] in the days of temptation while the children of Israel were in the wilderness.

8 Wherefore, we would to God that we could persuade all men not to rebel against God, to provoke him to anger, but that all men would believe in Christ, and view his death, and suffer his cross [*do whatever it takes to follow Him*] and bear the shame of the world; wherefore, I, Jacob, take it upon me to fulfil the commandment of my brother Nephi.

Next, Jacob talks briefly about the transition of power among his people, as far as their kings were concerned. Because the people loved Nephi so much, each of their succeeding kings was called Nephi (verse 11).

9 Now Nephi began to be old, and he saw that he must soon die; wherefore, he anointed a man to be a king and a ruler over his people now, according to the reigns of the kings.

10 The people having loved Nephi exceedingly, he having been a great protector for them, having wielded the sword of Laban in their defence, and having labored in all his days for their welfare—

11 Wherefore, the people were desirous to retain in remembrance his name. And whoso should reign in his stead were called by the people, second Nephi, third Nephi, and so forth, according to the reigns of the kings; and thus they were called by the people, let them be of whatever name they would.

12 And it came to pass that Nephi died.

Next, as stated above, Jacob redefines the terms "Lamanites" and "Nephites." It is important that we keep these new definitions in mind as we continue our Book of Mormon study. We will use **bold** to emphasize this point. Sometimes, in your scripture marking, you may wish to underline or highlight just a few words or phrases within a verse or set of verses, such that the underlined portion becomes a note in and of itself. This is what would happen if you were to underline the bolded portion of verse 14. You could even put a box around the words "Lamanite" and "Nephite," which would further clarify at a glance.

13 Now the people which were not Lamanites were Nephites; nevertheless, they were called Nephites, Jacobites, Josephites, Zoramites, Lamanites, Lemuelites, and Ishmaelites.

14 But I, Jacob, shall not **hereafter** distinguish them by these names, but **I shall call them Lamanites that seek to destroy the people of Nephi, and those who are friendly to Nephi I shall call Nephites**, or the people of Nephi, according to the reigns of the kings.

Next, Jacob leads up to the serious problem which is growing among his people wherein men are beginning to take plural wives, against the commandment of the Lord. They were under the same rules we are today, as far as polygamy was concerned (see Jacob 2:34 and 3:5). We will say a bit more about this in a few moments. We will continue to use **bold** occasionally for emphasis and for teaching purposes. As we continue now, we will see once again what we called the Big Three sins as we commented on 1 Nephi 13:7–9. These Big Three are well-used by Satan still today. They are:

1. Sexual immorality
2. Materialism
3. Pride

15 And now it came to pass that **the people of Nephi**, under the reign of the second king, **began to** grow hard in their hearts, and **indulge themselves somewhat in wicked practices, such as like unto David of old desiring many wives and concubines, and also Solomon, his son** [*sexual immorality*].

16 Yea, and they also began to search much gold and silver, and began to be lifted up somewhat in pride [*materialism and pride*].

Next, Jacob tells us that his sermon to his people was designed to alert them to these three major tools of the devil.

17 Wherefore I, Jacob, gave unto them these words as I taught them in the temple, having first obtained mine errand from the Lord.

18 For I, Jacob, and my brother Joseph had been consecrated priests and teachers of this people, by the hand of Nephi.

The terms "priests" and "teachers" as used here refer not to the Aaronic Priesthood, rather, to responsibilities within the Melchizedek Priesthood. Lehi and his descendants functioned by virtue of the Melchizedek Priesthood. The Aaronic Priesthood was not set up among the Nephites until the Savior's ministry to them as recorded in Third Nephi. Joseph Fielding Smith explained this as follows:

"The Nephites were descendants of Joseph. Lehi discovered this when reading the brass plates. He was a descendant of Manasseh, and Ishmael, who accompanied him with his family, was of the tribe of Ephraim (Alma 10:3)" (Smith, *Improvement Era*, 8:781; *Journal of Discourses*, 23:184).

"Therefore there were no Levites who accompanied Lehi to the Western Hemisphere. Under these conditions **the Nephites officiated by virtue of the Melchizedek Priesthood from the days of Lehi to the days of the appearance of our Savior among them**. It is true that Nephi 'consecrated Jacob and Joseph' that they should be priests and teachers over the land of the Nephites, but the fact that plural terms *priests and teachers* were used indicates that this was not a reference to the definite office in the priesthood in either case, but it was a general assignment to teach, direct, and admonish the people. Otherwise the terms *priest and teacher* would have been given, in the singular. Additional light is thrown on this appointment showing that these two brothers of Nephi held the Melchizedek Priesthood, in the sixth chapter, second verse of 2 Nephi, where Jacob makes this explanation regarding the priesthood which he and Joseph held: 'Behold, my beloved brethren, I, Jacob, having been called of God, and ordained *after the manner of his holy order*, and having been consecrated by my brother Nephi, unto whom ye look as a king or a protector, and on whom ye depend for safety, behold ye know that I have spoken unto you exceeding many things.'

"This seems to be a confirmation of the ordinations that he and his brother Joseph received in the Melchizedek Priesthood. All through the Book of Mormon we find references to the Nephites officiating by virtue of the Higher Priesthood (Melchizedek Priesthood) after the holy order." (Smith, *Answers to Gospel Questions,* 1:124)

19 And we did magnify our office unto the Lord [*we fulfilled the responsibilities of our offices and callings*], taking upon us the responsibility, answering the sins of the people upon our own heads [*considering that we were responsible for our people's sins*] if we did not teach them the word of God with all diligence; wherefore, by laboring with our might their blood might not come upon our garments [*that we would not be held accountable for their sins*]; otherwise their blood would come upon our garments, and we would not be found spotless at the last day [*on Judgment Day*].

JACOB 2

In this chapter, Jacob will go to the temple and teach his people. He will deal with three major topics, namely, materialism, pride, and sexual immorality. As he speaks about immorality, he will deal with the topic of plural marriage.

1 THE words which Jacob, the brother of Nephi, spake unto the people of Nephi, after the death of Nephi:

2 Now, my beloved brethren, I, Jacob, according to the responsibility which I am under to God, to magnify mine office [*to fulfill my calling*] with soberness, and that I might rid my garments of your sins [*not be responsible for your sins*], I come up into the temple this day that I might

JACOB 2

declare unto you the word of God.

> Preparing to deliver this particular sermon has been very hard on Jacob. He is a kind, tender man and does not like to place burdens on people nor hurt their feelings. He is like our modern prophets.

3 And ye yourselves know that I have hitherto [*up to now*] been diligent in the office of my calling; but I this day am weighed down with much more desire and anxiety for the welfare of your souls than I have hitherto been. [*He is really worried about them.*]

4 For behold, as yet, ye have been obedient unto the word of the Lord, which I have given unto you.

> As a prophet, Jacob can discern what is in the minds and thoughts of his people by the power of the Holy Ghost. It is his stewardship to do so. Our prophets do the same and we see it, especially as they address us at the General Conferences of the Church.

5 But behold, hearken ye unto me, and know that **by the help of the all–powerful Creator of heaven and earth I can tell you concerning your thoughts**, how that ye are beginning to **labor in sin**, which sin appeareth very abominable unto me, yea, and abominable unto God.

> The phrase "labor in sin" as used in verse 5, above, as a very interesting and insightful term. Sin creates much more stress and work (labor) than righteousness does. This is true both on an individual basis as well as on a national level.

> For instance, righteousness promotes peace and thus the labors and productivity of the people go to building up of the standard of living for everyone. On the other hand, wickedness requires the formation and financing of police, armies, self-defense, locks, security systems, guards, and so forth. In summary, righteousness builds, produces and creates prosperity, while wickedness consumes prosperity.

6 Yea, it grieveth my soul and causeth me to shrink with shame before the presence of my Maker, that I must testify unto you concerning the wickedness of your hearts. [*Jacob is ashamed of his people's behaviors.*]

7 And also it grieveth me that I must use so much boldness of speech concerning you, before your wives and your children, many of whose feelings are exceedingly tender and chaste and delicate before God, which thing is pleasing unto God;

> It is weighing heavily upon

Jacob's heart that many righteous members have come to the meeting expecting to be cheered up and encouraged, to have their day brightened by listening to their prophet. But it is not going to happen.

8 And it supposeth me that they have come up hither to hear the pleasing word of God, yea, the word which healeth the wounded soul.

9 Wherefore, it burdeneth [*weighs down*] my soul that I should be constrained, because of the strict commandment which I have received from God, to admonish [*teach and warn*] you according to your crimes, to enlarge the wounds of those who are already wounded [*by your sins*], instead of consoling and healing their wounds; and those who have not been wounded, instead of feasting upon the pleasing word of God have daggers placed to pierce their souls and wound their delicate minds.

10 But, notwithstanding [*in spite of*] the greatness of the task, I must do according to the strict commands of God, and tell you concerning your wickedness and abominations [*extremely serious sins*], in the presence of the pure in heart, and the broken heart, and under the glance of the piercing eye of the Almighty God.

11 Wherefore, I must tell you the truth according to the plainness of the word of God. For behold, as I inquired of the Lord, thus came the word unto me, saying: Jacob, get thou up into the temple on the morrow, and declare the word which I shall give thee unto this people.

First, Jacob teaches and warns them about materialism, in other words, making money and having things, personal wealth and possessions, a top priority in their lives. This leads to pride. We will continue to use **bold** for emphasis.

12 And now behold, my brethren, this is the word which I declare unto you, that many of you have begun to search for gold, and for silver, and for all manner of precious ores, in the which this land, which is a land of promise unto you and to your seed, doth abound most plentifully. [*There is lots of wealth available in this land.*]

13 And the hand of providence [*God*] hath smiled upon you most pleasingly, that you have obtained many riches; and because some of you have obtained more abundantly than that of your brethren **ye are lifted up in the pride of your hearts,** and wear stiff necks [*you won't bow your heads in humil-*

ity] and high heads because of the costliness of your apparel [*clothing*], and persecute your brethren because ye suppose that ye are better than they.

14 And now, my brethren, do ye suppose that God justifieth [*excuses*] you in this thing? Behold, I say unto you, Nay. But he condemneth you, and if ye persist in these things his judgments [*punishments*] must speedily come unto you.

15 O that he would show you that he can pierce you, and with one glance of his eye he can smite you to the dust!

16 O that he would rid you from this iniquity [*wickedness*] and abomination. And, O that ye would listen unto the word of his commands, and **let not this pride of your hearts destroy your souls!**

Next, Jacob teaches his people a simple method of overcoming pride and materialism.

17 **Think of your brethren like unto yourselves**, and be familiar [*generous*] with all and free with your substance, that they may be rich like unto you.

Some people think that wealth itself is evil. This is not the case. It is how individuals handle wealth and what goes on in their minds and hearts that counts. What Jacob says next is very important and quite well known among members of the Church today.

18 But **before ye seek for riches, seek ye for the kingdom of God**.

19 And after ye have obtained a hope in Christ ye shall obtain riches, if ye seek them; and **ye will seek them for the intent to do good**—to clothe the naked, and to feed the hungry, and to liberate the captive, and administer relief to the sick and the afflicted. [*In other words, if you remain loyal and faithful to God, and if you gain wealth, it will not ruin you because you will keep things in proper perspective.*]

20 And now, my brethren, I have spoken unto you concerning **pride**; and those of you which have afflicted your neighbor, and persecuted him because ye were proud in your hearts, of the things which God hath given you, what say ye of it?

21 Do ye not suppose that such things are abominable unto him who created all flesh? And **the one being is as precious in his sight as the other**. And all flesh is of the dust; and for the selfsame end [*purpose*] hath he created them, that they should keep

his commandments and glorify him forever.

> Jacob wishes that he could end his sermon at this point and let his people go home. It would be a great relief to him to do so. But one of the responsibilities of a leader is to deliver the word of the Lord to his people without diluting it. In the next verses, Jacob expresses this and then delivers the rest of the message.

22 And now I make an end of speaking unto you concerning this pride. And **were it not that I must speak unto you concerning a grosser crime, my heart would rejoice exceedingly because of you.**

23 But the word of God burdens me because of your grosser crimes. For behold, thus saith the Lord: This people begin to wax in iniquity; they understand not the scriptures, for they seek to excuse themselves in committing whoredoms [*sexual immorality*], because of the things which were written concerning David, and Solomon his son.

> Jacob's people have obviously read in the brass plates about David and Solomon and are using this as an excuse to violate the commandment which the Lord gave Lehi (see Jacob 3:5) that his people should not take up the practice of plural marriage which was still commonly practiced in Old Testament lands when they left Jerusalem in 600 B.C.

First, Jacob tells his people that they must not use David and Solomon as role models, because they both lost their souls as this practice got out of hand with them. For instance, David had Bathsheba's husband killed intentionally in battle so he could marry her as a plural wife after he found out she was expecting their child. Thus, David tried to cover up adultery with murder. As a result, David lost his exaltation (see D&C 132:39). David was not a good example for Jacob's people to follow at this stage of his life.

As for Solomon, 1 Kings 11:3 informs us that he had seven hundred wives and three hundred concubines (second class wives), and the Bible goes on to record that Solomon began worshiping idols, which was pleasing to many of his pagan wives. Thus, Solomon also apostatized from God because of his abuse of plural marriage. He too was not a good example for Jacob's people to follow.

No wonder Jacob told his people the following:

24 Behold, David and Solomon truly had many wives and concubines, which thing was abominable before me, saith the Lord.

25 Wherefore, thus saith the

Lord, I have led this people forth out of the land of Jerusalem, by the power of mine arm, that I might raise up unto me a righteous branch from the fruit of the loins of Joseph [*from the descendants of Joseph who was sold into Egypt*].

26 Wherefore, I the Lord God will not suffer [*allow*] that this people shall do like unto them of old.

> There are many rumors and false notions among members and non-members alike regarding the practice of plural marriage in the early days of the Church. Many try to come up with explanations of why the Lord commanded plural marriage. One of the most common is the notion that so many of the men were killed off by mobs, etc. that plural marriage was required for the remaining women to have a husband. Recent research has shown this not to be the case to any significant degree.
>
> As Jacob continues, he will give us the reason many of the early members of the Church practiced plural marriage. It is simple. The Lord commanded it.
>
> You may wish to put a box around verses 27 and 30, next, and tie them together with a line. They constitute the word of the Lord regarding plural marriage.

> Just a quick explanation about the word "polygamy," which is commonly used to refer to plural marriage. Technically, polygamy means having plural husbands or plural wives. Therefore, "plural wives" is a better term for us to use.
>
> Now on to the rules for plural marriage, as given by the Lord. We will use **bold** for emphasis.

27 Wherefore, my brethren, hear me, and hearken to the word of the Lord: **For there shall not any man among you have save it be one wife; and concubines he shall have none**;

28 For I, the Lord God, delight in the chastity of women. And whoredoms are an abomination before me; thus saith the Lord of Hosts.

29 Wherefore, this people shall keep my commandments, saith the Lord of Hosts, or cursed be the land for their sakes.

30 For **if I will, saith the Lord of Hosts, raise up seed unto me, I will command my people** [*to practice plural marriage*]; **otherwise they shall hearken unto these things** [*the rule given in verse 27*].

> "These things" in verse 30, above, refer to verse 27. In fact, you may wish to draw an arrow from "these things" back up

to verse 27 in your own scriptures.

A common question which comes up in classes is, "Will I be required to practice plural marriage if I attain exaltation?" The answer is "No." Bruce R. McConkie gives the answer as follows (**bold** added to point out the answer):

"From such fragmentary scriptural records as are now available, we learn that the Lord did command some of his ancient saints to practice plural marriage. Abraham, Isaac, and Jacob—among others (D&C 132)—conformed to this ennobling and exalting principle; the whole history of ancient Israel was one in which plurality of wives was a divinely accepted and approved order of matrimony. Those who entered this order at the Lord's command, and who kept the laws and conditions appertaining to it, have gained for themselves eternal exaltation in the highest heaven of the celestial world.

"In the early days of this dispensation, as part of the promised restitution of all things, the Lord revealed the principle of plural marriage to the Prophet. Later the Prophet and leading brethren were commanded to enter into the practice, which they did in all virtue and purity of heart despite the consequent animosity and prejudices of worldly people. After Brigham Young led the saints to the Salt Lake Valley, plural marriage was openly taught and practiced until the year 1890. At that time conditions were such that the Lord by revelation withdrew the command to continue the practice, and President Wilford Woodruff issued the Manifesto directing that it cease (Woodruff, *Discourses of Wilford Woodruff*, pp. 213–18).

"Obviously the holy practice will commence again after the Second Coming of the Son of Man and the ushering in of the Millennium (Isaiah 4).

"**Plural marriage is not essential to salvation or exaltation. Nephi and his people were denied the power to have more than one wife and yet they could gain every blessing in eternity that the Lord ever offered to any people**. In our day, the Lord summarized by revelation the whole doctrine of exaltation and predicated it upon the marriage of one man to one woman (D&C 132:1–28). Thereafter he added the principles relative to plurality of wives with the express stipulation that any such marriages would be valid only if authorized by the President of the Church (D&C 132:7, 29–66).

"All who pretend or assume to engage in plural marriage in this day, when the one holding the keys has withdrawn the power by which they are performed, are guilty of gross wickedness" (McConkie, *Mormon Doctrine*, 578).

31 For behold, I, the Lord, have seen the sorrow, and heard the mourning of the daughters of my people in the land of Jerusalem, yea, and in all the lands of my people, because of the wickedness and abominations of their husbands.

32 And I will not suffer [*allow*], saith the Lord of Hosts, that the cries of the fair daughters of this people, which I have led out of the land of Jerusalem, shall come up unto me against the men of my people, saith the Lord of Hosts.

33 For they shall not lead away captive the daughters of my people because of their tenderness, save I shall visit them with a sore curse, even unto destruction; for they shall not commit whoredoms, like unto them of old, saith the Lord of Hosts.

> Next, Jacob reminds the men among his people that they already know the commandments of the Lord to them on this topic. Therefore, they are accountable for going against God's law on this matter.

34 And now behold, my brethren, **ye know that these commandments were given to our father, Lehi**; wherefore, ye have known them before; and **ye have come unto great condemnation**; for ye have done these things which ye ought not to have done.

35 Behold, ye have done greater iniquities than the Lamanites, our brethren. Ye have broken the hearts of your tender wives, and lost the confidence of your children, because of your bad examples before them; and the sobbings of their hearts ascend up to God against you. And because of the strictness of the word of God, which cometh down against you, many hearts died, pierced with deep wounds.

JACOB 3

> Next, Jacob gives encouragement to those of his people who have not broken these commandments of God.

1 BUT behold, I, Jacob, would speak unto you that are pure in heart. Look unto God with firmness of mind, and pray unto him with exceeding faith, and he will console you in your afflictions, and he will plead your cause, and send down justice upon those who seek your destruction.

2 O all ye that are pure in heart, lift up your heads and receive the pleasing word of God, and feast upon his love; for ye may, if your minds are firm, forever.

> One of the most important messages of the gospel is the effectiveness of the Atonement of Christ. Jacob will now warn, invite and remind the wicked among his people to repent. It is not too late.

3 But, wo, wo, unto you that are not pure in heart, that are filthy this day before God; for **except ye repent** the land is cursed for your sakes [*unless you repent, you will be destroyed*]; and the Lamanites, which are not filthy like unto you, nevertheless they are cursed with a sore cursing [*because they have gone astray from the gospel*], shall scourge you even unto destruction.

4 And the time speedily cometh, that except ye [*the Nephites*] repent they shall possess the land of your inheritance, and the Lord God will lead away the righteous out from among you. [*He did have Mosiah I lead the righteous out of the land of Nephi to Zarahemla; see Omni 1:12–15.*]

5 Behold, the Lamanites your brethren, whom ye hate because of their filthiness and the cursing which hath come upon their skins, are more righteous than you; for they have not forgotten the commandment of the Lord, which was given unto our father—that they should have save it were one wife, and concubines they should have none, and there should not be whoredoms committed among them.

6 And now, this commandment they observe to keep; wherefore, because of this observance, in keeping this commandment, the Lord God will not destroy them, but will be merciful unto them; and one day they shall become a blessed people. [*We are watching the fulfilling of this prophecy today.*]

7 Behold, their husbands love their wives, and their wives love their husbands; and their husbands and their wives love their children; and their unbelief and their hatred towards you is because of the iniquity of their fathers; wherefore, how much better are you than they, in the sight of your great Creator?

8 O my brethren, I fear that unless ye shall repent of your sins that their skins will be whiter than yours, when ye shall be brought with them before the throne of God. [*They will be more pure and clean on Judgment Day than you.*]

> The illicit practice of plural marriage for the gratification of lustful desires among the Nephites at the time of Jacob's address to his people was a form of severe hypocrisy. They looked down at the Lamanites, yet they were guilty of gross sin themselves. Jacob explains this next.

9 Wherefore, a commandment I give unto you, which is the word of God, that ye revile no more against them because of the darkness of their skins; neither shall ye revile against them because of their filthiness; but ye shall remember your own filthiness, and remember that their filthiness came because of their fathers [*unrighteous traditions*].

10 Wherefore, ye shall remember your children, how that ye have grieved their hearts because of the example that ye have set before them; and also, remember that ye may, because of your filthiness, bring your children unto destruction, and **their sins be heaped upon your heads at the last day**.

> Just a quick word about the phrase "bring your children unto destruction" in verse 10, above. Remember that God is completely fair to all people, including children who are given bad examples, and thus grow up away from the gospel. If they do not get a fair chance in this life, such children will have a fair chance in the spirit world (see D&C 137:7–8; see also D&C 50:7 where the Lord tells us that those who are deceived by hypocrites "shall be reclaimed." This doctrine is very comforting.
>
> Next, Jacob gives one of the most eloquent calls to repentance found anywhere.

11 O my brethren, hearken unto my words; arouse the faculties of your souls [*wake up and think!*]; shake yourselves that ye may awake from the slumber of death [*death of your spirituality*]; and loose yourselves from the pains of hell that ye may not become angels to the devil, to be cast into that lake of fire and brimstone which is the second death [*being kept out of God's presence forever*].

12 And now I, Jacob, spake many more things unto the people of Nephi, warning them against fornication and lasciviousness [*all forms of sexual immorality*], and every kind of sin, telling them the awful consequences of them.

13 And a hundredth part of the proceedings of this people, which now began to be numerous, cannot be written upon these plates [*the small plates of Nephi*]; but many of their proceedings are written upon the larger plates [*the large plates of Nephi*], and their wars, and their contentions, and the reigns of their kings.

14 These plates [*this section of the small plates of Nephi*] are called the plates of Jacob, and they were made by the hand of Nephi. And I make an end of speaking these words.

JACOB 4

Engraving plates was a very painstaking task and next, Jacob takes a moment to call our attention to this.

1 NOW behold, it came to pass that I, Jacob, having ministered much unto my people in word (and I cannot write but a little of my words, because of the difficulty of engraving our words upon plates), and we know that the things which we write upon plates must remain [*will be permanent*];

2 But whatsoever things we write upon anything [*such as animal skins or whatever*] save [*except*] it be upon plates [*metal plates*] must [*will*] perish and vanish away; but we can write a few words upon plates, which will give our children, and also our beloved brethren, a small degree of knowledge concerning us, or concerning their fathers—

3 Now in this thing we do rejoice; and we labor diligently to engraven these words upon plates, hoping that our beloved brethren and our children will receive them with thankful hearts, and look upon them that they may learn with joy and not with sorrow, neither with contempt, concerning their first parents [*concerning us, their ancestors*].

Next, Jacob bears testimony to his descendants down through the ages.

4 For, for this intent have we written these things, that they may know that we knew of Christ, and we had a hope [*an assurance; see Alma 58:11*] of his glory many hundred years before his coming; and not only we ourselves had a hope of his glory, but also all the holy prophets which were before us.

Next, Jacob explains the purpose of the law of Moses.

5 Behold, **they believed in Christ** and worshiped the Father in his name, and also we worship the Father in his name. And for this intent we keep **the law of Moses**, it **pointing our souls to him**; and for this cause it [*the proper use of the law of Moses*] is sanctified unto us for righteousness, even as it was accounted unto Abraham in the wilderness to be obedient unto the commands of God in offering up his son Isaac, which is a similitude of God and his Only Begotten Son. [*Abraham was symbolic of the Father, and Isaac was symbolic of the sacrificing of the Son.*]

Next, Jacob teaches us a great lesson in the value of scripture study. Watch as he teaches the results of so doing.

6 Wherefore [*this is why*], **we search the prophets** [*the scriptures*], and **we have many revelations** and the spirit of prophecy; and having all these witnesses **we obtain a hope**, and **our faith becometh unshaken**, insomuch that we truly can command in the name of Jesus and the very trees obey us, or the mountains, or the waves of the sea.

7 Nevertheless, the Lord God showeth us our weakness that we may know that it is by his grace, and his great condescensions [*willingness to work with people who are so much less capable than He*] unto the children of men, that we have power to do these things.

8 Behold, great and marvelous are the works of the Lord. How unsearchable are the depths of the mysteries of him [*it is impossible for us to comprehend God at this point; but we will someday; compare with D&C 88:49*]; and it is impossible that man should find out all his ways. And no man knoweth of his ways save it be revealed unto him; wherefore, brethren, despise not the revelations of God.

9 For behold, by the power of his word man came upon the face of the earth, which earth was created by the power of his word. Wherefore, if God being able to speak and the world was, and to speak and man was created, O then, why not able to command the earth, or the workmanship of his hands [*us*] upon the face of it, according to his will and pleasure?

> Next is another famous quote among members of the Church. It reminds us to avoid telling the Lord how to run things, rather to listen carefully to Him so that we learn.

10 Wherefore, brethren, **seek not to counsel the Lord, but to take counsel from his hand**. For behold, ye yourselves know that he counseleth in wisdom, and in justice, and in great mercy, over all his works.

11 Wherefore, beloved brethren, be reconciled [*become at peace*] unto him [*the Father*] through the atonement of Christ, his Only Begotten Son, and ye may obtain a resurrection [*a celestial resurrection; see the next lines*], according to the power of the resurrection which is in Christ, and be presented as the firstfruits of Christ [*the best results of Christ's Atonement, namely, celestial*] unto God [*the Father*], having faith, and obtained a good hope of glory in him [*Christ*] before he manifesteth himself in the flesh.

> The last phrase of verse 11, above, is very significant doctrinally. It shows us that Christ's Atonement worked even before it was actually performed. Thus, Jacob's people could be forgiven of sins even though the Savior had not yet come to earth to serve His atoning mission.

12 And now, beloved, marvel not that I tell you these things; for why not speak of the atonement of Christ, and attain to a perfect knowledge of him, as to attain to the knowledge of a resurrection and the world to come?

> As mentioned previously, the word "prophesy" has at least two meanings in the context of the scriptures. For one thing, it means to foretell the future. Another definition is "teach." Both definitions seem to apply to verse 13, next.

13 Behold, my brethren, he that prophesieth, let him prophesy to the understanding of men [*so that people can understand what you are saying*]; for the Spirit speaketh the truth and lieth not [*truth is simple*]. Wherefore, it speaketh of things as they really are, and of things as they really will be; wherefore [*this is why*], **these things are manifested unto us plainly**, for the salvation of our souls. But behold, we are not witnesses alone in these things; for God also spake them unto prophets of old.

> You have probably noticed that many of Jacob's teachings are rather well known among Church members. Next, we see a rather famous statement, "Don't look beyond the mark." In other words, don't miss the obvious. Watch as Jacob teaches it.

14 But behold, the Jews were a stiffnecked people; and they despised the words of plainness [*they loved to complicate things*], and killed the prophets, and sought for things that they could not understand [*this is typical of many teachers of philosophy today*]. Wherefore, because of their blindness, which blindness came by **looking beyond the mark**, they must needs fall; for God hath taken away his plainness from them, and delivered unto them [*allowed them to come up with*] many things which they cannot understand, because they desired it. And because they desired it God hath done it, that they may stumble.

> Elder Neal A. Maxwell spoke of "looking beyond the mark" as follows:
>
> "In the Book of Mormon, Jacob speaks of ancient Judah as having rejected the words of its prophets because individuals

living then 'despised the words of plainness' and because they 'sought for things that they could not understand' (Jacob 4:14). Intellectual embroidery seems to have been preferred to the whole clothing of the gospel— the frills to the fabric. In fact, one can even surmise that complexity was preferred over plainness by some because in conceptual complexity there might somehow be escape, or excuse, for noncompliance and for failure. In any event, this incredible blindness which led to the rejection of those truths spoken by prophets and which prevented the recognition of Jesus for who he was, according to Jacob, came 'by looking beyond the mark.' Those who look beyond plainness, beyond the prophets, beyond Christ, and beyond his simple teachings waited in vain then, as they will wait in vain now. For only the gospel of Jesus Christ teaches us of things as they really are and as they really will be. There is more realism in the revelations than in reams of secular research, for secularism is congenitally shortsighted. Without revelation and its absolute anchors, The Church of Jesus Christ of Latter-day Saints would also follow the fads of the day, as some churches have done; but as Samuel Callan warned, the church that weds itself to the culture of the day will 'be a widow within each succeeding age.' This is but one of the marks of the 'true and living' Church: it is spared the fruits of fadism" (Maxwell, "On Being a Light," p. 1).

Pay close attention to what Jacob says in the next four verses. He will set the stage for Jacob, chapter five, in which the allegory of the tame and wild olive trees is given. The main point leading up to chapter five is, "How can the Jews (or any people, for that matter) who reject the Savior so completely, ever come back?" Jacob will pose this question specifically in verse 17.

15 And now I, Jacob, am led on by the Spirit unto prophesying; for I perceive by the workings of the Spirit which is in me, that by the stumbling of the Jews they will reject the stone [*Christ*] upon which they might build and have safe foundation.

16 But behold, according to the scriptures, this stone [*Christ*] shall become the great, and the last, and the only sure foundation, upon which the Jews can build.

17 And now, my beloved, **how is it possible that these** [*the Jews*]**, after having rejected the sure foundation, can ever build upon it** [*can ever return to Christ*], that it may become the head of their corner [*become the "chief cornerstone" of their lives; compare with Ephesians 2:20*]?

In verse 18, next, Jacob confides in us that he is quite nervous about getting his point across in chapter five. There is a message for us in this. If we get too anxious or worried about what the Lord asks us to do, we can ruin our ability to listen to the Holy Ghost and we may not get the job done right. While many of us will get nervous about teaching or speaking, we would do well to have sufficient faith to calm us down so we can be effective instruments in the Lord's hand.

18 Behold, my beloved brethren, I will unfold this mystery [*how the Jews can return to Christ*] unto you; **if I do not, by any means, get shaken from my firmness in the Spirit, and stumble because of my over anxiety for you**.

JACOB 5

Jacob 5 is often referred to as "The Allegory of the Olive Tree." An allegory is a story or parable which symbolizes things in real life. The allegory comes from the writings of Zenos (see verse 1), a prophet whose writings are not found in the Bible.

Since this is such a significant chapter in the Book of Mormon, and since it is referred to so often, we will take the time to give quite a bit of background which will help in understanding the various messages in this allegory. For instance, the "tame" olive tree is extremely significant as are the "branches" which are broken off from it.

Furthermore, as we actually get to studying the chapter itself, we will repeat the chapter twice, in order to point out that scriptural symbolism can be understood in several ways. It is said that scriptural symbolism is infinitely deep. In other words, through symbolism, the Lord can teach us many different things, depending on our need at the moment. It is important that we allow room for different interpretations of such scriptures. Otherwise, we may "miss the mark" ourselves, from one reading to the next.

First, we will get some background about olive trees, which are used extensively in this allegory. We will draw on the Institute of Religion *Book of Mormon Student Manual*, pp. 47–48 for this:

"The use of the olive tree as a symbol for the house of Israel is an excellent example of how God uses symbolism to teach his children gospel laws and principles. For centuries the olive tree has been associated with peace.

War and its grim attendants of destruction—rape of the land, siege, and death—were hardly conducive to the cultivation of olive orchards, that require many years of careful husbandry to bring into full production. When the dove returned to the ark, it carried an olive leaf in its beak, as though to symbolize that God was again at peace with the earth (see Genesis 8:11). The olive branch was used in ancient Greece and Rome to signify peace, and it is still used in that sense in the great seal of the United States where the American eagle is shown grasping an olive branch in its talons. The only true source of peace is Jesus Christ, the Prince of Peace. His peace comes through obedience to the laws and ordinances of the gospel. These laws and ordinances are given to the world through the house of Israel, symbolized by the olive tree. Someone once said that Israel was not chosen to be an uplifted people, but an uplifting people.

"There is further symbolic significance in the cultivation of an olive tree. If the green slip of an olive tree is merely planted and allowed to grow, it develops into the wild olive, a bush that grows without control into a tangle of limbs and branches producing only a small, worthless fruit (Moldenke and Moldenke, *Plants of the Bible*, p. 159). To become the productive "tame" olive tree, the main stem of the wild tree must be cut back completely and a branch from a tame olive tree grafted into the stem of the wild one. With careful pruning and cultivating the tree will begin to produce its first fruit in about seven years, but it will not become fully productive for nearly fifteen years.

"In other words, the olive tree cannot become productive by itself; it requires grafting by the husbandman to bring it into production. Throughout its history Israel has demonstrated the remarkable aptness characterized by the symbol of the olive tree. When they gave themselves to their God for pruning and grafting the Israelites prospered and bore much fruit, but when they turned from Christ, the Master of the vineyard, and sought to become their own source of sustenance, they became wild and unfruitful.

"Two other characteristics of the olive tree further illustrate how it is an appropriate symbol for Israel. First, though requiring nearly fifteen years to come into full production, an olive tree may produce fruit for centuries. Some trees now growing in the Holy Land have been producing fruit abundantly for at least four hundred years. The second amazing quality of the tree is that as it

finally grows old and begins to die, the roots send up a number of new green shoots that, if grafted and pruned, will mature into full-grown olive trees. The root of the tree will also send up shoots after the tree is cut down. Thus, while the tree itself may produce fruit for centuries, the root of the tree may go on producing fruit and new trees for millennia. It is believed that some of the ancient olive trees located in Israel today have come from trees that were ancient during Christ's mortal ministry. How can Israel be compared to an olive tree, which time and again seems to have been cut down and destroyed, yet, each time a new tree springs forth from the roots?

"Zenos was not the only prophet to use the olive tree as a symbol for the chosen people of God. Jeremiah, foreseeing the coming destruction of the Jews by Babylonia, compared the covenant people to a green olive tree consumed by fire (see Jeremiah 11:16). The apostle Paul used a brief allegory almost identical to that of Zenos's to warn the Roman Christians against pride as they compared their favored position to that of the Jews (see Romans 11:16–24). In modern revelation, the Lord uses the parable of a vineyard and olive trees to show his will concerning the redemption of Zion (see D&C 101:43–58).

Having studied the symbolism of the olive tree itself, above, we will now draw upon the same student manual, page 48, to point out several individual elements or parts of the allegory which symbolize specific things.

"An allegory or a parable should not be pushed too far in an attempt to correlate every item precisely with some outside reality. However, certain major elements need to be defined if the allegory itself is to be understood. The following items seem important in Zenos's allegory:

Key Features of Zenos's Allegory

Item	Interpretation
1. The vineyard	1. The world
2. Master of the vineyard	2. Jesus Christ
3. The servant	3. The Lord's prophets
4. Tame olive tree	4. The house of Israel, the Lord's covenant people
5. Wild olive tree	5. Gentiles, or non-Israel (later in the parable, wild branches are apostate Israel)
6. Branches	6. Groups of people
7. The roots of the tame olive-tree	7. The gospel covenant and promises made by God that constantly give life and sustenance to the tree
8. Fruit of the tree	8. The lives or works of men
9. Digging, pruning, fertilizing	9. The Lord's work with his children, which seeks to persuade them to be obedient and produce good fruit
10. Transplanting the various branches	10. The scattering of groups throughout the world, or restoring them to their original position
11. Grafting	11. The process of spiritual rebirth wherein one is joined to the covenant
12. Decaying branches	12. Wickedness and apostasy
13 Casting the branches into the fire	13. The judgment of God

One major message of Jacob 5 is that the Lord keeps working with us individually and as peoples and nations. He has some successes with each of us and some failures. Nevertheless, He keeps working and doing all He can, without violating our agency, to bring us back to the Father, permanently. As we go through the Allegory the first time, we will emphasize this theme. We will occasionally use **bold** to point things out. We will give some possible interpretations. We will note that the Lord of the vineyard makes four specific visits to His vineyard as follows:

1. Verses 4–14
2. Verses 15–28
3. Verses 29–51
4. Verses 52–77

1 BEHOLD, my brethren, do ye not remember to have read the words of the prophet Zenos, which he spake unto the house of Israel [*the Lord's covenant people*], saying:

2 Hearken, O ye house of Israel, and hear the words of me, a prophet of the Lord.

3 For behold, thus saith the Lord, I will liken thee, O **house of Israel, like unto a tame olive-tree** [*the Lord's covenant people*], which a man [*Jesus*] took and nourished in his vineyard [*the world*]; and it grew, and waxed old [*grew old*], and began to decay [*apostasy*].

4 And it came to pass that the master of the vineyard [*Christ*] went forth, and he saw that his olive-tree [*the covenant people*] began to decay [*go into apostasy*]; and he said: I will prune it [*cut off the most wicked; cut out false doctrines, etc.*], and dig about it, and nourish it, that perhaps it may shoot forth young and tender branches, and it perish not.

5 And it came to pass that he pruned it, and digged about it, and nourished it according to his word [*as He had promised to do when He sent us here from premortality*].

6 And it came to pass that after many days it began to put forth somewhat a little, young and tender branches; but behold, the main top [*the majority of His people at that time*] thereof began to perish [*had fallen away from Him*]. [*One possible fulfillment among many of this could be the apostasy of ancient Israel. Another could be Lehi's group over the centuries.*]

7 And it came to pass that the master of the vineyard [*Jesus*] saw it [*saw the apostasy*], and

he said unto his servant: It grieveth me that I should lose this tree; wherefore, go and pluck the branches from a wild olive-tree [*give the gospel to the Gentiles*], and bring them hither unto me; and we will pluck off those main branches which are beginning to wither away [*apostate Israel*], and we will cast them into the fire that they may be burned [*the punishments and destructions of God sent upon the wicked*].

> In verse 8, the Lord seems to be scattering various groups of people and also gathering some of them, as He has done throughout history. Remember, this allegory is quoted to show how the Lord works to save His people.

8 And behold, saith the Lord of the vineyard [*Christ*], I take away many of these young and tender branches, and I will graft [*scatter*] them whithersoever I will; and it mattereth not that if it so be that the root [*covenants*] of this tree [*the tame olive tree; Israel*] will perish, I may preserve [*gather*] the fruit thereof unto myself; wherefore, I will take these young and tender branches, and I will graft them whithersoever I will [*scatter them throughout the world*].

9 Take thou the branches of the wild olive-tree [*Gentiles*], and graft them in, in the stead thereof [*in place of Israel*]; and these which I have plucked off I will cast into the fire and burn them, that they may not cumber [*clutter*] the ground of my vineyard.

10 And it came to pass that the servant of the Lord of the vineyard did according to the word of the Lord of the vineyard, and grafted in the branches of the wild olive tree.

11 And the Lord of the vineyard caused that it should be digged about, and pruned, and nourished, saying unto his servant: It grieveth me that I should lose this tree; wherefore, that perhaps I might preserve the roots thereof that they perish not, that I might preserve them unto myself, I have done this thing.

12 Wherefore, go thy way; watch the tree, and nourish it, according to my words [*the gospel*].

13 And these will I place in the nethermost [*farthest away*] part of my vineyard, whithersoever I will, it mattereth not unto thee [*I know what I'm doing*]; and I do it that I may preserve unto myself the natural branches of the tree; and also, that I may lay up fruit thereof against the season [*I want to bring people home*

to Me forever], unto myself; for it grieveth me that I should lose this tree and the fruit thereof.

14 And it came to pass that the Lord of the vineyard went his way, and hid the natural branches of the tame olive-tree [*the scattering of Israel*] in the nethermost parts of the vineyard, some in one and some in another, according to his will and pleasure.

> You may have been "scattered" by the Lord in order to get you where He needs you to do His work.

15 And it came to pass that a long time passed away, and the Lord of the vineyard said unto his servant: **Come, let us go down into the vineyard**, that we may labor in the vineyard. [*The second visit referred to at the beginning of the chapter. A major message here is that the Lord constantly sends His prophets and missionaries to the world to give them chance after chance to hear and accept the gospel.*]

16 And it came to pass that the Lord of the vineyard [*the Savior is much involved with us here*], and also the servant, went down into the vineyard to labor. And it came to pass that the servant said unto his master: Behold, look here; behold the tree.

17 And it came to pass that the Lord of the vineyard looked and beheld the tree in the which the wild olive branches [*Gentiles*] had been grafted; and it had sprung forth and begun to bear fruit [*many of them accepted and lived the gospel*]. And he beheld that it was good; and **the fruit thereof was like unto the natural fruit** [*there is no difference between Israelite members of the Church and Gentile members of the Church, if they keep their covenants made at baptism, etc.*].

18 And he said unto the servant: Behold, the branches of the wild tree have taken hold of the moisture of the root thereof, that the root [*gospel covenants*] thereof hath brought forth much strength; and because of the much strength of the root thereof the wild branches have brought forth tame fruit [*the Gentiles are solid members of the Church*]. Now, **if we had not grafted in these branches, the tree thereof would have perished.** [*One possible meaning of this bolded phrase is that the European converts strengthened the early Church.*] And now, behold, I shall lay up much fruit, which the tree thereof hath brought forth; and the fruit thereof I shall lay up against the season, unto mine

own self [*I will bring many home to the Father*].

19 And it came to pass that the Lord of the vineyard said unto the servant: Come, let us go to the nethermost part of the vineyard, and behold if [*see if*] the natural branches [*the people of Israel whom we have scattered*] of the tree have not brought forth much fruit also, that I may lay up of the fruit thereof against the season, unto mine own self.

20 And it came to pass that they went forth whither the master had hid the natural branches of the tree, and he said unto the servant: Behold these; and he beheld the first that it had brought forth much fruit; and he beheld also that it was good. And he said unto the servant: Take of the fruit thereof, and lay it up against the season, that I may preserve it unto mine own self; for behold, said he, this long time have I nourished it, and it hath brought forth much fruit. [*Much success, with many souls brought home to heaven.*]

21 And it came to pass that the servant said unto his master: How comest thou hither to plant this tree, or this branch of the tree? For behold, it was the poorest spot in all the land of thy vineyard.

22 And the Lord of the vineyard said unto him: **Counsel me not**; I knew that it was a poor spot of ground; wherefore, I said unto thee, I have nourished it this long time, and thou beholdest that it hath brought forth much fruit.

> Verse 22, above, is a reminder that there are wonderful Saints who live in very poor circumstances.

23 And it came to pass that the Lord of the vineyard said unto his servant: Look hither; behold I have planted **another branch** [*another group*] of the tree also; and thou knowest that this **spot of ground was poorer than the first**. But, behold the tree. I have nourished it this long time, and it hath brought forth much fruit; therefore, gather it, and lay it up against the season, that I may preserve it unto mine own self.

24 And it came to pass that the Lord of the vineyard said again unto his servant: Look hither, and behold **another branch** also, which I have planted; behold that I have nourished it also, and it hath brought forth fruit.

> One important message from these verses is that the Lord has much success with many people, no matter where they are throughout the world. This is very encouraging.

Verse 25, next, seems to fit Lehi's group after they landed in America (see verses 43–45).

25 And he said unto the servant: Look hither and behold the last. Behold, this have I **planted in a good spot of ground**; and I have nourished it this long time, and **only a part of the tree hath brought forth tame fruit, and the other part of the tree hath brought forth wild fruit** [*apostasy*]; behold, I have nourished this tree like unto the others [*they have all been treated fairly and had opportunities to accept the gospel*].

26 And it came to pass that the Lord of the vineyard said unto the servant: Pluck off the branches that have not brought forth good fruit, and cast them into the fire.

27 But behold, the servant said unto him: Let us prune it, and dig about it, and nourish it a little longer, that perhaps it may bring forth good fruit unto thee, that thou canst lay it up against the season.

28 And it came to pass that the Lord of the vineyard and the servant of the Lord of the vineyard did nourish all the fruit of the vineyard.

Next, we have the third visit mentioned at the beginning of the chapter. There seems to be a feeling of urgency because time is running out.

29 And it came to pass that a long time had passed away, and the Lord of the vineyard said unto his servant: **Come, let us go down into the vineyard, that we may labor again in the vineyard.** For behold, **the time draweth near, and the end soon cometh**; wherefore, I must lay up fruit against the season, unto mine own self.

30 And it came to pass that the Lord of the vineyard and the servant went down into the vineyard; and they came to the tree [*Israel*] whose natural branches had been broken off [*scattered*], and the wild branches had been grafted in; and behold **all sorts of fruit did cumber** [*clutter*] **the tree**. [*Perhaps the universal apostasy with all kinds of churches and all kinds of false doctrines, creeds, and practices.*]

31 And it came to pass that the Lord of the vineyard did taste of the fruit [*judged the products of false churches*], every sort according to its number. And the Lord of the vineyard said: Behold, this long time have we nourished this tree [*from the beginning we have worked*

patiently with Israel], and I have laid up unto myself against the season much fruit [*and we have had much success*].

32 But behold, this time [*the great apostasy?*] it hath brought forth much fruit, and there is none of it which is good. And behold, there are all kinds of bad fruit [*there are all kinds of ways to be wicked*]; and it profiteth me nothing, notwithstanding all our labor; and now it grieveth me that I should lose this tree.

33 And the Lord of the vineyard said unto the servant: What shall we do unto the tree, that I may preserve again good fruit thereof unto mine own self?

34 And the servant said unto his master: Behold, because thou didst graft in the branches of the wild olive-tree they have nourished the roots, that they are alive and they have not perished; wherefore thou beholdest that they are yet good.

35 And it came to pass that the Lord of the vineyard said unto his servant: The tree profiteth me nothing, and the roots thereof profit me nothing so long as it shall bring forth evil fruit.

36 Nevertheless, I know that the roots are good, and for mine own purpose I have preserved them; and because of their much strength they have hitherto brought forth, from the wild branches, good fruit.

37 But behold, **the wild branches have grown and have overrun the roots thereof**; and because that the wild branches have overcome the roots **thereof it hath brought forth much evil fruit**; and because that it hath brought forth so much evil fruit thou beholdest that it beginneth to perish; and it will soon become ripened [*in wickedness*], that it may be cast into the fire, except we should do something for it to preserve it.

38 And it came to pass that the Lord of the vineyard said unto his servant: Let us go down into the nethermost parts of the vineyard, and behold if the natural branches have also brought forth evil fruit. [*Let's go see what is happening in the far away parts of the earth.*]

39 And it came to pass that they went down into the nethermost parts of the vineyard [*possibly America among the ancient Lamanites*]. And it came to pass that they beheld that the fruit of the natural branches had become corrupt also; yea, the first and the second and also the last; and they had all become corrupt.

40 And the wild fruit [*apostasy*] of the last had overcome that part of the tree [*the Nephites?*] which brought forth good fruit, even that the branch had withered away and died [*the Church had died out completely*].

41 And it came to pass that the Lord of the vineyard wept, and said unto the servant: What could I have done more for my vineyard?

42 Behold, I knew that all the fruit of the vineyard, save it were these, had become corrupted. And now these which have once brought forth good fruit have also become corrupted; and now all the trees of my vineyard are good for nothing save it be to be hewn down and cast into the fire.

43 And behold this last [*see verse 25*], whose branch hath withered away, I did plant in a good spot of ground [*America*]; yea, even that which was choice unto me above all other parts of the land of my vineyard.

44 And thou beheldest that I also cut down that [*the Jaredites?*] which cumbered [*cluttered with their wickedness*] this spot of ground, that I might plant this tree [*Lehi?*] in the stead thereof.

45 And thou beheldest that a part thereof [*the Nephites?*] brought forth good fruit, and a part thereof [*the Lamanites?*] brought forth wild fruit; and because I plucked not the branches thereof and cast them into the fire, behold, they [*the Lamanites?*] have overcome the good branch [*the Nephites?*] that it hath withered away.

46 And now, behold, notwithstanding [*in spite of*] all the care which we have taken of my vineyard [*the earth*], the trees thereof have become corrupted, that they bring forth no good fruit; and these I had hoped to preserve, to have laid up fruit thereof against the season, unto mine own self. But, behold, they have become like unto the wild olive-tree [*the wicked*], and they are of no worth but to be hewn down and cast into the fire; and it grieveth me that I should lose them.

47 But what could I have done more in my vineyard? Have I slackened mine hand, that I have not nourished it? Nay, I have nourished it, and I have digged about it, and I have pruned it, and I have dunged it; and I have stretched forth mine hand almost all the day long, and the end draweth nigh. And it grieveth me that I should hew down all the trees of my vineyard, and

cast them into the fire that they should be burned. **Who is it that has corrupted my vineyard?**

> The question at the end of verse 47 is an important one. We will **bold** the answer in verse 48.

48 And it came to pass that the servant said unto his master: **Is it not the loftiness** [*pride*] of thy vineyard—**have not the branches thereof overcome the roots** [*people are shallow in living the gospel*] which are good? And because the branches have overcome the roots thereof, behold they grew faster than the strength of the roots, **taking strength unto themselves** [*perhaps meaning not following the Brethren*]. Behold, I say, is not this the cause that the trees of thy vineyard have become corrupted?

49 And it came to pass that the Lord of the vineyard said unto the servant: Let us go to and hew down the trees of the vineyard and cast them into the fire, that they shall not cumber the ground of my vineyard, for I have done all. What could I have done more for my vineyard?

50 But, behold, the servant said unto the Lord of the vineyard: Spare it a little longer.

51 And the Lord said: Yea, I will spare it a little longer, for it grieveth me that I should lose the trees of my vineyard.

> Beginning with verse 52, we see the gathering of Israel in the last days.

52 Wherefore, **let us take of the branches of these which I have planted in the nethermost parts of my vineyard**, and let us **graft them into the tree from whence they came**; and let us pluck from the tree those branches whose fruit is most bitter, and graft in the natural branches of the tree in the stead thereof.

> As stated in verse 52, above, converts do not suddenly become "life long members." It takes time and effort to change old habits and break away from inappropriate traditions. But, with patience, and continued help from the Holy Ghost, it happens over time.

53 And this will I do that the tree may not perish, that, perhaps, I may preserve unto myself the roots thereof for mine own purpose.

54 And, behold, the roots of the natural branches of the tree which I planted whithersoever I would are yet alive; wherefore, that I may preserve them also for mine own purpose, I will take

of the branches of this tree, and I will graft them in unto them. Yea, I will graft in unto them the branches of their mother tree, that I may preserve the roots [*the original covenants, doctrines, etc.*] also unto mine own self, that when they shall be sufficiently strong perhaps they may bring forth good fruit unto me, and I may yet have glory in the fruit of my vineyard.

55 And it came to pass that they took from the natural tree which had become wild, and grafted in unto the natural trees, which also had become wild.

56 And they also took of the natural trees which had become wild, and grafted into their mother tree.

57 And the Lord of the vineyard said unto the servant: **Pluck not the wild branches from the trees, save it be those which are most bitter** [*how the Lord works with each of us*]; and in them ye shall graft according to that which I have said.

58 And we will nourish again the trees of the vineyard, and we will trim up the branches thereof; and we will pluck from the trees those branches which are ripened, that must perish, and cast them into the fire.

59 And this I do that, perhaps, the roots thereof may take strength because of their goodness; and because of the change of the branches, that the good may overcome the evil.

60 And because that I have preserved the natural branches and the roots thereof, and that I have grafted in the natural branches again into their mother tree, and have preserved the roots of their mother tree, that, perhaps, the trees of my vineyard [*all peoples of the earth*] may bring forth again good fruit and that I may have joy again in the fruit of my vineyard, and, perhaps, that I may rejoice exceedingly that I have preserved the roots and the branches of the first fruit—

> Verse 61 seems to denote the final gathering in the last days. The Lord calls many servants to help Him. We are in that number. Note that He is working closely with us.

61 Wherefore, go to, and **call servants**, that **we** may labor diligently **with our might** in the vineyard, that **we** may prepare the way, that **I** may bring forth again the natural fruit [*covenant people*], which natural fruit [*personal righteousness*] is good and the most precious above all other fruit [*all other lifestyles*].

JACOB 5

62 Wherefore, let us go to and labor with our might **this last time** [*our day, the dispensation of the fulness of times*], for behold the end [*of the world*] draweth nigh, and **this is for the last time that I shall prune my vineyard.**

63 Graft in the branches; begin at the last [*the Gentiles*] that they may be first, and that the first [*the Jews*] may be last, and dig about the trees, both old and young, the first and the last; and the last and the first, that all may be nourished once again for the last time.

64 Wherefore, dig about them, and prune them, and dung them once more, for the last time, for the end draweth nigh. And if it be so that these last grafts shall grow, and bring forth the natural fruit, then shall ye prepare the way for them, that they may grow.

> You've seen this next message several times in the allegory. It teaches that we must be patient with new converts, as well as lifelong members, and be very careful not to criticize them right out of the Church. This is how the Holy Ghost works with each of us.

65 And as they begin to grow ye shall **clear away** the branches which bring forth **bitter fruit, according to the strength of the good** and the size thereof; and **ye shall not clear away the bad thereof all at once**, lest the roots thereof should be too strong for the graft, and the graft thereof shall perish, and I lose the trees of my vineyard.

66 For it grieveth me that I should lose the trees of my vineyard; wherefore **ye shall clear away the bad according as the good shall grow,** that the root and the top may be equal in strength, **until the good shall overcome the bad,** and the bad be hewn down and cast into the fire, that they cumber not the ground of my vineyard; and thus will I sweep away the bad out of my vineyard.

67 And the branches of the natural tree will I graft in again into the natural tree;

68 And the branches of the natural tree will I graft into the natural branches of the tree; and thus will I bring them together again, that they shall bring forth the natural fruit, and they shall be one.

69 And the bad shall be cast away, yea, even out of all the land of my vineyard; for behold, **only this once will I prune my vineyard.** [*In other words, this*

is the last time the gospel will go forth to all the world, then the Second Coming will occur.]

70 And it came to pass that the Lord of the vineyard sent his servant; and the servant went and did as the Lord had commanded him, and brought other servants; and **they were few** [*relatively few members of the Church in the last days to carry the gospel to all the world*].

71 And the Lord of the vineyard said unto them: Go to, and labor in the vineyard, with your might. For behold, **this is the last time** that I shall nourish my vineyard; for **the end is nigh at hand**, and the season speedily cometh; and if ye labor with your might **with me** ye shall have joy in the fruit which I shall lay up unto myself against the time which will soon come.

72 And it came to pass that the servants did go and labor with their mights; and the Lord of the vineyard labored also with them; and they did obey the commandments of the Lord of the vineyard in all things.

73 And there **began to be the natural fruit again in the vineyard** [*the Church began to grow*]; and the natural branches began to grow and **thrive** exceedingly [*a description of the growth of the Church in the last days*]; and the wild branches [*false doctrines and wicked behaviors?*] began to be plucked off and to be cast away; and they did keep the root and the top thereof equal, according to the strength thereof.

74 And thus they labored, with all diligence, according to the commandments of the Lord of the vineyard, even until the bad had been cast away out of the vineyard, and the Lord had preserved unto himself that the trees had become again the natural fruit; and they became like unto one body; and the fruits were equal; and the Lord of the vineyard had preserved unto himself the natural fruit, which was most precious unto him from the beginning.

75 And it came to pass that when the Lord of the vineyard saw that his fruit was good, and that his vineyard [*the Church?*] was no more corrupt, he called up his servants, and said unto them: Behold, for this last time have we nourished my vineyard; and thou beholdest that I have done according to my will; and I have preserved the natural fruit, that it is good, even like as it was in the beginning. And **blessed art**

thou [*faithful members in the last days*]; for because ye have been diligent in laboring with me in my vineyard, and **have kept my commandments**, and have brought unto me again the natural fruit, that my vineyard is no more corrupted, and the bad is cast away, behold **ye shall have joy with me** because of the fruit of my vineyard.

> Verse 76 depicts the Millennium, followed by the "little season" at the end of the Millennium, depicted by verse 77.

76 For behold, for a long time will I lay up of the fruit of my vineyard unto mine own self against the season, which speedily cometh; and for the last time have I nourished my vineyard, and pruned it, and dug about it, and dunged it; wherefore **I will lay up unto mine own self of the fruit, for a long time** [*the Millennium*], according to that which I have spoken.

77 And when the time cometh that evil fruit shall again come into my vineyard [*the little season at the end of the thousand years*], then will I cause the good and the bad to be gathered; and the good will I preserve unto myself, and the bad will I cast away into its own place [*the final judgment*]. And then cometh the season and the end; and my vineyard will I cause to be burned with fire [*a quick review of what was said above*].

It is important to realize that parables or allegories with so much symbolism as Jacob 5 has, can be interpreted in many different ways. Because of this symbolism, the Holy Ghost can show you a different message each time you read it. For instance, suppose that you were a parent who has done all you can to raise obedient children, yet some have gone astray. You are reading your Book of Mormon and have come to Jacob 5. Your heart is heavy with worry and concern, even about your own status with the Lord. And as you read, the Holy Ghost comforts you by pointing out that the Lord knows how you feel and will continue to help you.

Without any commentary, we will simply **bold** some things that the Holy Ghost might point out to you about our Heavenly Father, a grieving parent.

Jacob 5:1–77
(Repeated for teaching purposes)

1 Behold, my brethren, do ye not remember to have read the words of the prophet Zenos, which he spake unto the house of Israel, saying:

2 Hearken, O ye house of Israel,

and hear the words of me, a prophet of the Lord.

3 For behold, thus saith the Lord, I will liken thee, O house of Israel, like unto a tame olive-tree, which a man took and nourished in his vineyard; and it grew, and waxed old, and began to decay.

4 And it came to pass that the master of the vineyard went forth, and he saw that his olive-tree began to decay; and he said: I will prune it, and dig about it, and nourish it, that perhaps it may shoot forth young and tender branches, and it perish not.

5 And it came to pass that he pruned it, and digged about it, and nourished it according to his word.

6 And it came to pass that after many days it began to put forth somewhat a little, young and tender branches; but behold, the main top thereof began to perish.

7 And it came to pass that the master of the vineyard saw it, and he said unto his servant: **It grieveth me that I should lose this tree**; wherefore, go and pluck the branches from a wild olive-tree, and bring them hither unto me; and we will pluck off those main branches which are beginning to wither away, and we will cast them into the fire that they may be burned.

8 And behold, saith the Lord of the vineyard, I take away many of these young and tender branches, and I will graft them whithersoever I will; and it mattereth not that if it so be that the root of this tree will perish, I may preserve the fruit thereof unto myself; wherefore, I will take these young and tender branches, and I will graft them whithersoever I will.

9 Take thou the branches of the wild olive-tree, and graft them in, in the stead thereof; and these which I have plucked off I will cast into the fire and burn them, that they may not cumber the ground of my vineyard.

10 And it came to pass that the servant of the Lord of the vineyard did according to the word of the Lord of the vineyard, and grafted in the branches of the wild olive-tree.

11 And the Lord of the vineyard caused that it should be digged about, and pruned, and nourished, saying unto his servant: **It grieveth me that I should lose this tree**; wherefore, that perhaps I might preserve the roots thereof that they perish not, that I might preserve them unto

myself, I have done this thing.

12 Wherefore, go thy way; watch the tree, and nourish it, according to my words.

13 And these will I place in the nethermost part of my vineyard, whithersoever I will, it mattereth not unto thee; and I do it that I may preserve unto myself the natural branches of the tree; and also, that I may lay up fruit thereof against the season, unto myself; for **it grieveth me that I should lose this tree and the fruit thereof.**

14 And it came to pass that the Lord of the vineyard went his way, and hid the natural branches of the tame olive-tree in the nethermost parts of the vineyard, some in one and some in another, according to his will and pleasure.

15 And it came to pass that a long time passed away, and the Lord of the vineyard said unto his servant: Come, let us go down into the vineyard, that we may labor in the vineyard.

16 And it came to pass that the Lord of the vineyard, and also the servant, went down into the vineyard to labor. And it came to pass that the servant said unto his master: Behold, look here; behold the tree.

17 And it came to pass that the Lord of the vineyard looked and beheld the tree in the which the wild olive branches had been grafted; and it had sprung forth and begun to bear fruit. And he beheld that it was good; and the fruit thereof was like unto the natural fruit.

18 And he said unto the servant: Behold, the branches of the wild tree have taken hold of the moisture of the root thereof, that the root thereof hath brought forth much strength; and because of the much strength of the root thereof the wild branches have brought forth tame fruit. Now, if we had not grafted in these branches, the tree thereof would have perished. And now, behold, I shall lay up much fruit, which the tree thereof hath brought forth; and the fruit thereof I shall lay up against the season, unto mine own self.

19 And it came to pass that the Lord of the vineyard said unto the servant: Come, let us go to the nethermost part of the vineyard, and behold if the natural branches of the tree have not brought forth much fruit also, that I may lay up of the fruit thereof against the season, unto mine own self.

20 And it came to pass that they

went forth whither the master had hid the natural branches of the tree, and he said unto the servant: Behold these; and he beheld the first that it had brought forth much fruit; and he beheld also that it was good. And he said unto the servant: Take of the fruit thereof, and lay it up against the season, that I may preserve it unto mine own self; for behold, said he, this long time have I nourished it, and it hath brought forth much fruit.

21 And it came to pass that the servant said unto his master: How comest thou hither to plant this tree, or this branch of the tree? For behold, it was the poorest spot in all the land of thy vineyard.

22 And the Lord of the vineyard said unto him: Counsel me not; I knew that it was a poor spot of ground; wherefore, I said unto thee, I have nourished it this long time, and thou beholdest that it hath brought forth much fruit.

23 And it came to pass that the Lord of the vineyard said unto his servant: Look hither; behold I have planted another branch of the tree also; and thou knowest that this spot of ground was poorer than the first. But, behold the tree. I have nourished it this long time, and it hath brought forth much fruit; therefore, gather it, and lay it up against the season, that I may preserve it unto mine own self.

24 And it came to pass that the Lord of the vineyard said again unto his servant: Look hither, and behold another branch also, which I have planted; behold that I have nourished it also, and it hath brought forth fruit.

25 And he said unto the servant: Look hither and behold the last. Behold, this have I planted in a good spot of ground; and I have nourished it this long time, and only a part of the tree hath brought forth tame fruit, and the other part of the tree hath brought forth wild fruit; behold, I have nourished this tree like unto the others.

26 And it came to pass that the Lord of the vineyard said unto the servant: Pluck off the branches that have not brought forth good fruit, and cast them into the fire.

27 But behold, the servant said unto him: Let us prune it, and dig about it, and nourish it a little longer, that perhaps it may bring forth good fruit unto thee, that thou canst lay it up against the season.

28 And it came to pass that the Lord of the vineyard and the servant of the Lord of the vineyard did nourish all the fruit of the vineyard.

29 And it came to pass that a long time had passed away, and the Lord of the vineyard said unto his servant: Come, let us go down into the vineyard, that we may labor again in the vineyard. For behold, the time draweth near, and the end soon cometh; wherefore, I must lay up fruit against the season, unto mine own self.

30 And it came to pass that the Lord of the vineyard and the servant went down into the vineyard; and they came to the tree whose natural branches had been broken off, and the wild branches had been grafted in; and behold all sorts of fruit did cumber the tree.

31 And it came to pass that the Lord of the vineyard did taste of the fruit, every sort according to its number. And the Lord of the vineyard said: Behold, this long time have we nourished this tree, and I have laid up unto myself against the season much fruit.

32 But behold, this time it hath brought forth much fruit, and there is none of it which is good. And behold, there are all kinds of bad fruit; and it profiteth me nothing, notwithstanding all our labor; and now **it grieveth me that I should lose this tree.**

33 And the Lord of the vineyard said unto the servant: What shall we do unto the tree, that I may preserve again good fruit thereof unto mine own self?

34 And the servant said unto his master: Behold, because thou didst graft in the branches of the wild olive-tree they have nourished the roots, that they are alive and they have not perished; wherefore thou beholdest that they are yet good.

35 And it came to pass that the Lord of the vineyard said unto his servant: The tree profiteth me nothing, and the roots thereof profit me nothing so long as it shall bring forth evil fruit.

36 Nevertheless, I know that the roots are good, and for mine own purpose I have preserved them; and because of their much strength they have hitherto brought forth, from the wild branches, good fruit.

37 But behold, the wild branches have grown and have overrun the roots thereof; and because that the wild branches have overcome the roots thereof it

hath brought forth much evil fruit; and because that it hath brought forth so much evil fruit thou beholdest that it beginneth to perish; and it will soon become ripened, that it may be cast into the fire, except we should do something for it to preserve it.

38 And it came to pass that the Lord of the vineyard said unto his servant: Let us go down into the nethermost parts of the vineyard, and behold if the natural branches have also brought forth evil fruit.

39 And it came to pass that they went down into the nethermost parts of the vineyard. And it came to pass that they beheld that the fruit of the natural branches had become corrupt also; yea, the first and the second and also the last; and they had all become corrupt.

40 And the wild fruit of the last had overcome that part of the tree which brought forth good fruit, even that the branch had withered away and died.

41 And it came to pass that **the Lord of the vineyard wept**, and said unto the servant: What could I have done more for my vineyard?

42 Behold, I knew that all the fruit of the vineyard, save it were these, had become corrupted. And now these which have once brought forth good fruit have also become corrupted; and now all the trees of my vineyard are good for nothing save it be to be hewn down and cast into the fire.

43 And behold this last, whose branch hath withered away, I did plant in a good spot of ground; yea, even that which was choice unto me above all other parts of the land of my vineyard.

44 And thou beheldest that I also cut down that which cumbered this spot of ground, that I might plant this tree in the stead thereof.

45 And thou beheldest that a part thereof brought forth good fruit, and a part thereof brought forth wild fruit; and because I plucked not the branches thereof and cast them into the fire, behold, they have overcome the good branch that it hath withered away.

46 And now, behold, notwithstanding all the care which we have taken of my vineyard, the trees thereof have become corrupted, that they bring forth no good fruit; and **these I had hoped to preserve**, to have laid up fruit thereof against the

season, unto mine own self. But, behold, they have become like unto the wild olive-tree, and they are of no worth but to be hewn down and cast into the fire; and **it grieveth me that I should lose them.**

47 But what could I have done more in my vineyard? Have I slackened mine hand, that I have not nourished it? Nay, **I have nourished it, and I have digged about it, and I have pruned it, and I have dunged it; and I have stretched forth mine hand almost all the day long**, and the end draweth nigh. And it grieveth me that I should hew down all the trees of my vineyard, and cast them into the fire that they should be burned. Who is it that has corrupted my vineyard?

48 And it came to pass that the servant said unto his master: Is it not the loftiness of thy vineyard—have not the branches thereof overcome the roots which are good? And because the branches have overcome the roots thereof, behold they grew faster than the strength of the roots, taking strength unto themselves. Behold, I say, is not this the cause that the trees of thy vineyard have become corrupted?

49 And it came to pass that the Lord of the vineyard said unto the servant: Let us go to and hew down the trees of the vineyard and cast them into the fire, that they shall not cumber the ground of my vineyard, for I have done all. What could I have done more for my vineyard?

50 But, behold, the servant said unto the Lord of the vineyard: Spare it a little longer.

51 And the Lord said: Yea, I will spare it a little longer, for **it grieveth me that I should lose the trees of my vineyard**.

52 Wherefore, let us take of the branches of these which I have planted in the nethermost parts of my vineyard, and let us graft them into the tree from whence they came; and let us pluck from the tree those branches whose fruit is most bitter, and graft in the natural branches of the tree in the stead thereof.

53 And this will I do that the tree may not perish, that, perhaps, I may preserve unto myself the roots thereof for mine own purpose.

54 And, behold, the roots of the natural branches of the tree which I planted whithersoever I would are yet alive; wherefore, that I may preserve them also for

mine own purpose, I will take of the branches of this tree, and I will graft them in unto them. Yea, I will graft in unto them the branches of their mother tree, that I may preserve the roots also unto mine own self, that when they shall be sufficiently strong perhaps they may bring forth good fruit unto me, and I may yet have glory in the fruit of my vineyard.

55 And it came to pass that they took from the natural tree which had become wild, and grafted in unto the natural trees, which also had become wild.

56 And they also took of the natural trees which had become wild, and grafted into their mother tree.

57 And the Lord of the vineyard said unto the servant: Pluck not the wild branches from the trees, save it be those which are most bitter; and in them ye shall graft according to that which I have said.

58 And we will nourish again the trees of the vineyard, and we will trim up the branches thereof; and we will pluck from the trees those branches which are ripened, that must perish, and cast them into the fire.

59 And this I do that, perhaps, the roots thereof may take strength because of their goodness; and because of the change of the branches, that the good may overcome the evil.

60 And because that I have preserved the natural branches and the roots thereof, and that I have grafted in the natural branches again into their mother tree, and have preserved the roots of their mother tree, that, perhaps, the trees of my vineyard may bring forth again good fruit; and that I may have joy again in the fruit of my vineyard, and, perhaps, that I may rejoice exceedingly that I have preserved the roots and the branches of the first fruit—

61 Wherefore, go to, and call servants, that we may labor diligently with our might in the vineyard, that we may prepare the way, that I may bring forth again the natural fruit, which natural fruit is good and the most precious above all other fruit.

62 Wherefore, let us go to and labor with our might this last time, for behold the end draweth nigh, and this is for the last time that I shall prune my vineyard.

63 Graft in the branches; begin at the last that they may be first, and that the first may be last, and

dig about the trees, both old and young, the first and the last; and the last and the first, that all may be nourished once again for the last time.

64 Wherefore, dig about them, and prune them, and dung them once more, for the last time, for the end draweth nigh. And if it be so that these last grafts shall grow, and bring forth the natural fruit, then shall ye prepare the way for them, that they may grow.

65 And as they begin to grow ye shall clear away the branches which bring forth bitter fruit, according to the strength of the good and the size thereof; and ye shall not clear away the bad thereof all at once, lest the roots thereof should be too strong for the graft, and the graft thereof shall perish, and I lose the trees of my vineyard.

66 For **it grieveth me that I should lose the trees of my vineyard**; wherefore ye shall clear away the bad according as the good shall grow, that the root and the top may be equal in strength, until the good shall overcome the bad, and the bad be hewn down and cast into the fire, that they cumber not the ground of my vineyard; and thus will I sweep away the bad out of my vineyard.

67 And the branches of the natural tree will I graft in again into the natural tree;

68 And the branches of the natural tree will I graft into the natural branches of the tree; and thus will I bring them together again, that they shall bring forth the natural fruit, and they shall be one.

69 And the bad shall be cast away, yea, even out of all the land of my vineyard; for behold, only this once will I prune my vineyard.

70 And it came to pass that the Lord of the vineyard sent his servant; and the servant went and did as the Lord had commanded him, and brought other servants; and they were few.

71 And the Lord of the vineyard said unto them: Go to, and labor in the vineyard, with your might. For behold, this is the last time that I shall nourish my vineyard; for the end is nigh at hand, and the season speedily cometh; and if ye labor with your might with me ye shall have joy in the fruit which I shall lay up unto myself against the time which will soon come.

72 And it came to pass that the

servants did go and labor with their mights; and the Lord of the vineyard labored also with them; and they did obey the commandments of the Lord of the vineyard in all things.

73 And there began to be the natural fruit again in the vineyard; and the natural branches began to grow and thrive exceedingly; and the wild branches began to be plucked off and to be cast away; and they did keep the root and the top thereof equal, according to the strength thereof.

74 And thus they labored, with all diligence, according to the commandments of the Lord of the vineyard, even until the bad had been cast away out of the vineyard, and the Lord had preserved unto himself that the trees had become again the natural fruit; and they became like unto one body; and the fruits were equal; and the Lord of the vineyard had preserved unto himself the natural fruit, which was most precious unto him from the beginning.

75 And it came to pass that when the Lord of the vineyard saw that his fruit was good, and that his vineyard was no more corrupt, he called up his servants, and said unto them: Behold, for this last time have we nourished my vineyard; and thou beholdest that I have done according to my will; and I have preserved the natural fruit, that it is good, even like as it was in the beginning. And blessed art thou; for because ye have been diligent in laboring with me in my vineyard, and have kept my commandments, and have brought unto me again the natural fruit, that my vineyard is no more corrupted, and the bad is cast away, behold ye shall have joy with me because of the fruit of my vineyard.

76 For behold, for a long time will I lay up of the fruit of my vineyard unto mine own self against the season, which speedily cometh; and for the last time have I nourished my vineyard, and pruned it, and dug about it, and dunged it; wherefore I will lay up unto mine own self of the fruit, for a long time, according to that which I have spoken.

77 And when the time cometh that evil fruit shall again come into my vineyard, then will I cause the good and the bad to be gathered; and the good will I preserve unto myself, and the bad will I cast away into its own place. And then cometh the season and the end; and my vineyard will I cause to be burned with fire.

There is no doubt that the Lord understands the feelings of a grieving parent.

JACOB 6

Jacob now explains some basic teachings of the Allegory of Zenos in chapter 5.

1 AND now, behold, my brethren, as I said unto you that I would prophesy, behold, this is my prophecy—that the things which this prophet Zenos spake, concerning the house of Israel, in the which he likened them unto a tame olive-tree, must surely come to pass.

2 And the day that he [*the Lord*] shall set his hand again the second time to recover his people, is the day, yea, even the last time [*the Restoration through the Prophet Joseph Smith*], that the servants of the Lord shall go forth in his power [*the final missionary work to gather the righteous before the Second Coming*], to nourish and prune his vineyard; and after that the end soon cometh.

3 And how blessed are they [*missionaries and faithful members*] who have labored diligently in his vineyard [*throughout the earth*]; and how cursed are they who shall be cast out into their own place [*the wicked; see D&C 88:114*]! And the world shall be burned with fire [*at the Second Coming*].

4 And how merciful is our God unto us, for he remembereth [*keeps His promises to*] the house of Israel, both roots and branches [*no matter where they have been scattered to throughout the world*]; and he stretches forth his hands unto them all the day long [*invites them to repent and return to Him*]; and they are a stiffnecked [*prideful*] and a gainsaying [*always rebelling and denying God*] people; but as many as will not harden their hearts shall be saved in the kingdom of God [*a simple fact*].

5 Wherefore, my beloved brethren, I beseech [*beg*] of you in words of soberness that ye would repent, and come with full purpose of heart, and cleave unto God as he cleaveth unto you. And while his arm of mercy is extended towards you in the light of the day [*while you have a chance to respond*], harden not your hearts.

6 Yea, today, if ye will hear his voice, harden not your hearts; for why will ye die [*spiritually*]?

7 For behold, after ye have been nourished by the good word of

God all the day long, will ye bring forth evil fruit, that ye must be hewn down and cast into the fire [*do you want to be destroyed*]?

8 Behold, will ye reject these words? Will ye reject the words of the prophets; and will ye reject all the words which have been spoken concerning Christ, after so many have spoken concerning him; and deny the good word of Christ, and the power of God, and the gift of the Holy Ghost, and quench the Holy Spirit, and make a mock of the great plan of redemption, which hath been laid for you?

9 Know ye not that if ye will do these things, that the power of the redemption and the resurrection, which is in Christ, will bring you to stand with shame and awful guilt before the bar [*the judgment bar*] of God?

10 And according to the power of justice [*the law of justice*], for justice cannot be denied [*cannot be robbed; see Alma 42:25*], ye must go away into that lake of fire and brimstone, whose flames are unquenchable, and whose smoke ascendeth up forever and ever, which lake of fire and brimstone is endless torment.

11 O then, my beloved brethren, **repent ye**, and enter in at the strait [*narrow*] gate [*repentance and baptism*], and continue in the way which is narrow, until ye shall obtain eternal life [*exaltation*].

12 O be wise; what can I say more?

13 Finally, I bid you farewell, until I shall meet you before the pleasing bar of God, which bar striketh the wicked with awful dread and fear. Amen.

JACOB 7

Sherem is the first of three antichrists whom we meet in the Book of Mormon. The other two are Nehor (Alma 1) and Korihor (Alma 30). Sherem is typical of many who oppose the Church today. You will see that he is well educated as far as the world is concerned and full of self importance. By studying his encounter with Jacob, we can learn several things to watch out for in such enemies of righteousness. We will use **bold** to point things out.

1 AND now it came to pass after some years had passed away, there came a man among the people of Nephi, whose name was Sherem.

2 And it came to pass that he

began to preach among the people, and to declare unto them that there should be no Christ. And he preached **many things which were flattering** unto the people [*things they wanted to hear*]; and this he did that he might overthrow the doctrine of Christ. [*He did this intentionally.*]

3 And he labored diligently that he might lead away the hearts of the people, insomuch that he did lead away many hearts; and he knowing that I, Jacob, had faith in Christ who should come, **he sought much opportunity that he might come unto me.**

> You may have noticed that many apostates today and others who are angry at the Church seek opportunities to debate the Brethren in public. Satan's methodology does not seem to change.

4 And he was learned, that he had a perfect knowledge of the language of the people [*he was very well educated and very skilled in public speaking*]; wherefore, he could use much flattery, and much power of speech, according to the power of the devil. [*The devil can inspire people and help them be skillful in leading people astray.*]

> Next, we see that Sherem was not very wise in choosing Jacob as his next victim.

5 And he had hope to shake me from the faith, notwithstanding the many revelations and the many things which I had seen concerning these things; for I truly had seen angels, and they had ministered unto me. And also, I had heard the voice of the Lord speaking unto me in very word, from time to time; wherefore, I could not be shaken.

> Perhaps you can picture Sherem swaggering up to Jacob and addressing him with a touch of sarcasm in his voice. He even calls him "Brother." Note the skill with which he attacks Jacob and the gospel with phrases designed to cast doubt.

6 And it came to pass that he came unto me, and on this wise did he speak unto me, saying: **Brother Jacob, I have sought much opportunity that I might speak unto you**; for I have heard and also know that thou goest about much, preaching **that which ye call** the gospel, or the doctrine of Christ.

7 And **ye have led away much of this people** that **they pervert the right way of God**, and keep not the law of Moses which is the right way; and convert the law of Moses into the worship of a being **which ye say** shall come many hundred years hence. And now behold, I, Sherem, declare

unto you that this is blasphemy; for **no man knoweth of such things; for he cannot tell of things to come.** [*No one can know the future. This statement will come back to cause trouble for Sherem in verse 9; also, among other things, he is denying the existence of true prophets.*] And after this manner did Sherem contend against me.

8 But behold, the Lord God poured in his Spirit into my soul, insomuch that I did confound [*stop, confuse*] him in all his words.

9 And I said unto him: Deniest thou the Christ who shall come? And he said: If there should be a Christ, I would not deny him; but **I know that there is no Christ, neither has been, nor ever will be.**

> In verse 7, above, Sherem claimed that no one can know the future. In verse 9, he contradicts himself. He says, in effect, that he knows the future and that there never will be a Christ.

10 And I said unto him: Believest thou the scriptures [*Old Testament*]? And he said, Yea.

> Jacob's approach to Sherem in verse 11 is rather gentle. He is trying to give him an "out" for what he has previously claimed. This is a kind approach because, if taken advantage of by Sherem, his ego is not so much at stake. Rather, he simply needs to be taught the truth. He will not take advantage of this opportunity to salvage his ego.
>
> Verse 11 is also a powerful reminder to us that the Old Testament, in its original, pure form, clearly taught about Christ.

11 And I said unto him: **Then ye do not understand them**; for they truly testify of Christ. Behold, I say unto you that **none of the prophets have written, nor prophesied, save they have spoken concerning this Christ.**

> Next, Jacob will bear pure, simple testimony to Sherem. This is a reminder to us of the power of this approach to teaching and spreading the gospel.

12 And this is not all—it has been made manifest unto me, for I have heard and seen; and it also has been made manifest unto me by the power of the Holy Ghost; wherefore, I know if there should be no atonement made all mankind must be lost [*compare with 2 Nephi 9:7–9*].

> Next, we hear the sarcasm in Sherem's voice as he rebuts Jacob's humble testimony and demands a sign.

13 And it came to pass that he said unto me: Show me a sign by this power of the Holy Ghost, **in the which ye know so much**.

14 And I said unto him: What am I that I should tempt God to show unto thee a sign in the thing which thou knowest to be true? [*Jacob knows by the power of the Spirit that Sherem is lying. Sherem knows Jacob is telling the truth.*] Yet thou wilt deny it, because thou art of the devil [*the devil is a liar*]. Nevertheless, not my will be done; but if God shall smite thee [*this is not the kind of sign Sherem had in mind*], let that be a sign unto thee that he has power, both in heaven and in earth; and also, that Christ shall come. And thy will, O Lord, be done, and not mine.

15 And it came to pass that when I, Jacob, had spoken these words, the power of the Lord came upon him, insomuch that he fell to the earth. And it came to pass that he was nourished for the space of many days.

> The fact that Sherem did not die immediately is a reminder of the kindness of the Lord even to the vilest of sinners. Despite Sherem's sarcastic attitude and damaging false teachings, he is an individual of infinite worth. The Lord shows tender mercy in giving him some time to think it over before he dies. It will work, according to verses 17–19.

16 And it came to pass that he said unto the people: Gather together on the morrow, for I shall die; wherefore, I desire to speak unto the people before I shall die.

17 And it came to pass that on the morrow the multitude were gathered together; and **he spake plainly unto them and denied the things which he had taught them, and confessed the Christ, and the power of the Holy Ghost, and the ministering of angels.**

18 And he spake plainly unto them, that he had been deceived by the power of the devil. And he spake of hell, and of eternity, and of eternal punishment. [*Sherem has a very good "gospel doctrinal vocabulary," probably indicating that he knew the gospel well before he apostatized.*]

19 And he said: I fear lest I have committed the unpardonable sin, for I have lied unto God; for I denied the Christ, and said that I believed the scriptures; and they truly testify of him. And because I have thus lied unto God I greatly fear lest my case shall be awful; but I confess unto God.

> Many students of the scriptures wonder whether or not Sherem would qualify to be a son of perdition. While final judgment is up to the Savior (John 5:22), we can note that one who becomes a son of perdition would think and act completely like the devil (see D&C 76:31–35) whereas Sherem has true remorse.

20 And it came to pass that when he had said these words he could say no more, and he gave up the ghost [*he died*].

21 And when the multitude had witnessed that he spake these things as he was about to give up the ghost, they were astonished exceedingly; insomuch that the power of God came down upon them, and they were overcome that they fell to the earth. [*Many were reconverted.*]

22 Now, this thing was pleasing unto me, Jacob, for I had requested it [*the reconversion of those who had followed Sherem*] of my Father who was in heaven; for he had heard my cry and answered my prayer.

23 And it came to pass that peace and the love of God was restored again among the people; and they searched the scriptures [*key to avoiding personal apostasy*], and hearkened no more to the words of this wicked man.

> Next, Jacob will lament the fact that they were unsuccessful in reclaiming the Lamanites of his day.

24 And it came to pass that many means were devised to reclaim and restore the Lamanites to the knowledge of the truth; but it all was vain, for they delighted in wars and bloodshed, and they had an eternal hatred against us, their brethren. And they sought by the power of their arms [*weapons*] to destroy us continually.

> Some people are very much opposed to building up weapons of defense. Here, the Book of Mormon applies to us in our day by advising us on this matter.

25 Wherefore [*this is why*], **the people of Nephi did fortify against them with their arms, and with all their might**, trusting in the God and rock of their salvation; wherefore, they became as yet, conquerors of their enemies.

26 And it came to pass that I, Jacob, began to be old; and the record of this people being kept on the other plates of Nephi [*the large plates*], wherefore, I conclude this record [*Jacob's portion of the small plates of Nephi*], declaring that I have written according to the best of

my knowledge, by saying that the time passed away with us, and also our lives passed away like as it were unto us a dream, we being a lonesome and a solemn people, wanderers, cast out from Jerusalem, born in tribulation, in a wilderness, and hated of our brethren, which caused wars and contentions; wherefore, we did mourn out our days.

> Next, Jacob will turn over the responsibility for keeping the plates and engraving upon them to his son, Enos.

27 And I, Jacob, saw that I must soon go down to my grave; wherefore, I said unto my son Enos: Take these plates. And I told him the things which my brother Nephi had commanded me, and he promised obedience unto the commands. And I make an end of my writing upon these plates [*the small plates*], which writing has been small; and to the reader I bid farewell, hoping that many of my brethren may read my words. Brethren, adieu.

> "Adieu," which means "Goodbye," may sound a bit strange in the Book of Mormon. Some critics of the Book of Mormon point out this use of a French word and use it against Joseph Smith. What they don't realize is that "adieu" was commonly used in Joseph Smith's day to bid farewell. In fact, American English is loaded with words adapted over time from several different European languages.

THE BOOK OF ENOS

Enos could well be referred to as "Enos Jacobson" because he is the son of Jacob. In this brief but powerful chapter, we will be taught much about many things, including having our faith strengthened for a specific occasion.

First, we will be reminded that the teachings of righteous parents often come to bless their children long after the teachings were given.

1 BEHOLD, it came to pass that I, Enos, knowing my father that he was a just man—for he taught me in his language, and also in the nurture and admonition of the Lord—and blessed be the name of my God for it—

2 And I will tell you of the wrestle which I had before God, before I received a remission of my sins [*a reminder that receiving forgiveness of our sins requires enduring effort on our part*].

3 Behold, I went to hunt beasts in the forests; and the words which I had often heard my father speak concerning eternal life, and the joy of the saints, sunk deep into my heart.

It appears that Enos was quite concerned about his standing with God. Thus, his thoughts of an adventurous day hunting turned into a deep yearning to be forgiven of sins and be clean before his Maker. Enos teaches us in verse 4 that these things often require persistence and patience.

4 And my soul hungered [*to be pure and clean*]; and I kneeled down before my Maker, and I cried unto him in mighty prayer and supplication for mine own soul; and **all the day long** did I cry unto him; yea, and **when the night came I did still raise my voice high that it reached the heavens**.

5 And there came a voice unto me, saying: Enos, **thy sins are forgiven thee**, and thou shalt be blessed.

6 And I, Enos, knew that God could not lie; wherefore, my guilt was **swept away**.

The phrase "swept away" in verse 6, above, is a wonderful reminder of the power of the Atonement to cleanse and heal. One can feel the power of his or her sins being "swept" away!

The speed and completeness of

this cleansing apparently startled Enos a bit, and caused him to marvel.

7 And I said: **Lord, how is it done?**

8 And he said unto me: **Because of thy faith in Christ**, whom thou hast never before heard nor seen. And many years pass away before he shall manifest himself in the flesh; wherefore, go to, thy faith hath made thee whole.

We are taught an interesting pattern here. First, we must be concerned with our own standing with God. When this is in proper condition, the Spirit enables us to be concerned about our immediate family. With that in place, our attention then goes to others, including our enemies. In other words, when we are at peace with God, we are then enabled by the Spirit to truly love others, including our enemies. We will see this clearly taught as we continue with Enos.

9 Now, it came to pass that **when I had heard these words** [*when I knew that I was acceptable before God*] **I began to feel a desire for the welfare of my brethren, the Nephites**; wherefore, I did pour out my whole soul unto God for them.

10 And while I was thus struggling in the spirit, behold, the voice of the Lord came into my mind again, saying: I will visit thy brethren according to their diligence in keeping my commandments. [*In other words, they have agency too, and I must not violate the rules of honoring agency as I deal with them.*] I have given unto them this land, and it is a holy land; and I curse it not save it be for the cause of iniquity; wherefore, I will visit thy brethren according as I have said; and their transgressions will I bring down with sorrow upon their own heads.

11 And after I, Enos, had heard these words, my faith began to be unshaken in the Lord; and **I prayed unto him with many long strugglings for my brethren, the Lamanites**.

12 And it came to pass that after I had prayed and labored with all diligence, the Lord said unto me: I will grant unto thee according to **thy desires**, because of thy faith.

13 And now behold, this was the desire which I desired of him—that if it should so be, that my people, the Nephites, should fall into transgression, and by any means be destroyed, and the Lamanites should not be destroyed, **that the Lord God would preserve a record of my people**, the Nephites; even if it

so be by the power of his holy arm, that it might be brought forth at some future day unto the Lamanites, that, perhaps, they might be brought unto salvation—

> Enos' desire has been granted by the coming forth of the Book of Mormon to the Lamanites in this dispensation.

14 For at the present our strugglings were vain in restoring them to the true faith. And they swore in their wrath that, **if it were possible, they would destroy our records** and us, and also all the traditions of our fathers.

> Referring back to the bolded phrase in verse 14, perhaps you've noticed that it is often the case with wicked dictators and their evil-minded followers, that they destroy or attempt to destroy written history, in fact, any history of the people over whom they wield unrighteous dominion. This has been repeated over and over again throughout history. It is Satan's way to destroy good ties with past generations.

15 Wherefore, I **knowing that the Lord God was able to preserve our records, I cried unto him continually**, for he had said unto me: Whatsoever thing ye shall ask in faith, believing that ye shall receive in the name of Christ, ye shall receive it [*compare with D&C 46:30 and 50:30*].

16 And I had faith, and **I did cry unto God that he would preserve the records**; and he covenanted with me that he would bring them forth unto the Lamanites in his own due time.

17 **And I, Enos, knew it would be according to the covenant which he had made; wherefore my soul did rest** [*I had peace about this matter of our records being preserved*].

18 And the Lord said unto me: Thy fathers have also required of me this thing; and it shall be done unto them according to their faith; for their faith was like unto thine.

19 And now it came to pass that I, Enos, went about among the people of Nephi, prophesying of things to come, and testifying of the things which I had heard and seen.

> As Enos finishes teaching us, he points out what happens to people individually as well as as a society when they reject the gospel. This has repeated many, many times throughout history and is happening in numerous manifestations today. One key indicator of this happening is that the farther

from God people stray, the more bizarre their dress and behavior.

20 And I bear record that the people of Nephi did seek diligently to restore the Lamanites unto the true faith in God. But our labors were vain; their hatred was fixed, and they were led by their evil nature that they became wild, and ferocious, and a blood-thirsty people, full of idolatry and filthiness; feeding upon beasts of prey; dwelling in tents, and wandering about in the wilderness with a short skin girdle about their loins and their heads shaven; and their skill was in the bow, and in the cimeter, and the ax. And many of them did eat nothing save it was raw meat; and they were continually seeking to destroy us.

21 And it came to pass that the people of Nephi did till the land, and raise all manner of grain, and of fruit, and flocks of herds, and flocks of all manner of cattle of every kind, and goats, and wild goats, and also many horses.

22 And there were exceedingly many prophets among us. And the people were a stiffnecked people, hard to understand.

> Enos reminds us how important it is that our prophets speak plainly to us about dangers to our well-being.

23 And there was nothing save it was exceeding harshness, preaching and prophesying of wars, and contentions, and destructions, and continually reminding them of death, and the duration of eternity, and the judgments and the power of God, and all these things—stirring them up continually to keep them in the fear of the Lord. I say there was nothing short of these things, and exceedingly great plainness of speech, would keep them from going down speedily to destruction. And after this manner do I write concerning them.

24 And I saw wars between the Nephites and Lamanites in the course of my days.

25 And it came to pass that I began to be old, and an hundred and seventy and nine years had passed away from the time that our father Lehi left Jerusalem.

> It appears that these people lived quite long lives. For instance, according to what Enos said in verse 25, above, we can calculate that Jacob and Enos spanned about one hundred and seventy-five years. So, they averaged about eighty-seven and a half years old.

26 And I saw that I must soon go down to my grave, having been wrought upon by the power of

God that I must preach and prophesy unto this people, and declare the word according to the truth which is in Christ. And I have declared it in all my days, and have rejoiced in it above that of the world.

27 And **I soon go to the place of my rest, which is with my Redeemer**; for I know that in him I shall rest. And I rejoice in the day when my mortal shall put on immortality, and shall stand before him; then shall I see his face with pleasure, and he will say unto me: Come unto me, ye blessed, there is a place prepared for you in the mansions of my Father. Amen.

Enos will have the kind of experience at the final judgment described in 2 Nephi 9:14, last half of the verse.

THE BOOK OF JAROM

We could refer to Jarom as "Jarom Enosson" because he is the son of Enos. He will review and remind us of many of the teachings of his father and grandfather.

1 NOW behold, I, Jarom, write a few words according to the commandment of my father, Enos, that our genealogy may be kept.

2 And as these plates are small, and as these things are written for the intent of the benefit of our brethren the Lamanites, wherefore, it must needs be that I write a little; but I shall not write the things of my prophesying, nor of my revelations. For what could I write more than my fathers have written? For have not they revealed the plan of salvation? I say unto you, Yea; and this sufficeth me [*this is sufficient for me*].

> It is clear from what Jarom writes that it is requiring every effort on the part of him and the righteous leaders of his people to stem the tide of apostasy among them. They are becoming increasingly spiritually insensitive.

3 Behold, it is expedient that much should be done among this people, because of the hardness of their hearts, and the deafness of their ears, and the blindness of their minds, and the stiffness of their necks; nevertheless, **God is exceedingly merciful unto them, and has not as yet swept them off from the face of the land.**

> It seems that their society is much like ours today. The righteous are becoming more and more righteous, and those who are sloppy about the gospel are getting farther and farther into the ways of the world.

4 And there are many among us who have many revelations, for **they are not all stiffnecked. And as many as are not stiffnecked and have faith, have communion with the Holy Spirit**, which maketh manifest unto the children of men, according to their faith.

5 And now, behold, two hundred years had passed away [*since Lehi left Jerusalem*], and the people of Nephi had waxed strong in the land. They observed to keep the law of Moses and the sabbath day holy unto the Lord. And they profaned not; neither did they

blaspheme. And **the laws of the land were exceedingly strict.** [*Good laws help preserve good people.*]

6 And they were scattered upon much of the face of the land, and the Lamanites also. And they were exceedingly more numerous than were they of the Nephites; and they loved murder and would drink the blood of beasts [*a direct violation of Old Testament law; see Genesis 9:4*].

7 And it came to pass that they came many times against us, the Nephites, to battle. But our kings and **our leaders were mighty men in the faith of the Lord**; and they taught the people the ways of the Lord; wherefore, we withstood the Lamanites and swept them away out of our lands, and began to fortify our cities, or whatsoever place of our inheritance.

> Next, we are taught and reminded that prosperity as a society is an inevitable result of personal righteousness among its citizens.

8 And we multiplied exceedingly, and spread upon the face of the land, and became exceedingly rich in gold, and in silver, and in precious things, and in fine workmanship of wood, in buildings, and in machinery, and also in iron and copper, and brass and steel, making all manner of tools of every kind to till the ground, and weapons of war—yea, the sharp pointed arrow, and the quiver, and the dart, and the javelin, and **all preparations for war.**

> Again, we have a guideline in these two verses, 8 and 9, that it is wise to be prepared for war, even in times of peace.

9 And thus **being prepared** to meet the Lamanites, they did not prosper against us. But the word of the Lord was verified, which he spake unto our fathers, saying that: Inasmuch as ye will keep my commandments ye shall prosper in the land.

10 And it came to pass that the prophets of the Lord did threaten the people of Nephi, according to the word of God, that if they did not keep the commandments, but should fall into transgression, they should be destroyed from off the face of the land.

11 **Wherefore, the prophets, and the priests, and the teachers, did labor diligently, exhorting with all long-suffering the people to diligence; teaching the law of Moses, and the intent for which it was given; persuading them to look forward unto the Messiah**, and believe in him

to come **as though he already was** [*as if He had already performed His earthly ministry*]. And after this manner did they teach them.

12 And it came to pass that **by so doing they kept them from being destroyed upon the face of the land** [*this is similar to what our prophets are doing for us*]; for they did prick their hearts with the word, continually stirring them up unto repentance.

13 And it came to pass that two hundred and thirty and eight years had passed away—after the manner of wars, and contentions, and dissensions, for the space of much of the time.

14 And I, Jarom, do not write more, for the plates are small. But behold, my brethren, ye can go to the other plates of Nephi; for behold, upon them the records of our wars are engraven, according to the writings of the kings, or those which they caused to be written.

15 And **I deliver these plates into the hands of my son Omni**, that they may be kept according to the commandments of my fathers.

THE BOOK OF OMNI

We could refer to Omni as "Omni Jaromson." The book of Omni covers many, many years. In it we will be given important background about Mosiah I and about King Benjamin. We will need this in order to understand the setting of the Book of Mosiah. We will see the passing of the small plates of Nephi from one record keeper to another, in rapid succession.

1 BEHOLD, it came to pass that I, Omni, being commanded by my father, Jarom, that I should write somewhat upon these plates [*the small plates of Nephi*], to preserve our genealogy—

2 Wherefore, in my days, I would that ye should know that I fought much with the sword to preserve my people, the Nephites, from falling into the hands of their enemies, the Lamanites. **But behold, I of myself am a wicked man** [*this is a sad confession*], and I have not kept the statutes and the commandments of the Lord as I ought to have done.

3 And it came to pass that two hundred and seventy and six years had passed away, and we had many seasons of peace; and we had many seasons of serious war and bloodshed. Yea, and in fine, two hundred and eighty and two years had passed away, and I had kept these plates [*the small plates*] according to the commandments of my fathers; and **I conferred them upon my son Amaron**. And I make an end.

4 And now I, Amaron, write the things whatsoever I write, which are few, in the book of my father.

5 Behold, it came to pass that three hundred and twenty years had passed away, and the more wicked part of the Nephites were destroyed.

6 For the Lord would not suffer, after he had led them out of the land of Jerusalem and kept and preserved them from falling into the hands of their enemies, yea, he would not suffer that the words should not be verified, which he spake unto our fathers, saying that: **Inasmuch as ye will not keep my commandments ye shall not prosper in the land.**

7 Wherefore, the Lord did visit

them in great judgment; nevertheless, he did spare the righteous that they should not perish, but did deliver them out of the hands of their enemies.

8 And it came to pass that **I did deliver the plates unto my brother Chemish.**

9 Now I, Chemish, write what few things I write, in the same book with my brother; for behold, I saw the last which he wrote, that he wrote it with his own hand; and **he wrote it in the day that he delivered them unto me.** And after this manner we keep the records, for it is according to the commandments of our fathers. And I make an end.

10 Behold, I, **Abinadom**, am the son of Chemish. Behold, it came to pass that I saw much war and contention between my people, the Nephites, and the Lamanites; and I, with my own sword, have taken the lives of many of the Lamanites in the defence of my brethren.

> Next, Abinadom makes a rather sad commentary about the status of continuing revelation among his people as they become increasingly wicked.

11 And behold, the record of this people is engraven upon plates which is had by the kings, according to the generations; and **I know of no revelation save that which has been written, neither prophecy**; wherefore, that which is sufficient is written. And I make an end.

> Amaleki will give us very valuable background about Mosiah the First, and also about King Benjamin. We will point out these things with **bold**.

12 Behold, I am **Amaleki,** the son of Abinadom. Behold, **I will speak unto you somewhat concerning Mosiah,** who was made king over the land of Zarahemla; for behold, **he being warned of the Lord that he should flee out of the land of Nephi**, and **as many as would hearken unto the voice of the Lord should also depart out of the land with him**, into the wilderness—

> There is symbolism for us in the fleeing into the wilderness. Sometimes, we must flee others or circumstances in which we find ourselves compromising the standards of the gospel. When we do so, we often find ourselves alone and out of our comfort zone, in a wilderness as it were. But, if we faithfully continue through the wilderness, we ultimately end up in a land of promise where the desired blessings and security are given us by God.

13 And it came to pass that

he did according as the Lord had commanded him. And they departed out of the land into the wilderness, as many as would hearken unto the voice of the Lord; and **they were led by many preachings and prophesyings.** And they were admonished continually by the word of God; and they were led by the power of his arm, through the wilderness until they came down into the land which is called the land of Zarahemla.

> Next, we are introduced to the Mulekites. Mulek was one of the sons of wicked King Zedekiah (see notes in 1 Nephi 1:4). According to the biblical account, all of the sons of Zedekiah were killed when he was taken captive and blinded. But, from the Book of Mormon account, we know that Mulek somehow escaped and, along with others, made their way to the New World. They are not referred to in the Book of Mormon as Mulekites but are commonly called by that name in gospel conversations.

14 And they [*Mosiah and his people*] discovered a people, who were called the people of Zarahemla [*Mulekites*]. Now, there was great rejoicing among the people of Zarahemla; and also Zarahemla did rejoice exceedingly, because the Lord had sent the people of Mosiah with the plates of brass which contained the record of the Jews.

15 Behold, it came to pass that Mosiah discovered that the people of Zarahemla [*Mulekites*] came out from Jerusalem at the time that Zedekiah, king of Judah, was carried away captive into Babylon.

16 And they [*the Mulekites*] journeyed in the wilderness, and were **brought by the hand of the Lord across the great waters, into the land where Mosiah discovered them;** and they had dwelt there from that time forth.

> In verse 17, next, we are reminded of the absolute necessity of having scriptures and written records.

17 And at the time that Mosiah discovered them, they had become exceedingly numerous. Nevertheless, they had had many wars and serious contentions, and had fallen by the sword from time to time; and **their language had become corrupted;** and **they had brought no records with them;** and they denied the being of their Creator; **and Mosiah, nor the people of Mosiah, could understand them.**

18 But it came to pass that Mosiah caused that they should be taught in his language. And

it came to pass that after they were taught in the language of Mosiah, Zarahemla gave a genealogy of his fathers, according to his memory; and they are written, but not in these plates [*the small plates*].

19 And it came to pass that the people of Zarahemla, and of Mosiah, did **unite together**; and **Mosiah was appointed to be their king.**

20 And it came to pass in the days of Mosiah, there was a large stone [*containing some history of the Jaredites*] brought unto him with engravings on it; and he did interpret the engravings by the gift and power of God.

21 And they gave an account of one Coriantumr [*the last Jaredite except for Ether*], and the slain of his people [*the Jaredites; see the book of Ether*]. And Coriantumr was discovered by the people of Zarahemla [*the Mulekites*]; and he dwelt with them for the space of nine moons [*nine months*].

22 It also spake a few words concerning his fathers [*ancestors*]. And his first parents came out from the tower [*the Tower of Babel; see Genesis 11*], at the time the Lord confounded [*confused*] the language of the people; and the severity of the Lord fell upon them according to his judgments, which are just; and their bones [*Jaredite bones*] lay scattered in the land northward.

King Mosiah I was King Benjamin's father. Next, Amaleki will give us some background concerning King Benjamin, whose famous address we will study in the book of Mosiah.

23 Behold, I, Amaleki, was born in the days of Mosiah; and I have lived to see his death; and Benjamin, his son, reigneth in his stead.

24 And behold, I have seen, in the days of king Benjamin, a serious war and much bloodshed between the Nephites and the Lamanites. But behold, the Nephites did obtain much advantage over them; yea, insomuch that king Benjamin did drive them out of the land of Zarahemla.

25 And it came to pass that I began to be old; and, having no seed [*children*], and knowing **king Benjamin** to be a just man before the Lord, wherefore, **I shall deliver up these plates unto him**, exhorting all men to come unto God, the Holy One

of Israel, and **believe in prophesying, and in revelations, and in the ministering of angels, and in the gift of speaking with tongues, and in the gift of interpreting languages, and in all things which are good; for there is nothing which is good save it comes from the Lord; and that which is evil cometh from the devil.**

> Amaleki bears strong testimony to us as he begins to draw his brief writings to a close.

26 And now, my beloved brethren, I would that ye should come unto Christ, who is the Holy One of Israel, and partake of his salvation, and the power of his redemption. Yea, come unto him, and **offer your whole souls as an offering unto him,** [*since Christ offered His "whole soul" for you*] and continue in fasting and praying, and endure to the end; and as the Lord liveth ye will be saved.

> What Amaleki tells us next is very helpful when we get to Mosiah 7:1–9. We will use **bold** to point these things out (and to demonstrate that you can carefully highlight or underline certain words in your scriptures as a way of making sentences or writing sentences).

27 And now I would speak somewhat concerning **a certain number** who **went** up into the wilderness **to return to the land of Nephi**; for there was a large number who were desirous to possess the land of their inheritance.

28 Wherefore, **they went up into the wilderness.** And their leader being a strong and mighty man, and a stiffnecked man, wherefore he caused a **contention** among them; and they were **all slain, save fifty**, in the wilderness, and **they returned again to the land of Zarahemla.**

29 And it came to pass that they also took others to a considerable number, and **took their journey again into the wilderness.**

30 And **I, Amaleki, had a brother, who also went with them; and I have not since known concerning them.** And I am about to lie down in my grave; and these plates are full. And I make an end of my speaking.

> In Mosiah 7:1–9, we will pick up the history of Amaleki's brother and those he went with to the land of Nephi, after seventy-nine years have passed.

THE WORDS OF MORMON

By referring to the chronology information on the lower right hand corner of the page in your Book of Mormon, you will see that Mormon is writing this about 385 years after Christ's birth. The Words of Mormon are a transition from the small plates of Nephi (1 and 2 Nephi, Jacob, Enos, Jarom, and Omni) to the book of Mosiah.

As we read, Mormon will explain that after he had abridged (condensed) the large plates of Nephi, leading down through history until the reign of King Benjamin (in the first part of Mosiah), he found the small plates of Nephi as he searched through all the plates he had. This small set of plates brought special feelings to his soul, so he included them (under inspiration) in what Joseph Smith would later be given by Moroni.

1 AND now I, Mormon, being about to deliver up the record which I have been making into the hands of my son Moroni, behold I have witnessed almost all the destruction of my people, the Nephites.

2 And it is many hundred years after the coming of Christ that I deliver these records into the hands of my son; and it supposeth me that he will witness the entire destruction of my people. But may God grant that he may survive them, that he may write somewhat concerning them, and somewhat concerning Christ, that perhaps some day it may profit them.

3 And **now, I speak somewhat concerning that which I have written**; for **after I had made an abridgment from the plates of Nephi, down to the reign of this king Benjamin**, of whom Amaleki spake, **I searched among the records** which had been delivered into my hands, **and I found these plates** [*the small plates of Nephi*], which contained this small account of the prophets, from Jacob [*including Lehi and Nephi*] down to the reign of this king Benjamin, and also many of the words of Nephi.

4 And **the things which are upon these plates pleasing me**, because of the prophecies of the coming of Christ; and my fathers knowing that many of them have been fulfilled; yea, and I also know that as many things as have been prophesied concerning us down to this day have been fulfilled, and as many as

go beyond this day must surely come to pass—

5 Wherefore, I chose these things [*the small plates*], to finish my record upon them, which remainder of my record I shall take from the plates of Nephi [*the large plates of Nephi*]; and I cannot write the hundredth part of the things of my people.

6 But behold, I shall take these plates [*the small plates*], which contain these prophesyings and revelations, and put them with the remainder of my record, for they are choice unto me; and I know they will be choice unto my brethren.

> Mormon is a great teacher, and next he teaches us that there are times when we are impressed by the Spirit to do something, even though we don't understand at the time why.

7 And I do this for a wise purpose; for **thus it whispereth me, according to the workings of the Spirit of the Lord** which is in me. And now, **I do not know all things**; **but the Lord knoweth all things** which are to come; wherefore, he worketh in me to do according to his will.

8 And my prayer to God is concerning my brethren, that they may once again come to the knowledge of God, yea, the redemption of Christ; that they may once again be a delightsome people.

9 And now I, Mormon, proceed to finish out my record, which I take from the plates of Nephi; and I make it according to the knowledge and the understanding which God has given me.

> Now, Mormon finishes telling us about the transition in the record to the reign of King Benjamin.

10 Wherefore, it came to pass that after Amaleki had delivered up these plates [*the small plates*] into the hands of king Benjamin, he took them and put them with the other plates [*the large plates and other records*], which contained records which had been handed down by the kings, from generation to generation until the days of king Benjamin.

11 And they were handed down from king Benjamin, from generation to generation until they have fallen into my hands. [*We understand from Journal of Discourses, volume 19, page 38, that there were the equivalent of several wagon loads of records.*] And I, Mormon, pray to God that they may be preserved from this time henceforth. And I know that they will be preserved; for

there are great things written upon them, out of which my people and their brethren shall be judged at the great and last day [*Judgment Day*], according to the word of God which is written.

12 And now, **concerning this king Benjamin**—he had somewhat of contentions among his own people.

13 And it came to pass also that the armies of the Lamanites came down out of the land of Nephi, to battle against his people. But behold, king Benjamin gathered together his armies, and he did stand against them; and he did fight with the strength of his own arm, with the sword of Laban.

14 And **in the strength of the Lord** they did contend against their enemies, until they had slain many thousands of the Lamanites. And it came to pass that they did contend against the Lamanites until they had driven them out of all the lands of their inheritance.

15 And it came to pass that after there had been false Christs, and their mouths had been shut, and they punished according to their crimes;

16 And after there had been false prophets, and false preachers and teachers among the people, and all these having been punished according to their crimes; and after there having been much contention and many dissensions away unto the Lamanites [*there had been much apostasy*], behold, it came to pass that king Benjamin, with the assistance of the holy prophets who were among his people—

> As Mormon describes and defines King Benjamin, it reminds us of what Enoch (see Moses 6:26 through 7:69) and what Melchizedek (Alma 13:14–19) accomplished among their people under the direction of the Lord.

17 For behold, king Benjamin was a holy man, and he did reign over his people in righteousness; and there were many holy men in the land, and they did speak the word of God with power and with authority; and they did use much sharpness because of the stiffneckedness of the people—

18 Wherefore, with the help of these, **king Benjamin**, by laboring with all the might of his body and the faculty of his whole soul, and also the prophets, **did once more establish peace in the land**.

SOURCES

Anderson, Richard Lloyd. *Investigating the Book of Mormon Witnesses.* Salt Lake City: Shadow Mountain, 1989.

Authorized King James Version of the Bible. Salt Lake City, Utah: The Church of Jesus Christ of Latter-day Saints, 1979.

Book of Mormon Student Manual, Religion 121 and 122. Salt Lake City: The Church of Jesus Christ of Latter-day Saints, 1989.

Church History in the Fulness of Times, Religion 341–43. Salt Lake City: The Church of Jesus Christ of Latter-day Saints, 1980.

Collier, John. *The Indians of the Americas.* New York: W. W. Norton & Company, 1947.

Dibble, Johnathan A. "Delivered by the Power of God: The American Revolution and Nephi's Prophecy." *Ensign*, Oct. 1987.

Doctrine and Covenants Student Manual, Religion 324 and 325. Salt Lake City: The Church of Jesus Christ of Latter-day Saints, 1981.

Holland, Jeffrey R. " 'This Do in Remembrance of Me.' " *Ensign*, Nov. 1995.

Jacobs, Wilbur R. *The Frontier in American History.* Tuscon, Arizona: University of Arizona Press, 1986.

Jacobs, Wilbur R. "The Indian and the Frontier in American History— A Need for Revision." *Western Historical Quarterly.* Jan. 1973.

Journal of Discourses. 26 vols. London: Latter-day Saints' Book Depot., 1854–86.

Kimball, Spencer W. "Our Paths Have Met Again." *Ensign*, Dec. 1975.

Kimball, Spencer W. "The Blessings and Responsibilities of Womanhood." *Ensign*, Mar. 1976.

Kimball, Spencer W. *The Miracle of Forgiveness.* Salt Lake City: Bookcraft, 1969.

Latourette, Kenneth Scott. *A History of the Expansion of Christianity, The Great Century.* Vol. 4. New York: Harper and Brothers, 1941.

Library of Aboriginal American Literature. Edited by Daniel Garrison Brinton. 8 vols. Philadelphia: William F. Fell & Co., 1890.

Ludlow, Daniel H. *A Companion to Your Study of The Book of Mormon*. Salt Lake City: Deseret Book, 1976.

Martin Luther edition of the German Bible, which Joseph Smith said was the most correct of any then available.

Maxwell, Neal A. "On Being a Light." Address delivered at the Salt Lake Institute of Religion, Jan. 2, 1974.

Maxwell, Neal A. "According to the Desire of [Our] Hearts." *Ensign*, Nov. 1996.

McConkie, Bruce R. *Millennial Messiah*. Salt Lake City: Deseret Book, 1983.

McConkie, Bruce R. *Mormon Doctrine*. 2nd ed. Salt Lake City: Bookcraft, 1966.

Moldenke, Harold and Alma Moldenke. *Plants of the Bible*. Mineola, New York: Dover Publications, Incorporated, 1986.

Nibley, Hugh. *Since Cumorah: The Book of Mormon in the Modern World*. Salt Lake City: Deseret Book, 1970.

Old Testament Student Manual, 1 Kings through Malachi, Religion 302. Salt Lake City: The Church of Jesus Christ of Latter-day Saints, 1981.

Petersen, Mark E. *The Great Prologue*. Salt Lake City: Deseret Book, 1976.

Reynolds, George and Janne M. Sjodahl. *Commentary on the Book of Mormon*. 7 vols. Salt Lake City: Deseret Press, 1976.

Richards, LeGrand. "Prophets and Prophecy." In Conference Report, Oct. 1975; or *Ensign*, Nov. 1975.

Richards, LeGrand. *Israel! Do You Know?* 4th ed. Salt Lake City: Shadow Mountain, 1990.

Smith, George Albert. In Conference Report, Apr. 1918.

Smith, Joseph. *History of The Church of Jesus Christ of Latter-day Saints*. Edited by B. H. Roberts. 2d ed. rev., 7 vols., Salt Lake City: The Church of Jesus Christ of Latter-day Saints, 1932–51.

Smith, Joseph. *Messenger and Advocate*, Apr. 1835.

Smith, Joseph. *Teachings of the Prophet Joseph Smith.* Selected and arranged by Joseph Fielding Smith. Salt Lake City: Deseret Book, 1976.

Smith, Joseph F., Anthon H. Lund, and John Henry Smith. First Presidency Statement. *Improvement Era*, August 1916.

Smith, Joseph F., John R. Winder, and Anthon H. Lund. First Presidency Message. *Messages of the First Presidency of The Church of Jesus Christ of Latter-day Saints.* 6 vols. Compiled by James R. Clark. Salt Lake City: Bookcraft, 1965.

Smith, Joseph Fielding. *Answers to Gospel Questions.* Compiled by Joseph Fielding Smith. 5 vols. Salt Lake City: Deseret Book, 1957–66.

Smith, Joseph Fielding. *Church History and Modern Revelation.* 4 vols. Salt Lake City: Deseret Book, 1947.

Smith, Joseph Fielding. *Doctrines of Salvation.* Compiled by Bruce R. McConkie. 3 vols. Salt Lake City: Bookcraft, 1954–56.

Smith, Lucy Mack. *History of Joseph Smith by His Mother.* Salt Lake City: Stevens & Wallis, Inc., 1945.

Talmage, James E. *Articles of Faith.* Salt Lake City: Deseret Book, 1981.

"The Family: A Proclamation to the World." First Presidency and Council of the Twelve Apostles. *Family Guide Book.* Salt Lake City: Church of Jesus Christ of Latter-day Saints, 1995.

Wasserman, Jacob. *Columbus: Don Quixote of the Seas.* Translated by Eric Sutton. Boston: Little, Brown, and Co., 1930.

Young, Brigham. *Discourses of Brigham Young.* Compiled by John A. Widtsoe. Salt Lake City: Deseret Book, 1954.

Notes

Notes

Notes

Notes

Notes

Notes

Notes

Notes

Notes

Notes

Notes

Notes

Notes

Notes

NOTES

Notes

About the Author

David J. Ridges taught for the Church Educational System for thirty-five years and has taught for several years at BYU Campus Education Week. He taught adult religion classes and Know Your Religion classes for BYU Continuing Education for many years. He has also served as a curriculum writer for Sunday School, seminary, and institute of religion manuals.

He has served in many callings in the Church, including Gospel Doctrine teacher, bishop, stake president, and patriarch. He and Sister Ridges served a full-time eighteen-month mission, training senior CES missionaries and helping coordinate their assignments throughout the world.

Brother Ridges and his wife, Janette, are the parents of six children and make their home in Springville, Utah.

0 26575 77256 2